((((((DOMESTIC SECRETS))))))

STUDIES IN LEGAL HISTORY

DANIEL ERNST &

THOMAS A. GREEN,

editors

Published by the University of North Carolina Press in association with the American Society for Legal History

WOMEN & PROPERTY

IN SWEDEN · 1600–1857

Domestic

(((((((((((((((((((((((((((((((((SECRETS))))))))

Maria Ågren

THE UNIVERSITY OF
NORTH CAROLINA PRESS
Chapel Hill

Designed by Courtney Leigh Baker
and set in Arno Pro by Rebecca Evans
Manufactured in the United States of America

The paper in this book meets the guidelines for
permanence and durability of the Committee on
Production Guidelines for Book Longevity of the
Council on Library Resources.

The University of North Carolina Press has been
a member of the Green Press Initiative since 2003.

Library of Congress Cataloging-in-Publication Data
Ågren, Maria.
Domestic secrets : women and property in Sweden,
1600–1857 / Maria Ågren.
p. cm. — (Studies in legal history)
Includes bibliographical references and index.
ISBN 978-0-8078-3320-9 (cloth : alk. paper)
1. Women — Legal status, laws, etc. — Sweden — History.
2. Marital property — Sweden — History. I. Title.
KKV517.5.A94 2009
346.48501'664 — dc22
2009022447

Portions of this work appeared earlier, in somewhat
different form, in "A Domestic Secret: Marriage, Religion
and Legal Change in Late Seventeenth-Century Sweden,"
Past and Present 194 (2007): 75–106.

13 12 11 10 09   5 4 3 2 1

THIS BOOK WAS DIGITALLY PRINTED.

IN MEMORY OF

my mother,

MARIANNE ÅGREN,

1933–2007

CONTENTS

ILLUSTRATIONS, TABLES, & MAP

PREFACE

Many years ago, I gave a lecture about past inheritance law in rural Sweden to a group of nonhistorians. I described how both sons and daughters were entitled to inherit land, although not on an equal basis prior to 1845, and I emphasized how this sort of inheritance system presupposed that one sibling (usually a brother) purchased the other siblings' shares of the farm. A man in the audience then asked, "Where did the money come from that allowed brothers to buy off their siblings in this way?" I answered to the best of my ability, but the question lingered on in the back of my mind. Where indeed did the money come from? As I immediately realized, this question was particularly relevant for the eighteenth century, when land prices were rising, and it must have been difficult to come up with the required sums. The question switched my interest from inheritance law as such to the marital union and to the rights, and lack of rights, of spouses. This book is an attempt to give a better answer to this question that has bothered me ever since.

I am indebted to the man who posed this question. But my debt of gratitude is larger than that. I want to thank Amy Erickson, who was the one who really made me realize how important married women's property rights are and have always been. It was in 1999–2000 that Amy spent a year at Uppsala University as holder of the Kerstin Hesselgren guest professorship, and ever since then, I have profited from her profound knowledge of English women's property rights in the early modern period. Without the new questions that arose as I attempted to explain to her (and to myself) how Swedish law differed from English law, I would not have been able to write this book. And without Amy's friendship and good humor, the exercise would not have been such a pleasant one. Thank you, Amy!

Speaking of pleasant experiences, I want to thank my editor, Tom Green, for the never-ending attention and sincere interest he has devoted to my manuscript. From our first contact in the fall of 2006, I have received more support, well-earned criticism, and language training from Tom than from anyone else. Even though we still have not met in person and only communicate via e-mail, Tom has become a much-cherished friend. Sitting in front of my computer, I have often laughed aloud at Tom's innumerable jokes, and I have tried to memorize all the words and idiomatic expressions he has taught me during our journey together. Thank you, Tom — I could not have written this book without you!

Writing in a language that is not your own is a great challenge. I have enjoyed every minute of this endeavor, but I am aware that without the help of my fellow historian Marie Clark Nelson the book would have been full of infelicitous phrases and sentences where the words come in the wrong order. With her perfect mastery of both English and Swedish, Marie has pruned and Americanized my language in a way few others could have done. When Tom was hurrying us on, Marie worked many late nights to have all chapters ready on time, but, characteristically, she never lost her temper, and, when she returned a revised chapter to me, it was always with words such as "How very interesting this book is!" Thank you, Marie — you are a pearl.

I am fortunate in being surrounded by so many skillful historians, who have generously read and commented upon earlier versions of this book. My former supervisor, Eva Österberg, and my predecessor, Rolf Torstendahl, have both taken the time to read and to formulate critical comments that have, as always, been right to the point. My colleague and friend Jan Lindegren has also been one of my readers; it is a privilege to have such an expert of early modern history in an adjacent office. Maria Sjöberg, Karin Hassan Jansson, and Rosemarie Fiebranz are all gender historians, early modernists and friends who have read the manuscript and shared their understanding of the past with me. Jonas Lindström, Cristina Prytz, and Gunnel Cederlöf have also been stimulating conversation partners. Sadly, Christer Winberg and Göran Inger died before the book was ready for publication, but they were both, in different ways, engaged in it, for which I am thankful. Peter Sjökvist helped me with some particularly convoluted passages of legal Latin, and Sören Edvinsson, from Umeå, and Claes Westling, from Vadstena, have helped me to gain access to demographic information and to probate inventories. I also want to thank the entire staff at the History Department in Uppsala — having you around me is a source of everyday inspiration and joy!

I want to thank the readers of UNC Press: Margaret Hunt, Hendrik Hartog, and Hilde Sandvik, who read the manuscript extremely carefully, identified weak points, and suggested remedies in a way that was not only helpful but intellectually stimulating as well. I am also grateful to John Östh, who drew the map of Sweden. Chuck Grench and Katy O'Brien at UNC Press have provided much valuable advice and support. My sincere thanks go to my in-house editor, Ron Maner, who has guided me and my manuscript through the production process in a very friendly and supportive way, and to my meticulous copyeditor, Eric Combest, who has been at great pains to make sure that not an iota was wrong.

As always, books cannot materialize if the material conditions are not favorable, that is, if the author cannot get some time free for writing. I want to thank the previous head of my department, Christer Öhman, and the present head of department, Lars M. Andersson, for being flexible and alleviating my teaching burden in the fall of 2006 and the spring of 2008. I also want to thank Kungliga Vitterhets Historie och Antikvitets Akademien for its support: thanks to the academy, and particularly to Ulf Sporrong. I was able to spend two weeks in complete isolation at Stjernsund Manor in 2006, and the academy also allowed me to profit from an exchange program with the British Academy in 2008. A grant from the Bank of Sweden Tercentenary Foundation made it possible to do the work upon which chapter 4 is based. The Swedish Research Council supported the publication of the book by providing support for the English language revisions. Publication was also supported by a generous grant from the Vilhelm Ekman Fund at Uppsala University.

A special thank-you is due my daughter Hanna, who checked and corrected the bibliography during her summer holiday. And, of course, the greatest thanks of all go to my whole family — Michael, Hanna, and Anders — for being my best friends and supporters.

UPPSALA
October 2008

((((((D O M E S T I C   S E C R E T S))))))

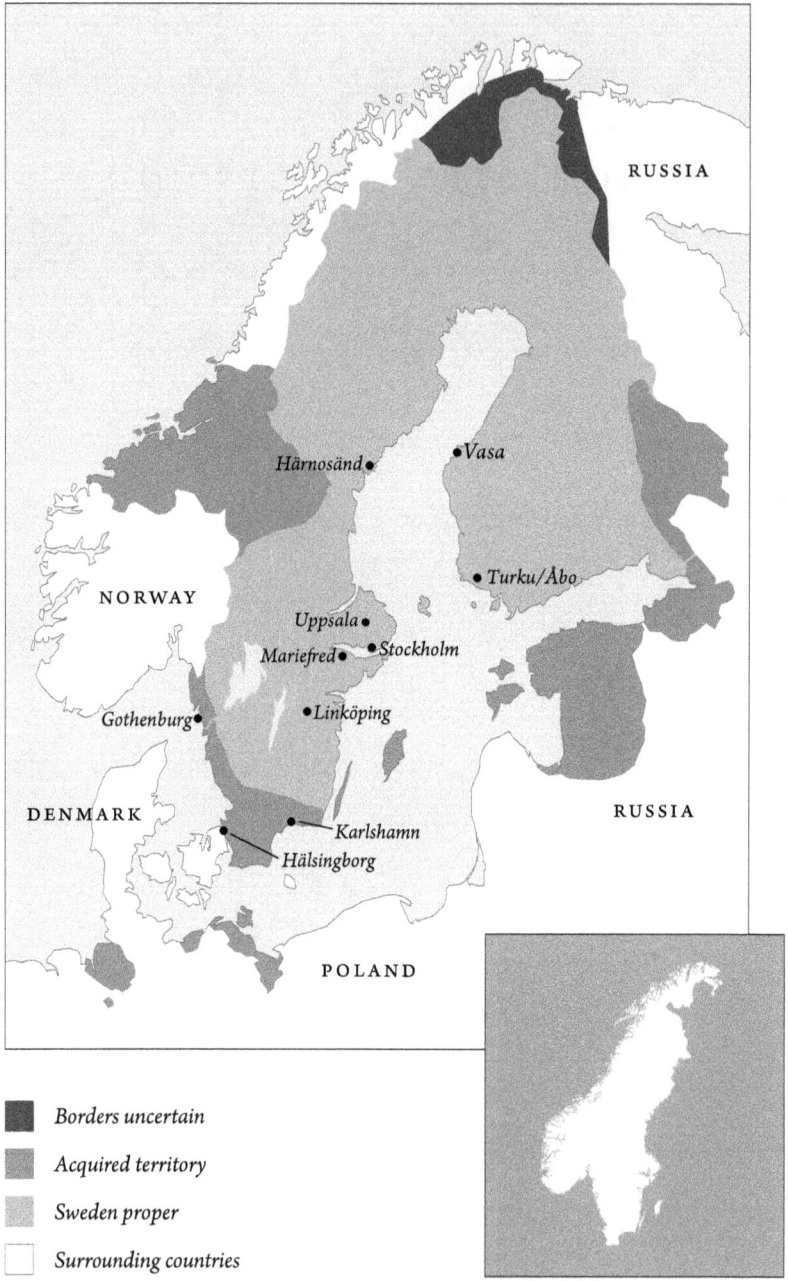

RUSSIA

•Vasa

Härnosänd•

• Turku/Åbo

NORWAY

Uppsala•
Mariefred• •Stockholm

Gothenburg• •Linköping

RUSSIA

DENMARK

Karlshamn
Hälsingborg

POLAND

■ Borders uncertain

■ Acquired territory

■ Sweden proper

□ Surrounding countries

Sweden, 1815–1905

DOMESTIC SECRETS

For centuries, families and households have been based on the union created through marriage, and, until recently, families and households have in their turn been the nuclei of society, the place where production took place and where new generations were raised. Even today, when marriage is not necessarily conceived of as a lasting engagement and when family members seldom work together to make a living, marriage nevertheless remains a predominant model for human life. Western culture has been and is still permeated with symbols and stories that underline the importance of marriage. Reading the Bible and listening to sermons, medieval and early modern people became closely acquainted with characters like Abraham and Sarah, Isaac and Rebecca, Esau and Jacob, and this reinforced their own sense of how childbearing, courtship and strategies of inheritance were vital parts of human life. A similar message is conveyed to modern people through the media's enormous preoccupation with the marital life of famous actors, and in these stories, the economic aspects of marriage are often writ large.

However, in spite of these continuities, marriage does not have exactly the same implications in all societies. The historical character of marriage does not preclude great variations and drastic change. These variations emerge primarily because marriage and its consequences have been regulated in very different ways over time and across cultures. When an English woman married in the seventeenth century, all her property (except freehold land) immediately became the complete and unconditional property of her husband, and, unless he made a will for her benefit, she ran the risk of becoming a destitute widow. By contrast, when a Swedish woman marries today, she knows that she will inherit everything left by her husband if he should predecease her (and the same applies to him). These two examples reinforce the conclusion that while marriage is a ubiquitous social institution, it cannot be properly understood if taken out of its legal and cultural context. The ways in which legal systems and cultural conceptions of gender define the roles and rights of spouses have significant repercussions not only on people's lives but also on society as a whole.

If these matters are considered, it soon becomes apparent that it is particularly important how the spouses' contributions to their joint partnership are conceived of in society. To be more precise, the extent to which men's and women's contributions are "seen" and acknowledged by law and social security systems is often crucially important for the meaning that marriage takes on for the individual. In the contemporary Swedish pension system, for instance, contributions in the form of childcare (traditionally associated with the wife) are poorly recognized, while the role as breadwinner (usually played by the husband) renders him more pension credits. Many find this inequitable and see it as a denigration of forms of work often performed by women. There is no reason to believe that this was any different in the past. The Church exhorted spouses to share all hardship that befell them, but did all wives really feel that they had shared the bitterness equitably and profited from work to the same extent as their husbands? The English example just mentioned suggests that when all was said and done, many women felt that they were the losers. To be sure, as we shall see throughout this study, the roles could be reversed; in eighteenth-century Sweden a man who married a rich heiress and invested his money and labor into the wife's property might have felt mistreated by the way in which these exertions remained unnoticed by the law.

The question as to how the economic contributions of spouses to the household have been respected in society is an issue of enduring importance, but often it is very difficult for the historian to uncover these secrets of domestic lives — some matters having been secret from others in their own day, others having once been known to the local community but then lost to posterity by the passage of time. I have over many years followed one of the few approaches available, that is, to focus upon how men's and women's economic contributions have been looked upon — or overlooked — in family law. In codifications, legal treatises, and, especially, court practice I have found it possible to observe how contributions of labor, skills, and property have been categorized as valuable or nonvaluable and how they have been made visible or turned invisible. Although at first glance these cultural processes have often left few traces that the historian can use, I have found more than sufficient evidence in extant legal sources to enable me to reconstruct these phenomena and thus to see patterns and long-term trends.

I have in the process brought to life many of the underlying conditions that define Sweden's place in the burgeoning field of the study of family, gender, property, and law in early modern Europe. Sweden is both instructive in its differences from other domains and yet similar to them in the ways in which it grappled with the effects of warfare and state building, with incipient commercialization and with the protracted course of modernization of the law. It was an important site for ideas that circulated throughout Enlightenment Europe, reflecting them both at the private domestic level and in the public sphere in its own distinctive ways that trace ultimately to medieval society with its strong focus upon rights in land and its propensity to invest such rights in kin groups rather than in individuals. To revive the Swedish past in the way that I do is at once to reconstruct a story all its own and to fill out, comparatively, a complex European historical experience.

My gleanings from the sources tell a large and intricate story in which legal, economic, cultural, and political forces meet. However, much of my early material operates at the case level — from modest individual cases I build up, over several chapters, a more panoramic view, one that is foundational for the ongoing story of the later eighteenth and nineteenth centuries that I tell in later chapters. The following example, found in seventeenth-century Swedish court records, shows both the potential and the difficulty of this early source material.

In the 1650s, a Swedish peasant by the name of Lars Andersson appeared before the local court to take issue with his stepmother Anna, who was then in possession of the family farm. Lars claimed that he and his siblings were entitled to at least six-fifteenths of the farm since this had been their late mother's share. He was also prepared, he declared, to buy off his siblings so that the entire share would rightfully be his. Through her legal representative, the stepmother contested this claim, arguing that she and her late husband had bought one part of the farm jointly and that her husband had devised yet another part of the farm to her, making her the largest shareholder and thus unassailable. Lars and his siblings protested vehemently. In fact, large parts of the farm had been purchased during their father's first marriage, and it was the inherited assets of their mother that had made the purchase possible. Lars proved his case by calling upon the testimony of a former servant of his father's, who remembered having delivered the payment in installments to the seller (Lars's aunt) while the first wife was still alive.[1]

This case brings to the fore married women's economic contributions to the early modern household. What is particularly interesting in the story is Lars's assertion, almost in passing, that the farm had been purchased with money his mother had inherited. In this way, Lars Andersson's narrative gives an indispensable glimpse of how the mother's property had been brought into the marital estate and used in a way her children disapproved of. The case is all the more interesting because it shows us how claims deriving from two different women were pitted against each other. The first wife was said to have contributed her inherited assets to the household, making it possible for the couple to buy a large part of the family farm from the husband's siblings. In this way, her children's maternal inheritance had been incorporated into the lineage property of their father. This would not have stirred any heated feelings, had not the father decided to remarry, apparently without having first paid to his children what was due them from their mother. The second wife argued, on the other hand, that the contested land had been purchased during her marriage to their father. The implication was twofold and unambiguous: the first wife had not made any economic contribution of relevance to the contested land, while the second wife had.

Regardless of which party was right, Lars Andersson's case epitomizes crucial aspects of seventeenth-century rural Sweden. This was a society with a bilateral inheritance system, giving sons and daughters strong (but not equal) rights to inherit from both their father and their mother. Since land was an important form of wealth, this was also a society where many women were potential, actual, or former landholders. Therefore, it must have been obvious to most people that women contributed to the marital economy by bringing their inherited assets into the estate — and it is also evident that cases like Lars Andersson's must have served as forceful reminders. Finally, the case is methodologically instructive, suggesting that vital information about women's property rights is scattered over innumerable unprinted legal documents where it has long failed to catch the attention of historians.

While highlighting the economic importance of women's contributions of property to the household, the case is remarkably silent on the economic importance of women's skills and labor. Had it been beneficial to the case, it is likely that Lars Andersson would have recounted the hard work his late mother had performed for the household, and the stepmother would probably have told a similar story about her own exertions. But such comments were accorded little legal significance in the seventeenth century, since early modern Swedish law was remarkably silent on the value of women's work for the benefit of the household — in sharp contrast to what was the case for other forms of work. It was not until the late eighteenth and early nineteenth centuries that the economic importance of women's work was placed on the agenda.

In 1770, for instance, an anonymous pamphlet was printed in Stockholm, addressing women's situation in society. The author exhorted "public opinion" to realize and acknowledge the economic value of women's contributions to society and to improve women's conditions by giving them access to better education. The author, who has been identified as the cookbook author Anna Maria Rückerschöld, condemned the sort of passive life that was then coming into fashion among upper- and middle-class women. Speaking up against what may have been a new ideal of domesticity, Anna Maria argued that society was highly dependent on the economic contributions of women.[2] These ideas would later, in the nineteenth century, be taken up both by other female authors and by male politicians.

Anna Maria Rückerschöld and Lars Andersson both emphasized the economic importance of women's contributions to the household and to society. However, their commitment was clearly fueled by different motives. Lars Andersson was not speaking on behalf of his mother (who had long been deceased) but for himself, his siblings, and his children. He was the mouthpiece for "the kin interest," ubiquitous in early modern Sweden, not for women's rights. If anyone was thinking of a woman and what would happen to her in her old age, it may have been Lars's father, who had made a special will for the benefit of his second wife. The local community, which in effect controlled the local court, may also have devoted thought to what would happen if the stepmother were left without assets with which to support herself. Costs for the poor would fall on the parish, in one way or other, if there was no other solution. Thus, pragmatic and self-interested considerations dominated the decisions of the court. By way of contrast, Anna Maria Rückerschöld, who lived at the time of the Enlightenment, broached the question of women's economic contributions as such, asking her readers what sort of role women should rightfully have in society. In doing so, she was one of the first to put the question into a political framework. Her approach makes it very clear that this was an issue subject to changing opinions. Over the period of 250 years that this book covers, Swedish women's economic contributions have continuously been reconceptualized and renegotiated in a process involving a wide gamut of interests and motives. Most of all, the need to protect Swedish women's economic assets was rethought, and the legal methods for doing so were reorganized.

This process forms the topic of this book, and the focal point is married women's property rights, both because women's economic resources were decisive for the creditworthiness and success of the household and because the extent to which these rights were well protected was decisive for individual women's lives. I pursue this theme by looking at Sweden in the period from 1600 to 1857. The seventeenth century was a period of intense state building and massive societal change in Sweden and Europe. An agrarian society with a small population and limited resources, Sweden nevertheless engaged in the continental wars which led to the loss of much manpower and to new financial challenges. The country also became a prominent producer of iron for the European market. It is natural to start in this period of thorough change but also useful in order to draw attention to some less well-known aspects of the transformative processes. In chapter 2, I show how married women's property rights were protected in this period, how the basic principles of medieval law remained intact, but also how at the same time new sociolegal practices started to develop on a grass-roots level. In chapter 3, I look closer at the standpoints taken in learned jurisprudence in the course of the seventeenth century, and how these views affected the legislative process preceding the new code of 1734, which introduced novel ways of conceptualizing married women's property rights. Chapter 4 sets a new scene: eighteenth-century Sweden, a country at peace, with a prosperous agrarian economy, and ruled by the four estates (until the 1770s). I explore the effects of these new conditions upon women's property rights, paying special attention to whether landed property and movable property were equally well protected by law, and to how ordinary people strove to make worthy arrangements for old women. In chapters 5 and 6, I study how these developments were reflected in various forms of public debate, and I argue that these debates are a missing link, the key with which the meaning of the early nineteenth-century emancipation reforms can be unlocked, while at the same time shedding new light on previous developments.

Protecting Women's Property Rights: The Existing Picture

Historical research has devoted considerable interest to women's economic contributions in the past. Within this field one central objective has been to clarify the quantitative importance of women's work, to find out whether women could make decisions about their own incomes, and, if so, how they used these incomes (for instance, for consumption or for investments).[3] Another, equally central ambition has been to analyze how well women's property rights have been protected in the past. In this context, the situation of the married woman has rightfully attracted special interest. Given that throughout Europe, and elsewhere, the married man was the one who managed household matters and wielded power in society, researchers have been particularly interested in what this meant for married women. To what extent could the husband use her property as if it were his own? Could a wife make legal complaints against a husband who abused his role as manager of the estate? What legal remedies were available? Was the marital estate a "black hole" from the point of view of the wife, where her resources effectively disappeared as they merged with those of her husband or were dissipated by him? This was what Lars Andersson claimed: that his mother's inherited assets had been incorporated into the family estate in a way that made it difficult to disentangle her (and her heirs') property from that of their father (and the stepmother and stepsiblings).

The "black hole theory" was vividly depicted by some nineteenth-century novelists. In *The Mill on the Floss* (1860), George Eliot paints a stark portrait of the unlucky Tulliver family, whose members are all deeply affected by the unwise investments and final bankruptcy of their father. Putting his mill up for sale does not suffice to cover all debts; the family also has to part with almost all their movable property, including linen and china the mother has brought into the estate. Even though she regards these goods as her own, they are the property of her husband according to the law and cannot be separated from the estate. The story suggests that Mrs. Tulliver becomes poor because of her marriage to Mr. Tulliver. Since no trust has been made to protect her separate estate, her property effectively disappears into the black hole of marriage.[4] In *Hertha* (1856), the Swedish novelist Fredrika Bremer presents a similar story of the talented and motherless Hertha Falk, who is barred from taking command of her own life by her despotic father. Mr. Falk is his children's guardian and has their property at his disposal. With his love for money and his miserly and insensitive attitude to his four daughters, he refuses to let the eldest, Alma, marry the man she loves, which eventually brings about her death. He is also reluctant to let the adult Hertha have access to her maternal inheritance. When she saves his life, he gives in and promises to grant her full legal capacity. However, Mr. Falk dies before having fulfilled his vows. Just like the Tulliver family, the Falk family is depicted as dominated and bullied by a man invested with too much power. And just like Mrs. Tulliver's linen and china, Mrs. Falk's property seems to disappear into a black hole from which her daughters are unable to retrieve it.[5]

Stories like these are both persuasive and pervasive. However, recent historiography suggests that they may be less representative of "the past" than we might think. In fact, medieval and early modern societies show us a wide array of subtle legal systems designed precisely to avoid the "black hole" scenario. One particularly illustrative example comes from fourteenth-century Venice. Here, the woman transferred her inherited assets — the dowry — to her husband upon marriage. As Linda Guzzetti has pointed out, the function of the dowry was dual: it was intended to defray the expenses of the household during marriage, and, as it was supposed to revert to the widow upon the death of her husband, it was also supposed to prevent women from falling into poverty. But to what extent did the dowry actually revert to the widow? Apparently very often, and the reason for this was that the Venetians had developed a formalized system for keeping track of wives' property. Upon marriage, husbands acknowledged receipt of the dowry through a so-called *carta securitatis*. With these instruments as evidence, Venetian widows found it comparatively easy to achieve restitution of their dowries through legal procedures. On the other hand, many husbands also seem to have acknowledged their debt to their wives in their wills, making a legal procedure superfluous. The system was not only advantageous to the widow and her heirs but to the husband's heirs as well. If the widow had been given presents by her husband during marriage, the value of these gifts was deducted from that of the dowry.[6] Thus, this was a highly formalized system, protecting both husband and wife from any negative effects that might ensue if his and her property were allowed to be combined.

Early modern Nantes provides another example of a legal system designed to keep track of what was his and hers. Here, members of the immediate family and the wider kin group played an important role in safeguarding the property interests of married women. When a marriage was negotiated, the two families involved could decide how much of the woman's dowry should count as separate property (*propres*) and how much as common, since this was not determined by the law. Thus, the notion that married women had the right to hold separate property was a cornerstone in Nantes, and the right was sustained by her relatives' strong self-interest in the matter. Moreover, the legal system supported married women whose husbands disregarded the property rights of their wives. A wife could apply for separation of her share of the common property, and she could also seek support from the local court and her kinsmen to retrieve her *propres*, if she could show that these assets had been badly managed or had been sold at "the instigation or persuasion" of her husband. As Julie Hardwick points out, women's *propres* were crucial to whether or not the household was regarded as creditworthy. Consequently, a wife could exert quite significant power by withholding her property from her husband.[7]

England is often seen as a country in which the property rights of married women were poorly protected; it is probably no coincidence that the Tulliver family lives in Britain. And it is true that English common law invested the husband with great economic power. He became the exclusive owner of everything his wife brought into the marital estate, with the exception of real property (that is, freehold land). However, since only a small minority owned freehold land in England, an even smaller minority of whom were women (because of the inheritance rules known as primogeniture), this exception was comparatively insignificant. The general rule was that all personal property (which was what most women had) became the exclusive property of the husband directly upon marriage.[8] On the other hand, Amy L. Erickson has pointed to the vast array of compensating practices deployed by early modern Englishmen to sustain and corroborate the property rights of individual women. There were many ways of circumventing the husband's power, like creating a trust for the married woman's "sole and separate estate." Through this legal device, married women could be protected against the evil effects of coverture. In fact, the result was that many women did have substantial property interests during marriage, in sharp contrast to what the doctrine of coverture would have us believe. Even if such trusts, or settlements, were not enforceable in common-law courts, equity courts protected them and sometimes even demanded that husbands create separate estates for their wives.[9]

These examples suggest that there were many different and often highly sophisticated ways of protecting married women's property rights in the medieval and early modern period, and that we would be well-advised in not attributing too much historical truth to nineteenth-century fiction. There is little evidence to support the argument that married women's property was generally, always, and everywhere incorporated into that of their husbands in a way that made their rights indistinct and, eventually, threatened to make them poor as widows. Still, the English case suggests that, to the extent that no special legal arrangements were made for the wife, her situation could be very precarious indeed. Lars Andersson's case (and other cases that we will encounter throughout this book) also shows that the "black hole" theory is not entirely inappropriate as a description of the Swedish situation. There were Swedish women whose property was in fact "swallowed" by that of their husbands. (But there were also Swedish men whose property was swallowed by that of their wives.) Understanding the mechanisms behind this phenomenon is vital. The various examples from different parts of Europe suggest that the mechanisms to be observed involve the role of kin and local courts, the use of oral proof as opposed to written evidence, and the role of individual legal arrangements (such as wills and trusts). They also alert us to the importance of studying in detail how these different systems worked, and how and why they changed over time. To what extent were marital estates "black holes" or, as seventeenth-century Swedish observers called them, "domestic secrets"? And did their roles as domestic secrets change in the course of the early modern period?

Domestic Secrecy as Simplification of the Law

In order to better understand historical change in this field, one has to bear in mind that in the early modern world family law was one of the main regulators of the redistribution of wealth in society. Inheritance law directed the flow of resources between generations, just as marital property law directed the flow of resources between spouses. In this way, family law could and did create tangible economic benefits for some, while seriously disadvantaging others. Family law also had huge repercussions for society's costs for care of the elderly. It is easy to see that a system that safeguarded widows' and widowers' property rights would reduce the need for communally organized poor relief, while poorly protected (or nonexistent) rights of the widowed would magnify the problem of poverty.[10] Moreover, family law affected economic life outside the family, for instance by laying down rules for how creditors' claims were to be balanced against those of the heirs. In a country such as early modern Sweden, where state finances depended largely upon taxes from small-scale peasant farms, it is obvious that the state was concerned with how inheritance law was implemented. It was not in the interest of the state to let farms be fragmented upon the demise of the former holder, since this was believed to jeopardize tax incomes.

Family law was thus nothing less than the hub of early modern economic life, both on a micro- and macro-level. Consequently, many actors had a keen interest in how family law worked and perhaps also in bringing about change. It is telling that such concerns surfaced precisely in the late seventeenth century when the Swedish Empire was at its zenith. With a vast territory (encompassing both sides of the Baltic as well as areas in northern Germany), a heightened sense of national importance, an increasingly commercialized economy, and large financial problems, Swedish society had been transformed in a way that put old truths under new pressure. Family law was definitely no exception.

Discussing the rules pertaining to marital property, Swedish appeals court lawyers in the late seventeenth century liked to refer to the marital estate as an *arcanum domesticum*, or a "domestic secret."[11] Using this expression, they indicated that outsiders had problems knowing who owned what within a household. An outsider could not assume that everything that was visibly in the hands of the husband was his sole property, the lawyers argued, because sometimes a husband had means at his disposal of which he was not the exclusive owner. As a matter of fact, the latter was regularly the case in early modern Sweden since women could inherit freehold land and since orphaned stepchildren often had unsettled inheritance claims. This situation made the legal position of husbands unclear, according to these lawyers. What was his actual authority when it came to carrying out commercial transactions? Could the husband sell everything that was in the estate? Could he mortgage it?

Who then were the "outsiders" these lawyers had in mind? In whose interest was it to make property arrangements within households less secretive and more transparent to those outside? The answer in the seventeenth-century context was obvious: creditors. It was creditors' interests that Swedish lawyers were considering when they described the situation as unfortunate. The lawyers believed that creditors lent their money to men in possession of large landed estates, assuming that these estates would provide security for their demands. However, many creditors would subsequently find out that they had acted under a misapprehension, since the estates in question turned out to belong to their debtors' wives. What was most important, lawyers asked themselves: to uphold the old principle of protecting married women's separate property or to improve the situation of creditors? Many, but not all, cast their votes for the latter alternative.

These debates displayed a vivid concern for the rights of creditors and, as a consequence, for the authority of married men. Paradoxically, what I have here described as a sign of sophistication in the legal system — that it made a clear distinction between his and hers and that it provided methods of checking that this distinction was not disregarded — turned into the main problem in the eyes of these lawyers. They did not see distinction and clarity; they only saw a bewildering and obscure bundle of intersecting and conflicting rights. Therefore, the solution they envisaged was to abolish the distinction between his and hers, and to define the marital estate as a unit of property at the complete disposal of the husband. This meant, by extension, that everything in the estate would become accessible to the husband's creditors.

But the lawyers did not consider this a quandary. In view of the mutual love that could be assumed to exist between spouses, they concluded, the law must be allowed to take for granted that the wife did not mind supporting her husband with that which she owned. The lawyers advocated that the law should simply take for granted that, for all practical purposes, everything in the estate belonged to the husband. Another solution could have been to require borrowers to specify collateral in writing and to hold those who listed a spouse's lineage property as defrauders. However, this was not what the lawyers opted for. Instead of finding ways of clarifying domestic secrecy, they chose to accept it. Had these ideas been fully put into practice (they were not, as we shall see), Swedish marital property law would have become more similar to the British system of coverture.

The seventeenth-century discussion about domestic secrets shows that early modern family law was far from impermeable to the interests of "outsiders." Instead, it was the battleground for many competing interests and ideas among which the concern for creditors was particularly salient. In this context, an overarching guideline seems to have been "simplification." Even if the lawyers did not use this word, they obviously felt that family law needed to be simplified, so that disputes could be avoided or, to the extent that they could not be avoided, more easily settled. To give husbands, and their creditors, greater leeway with respect to household property would be one way of achieving legal simplification, albeit at the cost of the wife (and her kinsmen).

Previous research has directed our attention to schemes of simplification and to the risks that may be inherent in them. In her study of women's property rights in the early American colonies, Marylynn Salmon proposed that, in the early modern period, the "semi-rights" of women often tended to be curtailed precisely because lawyers wanted to simplify the law.[12] On a more general level, James C. Scott has argued that modern states have often wanted to make society more transparent, or "legible," and that efforts to achieve that have invariably meant that crucial details of social life — knowledge, rights — were neglected, set aside, and forgotten. Interestingly, Scott notes in passing that not only high-modernist states have displayed this interest in transparency: early on, both the land market and the credit market presupposed legibility in the sense that entitlement had to be absolutely clear and unambiguous.[13] Thus, property law and credit law may be two of the earliest and best examples of the quest for transparency and legibility. Michael Roberts captures this idea of simplification eminently in his discussion about early bookkeeping practices. Roberts argues that bookkeeping (which was required, for instance, by Swedish bankruptcy law) made the economy "clearer than life." Thus, he suggests that legal and technical devices like bookkeeping and registration of titles allowed people outside the household (auditors, judges, creditors, curators of bankrupt estates) to gain a picture of the household which was easy to interpret but perhaps too simplified. It left out crucial aspects of economic life, such as the importance of women's and children's work and property rights.[14]

Looking at the early modern world, we are confronted with examples of family law according to which married women's property rights were distinct and well-protected. We are also confronted with examples where these rights were less distinct and where special legal arrangements were needed in order to secure them. Moreover, we see a tendency to "simplify" the law during this period and are alerted to the risks that such a tendency may have entailed. The drift toward simplification may have operated only on the surface of the legal system, among distinguished lawyers and judges, but not so much at the grass-roots level on which Lars Andersson, his family, and the local court operated. On the other hand, there is evidence to suggest that notions of the importance of "domestic secrecy" did appear among ordinary people, although later than the seventeenth century and with somewhat different connotations.

Domestic Secrecy as Privacy

Seventeenth-century Swedish lawyers looked at households from the perspective of outsiders. Instead of trying to find legal or technical solutions that would have made the marital property arrangements less opaque (as the Venetians had managed to do with the public registration of dowries), they settled for simplification. The complexity was reduced by assuming that the husband owned everything, a solution that was summarized in the term "domestic secret." However, the notion of domestic secrecy also appears with another and slightly different meaning: as the wish to protect the privacy of households in general and the privacy of married couples in particular. While surfacing occasionally in the early eighteenth century, this concern with privacy became much more pronounced in the early nineteenth century. Fredrika Bremer and her novel *Hertha* bear witness to the new ideals.

The novel elaborates on the theme of privacy to illustrate Hertha's situation: her home is described as "a dark mystery," concealing silently "the secrets of family life," so that they cannot be surmised by "the surrounding world." From these lines, it is obvious that Bremer thinks of privacy as something that militates against the interests of Hertha and her sisters. Had it been publicly known that their father withheld their maternal inheritance from them, and that he denied them the right to marry according to the wishes of their hearts, public opinion would probably have put pressure on him to change his behavior. And yet, Bremer's attitude to publicity was ambivalent. After the death of her father, some of Hertha's male acquaintances offer to help her petition the king to be granted full legal capacity (which was an option for unmarried women at the time). However, Hertha is unwilling to take this step since it would disclose to everyone her father's cruelty. Even if she resents his actions, she does not want to have her domestic secrets exposed to the public. According to the novel, then, privacy appears as something highly desirable. Even in a precarious situation, Hertha is willing to sacrifice her own economic interests to avoid public exposure of the family history. Privacy is also, the reader suspects, linked to notions of middle-class respectability. More than anything else, Hertha is anxious not to have the family's dirty linen washed in public.

Nineteenth-century legislators were not impervious to these ideas. Indeed, one of the most influential of them, Johan Gabriel Richert, vehemently opposed all legal solutions that would expose the married couple to the public. Publicity would hurt the delicate nature of marriage, he claimed. Marriage was not comparable to a company of shareholders; it was a very special union between two individuals, based on love, trust, and mutual support. To raise the issue of spouses' individual property rights, which presupposed technical solutions such as inventories that were a matter of public record, would be to inspire distrust in spouses and to undermine marriage, he argued. Consequently, information pertaining to marriage — such as how much each spouse had brought into the marital estate — should not be made public but remain a domestic secret.

In Richert's and other nineteenth-century jurists' minds, issues of legal simplification and marital privacy seem to have become woven together in ways that were not always clear-cut under the rubric of domestic secrecy. In Fredrika Bremer's mind, on the other hand, privacy was clearly an ambiguous concept that encapsulated both values of which she approved (like respectability) and implications of which she was highly critical (like women's vulnerable position). In her own life, Bremer increasingly dissociated herself from the middle-class confinement of women to the home and embarked upon travels that took her to the New World.

With its broad time span, this book moves from a period when ideals of privacy were unheard of (around 1600) to a period when they were at center stage (around 1850). In the world in which Lars Andersson lived, it was self-evident that the local community harbored knowledge about his family: that his father had been married twice, that his mother had brought property into the common household, and that his parents had acquired a certain farm during marriage. It was precisely because of this locally preserved knowledge, which made the distinction between public and private meaningless, that Lars Andersson turned to the local court. In the world of *Hertha*, this sort of information would instead have been stored in various forms of written documents, and it could have been widely disseminated through the medium of print, causing "scandal" and damaging respectability in ways that would have been inconceivable in the seventeenth century.

A major argument of this book is that over the 250 years under discussion, married women's property rights were affected by two different but closely interrelated social processes, both of which are captured by the expression "domestic secrets." One originated on the level of the state and its legislation and initially began to develop from the late seventeenth century onward; it targeted transparency and legal simplification and was closely linked to economic change. The other process originated within society and concerned the formation of new middle-class ideals from the turn of the eighteenth century; it centered on conflicting notions of privacy and public knowledge. Admittedly, these two social processes were not the only ones involved. As we shall see, commercialization and changing demographic realities also played very important parts in this story. However, at the heart of these matters lay changing notions of what domestic secrecy embodied.

Methodology

The following analysis combines a practical and a "technical" approach. The former focuses on how ordinary people disposed of property within the family. I am interested in unveiling and understanding everyday practices and in seeing to what extent any major changes occurred in this respect during the period under study. Inspired by the work of Martha C. Howell, Amy L. Erickson, and others, I assume that major legal change is seldom initiated solely from above but rather is usually the result of changing economic realities in local communities, experienced first and foremost by ordinary people.[15] Therefore, observing changes in local customs and in the uses of legal arrangements such as wills and retirement contracts is crucial.

The technical approach focuses on the legal system per se. It suggests that law is a social tool (probably the oldest social tool) that "looks" at society in a certain way, formulates norms for social life, and provides methods for the utilization and the enforcement of these norms. My point is that norms and methods must be considered together, and it is important to realize that certain norms are more difficult to enforce than others, because they are not supported by appropriate methods that enable their application. It is often useful to think about new legal methods (such as probate inventory) as means that allow the legal system to "see" new parts of society. In other words, new legal methods often serve to enhance legibility. On the other hand, we must employ a broad definition of legal methods and not restrict ourselves to what is familiar to us from modern society. In early modern local communities, orally transmitted knowledge and social control by neighbors were fundamental and often highly appropriate instruments that could be used to support the legal system. It is even possible to argue that these older methods functioned better than the new ones, since they were more attuned to the conditions of everyday life.[16]

Finally, the analysis concentrates on the legal protection of married women's separate property, not on women's rights of inheritance, nor on the economic situation of widows, although these matters will also be touched upon. This is a highly conscious choice, inspired by the work of Bina Agarwal. Agarwal has shown that in preindependence India, women's chances of inheriting land correlated significantly with the degree of control that their natal families could continue to exert over their land after marriage. In areas where women's families had the power to control land given to a daughter so that it could not be squandered or wasted by the son-in-law, women tended to inherit land. By way of contrast, in areas where families did not have this power, women rarely stood a chance of inheriting landed property. Agarwal suggests that this had something to do with "the critical importance of landed property in agrarian economies," which caused families to have a strong interest in making certain that their land would "remain within their overall purview."[17]

The methodological implication of Agarwal's comprehensive and detailed study is that, when investigating women's property rights in agrarian economies, we should look first at married women's property rights and the ways in which they are protected. Other rights, for instance, rights of inheritance, must be understood against the backdrop of how well-protected the married woman's rights were. In other words, women's different rights must be understood as being interconnected, but among all these rights the married woman's property rights are the most important, since they constitute the independent factor. Since early modern Sweden was also an agrarian economy where families and kin played important roles and where the notion of lineage property was very much stressed, it seems reasonable to assume that here, too, married women's property rights were particularly important within the broader framework of family law.[18]

Land, Population, and Courts

Domestic Secrets

———

19

Early modern Sweden was a large but sparsely populated country. We know that in 1571 the approximate size of the population was 639,000, a number that is believed to have risen to 1.3 million in 1700 and to 2.3 million by 1800.[19] In 1571, about 85 percent of all rural parishes had fewer than ten inhabitants per square kilometer, whereas in 1751 around 60 percent of the rural parishes had more than ten inhabitants per square kilometer.[20] The vast majority of the population consisted of peasants living in the countryside. In the sixteenth century, about 45 percent of the cadastral units (farms) were held by freeholders, and the rest by tenants of the Crown and the nobility. Around 1700 freeholders held about one-third of the farms and the latter two-thirds.[21] The nobility constituted less than 1 percent of the population in the period.[22] Towns and cities were few and small, and the urban population comprised only 7 percent of the total population at the beginning of the seventeenth century, rising to approximately 10 percent around 1700.[23]

Consequently, nearly everybody depended on access to land for survival. This was certainly true for the peasantry, who lived on what they could produce on their farms, but it was equally true for the nobility, who derived their incomes from their tenants (as well as from various entrepreneurial activities). This was also true for the early modern Swedish state: without taxes from the peasantry, the bureaucracy could not be fed and wars could not be waged. It is hardly surprising, then, that so much of seventeenth-century political strife focused on issues of land: how the state should use its own land, whether and under what conditions the nobility should be allowed to take over state land, the relationship between landlords and peasants, and whether the freeholding peasantry could endure increased taxes based on possession of land.[24] Nor is it surprising that property rights in land were accorded strong legal protection. Losing control of landed property was a serious matter.

Consequently, the law emphasized families' rights to their lineage land. In order to protect the family and the broader kin group against unwise disposition of this land by individual members, the law drew a very sharp distinction between land received through inheritance (*arve*) and land acquired through purchase (*avlinge*). An owner had no unconditional right to sell the former, since legally he was only holding it on behalf of his family, as a trustee. By way of contrast, owners had complete freedom of disposition as concerned noninherited land; for instance, they could devise such land by will.[25] These rules applied equally to all social strata living in the countryside, to peasants as well as to noblemen. The rules made it impossible for spouses to co-own lineage land, but all land that they acquired during marriage was considered their common property.

The law's concern with keeping land within families is epitomized in the crucial legal device known as *bördsrätt*.[26] This right gave members of the broader kin group the right to veto the sale of land by one of their kinsmen to someone outside the kin group. The following example from the court records of Uppland illustrates what this right could imply. Lars Olofsson of Sikhjälma came to court in 1638 and provided proof that he had purchased one-half of a farm in Sikhjälma for 100 copper *daler* from the heirs of Reverend Jöns in Rimbo. He also complained that, thus far, he had been unable to obtain a title deed. "Now, Bertil [from Sikhjälma] rose in front of the court and, adducing his *bördsrätt*, he argued that he should [be allowed to] reclaim the farm, and Lars's purchase should be annulled." And because Bertil had this right, Lars was content to surrender the farm to Bertil, providing that the purchase money was returned.[27]

Despite the fact that Lars had paid the heirs of the former owner a substantial sum of money, he was unable to get a title deed and in the end, he had to accept leaving the farm to someone who was obviously a distant relative of the sellers. His money was reimbursed, and, if he had already made any investments in the farm, Bertil would have had to compensate him for these as well. For all we know, Lars may have been completely satisfied with the final outcome of the affair. Still, the case would strike many people today as strange, precisely because it challenges ideals that are central to modern society, such as the freedom of owners to do what they like with what is theirs and the importance of providing owners with secure titles. The case is indicative of the crucial significance attached to kin and to lineage property in early modern Swedish society.[28]

However, the pervasive importance of the kin group should not be interpreted to mean that early modern Sweden was a sort of clan society, where every person belonged to and identified with one lineage only. Instead, all persons belonged to *two* lineages, the father's and the mother's, and were entitled to inherit from both lineages. This two-lineage identity is expressed very clearly in the Swedish language, which did not (and still does not) have a general word for "grandparents." Swedes have to use either the word for paternal grandparents (*farföräldrar*) or the word for maternal grandparents (*morföräldrar*). This two-lineage identity meant that a person could choose to stress different kin relations in different situations, depending on what suited his or her interests best. As we saw at the beginning of this chapter, Lars Andersson's basic argument was that he belonged to his mother's lineage, but in another dispute he may well have emphasized his father's lineage. Thus, the rhetoric of lineage and kin could be, and often was, used to sustain individual interests and claims.

Many Swedish farms had been abandoned in connection with the late medieval crisis,[29] and the problem of land desertion and shortage of manpower remained very significant in the early modern period. It was aggravated by new wars on Swedish soil[30] and by the fact that so many young men were conscripted and subsequently died as soldiers in the continental wars. Jan Lindegren has calculated that 30 percent of all young men born in the period from 1620 to 1720 died prematurely, drastically affecting sex ratios, particularly at the end of the protracted war period (around 1700).[31] This deficit of men must have improved women's chances of assuming responsibility for a farm (see table 5), and the results of a study by Magnus Perlestam corroborate this conclusion.[32] Seventeenth-century Sweden was a country where many farms were run by wives and widows.[33] This makes questions about how women's property rights were organized and protected during and after marriage particularly interesting.

Most peasants lived in rural settlements consisting of just a couple of farms, and many farms even lay in complete isolation. Only in some parts of the country (such as Skåne or Dalarna) were these settlements comparable in size to English villages. For most of them, the term hamlet is more appropriate, and I will use it throughout this book. The hamlets were not enclosed until the middle of the eighteenth century, when state-initiated enclosure reforms commenced. Therefore, when we think of seventeenth- and early eighteenth-century farms, we should not conceptualize them as compact but as a form of production unit where bits of land (and other material resources) were scattered in several places in the physical landscape and where cooperation between households was essential.

Just as peasants had to cooperate within hamlets, they also had to cooperate to combat crime and to settle internal disputes. Their arena for these legal actions was the local court (usually known as *häradsrätt*), of which there were approximately 250 in this period.[34] The local court dealt with all sorts of legal matters, and it could also take up other matters of interest to the local population. As the state became stronger in the course of the early modern period, it firmly asserted its presence in the courts, for instance, via bailiffs. Consequently, the early modern local courts catered to the needs of both local communities and the state. They could start the day by reading a few government announcements, then go on to hear witnesses in a fornication case, solve a dispute over fishing rights between hamlets in two different parishes, investigate the facts in a complicated case of conflicting inheritance claims, and finally register a will and a couple of land sales. Specialization was low, and lay participation high. Here, the twelve lay judges (denoted by the collective term *nämnd*) were crucial.

The lay judges were recruited from within the local community; typically, they would be well-established peasants of good reputation, often but not necessarily freeholders. These judges lacked formal legal training, but since they often served in the court for quite long periods of time (ten years was not uncommon), they gradually became acquainted with the content and meaning of the legal code. It should be emphasized that these men were judges, not a jury. They were an integral part of the court, taking part both in the interrogation of parties and witnesses and in the final interpretation of the law. One could even claim that the lay judges *were* the court. There was a legally trained chairman, but his influence is believed to have diminished in the course of the sixteenth and seventeenth centuries, when the regular holders of this office (noblemen) were often not on duty and were replaced by socially less-elevated persons.[35]

Not surprisingly, legal uniformity (in the sense that all courts interpreted the law in the same way) was low. At least this was the reason given for setting up the first royal court of appeal (*hovrätt*) in 1614, which was soon followed by three additional ones. Henceforth, a person who was not content with the outcome of his suit could appeal to these courts. In serious criminal cases a convicted person did not have the right to appeal, but the primary courts were required to submit these cases to the courts of appeal for scrutiny before a death sentence could be carried out. Moreover, all primary court records were submitted in their entirety to the courts of appeal annually, where they were closely read and checked for possible errors. Thus, the appeals court judges, all of whom were professional lawyers, must have possessed unique insight into how the law was understood and used throughout the country. In

1680 the king ruled that local court chairmen had to be on duty, increasing central control of the local courts even more.[36]

Usually, the local courts convened three times a year, but extraordinary sessions could also be arranged, for instance, in cases of homicide or suicide. As for civil cases, which greatly dominated the courts' work in the eighteenth and nineteenth centuries, the parties involved would have to await a regular session. It was not uncommon for such cases to become protracted, as oral testimonies or written documents were scrutinized and compared by the judges. Not infrequently, the disputes were never brought to a formal end. In some cases, the parties would turn up to inform the court that they had reached an amicable solution; in other cases, the parties just dropped out, presumably because they too had reached a private settlement. (That costs for taking one's case to court were low, or even nonexistent, encouraged legal activity.)[37] As Eva Österberg and others have pointed out, the guiding principle of the local courts seems to have been to establish socially sustainable solutions to local problems and not to press formal points of the law. Therefore, that people resorted to nonlegal solutions in the end was not perceived as a problem.

The parties usually appeared in the local court in person, and they also conducted their cases themselves. Women appeared in court, although not quite as frequently as men did.[38] Higher up in the legal hierarchy (the courts of appeal) and in the social hierarchy (the nobility) the use of legal representatives was more common and may have increased over time. Nevertheless, the court records offer us unique possibilities of hearing the actual words of people in the past, as they sought to convince the court and their neighbors that they had a solid case.

Early modern Sweden was characterized by literacy levels that were very high in comparison with most European countries. More or less all adult persons (men and women) are likely to have been able to read in the late eighteenth century. This was the result of concerted efforts initiated in the 1680s to bring the message of Christianity to the entire population and was based on a system whereby parents and heads of households were made responsible for the instruction of children and servants. Consequently, what people definitely knew was Luther's *Small Catechism*. It is the clergy's recording and grading of ordinary people's skills in reading and understanding Luther's work that scholars have used to measure literacy. Whether ordinary Swedes were also able to read and understand previously unknown texts has been the topic of some discussion. Daniel Lindmark has argued that, during the eighteenth century, a cleavage occurred in Swedish reading culture. Once based on Christian literature and common to everyone, the reading culture became divided into a bourgeois, upper-class segment and a popular one. The former welcomed and delighted in new types of texts, such as fiction, biographies, and scientific work, while the latter retained its focus on religious literature. It was not until the late nineteenth century, several decades after the introduction of compulsory education for everybody in 1842, that these two reading cultures visibly started to converge. Likewise, it was not until the nineteenth century that writing skills spread to the entire population.[39] Thus, it is possible that social differences with respect to reading and writing skills were particularly salient in the latter half of the period under investigation here. Still, the case of Anna Maria Rückerschöld (and others) shows that both reading and writing were mastered by women. In this way, women could affect how particular social and economic problems were broached and eventually politicized.

Sources

Previous research has provided ample evidence of the usefulness of probate material for the investigation of issues of property.[40] In Sweden, however, very little probate material survives from the seventeenth century. Probate inventories (*bouppteckning*)[41] became compulsory with the promulgation of the national legal code of 1734, and it is only after the middle of the eighteenth century that they have been preserved to an extent that makes possible analysis of large sets of data. For the seventeenth century, only occasional inventories have been preserved, usually from the higher echelons of society. Wills (*testamente*) do appear in the seventeenth and eighteenth centuries, but for various reasons, they are few and hard to come by. In this study, unprinted probate inventories are used systematically only for a period in the last half of the eighteenth century (for Rystad, an area near the city of Linköping). As for wills and contractual arrangements, I have made several investigations. One is based on a sample of unprinted seventeenth-century wills that were contested in the Svea Hovrätt (the royal court of appeal in Stockholm). Another is based on all preserved unprinted wills from a region in northern Sweden (Jämtland) from 1750 up to the early twentieth century. A third study builds on source material from eighteenth-century Roslagen (the coastal area north of Stockholm). Finally, I have used some randomly chosen wills from Värmland (Fryksdalen) and Dalarna (Stora Tuna).

The records from the rural primary court level are the most important type of source for an investigation of legal matters in the seventeenth century, at least if the main focus is, as here, on ordinary people.[42] Not surprisingly, these records have been used extensively by historians in Sweden and the other Nordic countries, but mainly within the field of history of crime, despite the fact that the bulk of their content consists of civil cases, not crime. There was even a tendency for rural primary courts to become increasingly involved with cases of litigation during the early modern period.[43] It must be stressed that the court records do not only include information on contested (and therefore possibly less normal) cases. They also include information on everyday matters that were never subject to dispute, such as registration of land transactions. In this study, I have used a sample of printed court records that represents various parts of the country (Uppland in central Sweden, Njurunda in northern Sweden, and Vedbo in western Sweden) and various periods.[44] I have also used various sources from the main court of appeal in Stockholm (Svea Hovrätt): court records but also documents where the lawyers discuss the interpretation of the law and the need for new legislation. I have made it a special point to relate the cases presented to the courts in detail because I am convinced that it is only through direct contact with the sources, what they actually say and how they say it, that we really understand past societies and are in a position to draw sound historical conclusions. We need to be able to visualize what kind of institution these courts were, and the best way of doing so is to read concrete cases.

The Swedish legal system was different in many ways from systems in other parts of Europe at the time. For instance, there were usually no notaries who registered property transactions, as in France, since all such matters were taken care of by the primary courts. (Stockholm differed in this respect.) Nor was there the same array of competing legal traditions and courts as in England, where common law existed alongside ecclesiastical law, manorial law, equity law, and statutory law. In Sweden, the ecclesiastical courts lost much of their power after the Reformation, and they were not in charge of the registration of probate inventories and wills. Very few manorial courts existed, and those that did were placed under the supervision of the courts of appeal, as were all other primary courts.[45] There were no special equity courts of the sort that existed in England; however, the appeals court judges did adduce *aequitas*. As we will see, considerations of what was fair and equitable (*billigt, skäligt*) under the circumstances are likely to have played a significant role not only in the courts of appeal.[46] Statutory law (*kungliga förordningar*) played quite a significant role, mainly because the legal code was becoming increasingly outdated and obscure, especially with respect to economic matters. Much of the new eighteenth-century credit legislation (which is of great interest in this context) was introduced through statutory law.

The main legal authority was the national legal code, which regulated central aspects of life, such as marriage, inheritance, landed property, relations within villages and hamlets, trade, crime, and the relationship between the king and his subjects. It also laid down procedural rules for the courts. The code dated back to c. 1350, when Magnus Eriksson was king, but had been slightly revised in 1442, during the reign of Christopher of Bavaria. Thus, it was the legal code named after King Christopher that was applied in the courts throughout the seventeenth century and up until 1736, when the new code, ratified by the four estates in 1734, was put into practice. Naturally, these codes are also used as sources in this study, as are relevant statutory law and drafts of new legislation.

In the eighteenth century, a new sort of "public sphere" emerged in Sweden. Its center was the capital, but due to new legal and technical possibilities (the freedom to print and printing techniques), it became nationwide. This public sphere had important and often beneficial consequences for women's legal and economic position in society since it offered new possibilities for making one's grievances known to others. Of course, reading and writing skills were particular assets in this context. The minor printed works published by ordinary people are the main sources for studying the public sphere. As for early nineteenth-century developments, the main sources are the minutes from the four-estate Diet (*riksdag*), which registered in detail the lengthy discussions that took place before the estates decided to grant equal property rights to women and men in 1845 and to abolish the system of lineage property in 1857. These minutes are supplemented by some case law and statutory law.

Throughout the book, I have endeavored to incorporate as much as possible of relevant research that is accessible only to those who read Swedish. Therefore, the book should be seen as a synthesis, which brings together not only my own research results but also those of other scholars who have worked in the field.

((2))

THE COUPLE BETWEEN KIN,
STATE, & LOCAL COMMUNITY

In early modern Sweden the marital union of husband and wife was depicted in two diametrically opposed ways. Christian discourse emphasized union, concord, and common interests and taught that it was the duty of spouses to live together in harmony and to give to one another "advice, comfort, and support." The idea that husband and wife could sometimes have contradictory interests was directly opposed to this notion; instead, spouses were supposed to be "one flesh." The Bible also declared, unambiguously, that a man should leave his parents upon marriage and stay with his wife.[1] The message must have been clear: marriage was an institution built on common interests, and loyalty to one's spouse was more important than loyalty to one's family of origin. Legal discourse, however, took a totally different view of marriage. With its strong focus upon landed property and its concern with preserving the status of lineage property, the law stipulated that inherited land brought into the marital estate by spouses could under no circumstances be merged. The husband was not the owner of his wife's lands, the law instructed, nor could the wife inherit lineage property from her husband.[2] Within this context, the marital union was seen merely as a temporary constellation of two persons and their property, soon to be dissolved by death and, if no children were born, leaving no visible traces. Even if the law only dealt with the economic side of marriage, and not the social or emotional aspects, these injunctions nevertheless smacked of a view according to which spouses had different or sometimes even conflicting interests.

The simultaneous presence of these two images created tensions in early modern society, but it also created opportunities, since it provided people with arguments for different situations and differing objectives. Sometimes spouses did have conflicting interests and allied themselves with people outside the household; sometimes spouses had common interests against the rest of the world. Depending on the situation, then, spouses could have an interest in claiming that property was either separate or common. And while the two views could be played out against each other, they could also be combined in inventive and unorthodox ways. In a society, where the printed legal code included the Ten Commandments, Christian arguments were patently relevant to the law. Moreover, while the law devoted most of its attention to safeguarding inherited land, it conceded that forms of property other than inherited land should be regarded as common to the spouses.

These two images were not employed in a social vacuum, however. People were deeply rooted in a concrete local context, where kinsmen, neighbors, and friends affected their lives and what claims could be made with respect to property. They were also deeply affected by their local communities being small parts of a nation with imperial ambitions and with an increasingly strong and demanding absolutist state. The state influenced the property system through its demands for taxes and for soldiers, just as it did through its various transactions and negotiations with the nobility. The state, nobility, and peasantry all chipped and tugged at the property system. On the whole, however, it remained a system that primarily saw to the interest of landholding kin groups. What sorts of property rights did rural women have in this type of society?

Protecting Women's Rights to Land: The Kin Veto

According to the Swedish legal code, all children born within wedlock were entitled to inherit a share of their parents' property. If the family lived in the countryside, as most people did, a brother would inherit a share twice as big as that to which his sister was entitled, but in urban areas, sons and daughters inherited equal shares. If the family had freehold land, both sons and daughters were entitled to have their shares in this form. In other words, girls were not barred by law from inheriting real property, even when there was a brother in the family.[3] In this respect, Sweden differed from its neighbor Norway, where the eldest son was always given possession of the farm in return for compensation to his siblings. Consequently, it was not uncommon for a Swedish woman to bring property, including land (or a claim to land), into her future marital estate. During marriage, the spouses could acquire more property through their own exertions, and the wife would be entitled to a third of this property which the spouses held in common.[4] Moreover, a woman was entitled to a gift from her husband when they started living together as husband and wife (the so-called morning gift).[5] Thus, a woman could and often did have means of her own, which her children would inherit upon her death: her inherited property, her share of the common estate, and the morning gift. This kind of inheritance system, where children inherit from both their father and mother, is commonly referred to as bilateral. The following example will show the way it worked in late sixteenth-century Sweden.

In 1578 Erik Matsson came to the local court in Boglösa and raised claims to ten *örtug* of land in Sundby that was in the possession of his elder brother and namesake, Erik Matsson. This land, the court records inform us, had been bought by the younger Erik's parents "when they had come together," after the death of the older Erik's mother. The plaintiff argued that he ought to have one-third of this land, which was his inheritance from his mother. Moreover, he and his sister were entitled to their inheritance from their father. The older Erik answered that he wanted to keep a brother's share in the land and reminded his brother that there was also a third brother, the issue of their father's third marriage. The court found in favor of the younger Erik, giving him the right to the ten *örtug* land but requiring him to pay his two half-brothers for their shares.[6] What were the judges' reasons for doing so?

The father of Erik and Erik had been married three times, having one son by his first wife (the older Erik), a son and a daughter by his second wife (the younger Erik and his sister), and one son by his third wife. The land in question had been purchased jointly by the father and his second wife, which made it their common property. Consequently, when the parents died, the land was divided into the father's part (consisting of two-thirds), to which all four children could claim a share, and the mother's part (consisting of one-third), to which only her two children held a legal claim. The younger Erik, however, had bought his sister's shares in both their mother's and their father's shares (The older Erik may not have known this prior to the court session), making the younger Erik the sole owner of his mother's third and the owner of three-sevenths of their father's share. With one-third of the entire estate plus three-sevenths of two-thirds, the younger Erik effectively owned about 60 percent of the land and won the case.[7] People had to be good at fractions in those days!

As this case shows, the fact that only two of the children were entitled to inherit the land through both their father and their mother had far-reaching implications for the outcome of the dispute. Had the entire estate been the father's inheritance, the younger Erik would only have inherited two-sevenths, and even if he had bought his sister's share, three-sevenths would still not have been quite enough to take possession of the farm. If, on the other hand, the estate had been the mother's inheritance, Erik would have received two-thirds, his sister one-third, and their half-brothers nothing. Thus, whether land was classified as inherited (and therefore separate) or acquired (and therefore common to both spouses) was profoundly important, and people had to keep track of these matters.

To an outsider with no access to local knowledge about the family history, the marital property arrangements would probably appear as impenetrable domestic secrets. Recourse to written documents would not necessarily clarify the matter. Buyers of land kept the sale document as a title deed. Minutes were taken at each court session, and one copy was to be kept under seal in the local community's "chest" (*häradskista*). The Crown kept written records in the form of cadastres, including information on each farm from which taxes were due. Seldom was the information detailed enough for anyone outside the local community to ascertain how the land had been acquired or, for that matter, where its precise borders were located. It is telling that the court of appeal in Stockholm often failed to retrieve the relevant information from the written documents only. When the judges turned to the royal archives for help, the archivists told them (after having searched the dusty shelves meticulously) that they could tell the judges no more than they already knew.[8] Obviously, the only way of clarifying such matters was to turn to old men (and sometimes women) who harbored memories of local conditions. A case from Uppland in 1638 vividly illustrates that this was how this system worked, but it also shows the shortcomings of this way of proving entitlement.

Karin in Löfsta came to court to complain about the way in which her deceased brother Nils had procured a title deed for what was actually her share in some houses and land. He had done this behind her back in 1622 and had inserted into the deed some words about Karin having been given twenty-one *daler* and a young horse for the property, all of which Karin adamantly denied having received. The assembly of lay judges now rallied to her support, saying that they knew nothing of this title deed. So did the men who had served as lay judges in 1622, and they also denied that they had ever issued a deed like this one.[9] Apparently, her brother had forged the title deed. The judges knew this, and they also knew that it was Karin who was the rightful heir to the land, although the latter point is unlikely to have been written down anywhere. Since the judges were obviously intimidated by Nils, they did not act in the matter until after his demise. Thus, even though Karin managed to collect her inheritance rights eventually, her situation had remained precarious for a long time.

In view of women's relatively strong rights of inheritance, we should expect not only local communities but also written law to take into consideration married women's rights to separate property. And this is indeed what we find. During marriage, the entire marital estate was managed by the husband, as if it were one unit. Yet, from the point of view of the law, it was no unit at all. Instead, the marital estate consisted of three distinct components: the husband's separate inherited land, the wife's separate inherited land, and the common property. The spouses' respective shares of the common property were called their marital rights (*giftorätt*). A main concern of the law was to make sure that these distinctions were not blurred, and it particularly sought to protect the separate property of the wife against possible abuse by the husband-manager. To that end, the legal code laid down a number of restrictions upon the husband's scope of action. The law allowed a husband to sell his wife's land in cases of acute emergency. If an army attacked the country and took either husband or wife as hostage, it was lawful for the other spouse to sell inherited land in order to pay ransom for the spouse kept in captivity. Likewise, it was lawful for spouses to sell inherited land if they were threatened by severe famine. In such cases, the local court would check afterward that an emergency had really been at hand.[10] In another part of the legal code, it was said that if a husband wanted to sell his wife's land, he had to offer it to her relatives and that he must sell twice as much of his own land at the same time.[11] In yet another part of the code, a husband was prohibited from substituting other land for his wife's land, unless the new land was of better quality and unless he had procured the prior consent of his wife and her close relatives, that is, her heirs.[12] While not identical to solutions chosen in other countries at the same time, it is still obvious that this "package," intended to protect married women's property rights, is a parallel to what we find in, for example, the French *système dotale*, where a husband had to offer a mortgage if he sold his wife's dowry.[13] A husband could alienate his wife's separate property, but in doing so he took a severe personal risk.

It is unlikely that the Swedish stipulations were understood as being all applicable to one and the same situation.[14] In other words, a husband did not have to point to an emergency, *and* to offer the land to the woman's relatives, *and* to sell a part of his own land, *and* to procure the consent of the wife and her close relatives. Instead, legislators must have had different cases in mind. First, they envisaged an emergency situation — a comparatively rare case — and, what was more, one closely surveyed by the local court. Second, they envisaged situations when spouses needed to reallocate land — a comparatively common case in a country where both husband and wife often brought land into the marital estate. Thus, if the spouses wished to sell her inherited land, perhaps because it was located far from their home, they were obliged to offer it to her relatives first. Perhaps keeping the relatives informed was what really mattered. Third, legislators regulated situations where the husband wanted to alienate the wife's land for reasons other than the ones outlined above. Here, consent was demanded of the wife and her close relatives. It is clear from the legal code that the sort of alienation medieval legislators had had in mind was substitution of land for land, but it is obvious from later legal practice that this stipulation was also applied (and perhaps foremost) when the husband wished to sell the land for money.

These stipulations gave a Swedish woman's natal family a considerable degree of control over the land that she had inherited and brought into her marital estate. Other legal rules gave kin other forms of influence over the young woman and her marriage. It was the father (or, in his absence, some other male relative) who accepted, or rejected, the future son-in-law, and who conducted the negotiations with his family. If the daughter married without the approval of her family, her parents could decide that she would be entitled to neither her paternal nor her maternal property.[15] This was one of the very few situations when the otherwise strong inheritance rights were undercut. Finally, *bördsrätt* always applied in cases concerning inherited land.

To what extent were the three stipulations actually used by ordinary peasant families to check the behavior of unwise sons-in-law or for other purposes? Did the legal protection accorded to married women's separate property really have any significance, or were the stipulations just dead letters in the sixteenth and seventeenth centuries? Scattered remarks in previous research suggest that people did invoke some of these stipulations, although not very frequently.[16] Disputes over claims of inheritance or claims of *bördsrätt* appear to have been much more common. Maria Sjöberg notes that the court records sometimes mention the wife's consent to the alienation of her land but that it was far more common for the court not to say anything on this issue. In her study of late sixteenth-century Dalarna, Sjöberg found no dispute caused by

TABLE 1. Husband's sale of wife's inherited land in a sample of late sixteenth- and seventeenth-century Swedish courts: number of cases and whether the legal restrictions upon the husband's scope of action are mentioned in the court records

Place	Time	Cases where wife's land is sold	Wife's consent mentioned explicitly	Relatives' consent mentioned explicitly	Other rules referred to	Total number of cases
PRIMARY COURT LEVEL						
Central Sweden						
Vendel	1615–45	6	1	0	0	c. 900
Uppland	1578–79	3	0	0	1	51
Uppland	1581, 1586	3+1(?)	1	1	0	188
Uppland	1638	4	1	0	0	407
Northern Sweden						
Njurunda	1609–72	6	2	0	0	c. 1,200
Western Sweden						
Vedbo	1613–25	9	0	0	0	not clear
Vedbo	1660–72	7	0	0	0	not clear
COURT OF APPEAL LEVEL						
Svea Hovrätt	1615–16	2	2	1+1(?)	0	not clear
Total		40+1(?)	7	2+1(?)	1	

Sources: *Vendels 1615–1645; Upplands Lagmansdombok 1578–79; Upplands Lagmansdombok 1581 och 1586; Lagläsaren Per Larssons 1638; Tingsprotokoll för Njurunda; Ur Vedbo härads domböcker.*

Comments: Court cases from the Svea Hovrätt have been located with the help of Becchius-Palmcrantz's collection of cases.

the husband's mismanagement of his wife's land.[17] She did find a case where a sale of land was registered at court (according to the normal procedure) and where it was recorded en passant that the husband had sold it in accordance with the rules of the legal code and then invested the money in new land (probably for his wife).[18]

A systematic study of a sample of late sixteenth- and seventeenth-century court records provides the basis for delving deeper into this matter. The records have been chosen so as to represent various parts of the country and various time periods. Areas which might have been affected by Dano-Norwegian law have deliberately been excluded.[19] Land sales outside the kin group were routinely registered at court, showing that land was alienable and that there was a land market.[20] However, the exact size and character of this market is hard to assess prior to c. 1700. Therefore, quantification in the strict sense is very difficult to achieve.[21]

It may seem surprising that so few cases were found of men selling their wives' land. Considering that the inheritance system was bilateral, many married women must have owned land, and one would have expected such land to have been a frequent issue in the courts. Could the relative absence of such cases reflect a situation where women's rights of inheritance were not respected and upheld? If few women received land, few married men would be in a position where they might want to sell such land. Numerous court cases show, however, that courts and local communities did *not* disregard the notion of female land ownership — on the contrary. It was carefully written down in the court records whether the land in question belonged to the husband or the wife. When Per Bengtsson of Åbyggeby told the court how he had come into possession of "his" farm (1621), he clearly stated that the farm had belonged to his wife's kinsmen and that, consequently, it was she who held the claim to it.[22] When Staffan Erichsson asked the court to issue a formal purchase deed, showing that he was the rightful owner of a certain farm (1625), Staffan proved his title by showing how his father had bought the farm from Hans Larsson for 64 *daler*, but it was added that the farm had actually belonged to Hans's wife Brita.[23] When Bengt Månsson offered land for sale (1639), the court record explicitly stated that it was his wife's "inherited share in houses and land" in Åkra.[24] Many other cases point in the same direction: people kept track of whether land belonged to husband or wife, and the courts respected this distinction.[25] The courts also acknowledged and protected women's rights of inheritance. For instance, when Per Mickelsson was dilatory in giving his sisters-in-law their shares, the court intervened and ordered him to pay at once.[26] When the sickly Ingeborg Eskilsdotter devised all her inherited property to her brother, against promise of care and support, the local court annulled the will, because that which Ingeborg had received from her brother was of such little value. Instead, the court ruled that the inherited wealth be divided between the siblings according to law. The decision indicates that the court thought Ingeborg had been cheated by her brother.[27]

In this context, a case brought to court in 1579 concerning whether or not Pär Månsson had had the right to sell a piece of his land to Erik Mickelsson is revealing. The plaintiff was Pär's grandson Erik Larsson, who adduced *bördsrätt*. It turned out that Pär Månsson's parents had mortgaged the land long ago and that Pär had subsequently paid the debt without any help from his maternal uncle and aunt (which suggests that the land originally came from Pär's mother's family). Later in life, when he was old and so poor that he could not pay his taxes and was incarcerated for this reason, Pär decided to sell the land to Erik Mickelsson. Erik promised to take care of Pär and his wife until the end of their lives, a promise he faithfully honored. None of Pär's relatives offered any help. One would perhaps think that this heart-rending story would provide sufficient evidence of Pär's right to sell his land to Erik. But the court took the time to check first that the land "was not his wife's nor his grandson's maternal inheritance."[28] The case shows that the court was aware of the fact that a head of household could have access to property belonging to many different persons (in this case the wife and the daughter-in-law) and to take this issue seriously. Even if the judges were outsiders to some extent, they did not accept being confronted with domestic secrets but carefully teased out all facts of the case.

Older research has not always paid sufficient attention to the strong notion of female ownership and rights of inheritance that we find in early modern Sweden. In his influential and comprehensive compilation of information on noble estates, J. A. Almquist frequently referred to land inherited by a woman as the property of her husband.[29] This misunderstanding testifies to an incomplete knowledge of the law, but it is easy to see how it could arise. Husbands could act *as if* they were the owners, except when it came to selling inherited land. What was more, early modern sources use a language which is brief and elliptical. Court records often refer to land as having "fallen through inheritance" to a certain man, or say that a man had received a piece of land "as inheritance with his wife."[30] A close reading of the cases usually reveals that what the scribe actually meant was that the husband came into possession of the land as a consequence of his wife having inherited it. According to the law, it was absolutely impossible for a man to inherit land from his father-in-law, even though the words of the court records may convey that impression when taken out of context.[31]

That married women's separate property was a reality and existed not merely in the letter of the law is also illustrated by the fact that spouses sometimes exchanged land with one another. This seems to have been particularly common within the nobility. For instance, Johan Bagge let his wife, Margareta Alfsdotter, have his land in Alleby, and in return, she transferred her farm near Falun to him.[32] Obviously, if husbands had been regarded as the actual owners of the entire marital estate, including the wives' inherited lands, practices such as this one would have been unnecessary and incomprehensible.

The notion of female landownership cannot be refuted. Still, table 1 does show that it was uncommon for people to adduce the legal stipulations restricting the husband's power. On the other hand, cases where the stipulations were adduced did occur. Therefore, it is unlikely that ordinary people (whom we meet in the court records) were unaware of what the law said on this issue. Previous research has shown that early modern people seem to have held the courts in high esteem[33] and that they had a surprisingly good knowledge of the law. That many ordinary men functioned as lay judges may explain this result. Of course, people could, and did, interpret the law in unorthodox ways. But it is unlikely that they were totally ignorant of its content, in view of the fact that, now and then, and in many parts of the country, the stipulations were indeed adduced. So, why was it uncommon for most people to use these legal possibilities, and why did some use them nevertheless? The answer seems to be that we are dealing with different types of land sales by husbands.

On the one hand, some land sales obviously involved the *implicit* consent by the wife or her relatives. Even if the husband had sold his wife's land without explicit consent, he had done it in a way that her relatives perceived to be in accordance with her, and their, interests and intentions. For instance, when Hans Larsson sold his wife's land to Staffan Erichsson's father, the money was used to pay for his wife's son's university studies in Germany. Whether Hans had asked for his wife's and her relatives' consent or not may have been beside the point; the point was rather that the money had been used in accordance with her wishes. Very likely, this is why the son's studies were mentioned in the court record: it was an oblique way of saying that consent had been obtained. Similarly, when Hans Bengtsson exchanged land with Olof Skinnare on behalf of his wife, no explicit consent was mentioned. However, the court records inform us that "this [land] did not reduce the heirs' lineage property since he [Olof] has given him [Hans] land for land."[34] In other words, Hans had not caused his children any harm through this transaction, since he had simply substituted new land for the property he had relinquished to Olof. Once again, it was an oblique way of legitimizing the transaction without explicitly mentioning consent.

In a similar fashion, whether consent had been given or not was seldom an issue in cases where husbands sold their wives' land to someone within the kin group (such as one of her brothers). The records from Njurunda provide an exception; here, we do find a few examples of how a husband sold his wife's land to his brother-in-law with her consent being explicitly mentioned.[35] Apart from these cases, such sales seem to have been routinely perceived as being in accordance with the wishes of the wife and her relatives, and consent was seldom mentioned. It is even possible that such sales were not always registered at court.[36]

On the other hand, the husband could act in a way that was directly opposed to the interests and intentions of his wife and her relatives. In these cases, people would not hesitate to adduce the stipulations of the law. When Jöns Olsson sold his wife Barbro's inherited land, her relatives came to court to lodge a complaint (1579). They argued that Jöns had had no right to do this, because poverty did not compel him to sell, nor had he sold parts of his own land at the same time "as law requires him to do."[37] The explicit reference to the law testifies to a quite precise knowledge of what the legal code said about cases like these. Obviously, Jöns had sold his wife's land without having consulted her relatives and then bought new land with the money, to which they strongly objected. As compensation, they wanted the new land to be given to them since, otherwise, land from their lineage would have been transferred to the husband and effectively lost, from their point of view.[38]

In another case, a dispute was brought to court involving Christopher in Nor on the one hand, and Anna Nilsdotter and her children, on the other (1615). It appeared that Anna's late husband had been in debt to Christopher and, as a consequence, he had sold her inherited farm to his creditor. In this case, the court ruled that the contract was illegal since Christopher had been unable to prove that Anna and her relatives had consented to the sale.[39] As in Jöns's case, the sale of the woman's land was perceived to be a net loss to herself and to her family: the land would have left the kin group permanently and ceased to be their lineage property. And just as in Jöns's case, reference was made to one of the three stipulations, once again giving evidence of a precise knowledge of the legal means that were available in a situation like this.

It is difficult to interpret the fragile and confusing evidence presented to us by late sixteenth- and seventeenth-century court records.[40] However, the results presented here along with those of other historians suggest that women's right to inherit land was widely acknowledged. Both contested and uncontested court cases often refer to women's inherited land. People — kinsmen, neighbors, and friends — kept track of whether land had been inherited by the wife or by the husband, and courts heeded this distinction and noted the information in the records. Moreover, the woman's natal family had many ways to ensure that her land was not lost from their overall purview during her marriage. They had a say as to whom the woman should marry, and the law gave them the right to veto unwise sales by the son-in-law. The son-in-law was also supposed to consult them when it came to reallocating the wife's inherited land.

Therefore, the fact that we find comparatively few cases where any of the three stipulations was explicitly adduced should not be interpreted to mean that they were accorded little significance by ordinary people. A more likely explanation is that the intent of the law was that families should be able to prevent transactions by which land was entirely lost from their point of view, and such transactions seem to have been uncommon, at least among ordinary peasants. Instead, there were numerous small transactions going on almost every day whereby land shares that had been split up into many hands as a consequence of death and the subsequent division of estates were reassembled and reallocated. Many of these transactions involved the sale of a woman's inherited land, but since such sales usually took place within the kin group, there was seldom reason for courts to inquire into whether the relatives had consented or not.

It can also be conjectured that husbands knew that the stipulations existed and that this awareness affected and limited their actions. If knowledge of the law was widespread, as many have argued, men would certainly take the law into consideration, not only in their roles as fathers, brothers, or judges, but also as husbands. In a society where land transactions were annulled almost daily, with reference to *bördsrätt*, a husband would surely realize that it was not at all unlikely that any possible sale of his wife's land would be annulled if he failed to present a satisfactory explanation of the necessity of this sale to his wife, his in-laws, or the local court.

In sum, Swedish property law had three distinctive features in the early modern period. First, the inheritance system was bilateral, giving both sons and daughters a right to inherit land (although not on an equal basis). Second, a woman's inherited land was looked upon as her separate property during marriage, and her natal family could exert significant influence over this property. Third, a married woman could claim one-third of her and her husband's common property. According to the work of Bina Agarwal, the first two phenomena were particularly important and should be conceived of as being closely interlinked, in the sense that women's rights of inheritance were dependent on, and corroborated by, the degree to which her land could be controlled by her kinsmen. Put more succinctly, strong control by the woman's natal family predicted for strong rights of inheritance for the woman. This relationship should not be thought of in terms of a strict statistical correlation, however. It is better to conceive of it as a kind of precarious balance, where changes in one factor were likely to affect, but not determine, the other factor. For seventeenth-century Sweden, strong rights of inheritance and marked influence by the woman's natal family were very prominent features.

It is important, however, not to be misled by this picture of the property system and to think of it as particularly "women-friendly," simply because women could inherit land and their husbands could not use it at will. The law implicitly depicted husbands as the ones against whom women might need protection, and the law consequently provided means by which the power of husbands was circumscribed. These means were primarily put in the hands of relatives, though, and only to a limited extent in the hands of the woman herself.[41] Moreover, the law took for granted that it was chiefly against her husband that a woman might need protection whereas, in fact, it was just as likely that her father, brother, uncle, or son would try to abuse their positions as spokesmen for the kin group. The case of Karin in Löfsta (mentioned previously) brings this out very clearly: her brother sold her inherited land behind her back, and the local court took no steps to assist her until the brother had died. "And [the lay judges] told how Karin always kept complaining about this land but that she was not successful as long as [the brother] was alive."[42] The quotation provides a clear illustration of the power with which the woman's male kinsmen were endowed and to what uses they could put this power. Other cases also show women who were at the mercy of their closest family members. For example, Olug Segolsdotter went to court to lodge a complaint about the way in which her two sons had sold her inherited land behind her back (in 1668).[43]

Similar examples can be found in the higher echelons of society. Klaus Fleming, one of the leading noblemen in sixteenth-century Finland, was the guardian of his sister and niece. He prevented both of them from marrying, presumably because he wanted to keep their property for himself. When his sister died, she made a will that benefited her niece, her fiancé, and the king, but as for her brother, she gave him nothing and spelled out very clearly her reasons for not doing so.[44]

While there is evidence of male abuse of power, exercised by brothers, there is also evidence of husbands who sought to defend the rights of their wives or of other women who depended upon their protection.[45] Anders in Vika went to court in 1638 to claim the inheritance of his stepdaughter, Elin, and Clemet Pedersson went to court in 1662 to claim his wife's inheritance, which her guardian had sold during her minority.[46] Contrary to the stereotype implied by real estate law, these husbands acted as the protectors of individual women. There were strong cultural norms emphasizing that married men should behave as good heads of the household, taking care of everyone under their roofs. The teachings of Paul were particularly important in this context, emphasizing that men who cannot control themselves and take care of their households cannot be responsible heads of the congregation. Paul's words were often invoked in seventeenth-century Sweden,[47] and it is hard to imagine that these religious tenets did not make an impression on ordinary married men and affect their actions and perceptions of themselves.

Obviously, asserting the property rights of a woman who belonged to one's household was also a way of increasing the resources that one could command. We should not romanticize these relationships by thinking of these husbands as acting merely from altruism or lack of self-interest. Nor should we entirely disregard the discrepancy between what many husbands did and how they were implicitly described in property law. When the law depicted husbands as threats and remained silent on the role played by fathers and brothers, it does not tell us anything about how real men actually behaved in these different roles. Men could protect women's interests or undermine them, regardless of whether they were acting as husbands or brothers and for egoistic as well as altruistic reasons. What the law tells us is simply how it construed, and constructed, domestic relations. It depicted the husband as someone who might represent a risk, not because married men were thought to be evil, but because husbands were in a position where they could threaten the property interests of the woman's kinship group. As we shall see, this was precisely where change and reconstruction would soon take place.

Protecting Women's Rights to Money: The Blind Spot

Let us go back to the case of Erik, who succeeded in court against his elder brother Erik after having bought his sister's shares in the contested farm. Let us imagine that Erik had married — what would happen then? If he married a woman from the same village or hamlet, the case would have been quite straightforward. The land that his wife brought into the estate would have been worked as part of Erik's farm. Since we are talking about the pre-enclosure period, the fact that fields and meadows were not spatially concentrated was not unusual. Thus, the wife's landholding would have become part of the estate. At the same time, it would have been visibly separate, and it would have been easy to tell those concerned (such as her children) where her property was. Everyone could have read the physical landscape, and they understood that this particular piece of land belonged to Erik's wife. It was a highly

Unenclosed hamlet with
field strips (Lantmäteriet,
Gävle, Sweden)

transparent system. If the wife's land had been situated in a more distant place, though, Erik might have found it complicated to work it. He would probably have tried to exchange it for land in his own hamlet. If that proved impossible, he would have tried to sell it, perhaps to his brother-in-law, and he would have bought new land for his wife in his own hamlet or nearby.

As long as Erik acted in any of these ways, his wife's property rights were safe and her relatives had little reason to complain. The "quality" of lineage property would be transferred to the new land bought by the husband for his wife. In this way, the protection of married women's separate property could be upheld even in situations where her land had to be sold. Sixteenth- and seventeenth-century court records unmistakably show that the quality of lineage property was not fixed to certain farms (like an entailed estate), but rather it was flexible and easily transferred from one object to another.[48] There was even a special phrase for money that an heir had received instead of land, "land money" (*jordapengar*),[49] indicating that the quality of lineage property rested temporarily in the money. However, the assumption was that the money would soon be reinvested in new land, and when this happened, the quality of lineage property was transferred to it, for which special terms were also used.[50] It is also possible that land money was de facto subject to the same restrictions as inherited land, that is, that the owner could not use it as he or she liked.[51] This was all in line with the spirit of the medieval legal code, epitomized in the three stipulations mentioned above. These stipulations did not forbid the sale of women's inherited land, merely regulated it so as to give her relatives a chance of making sure that the quality of lineage property was not lost but transferred to a new object. It is telling that Barbro's relatives did not complain because Jöns Olsson had sold her land; they complained because the land substituted for the previous plot was not given to them in compensation. Thus, the medieval protection of married women's rights to separate property was not incompatible with the market for land.

However, there seems to have been one blind spot in the system, one situation to which legislators appear to have been oblivious. What if Erik used his wife's monetary compensation for land to pay for his sister's and brothers' shares in his family farm? One might expect land bought in this way to have become the wife's lineage property, since the quality of lineage property normally followed the compensation. Alternatively, one might expect land bought in this way to have become the common property of the spouses, since it had been acquired during marriage. But neither of these two alternatives is correct. Instead, the land remained Erik's inherited, separate property, regardless of the fact that it had partly been purchased with his wife's land money. She no longer had land that was visible in the physical landscape, and the value of her land had been incorporated into that of her husband's. Her land had ceased to exist as an object in its own right. In cases like this, the quality of lineage property was not transferred but simply lost from the point of view of the woman and her relatives.[52]

Three legal principles were at a deadlock. Even if the quality of lineage property was normally transferred to the new land, and even if property acquired during marriage was normally regarded as common to both spouses, these two principles were barred by the prohibition against making a spouse co-owner of the other spouse's lineage property. In situations like these, a wife's property was extremely poorly protected simply because it did not take the form of land.

There was no discussion about this problem until around 1700, and there are few court cases illustrating the problem for the earlier part of the seventeenth century. Moreover, the court cases are often difficult to locate and to understand. This may be why their crucial importance and the underlying problem have not been stressed in previous research.[53] The cases that do exist suggest that people in the seventeenth century were in fact intensely aware of the precarious situation that a sale of this sort might cause a woman (or a man). The fear expressed and the precautions taken indicate that people perceived the legal protection of money and other personal property to have been insufficient precisely in this sort of situation.

In 1666 Nils Persson and his three nieces complained to the local court that the forest ranger Per Casparsson had prevented them from receiving their inheritance from their brother and uncle, Simon Persson. Per Casparsson was Simon's stepson, and his reasons for preventing the relatives from taking possession of the estate Åsen was that his stepfather had made two wills in his favor (in 1660 and 1665). In the wills, Simon had declared that, "when he bought the said [farm] Åsen, he had sold his wife Kerstin Andersdotter's inherited land . . . and used the money to pay for his own eighths in Åsen," that is, he had used her land money to free a farm from the claims of his relatives. What is more, Per had taken very good care of his mother and stepfather in their old age, when they could neither "move nor turn around," and none of the relatives had given Per any assistance. Provided that Per gave to his sister Karin what was due her, Simon wanted him to have all residual property for himself.[54] This case gives one clear example of how the wife's land money had been used to buy a farm to which the husband held claims of inheritance. But more importantly, it shows that Simon was aware of the dismal consequences this sale would have for his wife and for her children from a previous marriage. It was the stepchildren's maternal inheritance that was lost when Simon used the money to buy all the shares in his family farm. Because of their loss, and because Per had taken good care of his stepfather, Simon had drawn up the will. That the court records carefully mention what had happened to the land owned by Simon's wife also shows that the fate of the wife's land was highly relevant from a legal point of view. The court found in Per's favor, but the opposing party chose to make an appeal against the decision.

Other cases draw attention to the same problem. In 1651 a woman called Märit in Näs came to court to testify that her husband Lars had sold his own inherited land and invested the land money in the farm in Näs that seems to have been her inheritance. For this reason, she asked that he be allowed to keep the farm intact during his lifetime, without being troubled by her relatives.[55] The court found this a reasonable solution since Lars had "managed the farm well," which suggests that it attached importance to diligence and investment of labor. That the wife pleaded for him suggested, of course, that their marriage was loving and affectionate. Another illustration is found in 1666 when Lars Jönsson had sold all his inherited land to his stepdaughter, Börita, and her husband, Arne Torstensson. Strictly speaking, Lars did not have the authority to sell inherited land to people outside his kin group, but he explained his action to the court (in 1669) by telling the judges that he had sold his wife's inherited land, thus depriving Börita of her maternal inheritance. Lars never went into any details about how he had used the money, but upon entering a new marriage with Karin Persdotter, he made an agreement with Arne Torstensson to the effect that Arne and Börita would care for him until his death and that Karin's children could not claim any of the landed property.[56] Clearly, Lars was intent upon compensating Börita, but the contract was also a way for Lars to arrange for his own retirement.

All three cases show how one of the spouses had lost inherited land by investing its value in land that came from the other spouse's family. This could happen to both women and men, but since men generally inherited larger shares, it was less likely for a couple to choose to sell his part instead of hers. Märit, in the case cited above, may have been an only child. All three cases also show how the people involved were concerned with the adverse effects the situation could have for the spouse who had lost land. Märit was at pains to make sure that her husband would not be ejected by her relatives directly after her death, and Simon and Lars made arrangements to protect their deceased wives' children, who had been deprived of their maternal inheritance. In fact, the concern displayed and the precautions employed are important evidence supporting the interpretation that the quality of lineage property was *not* transferred to the other spouse's land.

Other cases are less clear but point in the same direction. In 1619 Erich Håkansson asked his brother Olof for his share in their family farm in Mjösund. After some discussion on which the court records remain silent, Erich announced that he renounced his claims in Mjösund and would be content with some minor lands in another hamlet. The court record continues: "Since Erich had sold his wife's land, and invested that money in the farm," he would be paid his 20 *daler* from his other siblings' inheritance.[57] Apparently, Erich had invested his wife's land money in the family farm in Mjösund, and it was now returned to him. Nothing was said about whether she or her relatives had given their consent to this way of using her money. As it turned out, they were actually fortunate that Erich did not win the farm from his brother but had to accept the money. In this way, the money could be invested in other land and would retain its quality as her lineage property. Similarly, Olof Elofsson in Ämtervik made a will (in 1652) for the benefit of his wife, giving her everything that was in the estate and claiming that he had acquired it "with his own labor." Then his wife, Karin Olofsdotter, testified that she had sold her inherited land herself and invested the value in their common estate. (In this way, she retained the right to at least one-third.). Presumably, this was a way of showing the court that her husband had not sold her land behind her back.[58]

The problem identified here was caused by inadequate legal categories for land. Swedish land law operated with two categories only — inherited land and acquired land — for which very different rules applied. One could do whatever one wished with acquired land, and such land became part of the common property to which one's spouse also held a claim. By way of contrast, inherited land afforded very little leeway for action, and one's spouse could under no circumstances have a share in it. But in real life, it was of course impossible to work with such rough labels. There were complicated and obscure intermediary forms that did not fit into these two standard boxes. In everyday language people were actually more sophisticated, making a distinction between purchasing land (köpa), inheriting land (ärva), and redeeming land, that is, taking over land from a relative in return for some monetary compensation (lösa).[59] This more fine-grained terminology was better adapted to the kind of society in which early modern people lived. As we have seen, the use of money to settle inheritance claims was often necessary at this time.[60] Moreover, spouses sometimes made wills that challenged the dichotomy of inherited/noninherited land. Finally, the transfer of much landed property in the first half of the seventeenth century from the state to the nobility, on varying and often unclear terms, did not exactly contribute to the clarification of these issues. Land granted to noblemen could not be classified as inherited, of course, but it was often far from self-evident that it should be looked upon as purchased land either, even though the donations were sometimes made in compensation for services rendered.[61] In sum, there was a wide discrepancy between the way in which the law described property and the many ways in which property was actually envisioned, discussed, and used.

In spite of these realities, however, and despite increasingly vociferous demands for a revision of the medieval legal code, the code remained unchanged for the duration of the seventeenth century. Consequently, the rich variety of methods for transferring landed property had to be fit into the simple dichotomy of inheriting or acquiring land.

This encouraged legal inventiveness. For instance, there was discussion at the time about whether a woman's morning gift should be looked upon as inherited or acquired. At least some legal commentators concluded that it was neither, admitting indirectly that the legal distinction was patently inadequate.[62] It certainly was, causing the status of redeemed land (*bördlöst jord*) to be ambiguous and open to various constructions. It was sometimes regarded as a form of inherited land, sometimes as acquired. Parties could profit from this lack of clarity, labeling redeemed land as suited their interests for the moment. But in view of how ordinary people often emphasized investment as a legal entitlement, it is likely that, to many, redeemed land would intuitively appear to be a form of purchased land and thus a form of property of which a spouse could become a co-owner. [63] It is impossible to map all the strategies that people may have employed in this respect. However, it is clear that spouses who sold their inherited land and invested the money in the family farm of the other spouse ran a very serious risk of losing their rights, since the property was no longer clearly discernible in the landscape. Therefore, the important thing for a woman's relatives was not to prevent all conceivable sales of her land; selling land was often necessary, as all parties would acknowledge. What was important for relatives was to prevent her land money from being invested in her husband's lineage property because, if it was, the land would be lost from the kin group's "overall purview."[64] But to the couple, the situation may have appeared in a different light. Their main identity may have been that of husband and wife, and they may have felt a desire to dissociate themselves from their kinsmen. Often, this spousal identity came to the fore in wills.

Separate or Together? The Right to Draw Up a Will

It has been suggested in Swedish historiography that wills became more commonly used in the latter half of the seventeenth century, at least within the higher strata of society. In an early twentieth-century study, C. G. Bergman pointed to some reasons for their increased popularity within the nobility. High mortality levels led to frequent remarriages, and as new children were born, the legal rights of children from previous marriages had to be defined more explicitly. Moreover, noblemen who served in the continental armies had the opportunity to take booty in the form of movable property; such property could be freely bequeathed.[65] Another obvious reason was that, according to the law, acquired land was devisable whereas there was an almost complete prohibition against devising inherited land. Noblemen were in a position

TABLE 2. Female plaintiffs in the Svea Hovrätt, as compared to the Court of Chancery, in the seventeenth century

	Svea Hovrätt, Sweden, 1614–1705 (a)		Court of Chancery, England, 1613–1714 (b)	
	N	%	N	%
Total number	1,408		2,400	
Men	965	69	1,663	69
Women	352	25	621	26
Indeterminate/corporate	91	6	116	5

Sources: Janus Regius, part 1, Svea Hovrätts arkiv, Riksarkivet; Erickson, *Women and Property*, 115.

Comments: The figures under (a) have been calculated on the basis of all cases registered under the letters A and C in Janus Regius. Erickson has calculated the figures under (b) with a similar method (Erickson, *Women and Property*, 116).

TABLE 3. Female litigants (plaintiffs and defendants) in will cases, the Svea and Göta Hovrätter, seventeenth century

	Svea Hovrätt, 1615–92		Göta Hovrätt, 1637–92	
	N	%	N	%
Total number	173		55	
Female plaintiffs	49	28	9	16
Female defendants	55	32	15	27

Sources: Bergman, "Testamentet."

Comments: The figures have been calculated by the author, on the basis of material presented in Bergman, "Testamentet."

where they could acquire landed property more easily than other social groups. The vast majority of the peasantry may have held inherited land only and was consequently completely barred from making a will.[66] Even when ordinary people did have the legal right to make a will, it is far from certain that they were aware of this option. The court records sometimes show us people going to court to make inquiries as to whether they were entitled to use their acquired property as they liked. This suggests that people may have taken for granted that no land was devisable.[67]

Wills often caused disputes, and noble women seem to have been particularly prone to engage in such litigation. They appeared as plaintiffs in one-fourth of all civil cases — exactly the same proportion as has been shown for England at the same time.[68] In cases involving wills, females accounted for roughly one-fourth in the Svea Hovrätt, while the rate was lower in the Göta Hovrätt. However, if their activity as defendants is also included, the figures rise quite considerably, and particularly so for the Svea Hovrätt. Since women were often the ones who were favored by wills, and who would thus appear as defendants if the wills were contested, it is reasonable to note their overall participation and not only their activity as plaintiffs. This suggests that wills were important to women and to noble women in particular (who were overrepresented in the courts of appeal). This is not surprising: noble women were disfavored by the tendency towards primogeniture prevalent in the seventeenth century, and they were particularly dependent on the individual arrangements that their fathers, husbands, or both made for them.[69]

New legal devices were often tried first within the higher echelons of society, partly because these people had access to legal expertise and advice in a way that ordinary peasants did not. The will drawn up by Count Jacob De la Gardie (in 1650) is revealing in this respect. In this will, De la Gardie described how he had given all his inherited property to his wife, Ebba Brahe, upon their marriage. He also described how he had sold some of her inherited property and bought other property instead, and how his main estate, Jacobsdahl, had been created with the help of her lineage property.[70] Apparently, this couple had paid no attention whatsoever to the legal restrictions upon the use of lineage property. Instead, they had let their respective property become confounded in a way that was clearly contrary to the law. (Another way of describing this is to say that they had exchanged lineage property with one another.) If their relatives had made complaints, they would probably have won, but it is obvious from the self-confident formulations of the will that the will-maker took for granted that no such complaints would disturb his plans.

Wills were sometimes used by ordinary peasants as well (even if the distinction between a will and a retirement arrangement was not always clear-cut),[71] particularly when the spouses lacked offspring.[72] People who had children must have trusted them not to demand immediate division of the estate as long as one parent was alive. Apparently, they did not always trust more distant relatives to be as considerate of the widowed spouse. While there is little to suggest that ordinary people used individual property arrangements (like wills) often, the ones we do find are of special interest since they testify to a view of the married couple that was profoundly at odds with the one emphasized by the legal code.

While the latter conceptualized the couple as a temporary constellation of two persons, with separate property and differing allegiances, the competing view suggested that husband and wife had common rather than conflicting interests, as their care for each other showed. For instance, wills often mentioned how the spouses' mutual love demanded that they show concern for each other's long-term well-being. While legal discourse subordinated the rights and interests of individuals to those of the broader kin group, the competing view suggested that it was legitimate for couples to make arrangements that benefited them and their close family. For instance, wills often drew attention to the value of spouses' common labor and argued that relatives had no rights to the fruits of that labor. Ultimately, the view expressed in wills claimed that, in seventeenth-century society, the couple (with its household) — not the kin group — was the most fundamental unit of society.

In many ways, this was true. The early modern system of taxation had made the peasant farm into the basic cadastral unit (*hemman*). Most taxes were calculated on the basis of farms and collected from the inhabitants of farms. Prompt payment of taxes presupposed that the farm was under cultivation, and for this one person would not suffice. It took a couple, often with children, servants, and grandparents, to maintain a farm and to pay all that was due to the state. Therefore, it is hardly surprising that disagreements about investment of labor often arose in legal disputes about land, as a conscious attempt to play down the importance of kinship. Why should a distant kinsman be entitled to take over a farm for which he had shown little interest in the past? Why should the present possessor and his wife be deprived of the fruits of many years' labor? Did not the widow have a stronger claim than the late husband's relatives? These were the kinds of sentiment that were expressed in litigation and that challenged the rights traditionally vested in the kin group.

The court records often remain silent on the fact that it was not only the husband who worked. In the individual arrangements that husband and wife made to protect each other in their old age, a more elaborate description was often offered of the contributions made by each party. Spousal wills are particularly useful in this respect. Here, men's *and* women's contributions of labor become more visible than they otherwise are. By means of a spousal will (or a "mutual will," Latin *testamentum reciprocum*)[73] a couple could decide that the spouse who lived longer should retain control of the property of the deceased spouse. This was a lawful arrangement as long as it only referred to acquired property, that is, to each spouse's share of the common property. Such a will would give a husband his wife's third and a wife her husband's two-thirds. Consequently, spousal wills normally gave more to women than to men. Since women generally lived longer than men, it is also likely that women benefited from spousal wills more often than men.

However, spousal wills were not lawful if the spouses tried to confer their entire property to each other, including their inherited separate property. Observations in the 1640s suggest that, nevertheless, some spouses tried to do just this. The legal commission of 1643 wrote that it was "very common" for spouses to draw up a mutual will, and that these practices did not always conform to the law. Spouses with no off-spring often decided that the surviving spouse should keep the entire estate intact until his or her death, "and we cannot approve of such a will since it damages the interests of the rightful heirs."[74] This authoritative statement was well-known in the seventeenth century; other influential lawyers concurred with it,[75] and references were made to it in various cases.[76] Still, there was much legal bewilderment as to which wills were lawful, and the distinction between inherited and acquired property was at the heart of many disputes.[77] What did spouses argue when their relatives refused to accept their wills and dragged them to court?

The childless couple Hans Kirs and Karin Pedersdotter had drawn up a spousal will in 1643, stipulating that the surviving spouse should keep everything in the estate. Since their relatives did not accept this arrangement, the couple ended up in the Svea Hovrätt. The will asserted that Hans had not inherited his property but had "acquired it honorably with the grace of God." It also appeared that Karin had received nothing from her parents. The couple went on to state before the court that they had acquired all their belongings "with the greatest trouble and toil in the sweat of their brow." The will had been drawn up "according to law and to legal immemorial custom," and Hans found it very odd if the opposing party should be able "to bereave me of my property through their claims of inheritance."[78] If such claims were accepted by the judi-ciary, he said, "who would then care to exert himself to save something for himself and his wife?"[79]

This pleading concisely sums up the main arguments that many couples used in similar situations. They argued that their legal arrange-ment conformed both to written law and to custom, and they depicted themselves as devout Christians, who acknowledged that man depends on God's grace and is supposed to act in accordance with the words of the Bible.[80] They denied having any obligations toward their kinsmen, since — as they alleged[81] — their property was not inherited. Finally, they argued that husbands ought to make special efforts to care for their wives and themselves and that the courts should not create negative incentives in this respect.

Erik Thomson and Marina Erichsdotter's will (drawn up in 1654) was similar, as was the dispute that arose when Marina's son suddenly turned up after having been gone for a long time. Erik had no inherited property, the spouses said in their will, and he wanted Marina to have everything that was in the estate on his death. Marina wanted the same for Erik, except that, if her son eventually turned up, Erik should give him 200 copper *daler*. They added that Christian love between spouses demanded that they show concern for each other's well-being. When summoned to court, Erik argued that their will conformed to "lawful and widely practiced custom." What was more, he continued, the city notary had helped him to draw it up, and, he asked, would not the notary have interfered if the will were illegal? Finally, Erik informed the court that his wife had turned ill shortly after their marriage so that he had devoted much time, money, and concern to nursing her. He had had little joy during the time they lived together.[82]

Many will-makers referred to their investment of labor. So did both Marina Jönsdotter and Barbro Persdotter. Marina claimed that she had inherited nothing but acquired all her property "with God's blessing and by the sweat of her brow." Barbro pointed out that the property had been acquired with "toil and labor" and claimed that her relatives had only caused her "anger and resentment."[83] The labor argument was particularly important to couples, since invoking *jointly* performed labor was an oblique way of saying that relatives had no rights. Moreover, by referring to Adam, who was the first to have worked "by the sweat of his brow" following the Fall, they placed themselves within a clearly religious context, while at the same time depicting themselves as self-made men and women, as it were, who had nothing to thank their relatives for.[84] Invariably, they also stressed their mutual love.

It is hardly surprising, then, that relatives who tried to have the wills declared illegal often tried to challenge the spouses on these two points. In the dispute caused by Anders Biörsson and Helena Hansdotter's will (1654), Helena's relatives told the court how the spouses had lived together "in great discord," referring to information obtained from the neighbors.[85] In the dispute between Karin Erichsdotter and Claes Nÿtinghoff, Karin's opponent claimed that she had been inconsistent in her love for her (now deceased) husband.[86] In the will by Karin Persdotter and her husband, it was said that the spouses only held property that they had acquired "in sweat and blood." But Karin's brother-in-law argued that his brother (who was a shipwright) had indeed received his inheritance from their parents. Armed with this initial capital and his great industry, the husband had achieved a "beautiful fortune," and his brother had assisted him with manpower, horses, and food each time a new vessel was to be built. But Karin, claimed her brother-in-law, had not contributed any property to the estate, and she had destroyed more than she had created within the household, referring to tales by friends and neighbors.[87] The brother clearly tried to depict himself as the real partner of Karin's husband, as someone who had assisted him unselfishly while the wife did nothing. (That she was said to have been in poor health was not commented upon by the brother.)

From a strictly legal point of view, the only thing that was relevant in these cases was whether the will referred to inherited property, in which case it was illegal. Acquired property was regarded as part of the common estate and spouses could dispose of it as they saw fit. If the husband wanted to give his entire share (two-thirds) to his wife, he was free to do so (and vice versa). Whether or not husband and wife had worked together diligently was of no legal importance; nor was the character of their feelings for each other. However, it is very clear from cases such as these that people did not know this or, perhaps even more likely, that they did not agree with the law on this point. It is revealing that Karin Persdotter's brother-in-law spent so much energy on trying to prove that she had been lazy and unfaithful, while only mentioning in passing that the property had been inherited by his brother. Likewise, couples would have been well-advised to present elaborate evidence of how they had come by the contested property, but in fact they spent more time on describing their married life. These practices suggest that ordinary people found it reasonable and equitable to pay attention to love, and investment of labor, too. As will be seen presently, the state and the local communities are likely to have concurred with this view.

Directly or indirectly, then, many of the cases regarding wills corroborate a view of the couple that has been proposed in previous research: that spouses should be loving and hardworking.[88] Extolling their own labor and love, spouses implicitly or explicitly sought support from important discursive authorities like the state and the church, both of which had a keen interest in well-functioning households and couples who lived together in harmony. In this way, preferences that were not inherent in the written law nevertheless put their imprint upon legal practice. It is striking how the rhetoric of these wills resembles that found in French, Belgian, and Scottish wills. In all these countries, spouses referred to their mutual love and hard labor in a way that raises questions about whether there was a common model to which people adhered.[89]

An indirect but crucial effect of these discursive strategies was the emergence of a new conception of the husband. The medieval land law depicted him as a person against whom a woman might need protection, while remaining silent on the possibility that fathers, brothers, sons, and uncles might also constitute threats to her and her property. The language of the spousal wills suggested that husband and wife had common rather than conflicting interests. It implied that spouses were capable of making individual arrangements for the surviving spouse that were more adequate than the ones that could be obtained through medieval law. Ultimately, it undermined the idea that the woman might need protection against her husband and portrayed him in a new light. While medieval law constructed the kin group as the protector of women's property rights, spousal wills suggested that couples preferred relatives not to interfere with what was none of their business.

Of course, this notion of the "good husband" was not entirely new. It was nurtured by the fact that every year in all courts throughout the realm husbands turned up to assert the rights of their wives, their stepdaughters, and their mothers-in-law. The legal construction of the husband as a possible threat had never been a true description of how husbands actually behaved. This construction was seriously challenged by new social practices and, even more, by new ways of speaking about the couple. Husbands' wills for the benefit of their wives (that is, unilateral rather than mutual arrangements) were important in this context, showing the husband as somebody who did not take advantage of his position but made careful provisions for his wife instead. Such wills have survived from almost all social strata, even though their total number (as with the number of spousal wills) is still unknown.[90] An armorer's apprentice could set up such a will,[91] as could an ordinary peasant,[92] or an aristocrat such as the chancellor Axel Oxenstierna himself. Even as extremely wealthy and powerful a person as the chancellor, who was de facto ruler during the minority of Queen Christina, legitimized his will by saying that he had received only a minor part of his property through inheritance and had acquired the major part "by the blessing of God, by the sweat of his brow and [through his own] labor."[93] Everybody was aware of the strong rights vested in the kin group, and even if many aristocrats expressed sympathy for *bördsrätt*,[94] they nevertheless tried to avoid its effects when it suited their interests, referring to arduous labor as the common lot of mankind.

Wills open a window on the sorts of arrangement that people wanted to be able to make. Invariably, they show us spouses planning for their old age, or the residual half of a couple planning for his or her remaining time on earth and for the future of their children. They strongly suggest that, contrary to the law, ordinary people did not think of property as something that belonged to the kin group but rather as their own. They vociferously objected when a kinsman tried to restrict the scope of their ability to give that property to whomever they liked. Finally, the wills are particularly interesting for showing us how one spouse could try to compensate the other for the labor invested during their life together. They suggest that people used their imagination and creativeness to achieve the ends they desired. At least some couples wanted to make known to the public hidden contributions to the household in the form of labor or property that could otherwise be easily ignored. The will proved to be one means of doing this.

State Impact upon Property Law

Swedish women's property rights were shaped in a context where concern with families' access to land was more fundamental than the notion of rights vested in individuals. It has even been argued that women were merely "bearers of wealth," transferring crucial economic assets from one generation of men to another but remaining largely unable to use these assets themselves.[95] This is true, but we should add here that men, too, were severely circumscribed in what they could do. Men could not sell their own inherited property to whomever they liked, without first checking that no kinsman was interested in taking over the land. Their freedom to act was particularly circumscribed as concerned their wife's land. Moreover, the notion of individual rights was not totally absent. It seems quite clear that old people were supposed to support themselves during widowhood with the help of their separate property; the court records frequently tell us about old women and men who have transferred their land to another person in return for a promise of care, support, and a worthy funeral. In such situations, it was preferable if the old person could find a close relative who was willing to help, because this would keep the land within the overall purview of the kin group. However, if this proved impossible, he or she could make a deal with anyone who volunteered to help. Thus, keeping the land within the family was not of such paramount importance as to deny women and men the right to a decent living in their old age.[96] It may be debated, of course, whether this acceptance of land transfers outside the kin group testifies to an acknowledgement of individual rights, or if it merely shows that local communities wanted to avoid increasing costs for poor relief.[97] However, for all practical purposes, old women (and men) did have some individual property rights; their share of the common marital estate is a conspicuous example of this.

Women's property rights, however, were not only shaped and colored by a context where kinship was important. They were profoundly affected by the early modern state's strong interest in stable and substantial tax incomes. Stability had to do with predictability or, in the words of James C. Scott, legibility.[98] The central state preferred a system where all farms liable to pay tax remained the same from one year to the next, because this allowed the state to set up comprehensive cadastral registers on the basis of which taxes could be calculated and predicted. The state opposed local practices that would upset the transparent order of the registers, such as splitting up farms or abandoning them — the fact that abandonment nevertheless occurred only shows that the state did not control rural society in detail.[99] The ultimate reason for this interest in stability and transparency was, of course, a concern with state finances and a wish to extract as much tax as the population could bear, particularly in times of war.[100]

Desertion of farms, or parts of farms, was an enduring phenomenon in the late sixteenth and early seventeenth centuries. Unoccupied farms yielded no incomes, and therefore, a family (or broader kin group) that failed to use its farm productively for three consecutive years had forfeited its property rights.[101] It is hardly surprising that both state representatives and the peasantry tried to avoid this. We find examples of how the local bailiffs exhorted particular members of the kin group to take responsibility for vacant farms. For instance, Olof Jåpsson was pressed to take over a certain farm in Uppland but was unwilling to do so, arguing that "if he would do so, then somebody will turn up who happens to have as strong *bördsrätt* as himself, and this person will then drive him away from his management and labor." This was actually exactly what happened, but the local court found in favor of Olof (1579), letting him keep the farm both because he owned a substantial part of it and because he had saved the farm from becoming entirely derelict.[102] In other cases, it was the members of the kin group themselves who tried to find a suitable person to take over the farm. Lars Hansson lived "in affluence" at his farm in Tensta when his kinsmen pressed him to take over another farm in Vendel in order to save it from being seized by the bailiff. He acquiesced to their wishes.[103]

It is clear that the state's insistence on prompt payment of taxes inserted a new component into the property-rights system of early modern

Sweden. The extremely strong legal rights vested in the kin group were modified by the fact that it seemed inequitable not to protect the rights of a person who had effectively invested labor, and possibly money, in a particular farm, and in addition paid taxes. It made sense from the point of view of the exchequer to protect owners who were present and diligent, rather than relatives who might or might not turn up to claim the land. It also made sense from the point of view of the local community (from which the lay judges were recruited) to support the claims of someone who had proved himself capable of paying taxes and supporting his household, because such a person was less likely to become a liability to the local community.[104] It did not always make sense from the point of view of relatives, as many court cases show,[105] but sometimes the dispute could be solved amicably, as when the brothers of a deceased man consented to pay their sister-in-law and her new husband for the ample investments they had made on the family farm.[106]

We may term this new component individualistic, since it accepted individual efforts and exertions as a basis for entitlement, rather than membership in a kin group. To a certain degree, this way of thinking could tap into real estate law with its insistence that a distinction be made between inherited and acquired property, between rights deriving from birth and rights deriving from exertion. However, the term "individualistic" is not entirely felicitous since it suggests that we are talking about the exertions of one person, whereas in fact, it was highly unlikely that a single person could put a neglected farm back into good shape. Even if the sources are often silent on this point, it must have been the exertions of the entire peasant household that made the difference. Thus, when the court in Njurunda determined that Erik Persson should be allowed to retain the meadows that Olof Mårtensson had claimed by adducing *bördsrätt*, it justified its standpoint by pointing to the fact that Erik was paying the tax for the land and that Erik had helped Olof when he was starving — once again a concrete reminder of how the court had access to local knowledge about what had happened in the neighborhood.[107] While the source presents the case as one where Erik was the person who paid and helped, it is of course highly unlikely that he could do either without a complete household behind him. As the spousal wills showed, couples would sometimes find it in their interest to stress this fact.

With its interest in tax incomes and stability, the central state sometimes had reason to favor claims that ran counter to demands made by kinsmen. Still, the notion that kinsmen did have a claim on each other's land remained very pronounced throughout the seventeenth century.

It was common for a person who had won a dispute about property to pay compensation to the kinsmen, even when he was under no legal obligation to do so, in order to be able to enjoy and keep the farm "with concord and love."[108] Behind these euphemistic words lay, no doubt, the harsh reality that the relatives would have made his life very uncomfortable if the compensation had not been forthcoming. This indicates that "individualistic" or household-oriented ways of thinking were contested and that kin rights were still relatively hard to challenge.

The state's impact upon the property rights system was even stronger with respect to the fragmentation of farms, and here the implications for women are more obvious and easily interpreted than in the case of land desertion. A number of investigations have shown that women's land was sold strikingly often.[109] There seems to have been a clear tendency for land to drift away from the women who had inherited it in the first place. This phenomenon reflects the prohibition against excessive fragmentation of farmland, which was laid down in statutory law in the fifteenth century and repeated over and over again in the course of the two subsequent centuries. These prohibitions underlined that farms should not be split up among too many owners since this would endanger payment of taxes; a minimum farm size was stipulated in 1684, and these prohibitions were not abolished until the middle of the eighteenth century.

Statutory law did not make it illegal for all siblings to inherit, but it exhorted owners of smaller shares to accept money (or personal property) instead of land. Naturally, this put women with brothers at a serious disadvantage, since their shares were always smaller than those of their brothers. We may recall the case of the two brothers Erik, where the younger Erik managed to gain possession of the contested land. His success was due to the fact that he could claim both his paternal and maternal inheritance in the landed property and that he had bought his sister's shares. Armed with this bundle of rights, his total share was worth approximately 60 percent of the farm, which was much more than his two half-brothers could muster. Consequently, the court gave him the right to take over the farm, but compelled him to pay the half-brothers for their shares. Naturally, his sister also had to agree to accept money instead. It is telling that she was not even involved in the dispute, which pitted two brothers against one another.[110]

The court records often bear witness to this drift of land away from women. In 1640 Olof Nilsson in Björkö demanded the right to buy the land that Kirstin had inherited in the same hamlet. He adduced the fact that he was the one who paid taxes on the land, and the court found in his favor. It appears that previously, and perhaps long ago, Kirstin's land had been split off from the farm that Olof now possessed, probably through inheritance. The taxes, however, had never been adjusted (they seldom were), leaving the owner of the farm with fewer resources but the same duties. It is easy to see why the court would want to restore the farm in its original form, although it had adverse effects for Kirstin.[111]

In 1586 Staffan Mårtensson came to court with his cousins and his two paternal aunts in order to settle claims of inheritance on land that lay in five different hamlets. The family had already divided the land among themselves some years before, but now one of the aunts expressed dissatisfaction, arguing that she and her sister should each have a complete farm just as their brothers did. She then proceeded to simply take possession of Staffan's father's land. When settling this dispute, the court stated that it was fair that a brother should have a share twice the size as his sister, and one of the aunts immediately agreed to accept money instead of land.[112] In both cases, land tended to end up in the hands of men rather than women, but this was only partly an effect of inheritance law. Equally important were the tax interests of the state and the ensuing prohibitions on land fragmentation.

Women were not the only ones who bore the brunt of this system. All owners of small shares were disadvantaged. When Olof Persson bought a farm in Alunda from the Crown, there was already a tenant on the farm by the name of Lass Olsson. Lass owned a small share and many times had been offered the opportunity to buy the whole farm. He always declined, saying that he would stay where he was regardless of who the (major) owner might be. But when Olof came back from Stockholm with his title deed, Lass assaulted him, "filling his mouth with earth and asking him whether he had enough land now."[113] Probably, Lass understood what would happen now that Olof had become the major owner, and this was his way of protesting. As could be expected, the court found that the farm was too small to have two owners, and Olof was required to buy all residual land, that is, Lass' share.[114]

Thus, the early modern property system often tended to favor individual households that functioned well or individual owners who held large shares of farms. In both cases, it was the interest in upholding cadastral stability that explained the tendency, and this interest was at least partly common to local communities and to the state. As a consequence, land tended to drift away from women, whose inheritance shares were smaller. Because of the strong inheritance rights, women (as well as many men) were instead compensated with money or other forms of personal property, but unfortunately, such forms of property were not as well-protected by the law as was land.

In the Local Public Sphere

Swedish women's property rights hinged upon the protection these rights enjoyed in the local community, just as the support an individual woman could muster for her sake depended upon how other people — kinsmen, neighbors, and friends — viewed her case. If her husband tried to sell or mortgage her separate inherited land, her relatives could use their veto to stop him, but, if they neglected to do this in time, it would be difficult for the woman to take action on her own. If her husband had sold the land, arguing that severe famine had forced him, the local court could subsequently annul his sale if it found that the situation had not been as serious as he claimed. But if the members of the court feared reprisals by the husband, they may have refrained from taking action. Thus, loss of memory and timidity could affect the legal situation of women most palpably.

Similarly, both women's and men's rights were affected by the fact that, in legal practice, property rights were often understood as being dependent upon, or at least improved by, virtues such as diligence, the capacity to work hard, love, loyalty, and faithfulness. Qualities of this sort cannot be proved in any "objective" way but rather have to be attested to by other human beings. Consequently, local people's perceptions of who had worked hard and who had shown love for her husband inevitably influenced courts in their decision making. In their deliberations, the local courts listened to local stories, or even gossip, and these "facts" played a part when they decided what was reasonable. Since the majority of the court consisted of lay judges — usually older peasants — this susceptibility to locally held opinions became even more pronounced. It is often hard to distinguish between what the lay judges said in their capacity as local inhabitants and what they said in their capacity as judges. The following example gives a vivid illustration of these mechanisms.

In 1579 Jåp Olsson of Munga came to court to solve a conflict he had with his younger brother, Pär, about their family farm. Pär wanted to take over the farm, claiming that when the brothers had drawn lots for the farm, he had won. Moreover, there was another brother and an ailing sister (who lived with Pär), both of whom had consented to selling their shares to Pär. But Jåp answered that he had expended a substantial amount of labor on the farm. He had stayed with his father for the duration of his lifetime, and his father had wanted him to take over the farm, since he had worked harder on it than any of his siblings. The twelve lay judges affirmed that he had worked tirelessly and they argued that, consequently, Jåp must have a better right to this farm than any of his siblings. Here, the lay judges acted as witnesses and judges at the same time. Subsequently, "all men who had assembled at court" testified that he had supported his father in his old age. At this point, one senses, the scales turned in favor of Jåp. Despite the fact that Pär must have owned a larger share of the farm, the court found in favor of Jåp, arguing that he should keep the farm since he had "invested all the strength of his youth" in the farm, while his brothers had "walked away and been more concerned with their own well-being" than with that of their old father.[115] The sizes of the shares were accorded little interest; it was more important to encourage people to be diligent laborers and good sons. Here, we may recall the case of Simon Persson, where it was explicitly pointed out that the stepson, Per Casparsson, had taken good care of his parents, which entitled him to keep the farm, while Simon's *relatives had given no assistance.*

It made sense from the point of view of both the central state and the local community to let those who were hardworking resume responsibility for the farms. But the state had no way of knowing who had worked hard and who had not. Only local people like the lay judges or the men assembled at court (often called "the common men") could know this. This knowledge gave them considerable power over cases where this sort of memory-based information was needed. It turned them into a local authority to which parties might want to appeal. What common men knew, or believed to be true, became "public opinion." Therefore, people who appeared before the court would often have an interest in influencing and persuading these men.[116]

When Jöns Grelsson tried to prove that his half-sister Kirstin had not been born within wedlock (which would have meant that she had no rights of inheritance), "all common men" and "the twelve judges" testified that they had never heard anything that would suggest that Kirstin's parents had not been betrothed.[117] In a very complicated dispute over land, Erich Olufsson claimed to have *bördsrätt* on behalf of his wife and, consequently, to be entitled to take over land that two other men claimed was theirs. These men, however, promptly produced a detailed account of how the land had been handed down to them from a previous owner, and the lay judges confirmed their story. Therefore, the court found in their favor and fined Erich for unlawful use of the land and for having caused trouble. But when Erich himself pleaded his case, and when the lay judges, somewhat surprisingly, supported him, he was granted a pardon.[118] When Nils in Söderby went to court to claim a strip of land, the lay judges testified that "no man any longer remembers how this strip of land" was lost from Söderby, implying that Nils had acted too late.[119]

All three cases show the lay judges to have been local authorities, whose support was important to obtain, and whose knowledge, or lack of knowledge, was crucial to the outcome of the case. Karin in Löfsta, whose brother had sold her land behind her back, also experienced how the judges' lack of support (as long as her brother was still alive) made it impossible for her to win her case. It is easy to see the disadvantages of this system: the ways in which it offered opportunities to unscrupulous persons for manipulating justice by putting pressure on the judges. But it is equally important to see its advantages: the flexibility with which the courts could adapt to local circumstances in order to arrive at fair and reasonable verdicts. When Anna in Ugglebol was taken to court because she could not verify her property rights, the court ruled that she should be allowed to keep the lands she had held for eleven years. That she had "imprudently" neglected to acquire a proper title deed was of little importance, since the court knew that she had held the land in "peaceful possession." Similarly, when a man called Mårten wanted to rescind an exchange of land which his ancestor had made 101 years previously, the court allowed the case to be reopened in spite of the fact that, by all conceivable standards, it was far too late. Not surprisingly, Mårten lost the case. But the facts presented by Mårten suggest why the case was reopened. It turned out that twenty years prior to that time, the local bailiff had (for unknown reasons) confiscated the land Mårten's ancestor had received through the contested exchange. Very likely, many people in the local community, including the lay judges, had compassion for Mårten and resented what the bailiff had done. Therefore, they wanted at least to investigate whether Mårten could be compensated in some other way.[120]

Swedish local courts were characterized, then, through lay participation and attention to solutions that were socially sustainable and "fair," by flexibility, and, sometimes, by disquieting relations of power.[121] This was the context in which women's property rights were interpreted and upheld. Like all family matters, women's property rights were of interest to everybody in the local community. Attending a court session, people would hear their neighbors explain how they were related to each other, how they had obtained a certain piece of land, and why they had failed to pay their debts. Consequently, people possessed surprisingly broad and detailed knowledge about what we might call local history. The basic

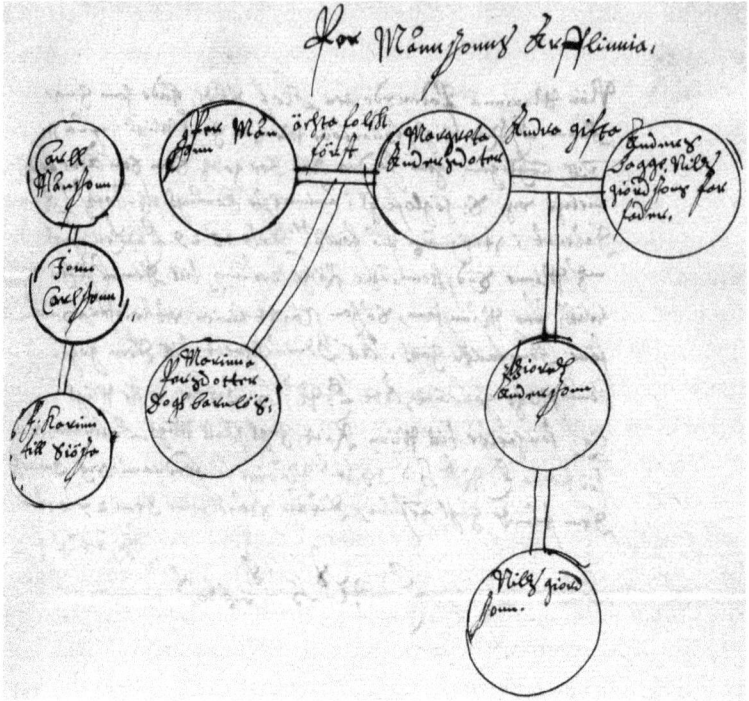

Handwritten family tree (Riksarkivet, Stockholm,
Sweden; photograph by Kurt Eriksson)

structure of these local histories was how people had married and re-married in the past, how landed property had been transferred between various persons and families, how farms had been split up and reunited, and what property parents had wanted their children to have. As they grew older, people acquired a profound knowledge of local history, a knowledge that they did not write down but carried within them. It was only when the court found it impossible to understand all intricacies that family trees were drawn up and attached to the court records.[122]

Family matters were not private matters in sixteenth- and seven-teenth-century local communities. People knew a lot about their neigh-bors and friends, not because they were particularly prying but because comprehensive knowledge was necessary in order to be able to assert one's own rights, and because such knowledge was unavoidable if one attended the local court regularly. The local community constituted a local public sphere where the distinction between private and public had no meaning and where "public opinion" affected the outcome of private disputes.[123] Consequently, there could be no, or only very few, domestic secrets from the point of view of local people.

From the point of view of the central state, the situation was different. One might think that title deeds and other forms of written records would have allowed centrally placed judges (in the courts of appeal) to settle property disputes on their own, without having recourse to additional local information. Would not the early modern absolutist state have produced cadastral registers and lists of taxation that sufficed to give courts complete insight into local property arrangements? The truth is that the early modern Swedish state was very much in the same position as the people of Saumur, who appear in Balzac's novel *Eugénie Grandet*. The townspeople could see that the miser Grandet had a large house, and they inferred from this fact that he was wealthy, but in fact they knew nothing about his liquid capital or the internal property arrangements of his household. In the same way, the Swedish state had registered all farms liable to pay taxes and knew the names of the men who represented the households in charge of the farms. Less was known about what parts of the physical landscape belonged to each farm and virtually nothing about whether the farm belonged to the husband, the wife, or to both. The state lacked "the information and the administrative grid" that would have allowed it to establish full control over society.[124] To the state, all households were essentially domestic secrets. To judges in the courts of appeal, who were at some distance from the local communities, households were equally obscure, and they were utterly unable to solve property disputes without aid from the local communities.[125]

Therefore, when complaints about lacking transparency were voiced in the latter half of the seventeenth century, they must not be interpreted as signs of problems inherent in local society. Rather, these complaints indicate that economic life was no longer confined to and limited by local communities. Instead, it took place within wider and more anonymous frameworks, where neither seller nor purchaser knew the other, and where landed properties may have been sold so often that their "pedigrees" were lost. The next chapter explores the implications of this situation for women's property rights.

Conclusions

The analysis presented in this chapter is based on sixteenth- and seventeenth-century court records (including wills). These are not ideal sources if one wants to know how ordinary people generally disposed of and thought about property. Every court case is unique in some sense, which makes it difficult to establish a set of cases that is sufficiently large and coherent to allow for any general conclusions. But for all their shortcomings, court records are still the best sources available for this period. With their help, it has been possible to determine some basic characteristics of the Swedish property system and what the implications for women were.

It is clear that a rhetoric of kinship played a very prominent role in early modern Swedish society. With the help of *bördsrätt*, members of the kin group could exert considerable influence over land that was for the moment in the hands of one of their kinsmen, or land that this kinsman tried to sell to somebody outside the kin group. In addition, the legal code laid down three concrete stipulations, which allowed a woman's natal family to continue to control land that she had brought into her marital estate. In this way, owners (that is, husbands) were significantly circumscribed with respect to what they could do with "their" landed property. Even if the sources tell us more about how *bördsrätt* was adduced than about how the three other stipulations were used, the conclusion may still be drawn that in Sweden, as in many other countries at this time, families and kin groups wielded considerable power over land and that this power was reinforced by the ways in which local communities and local courts functioned. This power of families and kinsmen may explain why Swedish women had comparatively strong rights of inheritance. Women's property rights *could* be strong precisely because their families did not normally risk that land given to a daughter would be lost "from their overall purview," as Bina Agarwal has succinctly put it.

The marked presence of the kin group, epitomized in the concept of lineage property, was considerably modified in the early modern period by two other authorities: the state and the Christian Church. The state tended to favor taxpayers and diligent workers, and the Church favored the hardworking spouses, united in their love for each other. Through their respective rhetoric, state and religion provided battering rams, as it were, to those who wanted to argue for their right to use their property as they liked, disregarding the claims of relatives. When even the law itself admitted that acquired property could be used at will, it more or less invited owners to use arguments based on the value of their invested labor. Those who took advantage of these opportunities were peasants, in disputes with each other, but also married couples, who adduced the value of labor when they wanted to argue for their right to care for each other by drawing up a will. From the very top of society down to ordinary peasants and townspeople, owners referred to their hard work and their unfailing love, not only because they no doubt saw themselves in this light, but also because property law, the tax system, and religious discourse made it likely that such arguments would meet with success. In the long run, these arguments, presented to courts all over the country, undermined the notion that kinsmen were the ones who were best at protecting couples' and individuals' legal rights and economic well-being.

In sharp contrast to landed property, personal property was poorly protected by Swedish law, and even if this could have an impact on both men and women, it was more likely that women would be affected. For instance, if a couple had sold the inherited land of the wife and invested the money in the lineage land of the husband, her rights were effectively extinguished. For relatives who wanted to keep a woman's property within the lineage, it was particularly important to intercede before this had happened. This was the blind spot of Swedish property law, a situation that medieval legislators had not foreseen and that could have disastrous effects for individuals. In a situation like this, making a will for the wife was particularly important, and some ordinary people did just that.

In her study of medieval Douai, Martha Howell showed that the radical change that gradually took place within Franco-Belgian family law was not the result of new statutory law or any order from above. What happened was that ordinary people started to act in new ways as they perceived changes in their economic situation, and the accumulative result of these new social practices was legal transformation. Her results are thought provoking. When people do not remain inactive but start making new types of arrangements for themselves and their families as a consequence of new economic realities, laws will change, albeit very slowly at first. Practices that have been observed in seventeenth-century Sweden may not have been very common. Every couple did not make a spousal will, nor did all couples describe themselves as united by mutual love and care. Every husband did not sell his wife's inherited land, nor did all husbands compensate their wives for losses of this type. Not everybody engaged in property litigation, nor did all Swedes laud their own labor. But these practices were common enough to be important for us to observe, and they would become increasingly influential as time wore on.

((3))

SUBTLE CHANGES

Johan Skytte was reputed to be the most erudite of all Swedish men of his time. He had traveled widely in Europe and attended the University of Marburg. Upon his return to Sweden he was appointed tutor of Crown Prince Gustaf Adolf. Later, he became chancellor of Uppsala University and first president of the court of appeal for southern Sweden — not to mention all his political offices.[1] In 1608 Johan Skytte wrote a commentary on Swedish law. In this work, he mentioned the stipulation of the legal code which stated that a man must procure the consent of his wife and her relatives before he can sell her inherited land. This injunction, Skytte commented, was "somewhat harsh." He went on to give reasons for his standpoint: "Were one's relatives to have such powers over one's estate, while the owner is still alive, so that one would have to secure their consent, then much trouble would ensue, [if] they would be regarded as owners while the owner was still alive."[2]

Skytte's opinion is thought provoking. It suggests, first, that he operated with a definition of ownership that was somewhat at odds with the one prevailing in Sweden at that time. As has been seen, *all* owners were surrounded by relatives who were regarded as "owners while the owner was still alive" and who would not hesitate to interfere with what the owner did, should his actions in any way harm their interests. There was nothing exceptional in this: all relatives were latent owners, as it were, as an effect of the *bördsrätt*. Due to his foreign education, Skytte had adopted a conception of ownership which focused on the absolute and unrestricted rights of individuals. This form of ownership hardly existed in Sweden at that time.

Skytte's opinion is also interesting for the hypothetical form in which he framed it. Instead of criticizing the fact that the wife's relatives had such extensive powers, he argued that much trouble would ensue *if* her relatives had such powers. Evidently, Skytte thought that this stipulation was a dead letter. There may have been some justification for his interpretation. Some husbands may not have bothered to acquire the explicit consent of their in-laws before selling the wife's land. On the other hand, some husbands obviously did. Moreover, it is unlikely that the medieval protection of wives' lineage land had become completely obsolete in the seventeenth century, simply because it would be hard to account for all the ink and ingenuity that was spent on the issue if it no longer mattered at all. It would be particularly incomprehensible why another man, who was also famous for his great erudition, would spend so much energy defending not only the protection of married women's separate property rights but also women's share of the common marital property. The name of this man was Claes Rålamb, one of the most articulate and influential lawyers and statesmen of his time.

The chronological emphasis of this chapter will be on the latter half of the seventeenth century, even though it extends as far as 1734. In social terms, the focus is on the upper strata of society, on social groups that possessed considerable capital, either in the form of land and money or in the form of knowledge. Women's property rights will be viewed from the perspective of these highly placed persons, not only because women's property rights may have played a different role for them than for the peasantry, but also because such persons were in positions where they could bring about legal change. Their arguments and opinions are of considerable interest even in a book where the main focus is upon "ordinary" people. What kinds of legal problems did they see in late seventeenth-century society, and what did they fail to see? From whose perspective were they viewing these problems?

The Dynamic Aspects of Property

As early as around 1600 there was much complaint about the Swedish legal code being obscure, muddled, and confusing. As the century wore on, these complaints had far from abated; they became increasingly vociferous. A number of law commissions were set up with more or less far-reaching mandates but with fairly modest results. It was not until 1686, when the so-called Great Law Commission was instituted, first under the chairmanship of Erik Lindschiöld, that any permanent results were achieved. This commission succeeded in bringing about a complete overhaul of the medieval code, resulting in the new code of 1734.[3]

Even if criminal law also needed to be modified, it is no exaggeration to claim that the necessity for legal change was most acute in legislation governing economic affairs. A large number of complicated problems had to be solved, many of which were situated at the intersection of real estate law and credit law. The former was old-fashioned and rigid, with its rough dichotomy of lineage versus acquired land, while the latter was very rudimentary. The medieval legal code had no special section dealing with credit and the recovery of debts; the few rules that were to be found were interspersed in other matters and were not sophisticated enough to fit a more well-developed credit market. The most basic problem may have been that the law did not fully acknowledge the ways in which investments and debts affected property rights. In the eyes of the law, property equaled land and was regarded as something essentially static, as an object whose value was more or less impervious to the actions of humans. The law was poorly adapted to dealing with the dynamic aspects of property, such as how the value of land could be increased by investing labor and money in it or how the value could be reduced by mortgages. That land could be transformed into personal property or liquid capital, and vice versa, was something medieval law hardly took into account. Seventeenth-century lawyers attributed these shortcomings of the law to the fact that their ancestors had not used credit but always paid in cash.[4] This was a conclusion that is hardly compatible with the historical evidence but that does bear witness to the keen sense that seventeenth-century people had of living in a modern society where the use of credit and liquid capital was more pronounced than ever before.

The first problematic issue, the effect of investments upon property rights, manifested itself in several ways. For instance, a person who had bought land and made improvements on it but lost it shortly afterward because of claims of *bördsrätt* made by relatives of the previous owner would, of course, want all his money back, including the value of the investments. This case was quite straightforward; what the owner said was simply that he wanted compensation for any labor and extra money he had expended. Such claims were often voiced by ordinary people in the primary courts, and courts heeded these arguments. When similar claims were raised within the nobility and in front of the courts of appeal, they were usually labeled with the Latin term *melioratio*. Naturally, melioration never referred to labor expended by the noble owner himself but to money he had invested by paying, for example, carpenters and joiners for their work on beautifying the estate. Such claims for compensation were usually unproblematic as well, unless the owner had indulged in sumptuous and extravagant investments. In such cases the court would make a distinction between necessary and unnecessary improvements, of which only the former were entitled to compensation.

Investments became more difficult to handle if they had been made on the inherited landed property of the owner. Was it not reasonable to acknowledge such investments as well, and should not the owner be allowed to make the investments he preferred? If he had chosen to acquire new land instead of investing his money in the lineage land, he would have had complete leeway with respect to its disposition. For instance, he could have willed it away to someone. Therefore, it seemed unjust if the owner were barred from this freedom simply because he had decided to improve his inherited lands. Such laws would certainly create negative incentives in regard to the family estate, the argument ran. The essence of this issue was that owners should be allowed to distinguish between object and value and that they should be allowed to use the value as they saw fit. To some extent, this distinction already existed in the form of land money, designating the value of the inherited land rather than the land itself. However, it was still rather complicated to make this distinction, precisely because landed property was conceptualized as a static object. How could the distinction be made between the object as it had once been (a couple of farms) and the object in its current state (a palace surrounded by extensive parks), and how could the owner be allowed to use the difference in value as he liked without affecting the object as such?[5] Questions such as these led into a veritable jungle of convoluted jurisprudence. These problems were only relevant to the tiny fraction of the population that the nobility constituted, but they nonetheless consumed much court time as the nobility, however small, was very active in the land market.

Thus, the issue was complicated if the money was not used to buy new land but was invested in land the owner had inherited. The situation became even more intricate if the invested money was not attributed to the owner but to his wife. This was the trickiest issue of all, as has been seen in chapter 2, and its implications even more far-reaching. In principle, it could affect all owners, not only noblemen. Some people dealt with this problem by drawing up wills in the hope that relatives and courts would accept them. Still, it was obviously very difficult to find a way of accommodating the demands of the legal code, which said that land bought from a relative should be classified as lineage property regardless of the origins of the money.

The effects of debts upon property rights were potentially sweeping and entailed a number of related problems. The legal code stipulated that when a man died, all his debts first had to be paid from his undivided estate before his heirs could have their shares.[6] Thus, the law stipulated that creditors' rights should be given precedence before those of heirs and relatives. In principle, therefore, the rights of kinsmen were far from absolute. This was precisely why *bördsrätt* was so valuable; adducing this right, a kinsman could reclaim the property from the creditor, provided that he could pay the amount that was due.

The law, however, provided no clear guidelines as to what constituted "his undivided estate." Some argued that "his estate" should be understood literally as the property he owned. For a married man living in the countryside, this meant his inherited lands and his two-thirds of the common property. Others argued that "his estate" meant "the couple's estate," and the implications were that her inherited lands and her one-third of the common property could be used to cover the husband's debts.[7] If the latter interpretation were correct, then the question would arise as to whether the wife and her relatives should give their prior consent to any debts that the husband might want to incur. If the three stipulations protecting women's property rights were invoked, it would be logical to require such consent. However, since the demand for explicit consent may not have been respected by everybody in the seventeenth century, requiring such consent was almost tantamount to requiring a new legal practice. In fact, the increasing concern with issues regarding debt may account for the interest awakened in the seventeenth century in whether or not relatives' consent should be required.

Nor was there an unequivocal definition of "debt." If an owner had borrowed money from someone outside the family or kin group, the case was rather uncomplicated. It became more complex as it began to be argued that the wife's morning gift was a form of debt, creating a preferential claim upon the husband's property.[8] The question became even more convoluted and contested when it was said that wills should also be looked upon as debts.[9] If wills were categorized as debts, then the beneficiary of the will would be able to take out his share before the legal heirs, and there would always be the risk that nothing would be left when all creditors had taken their due. Such an interpretation of the law would seriously undermine the *general* right of family members and kinsmen to inherit, some feared, while giving to owners the privilege of favoring particular individuals within or outside the family.

These issues were highly controversial and they caused much heated debate in the seventeenth century. They all bear witness to the enduring and crucial importance of lineage property as a fundamental legal institution, while at the same time showing how this institution incessantly clashed with the social ambitions of the nobility, with the increasingly vital credit market, and with the interests of wives. Was a wife liable to pay debts incurred by her husband, even if he had not procured the consent of both wife and relatives? Did wives' contributions of land money give them any rights to the land in which the money had been invested? The debates were rife with gendered notions and ideas that touched upon concepts of what men and women were like and how men and women ought to behave. In what follows, some aspects of these debates will be viewed more closely, since they provide a unique window upon the struggles that eventually caused legal change.

The Veto Debate: Can a Husband Use His Wife's Property to Cover His Own Debts?

Johan Skytte not only wanted to strengthen owners' rights and restrict the influence of relatives, he also emphasized debtors' duty to honor their debts. It was hardly a coincidence that he adopted these two standpoints. Relatives' consent was particularly pertinent in cases where the husband had sold the wife's lands to someone outside the kin group, for example, to a creditor. Therefore, a commitment to improving the legal position of creditors was almost inevitably bound to lead to opposition to the stipulation about relatives' consent. Likewise, such a commitment could have implications for the wife's share of the common property that was not protected by the relatives. Was it equitable entirely to exempt the wife's one-third from debt responsibility, or must she pay with what was hers?

Skytte was not alone in his concern with prompt debt payment. The prominent legal scholar Johan Stiernhöök displayed a similar standpoint in his legal commentaries.[10] The legal code was unequivocal concerning inherited land, Stiernhöök wrote. A wife could not become the co-owner of her husband's lineage property, nor could he become the co-owner of hers, "so that the husband does not have anything more to do with his wife's real estate than would a complete stranger." Consequently, the husband should act as a trustee with a view to improving his wife's property; should he fail to do so, he must be held responsible and pay for whatever losses she might have incurred. But the credit market complicated the matter. It often so happens, Stiernhöök went on, that the wife consents to the alienation of her own estate and signs the debt bond together with her husband. The question then arises whether her real estate can be sold to cover the debts, regardless of whether her relatives have given their consent or not. In such a case, Stiernhöök maintained, "it seems as if the rights of creditors must be honored before those of the heirs." To support his standpoint, he referred to a legal case from 1663, in which the widow of the owner of an ironworks had been forced to pay his creditors.[11]

It was not incidental that Stiernhöök addressed the problem of indebtedness in relation to the iron industry. This sector of the Swedish economy dated back to the Middle Ages (or even earlier), but it was in the seventeenth century that iron production expanded rapidly, making Sweden Europe's most important exporter of iron. Much of the iron used in England and the Netherlands at this time was of Swedish origin. Somewhat later, in the period 1720–50, no less than 40 percent of all iron consumed in England was imported from Sweden. Swedish iron production was organized on the basis of a large number of small-scale units (*bruk*), combining various methods of attracting local labor. In this context, debt bondage was quite pronounced. However, the workers were not the only ones who were indebted: so were the ironmasters, who needed large amounts of capital to keep production going while they were waiting for payment for their products. Often, they were indebted to the merchant houses in Stockholm and Gothenburg.[12]

In sharp contrast to the agricultural sector, which was still comparatively stable and in the hands of small-scale peasant production, the flourishing iron industry could not exist without credits and investments, and credits and investments demanded a conception of ownership which was both more dynamic and at the same time more individualistic. Merchants and moneylenders took note of the possessions of the ironmaster seeking credit, and, if these were visibly substantial, they granted the loan, only to be bitter at the deception should they learn that parts of the marital estate were owned by the wife and therefore unassailable. It was in the interest of moneylenders that entitlements should become unambiguous.

It could not come as a total surprise to Swedish moneylenders that some wives had separate property; indeed, this was a central tenet of real estate law. But for various reasons this circumstance, nevertheless, developed into a problem at this time. A Swedish creditor could be indebted, in turn, to a foreign creditor who was unaccustomed to wives having property of their own. As chains of debt extended beyond national borders, the risk that one of the links would fail multiplied. And even when the credit nexus was confined within Sweden, problems could ensue due to low legibility. In other words, there was no uncomplicated way for an outsider to find out who owned what within marriage. Wives' property rights were seldom explicitly defined and regulated in contracts. They were the automatic effect of the woman being the daughter of her parents. In order to ascertain what might be hers, it was necessary to have access to local knowledge.

Ironmasters were one group for whom access to credit was essential; consequently, they were highly susceptible to the creditors' perspective. There were other actors who may have been equally susceptible. Aristocratic landowners were often dependent on credit, either because they were easily affected by fluctuating grain prices or because they wanted to display a sumptuous lifestyle, one for which they lacked the adequate liquid means.[13] Regardless of the reasons for their indebtedness, they always sought to retain their good name. Highly placed aristocrats like the chancellor Axel Oxenstierna or the chief admiral Karl Karlsson Gyllenhielm (the illegitimate half-brother of King Gustaf II Adolf) were at great pains to explain to their heirs the necessity of honoring any debts that might be in the estate after their deaths.[14] Payment of debts was seen as vital, both as a way of sustaining one's future creditworthiness and as a means of defending one's honor. In order to be honorable, a man had to dispel all doubts about fraudulent manipulations involving his wife's property.

The absolutist state also displayed an increasing interest in ameliorating the conditions of creditors in order to make credit more accessible. To some extent, this interest was directly linked to costly state projects such as warfare. Even if early modern states seem to have managed to force those who lived near the battlefields or future generations to bear the costs of war, they were still highly dependent on those who could provide ready cash.[15] It is no surprise that the statutes providing creditors with the best conditions were the ones promulgated at the inception of the Nordic Wars.[16] Clearly, they were designed so as to tempt creditors to lend their money, preferably to the state. However, the state, or the kings, also showed a more general interest in the ways in which the credit market worked and assumed responsibility for making credit law clearer and less ambiguous. The fact that the royal courts of appeal had to use so much of their time in settling debt disputes must have made the monarchs increasingly aware of the importance of well-functioning credit law.[17] This awareness manifested itself in the intense activity with which new statutory law was enacted in this field. Only warfare resulted in more new legislation in the period 1600 to 1679 than did credit.[18] Several of these statutes dealt with the extent to which spouses could be held legally responsible for each other's debts. Because of the complicated nature of Swedish real estate law these rules were often extremely intricate, making distinctions between yields from lineage land as opposed to yields from acquired land, between debts from which both spouses had benefited as opposed to debts that only benefited one of them, and so on.[19]

Both debtors and creditors were thought to be insufficiently protected by law, and both were believed to take advantage of loopholes and contradictions in existing credit legislation. On balance, however, complaints focused more on the situation of creditors. They were said to have to wait for insufferably long periods of time before they could recover their money. Sometimes they had to accept payment in kind and would then have the trouble of selling the products themselves; sometimes, they were unable to recover the full value of what they had lent. It was frequently claimed that debtors were prone to fraud and embezzlement. They tried to conceal what property they had, or to mortgage the same property several times. It is hard to know whether these narratives were entirely true, but it is obvious that they affected leading actors and their perceptions of what needed to be done. The conclusion was concisely summarized in a statute issued by King Karl XI in 1684, in which the king stated that "if any damage is to ensue from this regulation, then it is better that he suffers, who has an obligation to another man, than he, who in good faith lent of his own."[20] Creditors were the ones who should be favored.

Thus, many powerful actors were strongly committed to improving the legal position of creditors in the latter half of the seventeenth century or, in other words, to enhancing legibility. It was in this context that the question of married women's property rights came on the agenda. Some believed, rightly or not, that separate inherited property for married women could be a way of concealing property from creditors. Moreover, it was argued that wives' share of the common property must be made available to creditors, since wives, too, profited from the loans taken by their husbands. The king had to take these views and arguments seriously. On several occasions, he exhorted the appeals court judges to submit their opinions on how the law should be interpreted and whether any changes or amendments needed to be made. In these debates, which took place in the 1660s and 1680s,[21] the majority of judges argued that legal practice had already changed. In the practice of the time, they said, the entire common property of the couple was used to cover the husband's debts, and the consent of relatives to the alienation of wives' lineage property was not generally acquired. With all due respect for the old law, its provisions with respect to wives' property rights were obsolete, and there was no convincing reason for reintroducing these outdated provisions, since they were "too harsh for these modern times"[22] — once again a reminder of the historical consciousness of seventeenth-century people and how they used the past to define themselves as modern.

What these modern times demanded in their eyes, then, was the improvement of the creditors' legal position, and to achieve this, it was necessary to have satisfactory knowledge about the security offered for their loans. Many judges claimed that households were inscrutable from the point of view of outsiders. For them, it was impossible to know whether the husband owned everything within the marital estate or if some parts were the separate property of his wife, and so not to be counted on. These matters were opaque and, as these judges frequently emphasized, it was best to leave them that way. The technical problems involved if one wanted to reduce inscrutability were insurmountable, so why not just define property relations within households as *arcana domestica* — "domestic secrets"? Why not just simply accept inscrutability and regard the entire marital estate as if it were one unit, for all practical purposes owned by the husband?[23]

The technical side to the matter was central to how these judges assessed the legal problem, but they buttressed their standpoint further by adding arguments that targeted issues of equity. It would be unfair, these judges argued, to make the husband responsible for all debts, given that wives benefited from the possessions that their husbands bought with borrowed money and, what was more, that wives were often the ones most prone to lavish consumption. Did not fairness, they argued, demand that there be a balance between the rights and duties of spouses? Otherwise, marriage would be nothing but a "lion's society," a company in which one partner was allowed to exploit and destroy the other. Husband and wife had to share the good and the bad times. Thus, the wife should not shirk her responsibilities when the husband was haunted by creditors. Further, it was reasonable to expect from a woman that she should choose her husband with care, listening to advice from relatives, so as to avoid marrying a profligate. Whether women were indeed presented with a choice may have been another matter, but the majority of judges argued as if women did have a say. Therefore, they concluded, a woman could not claim to be unaware of her future husband's economic situation when she married him, and knowledge entailed responsibility.[24] Finally, the majority employed many biblical locutions that suggested that it was wrong for a woman to assert her rights against those of her husband. The Bible clearly said that spouses should be "one flesh," the majority pointed out, and as this was by necessity true, then it must be lawful for spouses' separate properties to merge, in much the same way as their carnal bodies were joined during marriage.[25]

While the majority of judges argued for married women's responsibility for their husbands' debts, the dissenting minority was both erudite and eloquent in its plea for the sole responsibility of husbands for their debts, for their patriarchal responsibility for their wives, and for their irrefutable responsibility for themselves as adult men. The dissenting minority did not deny that legal practice had started to change, but contrary to their opponents, they did not want to accept this state of affairs. Their aim was to resuscitate the literal and, as they saw it, correct meaning of the old law. This included the requirement for relatives' consent to the alienation of wives' lands as well as a stricter definition of "his undivided estate." Emphasizing these two tenets of medieval law, they strove to protect both women's landed property and their share of the common property.

The most prominent spokesman for this group was the nobleman Claes Rålamb, president of the court of appeal for southern Sweden in the 1680s.[26] Widely read in vernacular and foreign law, Rålamb thought little of the skill of his opponents in matters of jurisprudence, and he used all of his learning to refute their arguments. He argued that property spouses had held before marriage did *not* become "one mass, belonging to one of them" upon marriage. Moreover, that a wife could claim one-third of the common estate was because the law assumed her to have paid for one-third of what was in that estate.[27] In this way, Rålamb tried to show that Swedish law had always kept track of what each spouse owned and did. Thus, in practice, spouses' property was not a unit, nor was the wife's share given to her by mercy but instead was granted as just compensation for her contributions. With his international experience, Rålamb may have been thinking of the English coverture system, to which he contrasted the Swedish system wherein married women had clearly discernible rights. A Swedish married man did not own his wife's property in the same way English husbands did. This conclusion presupposed that Swedish wives frequently held freehold land whereas English wives did not — which may very well have been true at this time.

Moreover, a Swedish married woman did not have the same legal authority as her husband. Therefore, Rålamb argued, his opponents' contention that spouses must share responsibility for debts was invalid for the simple reason that married women were like minors, subordinated to their husbands. As such, they did not have the authority to prevent their husbands from becoming indebted, and it would be inequitable for the law to demand responsibility for an unlawful or immoral action from a person who had never been able to stop it. When his opponents remarked that it certainly did happen that wives acted as if they were of age, and that much indebtedness was the result of women's extravagance, Rålamb retorted that in such unfortunate cases the husband must blame himself for not having controlled his wife properly.[28]

Rålamb expected men to be circumspect and prudent in all their daily tasks. Already as young men, they had to discipline themselves in all possible ways. From this perspective, the law that made wives responsible for their husbands' debts, including the ones he had incurred prior to marriage, was highly undesirable, because it would remove all incentive for young men to act responsibly. If they could count on heaping their debts upon their future wives (or the wives' kin), he reasoned, these young men would have no reason to curb their impulses. Therefore, the law must not encourage irresponsible behavior but rather send a clear signal that such behavior would always be chastised. As for the argument about the need for a proper balance between spouses' rights and duties, Rålamb totally agreed but arrived at a different conclusion than did his opponents. It was the husband, Rålamb claimed, who had most to win from getting married, since he came into a position where he could use his wife's property and even consume the yields of her lands. Consequently, it was the husband rather than the wife who could be suspected of exploiting the other party, and it was only reasonable for the law to place restrictions upon his power. As for spouses being "one flesh," Rålamb thought this argument reflected a fatal misunderstanding of the Bible. To be one flesh only referred to the carnal union of spouses and did not have any bearing whatsoever on the internal property arrangements of the household.[29]

These debates were literally packed with ideological conceptions about society, law, religion, and gender. Clearly, Rålamb's perception of marriage was profoundly patriarchal. Assuming women to be less knowledgeable than men, Rålamb placed the married woman in a subordinated position, while her husband was construed as her spokesman, trustee, and supporter. But Rålamb was very explicit about the risk that a husband might abuse his position in a way which could be profoundly detrimental to both the woman and her natal family. Drawing on canon law, he argued that a woman was likely to become *miserabilis* (that is, unprotected) if she were given responsibility for the payment of her husband's debts. A husband was in a position where he could apply persuasion or force, and in this way she could be deprived of her means. Since the law "gave men so much power over women . . . it had an obligation to protect women when husbands abused that power."[30] These words of Marylynn Salmon refer to the view of non-Puritan American lawyers, but they also capture the view of Claes Rålamb. Like medieval Swedish law, he focused upon what unscrupulous husbands might do and thought it his duty to protect women's legal position against what he saw as dangerous attacks. However, he was notably silent on the possibility that a woman's male relatives might also abuse their power.

Rålamb's opponents shared his fundamental assumptions about society being, rightfully, a patriarchal organization. However, where Rålamb stressed men's duties and women's absence of rights, his opponents stressed men's rights and women's duties. While Rålamb explicitly acknowledged the risk that married men might use persuasion or violence to force their wives to give consent, his opponents tended to make light of this scenario. Like the Puritans of New England, they did not want law explicitly to admit that spouses could have conflicting interests. Rålamb's opponents either emphasized woman's irresponsible behavior or depicted the married couple as a unit of mutual love and common interests. The couple should be "one flesh," bound together by "the same yoke."

These intense debates did not focus directly upon women's legal position and property rights, but they did force all participants to articulate how they conceived of the gender order, both inside marriage and in society as a whole. It is also obvious how the debates were linked to the credit question. In fact, it was the king's interest in this question that triggered the discussions. The majority of judges agreed that the legal position of creditors needed to be improved. Consequently, they condemned what they saw as the spouses' fraudulent manipulations of the marital estate, and they were even willing to accept a legal practice that made wives coresponsible for husbands' debts. Rålamb and a few other judges were less interested in the rights of creditors, who had, they argued, a responsibility for being vigilant and careful themselves. According to this view, it was more important for the law to protect women and, most of all, the long-term interests of families with landed property.

These debates were considered by the Great Law Commission, within which, as elsewhere, opinion was divided.[31] Two of the more prominent members had totally different views on the problem. Erik Lovisin maintained that, if the woman had given her explicit consent by signing a debt bond, she was obliged to stand by her word, with the possible consequence of her separately owned land being lost. On the other hand, the first chairman of the commission, Erik Lindschiöld, maintained that such laws would be risky, since great harm might be caused to the woman's natal family. Selling her land would be acceptable only if an emergency made it absolutely necessary.[32] Clearly, Lindschiöld saw the problem from a point of view resembling that of Claes Rålamb. He wanted to protect the interests of landed families, and he saw the stipulations of the old law as a means of attaining this objective. Lovisin, on the other hand, argued in a manner similar to that of Johan Stiernhöök and the majority of late seventeenth-century judges: a woman must keep her promises, no matter what the consequences might be.

The crucial question thus remained whether the law should retain the old requirement that the relatives give their consent. As early as in 1688, the commission wrote that such consent was really superfluous since all land sales outside the family had to be publicly announced and registered at court.[33] In this way, the woman's family would hear of the projected sale anyway and could use the *bördsrätt* to intervene. When the first draft of the new code was referred to a number of state bodies for consideration in 1690, two of them made explicit remarks concerning the abolition of the relatives' consent. The Svea Hovrätt did not want relatives' consent to be reintroduced, which was entirely in line with the position the court had taken in the past.[34] The county government of Östergötland was more worried about the absence of relatives' consent and stressed how the new rules could harm the woman's family. It also pointed out that a general principle of Swedish law was not to merge the property of husband and wife, and it was argued that the proposed new law would make it easier to "squander the value [of property] in an inequitable way." The emphasis on "the value" should be noted; apparently, the county government was aware of how badly protected land money would be if the bill met with approval.[35]

In 1714 new members had joined the commission, and the question about the consent of relatives once again was placed on the agenda. The two new members, Scheffer and Thegner, argued that, even if a wife had signed a debt bond, it was highly dubious if it made her liable to pay, since it was a fundamental principle of law that a husband could not use his wife's property for his own ends. Thus, whether she had consented and whether this consent was freely given was of no legal importance. Two other members objected, but without addressing the issue of consent. Instead, they argued that marital love (*amor conjugalis*) compelled the wife to support her husband "in his poverty." Consequently, she had to honor the debt if she had signed the bond after having come of age.[36] The new chairman, Gustaf Cronhielm,[37] replied that the question was highly delicate and went on to list all arguments for and against female debt responsibility.

Arguments against were more numerous. The wife was subordinated to her husband and owed him obedience, the chairman pointed out. For this reason, it was unlikely that she would refuse to sign a bond if he asked her. She was also less knowledgeable and would "often not comprehend what consequences such a signature might entail." Moreover, it was highly unlikely that either the husband or his creditor would give her correct information: "One must presume that a husband who is intent upon deceiving his wife in this way, or a creditor who wants to retrieve what is his, will not disclose or explain the dangers to her." These arguments suggested that, almost by definition, a woman's consent could never be informed and freely given.

On the other hand, the chairman went on, a married woman was not to be regarded as a minor. Therefore, if she committed herself to something that was detrimental to her or her children, she must be held personally responsible. But since "we know for certain, that all wives are not as intelligent as a man," a solution could be for the law to demand not only her signature but also that of her closest relatives. In this way, the relatives' consent was brought back into the debate.[38] But unlike Lindschiöld, whose arguments were shaped by an interest in preserving lineage property, Cronhielm seems to have conceived of the problem from the point of view of the woman. He wanted to reintroduce relatives' consent, not to increase their power, but to balance the unequal power relations between husband and wife.

Apparently, Cronhielm's suggestion did not meet with unwavering support.[39] Instead of reintroducing relatives' consent, the commission started to think of other ways of protecting the wife against pressure exerted on her by the husband or his creditors. A draft written as early as 1690 stated that a husband must not be allowed to exchange, mortgage, or sell his wife's lands, unless she had given her consent of her own free will. In 1692 the commission added that she must also sign the deed herself. In 1713, after Cronhielm had become chairman, a new amendment was added to the effect that she could also give her consent orally in court.[40] Clearly, the commission was heading for a solution resembling the laws that could be found in some other countries at this time.[41] This new way of constructing legal protection for married women's separate property emphasized that a married woman was not a minor. She was subordinated to her husband, but this did not deprive her of all legal responsibility. Of course, this definition of the married woman was highly ambiguous. When was she responsible and when was her husband responsible? Women's legal capacity was construed as contingent — it depended on the sort of situation she was placed in.[42]

The question of contingency spawned debate, and in this, Erik Lovisin was one of the members who insisted most on female responsibility.

By constructing hypothetical cases, Lovisin tried to prove that if the law did not require wives to take responsibility for the household, it became inequitable. "If my wife comes to me as a poor woman, and I am able to acquire a lot, [then] she will enjoy it with me; however, she is not willing to share my burdens, as where I have given a personal guarantee [for a friend], but puts all responsibility on me or the heirs." Another member argued that this was entirely in accordance with the old law. Husbands bore the responsibility, for better or worse. Lovisin retorted, emphatically, that he was thinking of cases where the husband's actions had been irreproachable and his indebtedness simply unfortunate. In such cases, the wife ought to stand by her husband and share good times and bad times, no matter what the old law said. And what was more, he added, it was the job of the commission to propose the *new* law.[43] Here, Rosamund in George Eliot's novel *Middlemarch* might be brought to mind. She does not break any law, but her behavior is still objectionable in a more general sense, since she does not stand by her husband when he needs it most. Even if one could argue, as some members did, that husbands had a responsibility for supporting their wives, which wives did not have for their husbands,[44] to someone like Erik Lovisin it still seemed contrary to justice and to the meaning of marriage if a woman was able to absolve herself of all responsibility for debt. The essence of his argument was that there should be a balance between the spouses. In order to uphold equity — a word close to equilibrium — spouses must be, and behave, as equals. His predecessors in the Svea Hovrätt had argued that "he/she who has the benefits must also accept the drawbacks,"[45] and Lovisin now rephrased the same principle as "to the extent that she participates in the incomes, she must also participate in the damages."[46]

Throughout the period, the discussion about the wife's responsibility for debts hinged ultimately upon perceptions of what was good for creditors and the credit market. Yet some legislators did have reservations with respect to creditors, suggesting that they lent their money imprudently and that, therefore, they had themselves to blame if they were sometimes deceived. Claes Rålamb was one of these. Gustaf Cronhielm also maintained that if the new law explicitly stated that a wife was not responsible for her husband's debts, then "creditors, who are otherwise prone to covet other people's [property], particularly real estates, *will learn not to lend their money so easily* to him, on whose paying capacity they have been unsure, unless they can take recourse to the wife's property."[47] Cederhielm, another member of the commission, was even blunter. He argued that it was highly necessary to "*make conditions very hard* for the person who is a moneylender, in order that he be more careful." In this way, many owners would be able to keep their property, and this would be in the interest of the state.[48] Clearly, this way of looking at creditors was squarely against the view adopted by the king in 1684. Still, the view was not pervasive enough to make the law "very hard" on creditors.

By the time the proposal for a new national legal code reached the four estates, a certain amount of fatigue seems to have characterized its reception. Unlike with the first drafts, which were circulated throughout the country and gave rise to some critical observations, few remarks and responses were recorded with regard to the final version. This is surprising in view of some of the formulations found in the section dealing with the marital estate.

The new legal code emphasized that the husband could not alienate the wife's landed property and that debts made before marriage were to be kept separate for each spouse.[49] In this regard the new law adhered to the old principle of keeping track of what was his and what hers. However, the husband no longer needed to consult his wife's kinsmen before selling her landed property. This stipulation had been completely abolished. Now, it was enough to have obtained her consent, which had to be given voluntarily and was not to be the result of persuasion or threats. Therefore, the law required two honorable men to be present when consent was given. Alternatively, the consent could be given orally in court.[50] This legal construction took the issue of male abuse of power seriously, as the old one had, but chose new methods of checking it, substituting public supervision for control by the wife's relatives. However, if the wife's land had been sold in good order, with proper attention to her free will, the law had little to offer if it turned out to have been an unwise decision. The importance of female responsibility was explicitly underlined:

> If there remains neither land nor chattels [in the estate], and the
> wife's land was sold with her consent; in that case, *the burden must
> fall on her*. If the husband has sold her land without her consent
> and approval, let her then seek to have it back through law within
> a year's time, counting from the day when she received informa-
> tion about this; and the person who bought [the land] must
> blame himself. If the wife should die before her husband, let her

heirs seek to get [the land] back within a year's time, counting from her death.[51]

Here, legislators had clearly chosen sides as regards the question of women's essential qualities. Instead of arguing that the woman was the weaker vessel or the less well-informed sex, they depicted her as perfectly able to take responsibility for herself and, by extension, for her children. Women who failed in this respect by letting themselves be cajoled into giving their consent in public had forfeited their rights. The new legal construction depicted woman as highly capable of thinking rationally and, if necessary, as capable of dissociating her interests from those of her husband.[52] It said less about social conditions and power relations that might affect her behavior and, by extension, her opportunities for asserting her rights. It was logical, then, that the husband was no longer depicted as someone against whom the woman might need special protection. In a gender-neutral way, the new legal code said that if the husband sold his wife's lineage property for his own benefit, or if she sold his for her own benefit, then the guilty party would have to compensate the aggrieved party.[53] This clause had been inserted to replace two of the medieval stipulations: those by which the husband could only sell his wife's land in certain emergency situations and only on condition that he sell twice as much of his own land at the same time.[54] According to the new code, then, marriage was a partnership between two equals, neither of whom was *particularly* suspected of taking advantage of the situation.

This solution to a problem which had been discussed for more than a century caused little debate. Little was said in the Diet when the new code was on the agenda in 1731. Only one member of the noble estate made a more substantial speech, saying, "No man must mortgage or sell his wife's real estate, either *with or without her consent*, because a man can induce her to give her approval by enticing or intimidating her."[55] The name of the speaker was Colonel Bror Rålamb, a son of Claes Rålamb. After a short period as auditor (*auskultant*) in the Svea Hovrätt, Bror had chosen a military career. He was among the Swedes taken hostage after the humiliating defeat at Poltava in 1709 in Sweden's war against Russia. With his strong religious convictions, he became an important leader for the Swedish soldiers both in the prison camp and afterwards on their way back home to Sweden.[56] Bror Rålamb is not known as a legal expert, nor is he famous as someone who was particularly engaged in the rights of women. Still, he was the only one who spoke up on this occasion, and he did so with words strikingly similar to those his father had employed on the same question several decades before. Both father and son emphasized that it was not enough for the law to demand testimony of the wife's consent, because the husband could have "kissed or kicked" it out of her. It is difficult not to think that Bror had taken over the arguments his father had once formulated, either from his writings[57] or, directly, by word of mouth. Considering the length and meticulous detail of Claes Rålamb's *Observationes*, the latter alternative is more plausible. It is hard to imagine that even the most devout son would study this work so assiduously as to remember every argument in it. By way of contrast, it is easy to envisage Claes Rålamb being so deeply engaged in the matter that he frequently spoke about it in the family. As a consequence, his son had become keenly aware of his father's standpoint and felt a special responsibility for keeping it alive after his father's death. But with all their knowledge and commitment, neither father nor son succeeded in preventing a reform they regarded as unwise or even sinister.

The Increasing Importance of Privacy

While late seventeenth-century legislators, judges, and kings spent much time and energy on discussing the credit market, they said much less on the other dynamic aspect of property: investments. More importantly, they said almost nothing at all about women's contributions of labor to the household,[58] even though investment of labor was often used by litigants as an argument for the right to keep land or to be compensated for the loss of land and even though lawyers used the labor argument to explain why owners had a legal right to use acquired land without any restrictions. Evidently, the argument that labor improves property rights was used very selectively, in a way that suggests a gender bias in the law. Only some forms of labor were regarded as legally relevant.[59] Nor did legislators say anything about the specific "blind spot" identified in the previous chapter, namely, that a spouse who let the other spouse use his or her land money (but it was usually the wife's) to redeem lineage land from relatives was badly protected by law. People like Simon Persson had been farsighted enough to compensate his wife by drawing up a will for the benefit of her children, but the Great Law Commission devoted no special attention to this issue.

It is intriguing that these two problems were accorded so little legal attention at the time. One reason could be that they were, after all, unusual. Perhaps most families managed to transfer property between generations without taking recourse to the land money of one of the spouses. It is difficult to know, not only because inheritance practices are not as well explored as could be wished, but also because the written sources seldom give information about details of this sort. Another reason may be that peasant women were the ones who were most likely to suffer, and they were not in a position where they could easily express dissatisfaction.[60] Still, the silence on these issues remains something of a conundrum.

The silence becomes more understandable, however, if the implications of the more debated issue of debt are considered. As has been seen, most legislators and judges wanted to abolish the requirement for relatives' consent and to emphasize that adult women had to accept full responsibility for their own actions. With this view of women, it was rational not to worry about the possible consequences of a wife's acceptance of having her land money used for her husband's ends. It would have been simply illogical and contradictory to try to prevent such uses of her assets, since it would have suggested that women were minors, while other parts of the law expressly said they were not. Thus, the ambition to make the new legal code speak with a consistent voice may account for the law's reticence in this respect.

The silence should also be understood in the context of a general tendency around 1700 to protect the nuclear family, the couple, and household privacy.[61] When the consent of relatives was ruled out, it was another way of saying that husband and wife had to decide what property arrangements were best for them and that relatives had no business meddling in their affairs. This shift was rather subtle but can be observed in other areas of law as well. In 1720, for instance, the *bördsrätt* was reformed in a way that made it considerably less common and sharp as a weapon in the hands of relatives. Through new statutory law, the group of kinsmen who were entitled to adduce *bördsrätt* was restricted. Henceforward, only a close circle of relatives had any legal claims upon the land and thus the right to insight into the household's economic matters. Moreover, a person who wanted to veto a sale of land in this way had to give full compensation to the first purchaser, that is, to pay a market price.[62] In this way, the economic value of kinship was reduced, and so was the influence kinsmen could exert over individual households. Similarly, the responsibility for taking care of elderly people was recast around 1700. Previously, it had been the broader kin group that was made responsible for the care and support of their older members, but from 1734 and onward the responsibility was placed on the nuclear family and often formalized through written contracts.[63] New legislation in 1669 had also given parents a stronger right to appoint the people they preferred as guardians for their children, rather than necessarily kinsmen. This, too, should be seen as an example of how the influence of the kin group was gradually undermined.[64]

Another example of the propensity to choose legal arrangements favoring privacy was the discussion about how the law should treat cases where one spouse had taken movable property out of the marital estate (*bodräkt*). The question was whether or not such behavior should be classified as theft and, if it was theft, on whom it was incumbent to bring legal action. Legislators argued that "nothing good will come out of it, if husband or wife should be called a thief," particularly not if someone outside the household had the right to bring action.[65] This kind of case was delicate, they felt; the marital estate belonged to both spouses (here, it concerned not land but movables), and it was not possible to say that one spouse took from the other if one alienated property. What was more, "men often deny their wives the necessities of life," which could force a "sensible woman" to use some of their common property to support herself and her children.[66] In such a case, it would be unreasonable to brand her a thief. Legislators had a sense that such matters should not be regulated by law, particularly not by labeling such practices theft, because it was difficult to know anything about what had actually happened. Therefore, they retreated, leaving the household to remain or, rather, to become a private sphere. In a similar vein, legislators briefly discussed whether or not the law ought to continue prescribing that the local courts check if poverty had indeed been imminent when a husband sold his wife's land. In a manner indicative of the increasing emphasis on privacy and male integrity, one member of the commission argued that it would look odd if somebody else should prescribe what an honest man should do. He did concede, however, that such a stipulation could be called for with respect to profligates.[67]

Jonas Liliequist has brought to our attention that, from 1734 onward, legislators were loath to accept that an outsider could bring action in cases where the husband abused his wife physically. In this way, the law divested itself of its means of interfering in households where violence was used against the wife.[68] It is hard not to see this as a direct parallel to the reluctance to let outsiders bring action against the alienation of movable property or to prescribe through law how adult men should behave. Together, these trends suggest that there was an increasing emphasis on marital privacy and, at the same time, a propensity to reduce the role previously played by kinsmen. These trends can be seen as an expression of the "disembeddening" of the nuclear household (to use a term coined by Karl Polanyi). They meant that some of the ties to the kin group were loosened and portended the later tendency to romanticize conjugal love.

Adapting Law to a Commercialized Society

Even if legislators remained silent on how women's investments affected property rights and on many other private issues, they did touch upon the problem in a more abstract way when they discussed the rough and unfortunate distinction between inherited and acquired property. The tricky question was how to classify redeemed (*bördlöst*) land, particularly if the husband's family land had been redeemed with the help of his wife's land money (or vice versa). Thus, the distinction between inherited and acquired land was highly relevant to women's property rights, although this was not openly acknowledged in the discussions at the time.

Even if the medieval legal code was often confusing and hard to interpret, it nonetheless was clear that redeemed land was to be classified as lineage land.[69] It is another matter how this clause was construed in the seventeenth century. Court practice attests to a certain amount of legal bewilderment where redeemed land was sometimes classified as acquired, which could be devised by will, and sometimes as inherited, which could not be included in a will.[70] The Law Commission emphasized the literal meaning of the old legal code, arguing that redeemed land should be looked upon as a form of inherited land.[71] This caused very little debate, but when the final version of the new code reached the Diet in 1731, Lilliegren argued that redeemed land ought to be classified as acquired land and, consequently, as available for testamentary disposition. The response to this was that a distinction had to be made between "purely acquired land" and redeemed land. "Since kinsmen are always entitled to redeem lineage land, we must conclude that once it has been redeemed, no testamentary disposition can be made to the detriment of the heirs, apart from the value and the improvement."[72] The answer shows that the commission did admit that redeemed land had a sort of intermediary character and that they tried to deal with this by making a distinction between object and value. The object (the land) could not be disposed of at will, as in the case of ordinary inherited land, but the value could be, as in the case of acquired land. What this stipulation would mean in real life is somewhat hard to understand, but probably the commission wanted an owner to be able to sell the land to his kinsmen and then to be free to will the money to whomever he liked. Nobody in the Diet asked whether the redeemed land should become part of the spouses' common property, which would have been a rather natural assumption, given that this was how purchased land was normally categorized. If it had been classified as common property, this would have had highly beneficial consequences for spouses.[73] However, it is clear from later jurisprudence that for all practical purposes redeemed land was still looked upon as inherited land.

While legislators devoted most of their attention to landed property and its devolution by way of inheritance, they nevertheless had to admit that some people received their inheritances in the form of money or movable property. Such land money could be reinvested in land, in which case the new land acquired the character of lineage property. But what if the heir chose *not* to reinvest in land? What if one chose to consume the value or to transfer it by will to someone outside the kin group? If this became common practice, significant economic assets would be lost from the overall purview of the kin group, and the stipulations concerning the preservation of lineage property would be to little avail.[74]

To prevent such "leakage" legislators decided to introduce what a later observer called "the regulator of the system."[75] If a person had consented to receiving an inheritance in the form of money instead of land, the law stipulated that this person must substitute new land ("surrogate") for the money received, before being allowed to make a will. What was new was the explicit wish to protect the rights of heirs to such money.[76] Just as an owner could not and had never been able to will away inherited land, he now could not will away inherited money either. It was a rather convoluted way of retaining the special status of inherited resources, while at the same time admitting that society was now commercialized and highly dependent on money transactions. The stipulation about surrogates was complex and hard, both for judges to apply and for ordinary people to understand. It also created strange relations of debt within families (as we shall see).

Table 4 shows the legal situation with regard to landed property from 1734 onward. The two first cases show that the same rules continued to apply for inherited and acquired land. The other two cases show where clarification (case 3) and innovation (case 4) took place. Interestingly, the two latter cases were also the ones that were most pertinent to the situation of women. Redeemed land could not be made part of the common property of the spouses (even if the wife's money had been used), which had potentially adverse effects for wives. Persons who received money instead of land were not at liberty to will that money as they liked, and this was likely to be the case for rural women, since

TABLE 4. Rules pertaining to property from 1734

| | FORM OF ACQUISITION | | |
Form of property	Inherited	Acquired	Redeemed
Land	Not devisable. Not part of common marital property.	Devisable. Part of common marital property.	Value but not object devisable. Not part of common marital property. (This changes in the nineteenth century.)
Money	If received instead of inherited land: no right to will away unless substitute is provided.		

Consequences:

If husband dies, then his inherited land goes to his children or, in their absence, to his relatives. It will never go to his widow. The common marital property is divided so that his children (or relatives) take two-thirds and the widow one-third. If, however, the couple has made a mutual will, the entire marital estate goes to the widow. Apart from her third, the widow will retain her own inherited land and her morning gift (given to her by the husband).

If the widow's inherited land has been alienated during marriage for the benefit of the household, she will need to prove this before her husband's estate is divided, in order to receive compensation. If the widow inherited money instead of land from her natal family, she might be asked to provide "surrogate" if she wants either to make a will or in any case (the law is not clear on this point).

If wife dies, the procedure will be the same except (a) the widower will not have a morning gift to retrieve from the household, and (b) his share of the common marital estate is two-thirds.

their shares were always smaller than those of their brothers. Thus, even though husband and wife were now portrayed as equals in some parts of the law, there is much to suggest that the wife's property rights had been effectively diluted in other parts of the law. As we shall see, however, the concept of surrogate tended to be used in two different contexts in the subsequent century. It not only referred to compensations given from an heir to his or her family of origin; it was also used to designate a pecuniary compensation given to a spouse for lineage lands.[77]

TABLE 5. Size and composition of Swedish population in 1620, 1718, and 1800

	1620	1718	1800
Size of whole population	916,379	1,446,698	2,347,000
Adult women (over fifteen years) in whole population	317,993	561,588	830,000
Rural population	852,232	1,302,028	1,838,147
Landowners	284,077	434,010	676,000
Married men	45,448	67,392	144,000
Unmarried men	43,726	48,995	66,000
Married women	45,448	67,392	144,000
Unmarried women	53,130	101,085	68,000
Children under fifteen years	96,325	149,146	254,000

Sources: For 1620 and 1718, Professor Jan Lindegren's population model (Uppsala University); for 1800, contemporary statistics (printed in *Emigrationsutredningen* IX).

Assumptions: (i) that the rural population comprised 93 percent of the whole population in 1620 and 90 percent in 1718 (based on Palm, *Folkmängden*, 88); (ii) that the landowning part of the rural population was 33 percent in 1620 (we know that it was 33 percent around 1700); (iii) that the entire nobility and 50 percent of the peasantry and the crofters owned land in 1800.

In spite of these facts, the legal discussions around 1700 failed to take into account the position of women or to show in what ways these rules were particularly relevant to them. There were not even comments on the simple fact that the distinction between inherited and acquired property had profound implications for married women's rights to the common part of the estate. One possible explanation of this silence could be the demographic situation around 1720. After a century of devastating wars, sex ratios were strongly skewed, with a significant lack of adult men (table 5). In this situation women's chances of inheriting land and of taking over the headship for farms and manors must have been better than ever. Indeed, there are strong reasons to assume that female landowners had never been (and would never again be) as numerous as they were around 1720.

Not only did the adaptation of law to a more commercialized society manifest itself in the introduction of surrogates. Many other legal innovations adopted at this time must also be seen in this light, and several of them can be conceived of as ways of increasing transparency in the economic sphere. These new schemes aimed at enhancing legibility and reducing what outsiders thought of as domestic secrecy. The lively interest devoted to these matters further underlines how problematic nontransparency was believed to be at this time.

The probate inventory had increasingly come on the legislative agenda in the course of the seventeenth century, often in connection with making wills. To the extent that a will referred to personal property, it became necessary to have the estate inventoried. Contrary to land, which could not be embezzled and which was easily observed by people in the local community, personal property could be hidden to the detriment of heirs (and particularly to underage children). That executors were rarely used in Sweden also tended to make the inventory important.[78] It provided a solution to the technical problem of knowing what was in an estate. That inventories did not become compulsory until 1734 suggests, once again, that previous law had mainly been concerned with landed property.

The debate about wills among legislators clearly shows that the probate inventory was seen as something of a panacea to the problems caused by domestic secrecy. Early on, the Great Law Commission agreed to make inventories compulsory, even in cases where no dispute and no underage heirs existed. Inventories would be useful and convenient in any case, the commission argued, for instance, if the estate of the deceased was later found to be indebted.[79] Erik Lovisin was a particularly ardent advocate of probate inventories. He hoped that they would make it possible to apply the distinction between inherited and acquired property to personal property as well — a hope which may have reflected a concern with keeping track of inherited wealth in a society where landed property was easily transformed.[80] When his colleague Törne asked, "Is it at all possible to make this distinction [for personal property]?" Lovisin exclaimed enthusiastically, "Why not, we have the inventory!"[81]

Another technical method that aroused interest was the public registration (*inteckning*) of mortgages and prenuptial agreements. Public registration of land transactions outside the family had been compulsory since the Middle Ages, because it provided a means of checking that the *bördsrätt* was not violated, but there had been nothing similar for debts.[82] This fact illustrates, once again, how the law was only concerned with the static and not the dynamic aspects of property. Because indebtedness was believed to have become more common, the lack of public registration appeared increasingly problematic. Even a central credit institution like the Bank of Sweden had problems in the late seventeenth century with debtors who mortgaged the same property several times.[83] Prenuptial agreements were subject to severe criticism, since they were often kept secret and were believed to hurt third parties.[84] Even wills were believed to cause "frustration" unless they were publicly registered.[85] Thus, making such documents public was seen as the solution to many problems.

However, there was not unanimous enthusiasm for the public registration of debts. As in Denmark and France, the aristocracy was often adamantly opposed to systems that disclosed their debts to the public. They did not like to have their domestic secrets unveiled to everyone, since it could tarnish their honor and, what was more, drastically reduce their creditworthiness.[86] Of course, this was the whole point of having debts publicly registered: creditors would have a reliable means of checking whether a person had security for his loans or not, and credit could be denied to less trustworthy clients, regardless of their social position. Therefore, those who had most to win from a system built on public registration of debts and mortgages were creditors who had economic assets at their disposal but lacked the social and political power to force their socially superior debtors to pay. A good example of such a debtor was Magnus Gabriel De la Gardie, who died in 1686, leaving huge numbers of creditors behind him.[87] According to the Italian diplomat Lorenzo Magalotti, who had met De la Gardie some ten years before, the Swedish aristocrat had very large debts but could not be forced to pay since his social standing was so high and credit law so poorly developed.[88] Another example was the chancellor of the exchequer (*riksskattmästare*), Sten Bielke, who died in 1684, leaving his creditors to sue his estate in the Svea Hovrätt. Many of the creditors were ordinary tradesmen or craftsmen, who had provided Sten Bielke with chocolates, wine, medicine, and other items.[89] If the debts of De la Gardie and Bielke had been publicly registered, new credit might not have been easily forthcoming.

In this context, Erik Lovisin himself is an instructive case in point. Because of his demanding job, in the Great Law Commission, for example, Lovisin had earned very handsome incomes in the 1680s, and he lent some of this money to aristocratic families with their real estate as security. He was also married to a merchant's daughter who had inherited large claims on the state from her father.[90] Against this backdrop, Lovisin's interest in improving the legal position of creditors is not surprising. Like many other higher civil servants, he owed his position in society to his own achievements, and he was dependent on his salary in a way that owners of large numbers of inherited landed estates were not. These "self-made men" had little compassion for the economic distress of the aristocracy, and they supported the autocratic king when he proposed a far-reaching repossession of Crown lands as a means of ameliorating state finances (*Reduktion*).[91] Lovisin's enthusiasm for the probate inventory, and his concern with whether the distinction between inherited and acquired could be applied to personal property as well, is only what could be expected from someone who was "un homme noveau." When men of his sort argued that an owner should be allowed to use his acquired property as he liked, and legitimized their standpoint by pointing to work "by the sweat of his brow," this was an implicit but scathing critique of those who had received their property without really exerting themselves, that is, the old aristocratic families.

The introduction of new methods of obtaining knowledge about what was in an estate, in turn, provides information about the increasing complexity of society and how people from different social groups and various parts of the country were now coming into commercial contact with one another. Within local contexts and among people who knew each other well, there already existed various customary methods of keeping track of property. Local people knew what family had used what land, and this knowledge was transferred from one generation to the next and could be called upon when a land dispute erupted.[92] Before mortgages were introduced, people relied on personal guarantees (*borgen* or *caution*).[93] Studies of other countries have also shown how people were accustomed to marking their personal property to make sure that it was not mixed up with other people's property; women, in particular, marked their goods.[94] There is no reason to think that Swedes did not use such methods. Consequently, it should not be assumed that people did not feel the need to control property before the introduction of inventories and the public registration of debts and mortgages. Instead, these new methods provide information about the increasing difficulty of surveying what people were doing when they acted within a wider social space than before.[95] Those who experienced the worst problems in this respect may have been small actors, people who lent their money on trust alone, only to find that the debtor was untrustworthy. To make commercial contacts work, the inventory and, most of all, the public registration of mortgages were believed to be necessary. In Sweden those who did not approve of such methods were not powerful enough to prevent their introduction. Consequently, from 1730 the public registration of all mortgages was required. These new practices enhanced legibility and were closely connected with the introduction of a modern credit system.[96]

The obvious tendency toward making property arrangements more transparent is inconsistent with the previous observation that legislators were strongly inclined to respect marital privacy. In fact, it is something of a paradox that domestic secrecy seems to have both decreased and increased at the same time. A closer look at the ways in which men and women were portrayed at the time will, if not erase, at least illuminate the paradox.

Male and Female Responsibilities

When Claes Rålamb discussed real estate law, he portrayed married women as vulnerable and less well-informed than men. Women were, according to the words of Paul, "the weaker vessel," for whom men (husbands, fathers, brothers, and sons) had special responsibility. Should the latter fail to live up to the standard required from "a good housefather," it was incumbent on the law to provide the means by which male behavior could be checked. Women were also, according to Rålamb, the less intelligent sex — a notion he borrowed from the Roman digests when it suited his purposes.[97] In other situations, however, Rålamb conceded that a married woman might be better informed than her husband and that he should listen carefully to her opinion.[98] Thus, Rålamb's views of women's capacity seem to have been contingent and shaped by the sort of legal problem he had in mind.

Similarly, his opponents did not operate with a single view of women. Some of them emphasized women's moral flaws and saw these as valid reasons for increasing women's legal responsibility. The Åbo Hovrätt pointed out that Mosaic law gave to husbands the right to repudiate their wives at any time; yet, it prescribed shared debt responsibility for spouses. When Jews could put debt responsibility upon their wives, "then should not we have the same right, and to an ever higher degree — we, who have to put up with [our wives'] mischief until our death?"[99] Obviously, there was a certain misogynist attitude at work here, and it becomes even more striking in a statement made by one of the appeals court judges in the case of Maria Wrangel:

> There are many rocks [in matrimony] upon which one may
> easily hit, when one plumps into [it] without first thinking; and
> such rash behavior is particularly insufferable in women who
> are at complete liberty to choose whomever they like [for their
> husband], with the advice of their relatives and friends, which
> is easier for them to do than for men, since the reputation and
> skillfulness and all other properties that women love and seek in
> men can be seen by everybody in public, whereas the qualities of
> a woman are hidden in the domestic sphere and are difficult to

discover and find out because of [women's] arts of dissembling
and their tricks of imitation.[100]

Clearly, this judge saw women as an irresponsible lot, who benefited
from the fact that the qualities of men were publicly displayed but who
would nevertheless moan and complain when they made an unwise
decision in the choice of husband, leading to economic problems for
themselves and their children. However, scolding of the female sex was
less common. Most of Rålamb's opponents merely pointed to the fact
that the husband and wife formed a company together and that both
parties had to take their share of both problems and revenues — to share
good times and bad times, just as the Bible taught.[101] They regarded the
legal responsibility of adult women as a simple issue of equity. Thus,
there was not a single, unambiguous view of the female sex.

In a similar fashion there was not one view of the husband. Medieval
law constructed the husband as a potential threat to the woman and
to her natal family, and Rålamb vociferously concurred with this view.
On the other hand, those who wanted to change the law saw the husband as the obvious and (usually) unproblematic head of household,
for whom the law should show a certain amount of respect, even though
they admitted that special rules were required with respect to men who
were profligate.[102] In wills, husband and wife were often portrayed as
good and loving partners. In this way, the practices applied by ordinary
people tended to lend support to a more positive picture of both men
and women.

Consequently, the importance of the different assessments of men
and women that were articulated in the debates should not be exaggerated, precisely because these assessments were contingent upon circumstances and depended on the judges' opinions on other legal questions. When some judges wanted to change the law, it was not because
of any specific qualities inherent in women. They wanted to modify
the law for other reasons, but they used images of women as discursive
means of attaining their objectives. Likewise, those who preferred the
law to remain unchanged used arguments that were related to women's
character, but their main objective had more to do with keeping control
of landed estates. That a forceful gendered imaginary was called forth on
both sides testifies to the importance ascribed to these legal issues,[103]
and the ways in which this imaginary was linked to issues of responsibility are particularly interesting.

Previous research has shown that it was precisely during this period that the issue of gendered responsibility arose in relation to other

legal problems as well. A case in point is sexual crime. Medieval law had placed the responsibility for premarital sexual intercourse upon the man, who had to pay the fines and to compensate the woman and her family for the harm inflicted upon her. It is telling that the crime was labeled "violation of a virgin." In the late seventeenth century, however, the law was changed to the effect that both man and woman had to pay fines for what became labeled "fornication."[104] Similar concerns about responsibility for economic matters surfaced in the very same period. Could married men be trusted to take responsibility for their wives and their separate property? was one disquieting question. Would it not be reasonable for married women to take a greater responsibility for the common marital economy? was the rejoinder. Men and women had responsibilities both to people outside the household, like bailiffs and creditors, and to those who were inside the household, like children and stepchildren. These intersecting responsibilities had to be balanced against each other in a way that, ideally, did not harm anyone. What lawyers disagreed about was essentially how this balance should be struck, and whether one needed to increase or decrease the particular part played by husband or wife.

It was in this context that women's consent to the sale of their separate property became an issue of intense interest. It is true that wives' consent to land sales was not something completely new around 1700; it had been required in the Middle Ages as well. Their consent, however, was put into greater relief when no longer accompanied by the simultaneous requirement for relatives' consent. Female consent now came to indicate full legal responsibility for women, because consent could only be legally relevant if it was given freely by someone capable of full legal responsibility. Thus, there was a tendency in law, albeit not undisputed, to stress female responsibility and to underline (as Cronhielm did) that adult women should not be regarded as minors. The paradoxical effect of this tendency was to make many women more vulnerable, both when accused of sexual crime and when faced with the task of deciding whether or not her property should be sold.

The issue of responsibility somehow reconciled increasing domestic secrecy with decreasing domestic secrecy and accounted for the simultaneous emphasis upon privacy and transparency. If the woman was emphatically described as someone who could be expected to take full legal responsibility for herself and to assert her rights even against those of her husband, there was no longer any need for relatives to intervene and have a say. The woman needed no special protection other than that provided by the courts, since marriage was no longer conceived of as a partnership between unequals: a possibly unreliable man and a weak vessel. Now, it was a partnership between two equals. Having solved this part of the balancing problem, the law could concentrate on removing everything that obscured the household from the point of view of creditors, such as introducing the public registration of debts and mortgages.

Conclusions

In the late seventeenth and early eighteenth centuries, Swedish law underwent a number of important changes. The modifications discussed in this chapter — the ways in which the protection of married women's property was recast — were rather subtle and have occasioned little attention in previous research. However, if the general tendencies are compared to other legal trends at work in the same period, it is clear that this change had a great potential for shifting the balance of power in society. It affected and reorganized the relations between generations, between kinsmen and couples, between creditors and debtors, and between husbands and wives. It is the accumulated effects of these changes that are important to evaluate with a view to understanding whether women's legal and economic position deteriorated in the early modern period.

Those who took part in changing Swedish law around 1700 were men from the upper strata of society. They were neither women nor peasants. Their specific place in society shaped their views of what the relationship between spouses should be like and how households should interact with the rest of society. Despite many appeals court judges having excellent insight into how law was applied on the primary court level and what sorts of legal problems ordinary peasants had, their perspective was inevitably colored by their own personal experiences, professional training, and lifestyle. The one-sidedness of their outlook was particularly salient on two points. First, they all agreed that a husband had a duty to support his wife. Second, they paid much more attention to the impact of credit upon spouses' property rights than to the effect of investments.

Had the legislators been members of the peasantry, representing more than 90 percent of the population, they would hardly have claimed that husbands had to support their wives. Within the peasantry, it was self-evident that husband and wife had to work together in order to support themselves. It was equally obvious that other members of the household had to make their contributions as well. In the prevailing small-scale subsistence economy there was no room for an ideal of domesticity. The results presented in the previous chapter suggest that joint investment of labor was something spouses would often adduce when arguing for their rights to keep property undivided in their old age. They also suggest that peasants often referred to investment of labor when arguing for their right to keep a certain piece of land. The kind of domestic ideal envisioned by leading lawyers was a far cry from the one common to most Swedish households at the time, where the laboring couple was a central cultural symbol. The latter, however, did not succeed in making an imprint on the law.

Had the legislators been peasant women, representing close to 50 percent of the population, it is possible that they would have been especially interested in the effects of investment upon property rights. Women's input of movable property or inherited money is likely to have been absolutely vital when property was transferred between generations. Moreover, peasant women's contributions of labor to the household were essential, but were often invisible to or unnoticed by people outside that household.

It is slightly paradoxical that these kinds of contributions were poorly protected by Swedish law, because lawyers were not impervious to the argument that investment of labor or money improves a person's property rights — on the contrary. Indeed, it is striking to what extent this argument was used by lawyers and others to underpin the claim that an owner was free to do whatever he liked with his acquired property. And yet, despite the fact that this was one of the central tenets of Swedish real estate law, lawyers were oblivious to the fact that some forms of investment rarely received any compensation at all. The expert in jurisprudence, Claes Rålamb, recognized women's right to one-third of the common property by reference to what women had paid to the estate. Yet even Rålamb never seems to have thought of the possibility that the wife could have contributed *everything* that was in the common estate. In such a case, losing two-thirds to the husbands' creditors was better than losing everything, but it was still an unfavorable outcome.

The female contribution to the household — or its precise extent — tended to be absorbed, obscured, and turned into a domestic secret, known only to the household members, the kinsmen, or the woman herself. Like Mrs. Tulliver in another of George Eliot's novels,[105] Swedish women may have kept track of what was theirs, but there were few means to register such investments or make them legible to outsiders, simply because outsiders were seldom interested in these contributions. "Outsiders" were often the same as creditors or representatives of the state, and their interest consisted more in playing down the importance of anything that might give rights to anyone other than the male head of household. Outsiders were more interested in clarifying household authority. Together, the credit market and the state encouraged transparency and legibility, but it was a form of transparency that offered a simplified picture and left out important aspects of everyday life. It is true that Swedish law did not go so far as to regard the entire marital estate as the property of the husband; it continued to make a distinction between his and hers, both in terms of property and in terms of debts. Still, with its scant interest in how money and personal property were used inside households, the law cleared the way for a deterioration of women's rights in the eighteenth century. The law had always been blind to the fact that marital estates could contain valuable movable property. From the early eighteenth century, it also became less attentive to the fact that the marital relationship could be a relationship of power.

((4))

DETERIORATING RIGHTS &
COMPENSATING PRACTICES

The Eighteenth-Century Transformation

In 1815 the widow Ulrica Helena Funck appealed to the Svea Hovrätt in Stockholm, asking the royal court of appeal to grant her daughter, Mrs. Anna Maria Wennerstedt, separation of property. Anna Maria was married to the nobleman Ludvic Boye, and the reason for the application was his insolvency. He had squandered the large fortune which Anna Maria had brought into their marital estate, and he had also forced her to sign bonds that made her responsible for very large debts. To make matters worse, he had always treated her "harshly and unkindly," abusing her physically, so that her mental state made her unable to take care of herself and her children. Consequently, Ulrica Funck saw it as her maternal duty to take her daughter and grandchildren out of the house of Ludvic Boye.[1]

This case seems to be Claes Rålamb's worst nightmare come true. When the wife's relatives no longer could veto sales of her property by the son-in-law and when he no longer had to prove that he had sold twice as much of his own property, the wife became *miserabilis*, that is, legally unprotected. In this particular case, she appears to have become highly miserable indeed, being exposed to physical and mental abuse at the hands of her husband. Apparently the new forms of protection provided by the legal code, that is, the requirement that the local courts check to see that the woman had not been forced to sign contracts or bonds, had failed in this instance.

For all its spectacular qualities, however, this case was hardly representative of the married woman's situation after 1734. A much less dramatic but arguably more common case was the dispute between Bertha Åkesdotter and her late husband's nieces in the 1830s. Bertha's husband, Sven, had inherited parts of the farm Påtorp from his father and his two brothers, and he had redeemed the residual parts from his sisters. To do this, he had used money that his wife Bertha had brought into the marital estate. Later on, Sven and Bertha decided to sell Påtorp to Bertha's son, Abram Gummesson, in compensation for the money which had been used to redeem Sven's farm. Abram, in turn, had not yet received his paternal inheritance, which may have constituted a part of the money his mother had put at Sven's disposal. But Sven's nieces filed a complaint in the local court, arguing that Sven had divested them of their legal shares of their inheritance in Påtorp. Thus, the relatives' claims for compensation for their lost inheritance were pitted against the wife's claims for compensation for invested money. It was an extremely convoluted case, but the problems it illustrated were far from uncommon. The Supreme Court found in the nieces' favor, imposing on Bertha and Abram the duty of compensating them.[2]

The cases of both Anna Maria Wennerstedt and Bertha Åkesdotter, which occurred in the early nineteenth century, nevertheless reflect eighteenth-century developments and could not have happened in the seventeenth century. Anna Maria's mother took advantage of the legal device of separation of property, which became an integral part of Swedish law in the course of the eighteenth century. Bertha Åkesdotter claimed compensation for the money she had invested in her husband's farm and managed to take her case to the court of last instance. Although the court never questioned the principle that wives were entitled to such compensation, it ruled that this principle was not applicable in this particular situation. Relatives did have a right to a "surrogate" — an innovation in the legal code of 1734.

The two cases show why a married woman's economic situation could be precarious in the eighteenth century. It had to do both with the secretive character of the household and with the complexities of law. Few knew and could interfere with what happened between Boye and his wife, and few understood the law well enough to predict the outcome of Bertha's suit. The cases also show the importance of individual arrangements to improve the economic and legal situation of women. Sven acknowledged the rights of Bertha and her son, and he tried to compensate them by transferring his father's farm to his stepson. Anna

Maria's parents would have been well-advised to have made a prenuptial settlement for their daughter, because it was the absence of such an arrangement that had exposed her to the thoughtlessness and cruelty of her husband. What the cases do not illustrate, however, is how commercialization and shifting sex ratios impinged upon women's access to property. As we shall see, these trends were at least as important as the legal changes.

What were, on balance, the overall effects of these different developments? Could Swedish husbands sell their wives' property more easily, more often, and with more sinister effects in the eighteenth and nineteenth centuries than previously? This is a plausible hypothesis, certainly, but methodologically, it is very difficult to present quantitative evidence that either refutes or confirms it. In principle, it would be possible to compare the number of sales registered in the courts at various points in time, but apart from the fact that it is extremely time-consuming to carry out such a study, the results would be difficult to evaluate, since regional variation might blur chronological change.[3] The outcome of such a procedure would be dubious. Instead, the method I will use in this chapter is, first, to identify background factors that are likely to have increased the general need to sell wives' land. Then, I will discuss social practices that appear to have become more common and that may best be explained as reactions at this time to a growing number of women lacking adequate protection for their inherited land.

Understanding what happened to married women's property rights in the eighteenth and early nineteenth centuries is not easy, precisely because trends that must have undermined these rights were balanced by opposing trends that have not been evaluated in previous research. What historians should now focus on are the overall effects of a process that may have implied deteriorating rights and a tendency toward developing compensatory practices. Moreover, the even more complicated question of whether women's rights of inheritance were undercut in this period should be addressed. Mechanisms identified by Bina Agarwal and Jack Goody suggest that in agrarian societies the elder generation became less inclined to transfer land to daughters if they feared that the property would not remain in the possession of their daughter or her children.[4] If such mechanisms were at work in Sweden, then the assumption that women's inheritance rights were undermined after 1734 would be justified. Whether this was the case or not is an open question. To start disentangling these matters, a helpful key may be found in a reform carried through in 1807.

In the early nineteenth century legal reform was once again on the agenda, and new legal commissions were appointed with various mandates. With respect to inheritance law and marital property rights, their work did not come to fruition until the middle of the century, a subject to which we will return in chapter 6. However, in the early years of the century, important but as yet little-studied discussions took place that suggested the kinds of social and legal practices that had developed in the preceding period.

In 1806 the legal commission headed by Count Wachtmeister discussed the issue of marital rights to redeemed land. Almost all members of the commission expressed the view that no change was called for. A spouse did not then have any right to land the other spouse had redeemed from relatives during marriage, and this was just the way it should be, in their opinion. The lawyers buttressed their view with references to appeals court practice and to what K. Maj:t[5] had said in the past. However, the vice chairman of the commission, Leijonmarck, did not agree.[6] He could not understand, he said, why a father-in-law could not sell his land to his son-in-law, when he could sell it to nonrelatives. In the latter case, relatives could veto the sale by adducing the *bördsrätt*, and they were perfectly free to do the same in the former as well. But if they had failed to do this in due time, he could not see any reason why the sale should not be regarded as an ordinary legal sale. Consequently, he did not understand why the buyer could not be allowed to look upon the land purchased as acquired. And if it was acquired, the buyer's spouse must be accorded marital rights to that property. He refuted the majority's interpretation of the legal code, arguing that marital rights applied to all forms of acquisition *except* pure inheritance.[7]

Shortly afterward, in March 1807, King Gustaf IV Adolf issued a new statute, the preamble of which elaborated on the need for legal reform and clarification. The legal code of 1734 was said to be good, just, and equitable and its injunctions to have been sufficiently clear at the time of its promulgation. However, "growing population, increasing enlightenment, expansion of the country's culture, through agriculture [. . .] and other useful enterprises, have recast many of the objects, with which the law deals, as well as added new ones, which could not be regulated then [that is, in 1734]." In brief, society had changed, and legislators and the judiciary needed to take this into account. Thanks to "the improvement of language," the statute went on, "expressions and locutions that used to be subject to doubt and various interpretations have now become firmer." Thus, nineteenth-century people had better linguistic means at their disposal that could be used to make the law less ambiguous. The king consequently announced his intention to collect all regulations and statutes in a comprehensive volume to allow for a better understanding of the law. But some issues were too important to wait for this project to be completed. The first of these was the question of whether or not a spouse ought to have marital rights to land the other spouse had redeemed from relatives. Without much further ado, the king simply announced that marital rights did apply in such cases, unless the spouses had made a special agreement to the contrary. Obviously, the king had listened to Leijonmarck.[8]

It is revealing that this question was the very first to make it onto the agenda. It strongly suggests that family law was not only unclear but that it was not believed to work as it should and, furthermore, that it was inequitable. Even if Leijonmarck was the only member of the commission to articulate this view at first, it is highly unlikely that he was the only Swede at the time who held this opinion. Studies of Uppland suggest that some farmers immediately availed themselves of the opportunity to register their wives as co-owners of redeemed estates when the reform of 1807 made this possible.[9] Clearly, this option was highly coveted and, compared to some other countries, it was introduced rather late.

Land, however, had been redeemed by couples in the seventeenth century as well, and, unless the husband made a special will to compensate his wife for the inheritance she had thus lost, such practices had entailed adverse effects for her.[10] Yet this situation had not caused legislators to make any amendments to the law. Indeed, they were noticeably silent on this issue. Even if nineteenth-century people thought of themselves as being enlightened in a way their forebears had not been, it is hardly likely that the degree of enlightenment can explain the new concern with the way in which redemption of land worked. Instead, there is reason to believe that the quantitative importance of this phenomenon had grown in the course of the eighteenth century and that it was the magnitude of it that prompted the legislature to take action. As will be shown, the character of eighteenth-century society explains why the issue appeared increasingly problematic.

Factors Promoting the Sale of Married Women's Inherited Lands

No doubt, husbands had stronger needs to sell their wives' inherited land in the eighteenth century than in the previous one. For one region in western Sweden Lars Herlitz has shown how prices for taxable freehold land (*skattejord*) increased markedly and steadily in the period from 1722 to 1777, especially after 1740. Janne Backlund has provided evidence for a similar process in central Sweden in the period from 1684 to 1748.[11] In this context it is particularly important to note that land sales between relatives displayed the same pattern as did land sales between people who were not related to each other. Even if prices were somewhat higher within the latter segment of the land market, there was a very clear tendency for prices to rise even when the seller and the purchaser were kinsmen.[12] In the long run the two segments of the land market seem to have converged, providing yet another indication of how the special status of lineage property and kinsmen was gradually undermined. The long-term effect of these processes was a drastic reduction of the price difference between taxable freehold land held by peasants and nontaxable (or lightly taxed) freehold land held by the nobility.

To many people in rural Sweden, the tendency for land prices to rise within families must have been one of the things that affected their economies most. It is likely that almost every peasant couple, excepting the ones where the spouses had no siblings, was confronted with the need to find money to pay off inheritance claims. No doubt these payments were a tangible burden on newly established peasant households and a problem that could harass them for long periods of time. Toward the end of the eighteenth century, voices were even raised in the Diet, claiming that young peasants had difficulties paying their taxes because of the costs of redeeming family land. Demands were made that the eldest sons should always be chosen successors and, what was more important, that the sums they paid to their siblings had to be fixed below the market price level. It was believed that the problem of competition over land and ensuing indebtedness could be solved in this way, but the proposal did not meet with approval.[13]

What accounted for this marked rise in land prices? Lars Herlitz, who was the first to establish that a price increase had taken place and whose view of the process has become very influential, argued that it was a consequence of a decreasing tax burden upon taxable freehold land, which originated during the late seventeenth-century *Reduktion*. The mitigation of taxation allowed for greater profit margins for peasant producers, Herlitz concluded. When peasants could keep a larger share of their yields, to eat or to sell, their profit expectations grew, and gradually they were prepared to pay more for land.[14] There is no reason to question this interpretation as such, but it should be supplemented by other factors. First, population growth may also have boosted demand for land, although this effect is likely to have been more visible in the nineteenth century. Second and more important, prices cannot escalate if there is no capital available. Even if common men did believe that buying land was a safe and profit-yielding way of investing their assets, prices could not rise if nobody could come up with capital. While no doubt valuable, Herlitz's explanation needs to be complemented. The question is where eighteenth-century peasants got the money that allowed them to pay more for land.

Since there is little to suggest that formal credit institutions were easily available and attractive options in the first part of the eighteenth century,[15] there must have been hidden sources of capital in agrarian society to which peasants could have recourse. For instance, eighteenth-century probate inventories suggest that some peasant households possessed considerable amounts of silver.[16] Such observations strongly suggest that there must have been such resources within preindustrial agrarian society that allowed peasants to react to price incentives without necessarily becoming dependent on moneylenders or banks.

The most important "internal" source of wealth, however, seems to have been marriage alliances. Marrying a wealthy woman was arguably the best way of boosting a man's economic position, giving him the necessary resources with which to act in the land market.[17] The economic importance of marriage has of course been pointed out many times before, and not only for the early modern period. Still, it appears that a vital distinction has frequently been overlooked, namely, the distinction between whether the husband was only able to *use* the property of his wife or whether he could dispose of it as if he were the absolute owner. In the former case, marriage gave men access to the returns on the property, which could certainly be substantial, but it did not make it easy for them to mortgage or sell. In the latter case, marriage could mean something completely different. It could become a crucial source of capital accumulation. This alerts us to the profound importance of the new rules codified in Sweden in 1734. Before that year, a husband was only allowed to use the yields from his wife's inherited landed property. When it came to selling or mortgaging the land, his actions were severely circumscribed, and he had little room to maneuver. After 1734 he had much more leeway. Even if the law still made it clear that he did not own her lands, and even if he could not use her property to cover debts he incurred before marriage, it was now up to his wife alone to stop him if he tried. Her ability to dissociate her own interests from those of her husband and her strength to withstand persuasion were now all that barred him from using her land as if it were completely his own. And why should she stop him? If he proposed to sell her land in order to raise capital to pay off his siblings' claims on the family farm, this would probably seem a very sensible thing to do in the eyes of many women. Thus, rising land prices prompted families to use the wife's inherited means in new ways, but these practices fueled land prices even more.

Consequently, the wife's inherited wealth must be regarded as one of the hidden sources of capital in preindustrial agrarian society. This resource had de facto become much more easily accessible to husbands with the reforms of 1734. Many peasant households were under strong pressure to find capital with which they could pay off relatives. Likewise, the need to raise capital increased within the nobility, as men had to pay ever higher prices for a position as a salaried officer.[18] Therefore, taking recourse to the wife's lands or her personal property must have been a tempting solution to many married Swedish men in the eighteenth century. That women from landholding families married to a much greater extent than did women in general suggests that these women were more attractive in the marriage market precisely because of their material assets.[19]

Not only did the eighteenth century witness a steady rise in land prices; the land market also expanded, in the sense that there was a drastic increase in the amount of land that was offered for sale. The main reason for this increase was the government decision to sell off Crown-owned farms, primarily to tenants, a process that started in the early decades of the century and continued, albeit with some breaks, until around 1800. As a consequence of these developments, approximately 60 percent of all cadastral units (farms) were owned by freeholder farmers by 1850. This reform, which had parallels in Denmark, turned many tenants into freeholders, particularly in the southern parts of the country. These developments were vitally dependent on the ability of the tenants to raise the necessary capital. Prices for Crown land were usually lower than those paid for ordinary freehold land, but it remained a difficult matter to come up with the required sums.[20] Court records sometimes disclose that tenants who wanted to buy their farms were able to raise cash from children or neighbors;[21] apparently, there was room for saving money even among ordinary agricultural workers. In this context the monetary contributions of wives could be a particularly important source of cash, as a 1725 will from the rural parish of Asker demonstrates. An elderly widow informed the court that her son had managed and paid taxes for their tenant farm for many years. She explicitly mentioned how he had

TABLE 6. Husband's sale of wife's inherited land in a sample
of eighteenth-century Swedish courts (primary court level)

Place	Time	Population size (1751)	Cases where wife's land is sold	Wife's consent mentioned explicitly	Money invested in husband's land
Central Sweden					
Vendel	1736–37	1,963	2	1	—
Stora Tuna	1741–45	6,000	3	—	2
Roslagen	1750–54	17,966	6	—	4
Northern Sweden					
Undersåker (a)	1750–64	1,583	1	—	1
Undersåker (b)	1763–99	1,583	2	2	2
Total			14	3	9

Sources: For population figures, see Palm, *Folkmängden.* For court records, see *Vendels 1736–37;* Kopparbergs läns häradsrättsarkiv, Domböcker för Stora Tuna 1741–45, Uppsala landsarkivet; Svea Hovrätts arkiv,
Renoverade småprotokoll för Bro och Vätö skeppslag, Frötuna och Länna skeppslag, Väddö och Häverö
skeppslag, and Frösåkers härad, 1750–54, Riksarkivet; Jämtlands läns häradsrättsarkiv, Domböcker för
Undersåker 1750–64 (a) database of wills (b) Östersunds landsarkiv.

Comments: In Stora Tuna, one case was found where the husband "had been forced" to sell his lands
during marriage (Dombok Stora Tuna 1744, 24 September).

finally bought it from the Crown with money he had acquired by selling his wife's land. For these reasons — the investment of money and
hard work — she wanted this son and his children to take over the farm,
rather than her daughter.[22]

The land market, however, was not the only factor that affected married women's property rights. Another factor, which has as yet received
little attention, was the enclosure movement. While preceded by some
locally initiated and locally restricted enclosures in the seventeenth century, enclosure proper started around 1750, as the result of new statutory
law, and continued into the nineteenth (and even twentieth) century.[23]
The long-term objective of these reforms was to avoid a strip field system with scattered holdings, which was believed to be economically
inefficient, and to create compact farms instead. It is known that the
peasants were engaged in the implementation of the reform and that
many of them explicitly advocated this reorganization of landholding.
However, the point here is that enclosure made it more difficult to keep
track of small but distinct pieces of land owned by household members
other than the head of the household. By way of contrast, the unen-

closed hamlet had been well adapted to a legal system where the wife could have a piece of land of her own. When all farms had a large number of different holdings scattered in the landscape, there was nothing strange about the fact that yet another odd holding was added when a new household was established. It could even be an advantage: the wife's land was clearly visible in the landscape, and kinsmen and the local community could easily keep track of it. The creation of more compact farms is likely to have complicated matters, and it provided yet another impetus to sell the wife's land and to invest the money in the husband's family farm instead. Both spatial and financial concentration of household resources probably affected married women's chances of retaining their actual plots of land.

Thus, the vitalized land market and the incipient enclosure movement are indispensable background factors in the discussion of married rural women's property rights in the eighteenth century. They both suggest, unambiguously, that it had become harder than before to keep a married woman's inherited land as a separate unit. These developments also imply that it must have seemed wise to many peasant couples to transform her land into liquid capital. It is important to spell this out before proceeding to a closer study of these matters, simply because the marital estate was a domestic secret, even to us, and we may fail to spot important evidence if we do not know what to look for.

Were women the only ones who ran the risk of being disfavored by the new situation? Not necessarily. The husband and wife could choose to retain *her* family farm and to invest his inherited wealth in it. In families where there was no son, a daughter and a son-in-law would normally take over the farm, and even in families where there were sons, nothing prevented the parents from choosing the daughter and son-in-law instead (in contrast to the situation in Norway).[24] In such cases, it was the son-in-law who courted the risk of being barred from ownership of the farm, as the following case, which formed a precedent, shows. A man had sold the family farm to another peasant in 1788 without having first acquired his wife's consent. She filed a complaint with the local court, pointing out that she and her husband had bought the farm jointly from her parents in 1785. This case caused considerable bewilderment within the judiciary, but in the final instance, K. Maj:t ruled that one-quarter of the farm should be regarded as the wife's inheritance (apparently, she had three sisters). As for the remaining three-quarters, which the spouses had bought, "the husband does not have any marital rights to them, because the law makes a clear distinction between acquired land

and redeemed land." Despite the fact that the farm had been bought, it was not classified as acquired but as redeemed, and therefore it was not part of the spouses' common estate. It belonged to the wife.[25] Referring to what the legal code said about unauthorized selling of land belonging to someone else, K. Maj:t made it very clear that the husband did not own any part of the farm and that he had had no right to sell his wife's property.[26] The case does not spell out explicitly where the couple had found the money to buy the farm from the woman's parents, but it would not be too far-fetched to assume that the husband had contributed at least some of it.

Both men and women could be affected, then, if their money was used to redeem the other spouse's land. Still, it was more likely that the wife would suffer, simply because daughters' inheritance shares were only half the size of what sons received. Men were advantaged, since it cost less to keep a brother's share and buy off his siblings than for a woman to keep a sister's share and buy off her siblings. Only in cases where a daughter took over the farm could the son-in-law become the victim. That women inherited smaller shares than men in the rural areas was nothing new, but what was new to the eighteenth century was that the odds had grown against married women being able to retain their inherited wealth as separate property. How did ordinary rural people deal with this situation, and what part did the law play?

Guarding Widows' Rights

The rural parish of Rystad, located near the episcopal see of Linköping, was not an isolated enclave but an area upon which the greater societal developments left their imprint in the late eighteenth century. As in the rest of the country, land prices were increasing in an unprecedented way. It is telling that, when a deceased farmer's estate was inventoried, the assessors noted, almost apologetically, that land was now generally very expensive.[27] When another estate was inventoried and found to have included neither claims nor debts, the assessors wrote that this was "truly remarkable."[28]

Thus, rising land prices meant that it was more common for farming households to have to incur debts. Another reason for indebtedness was the pervasiveness of inheritance claims. Almost all households in Rystad were indebted to one or several young men or women who had not yet received their inheritance shares. Not all such claims were irregular; when a person lost a parent at a tender age, an inheritance would normally be placed in the hands of a guardian (often an uncle) who would then keep it, with interest, until the child reached a more mature age. In this way, guardians functioned as a sort of small bank, and, since many men were commissioned as guardians, they often had debts to their wards. Some inheritance debts were different in the sense that the claimant had obviously come of age and perhaps even married without yet having received his or her share. When Måns Larsson's wife died in 1794, her inheritance had been due from her guardian at least since 1792, when she married; it is unclear how long she had waited for it prior to this date.[29]

Landowners in Rystad had inherited their land, redeemed it from their relatives, or purchased it on the open market, although often the first two forms of acquisition were combined.[30] Inherited land was kept strictly separate, both for women and men, in full accordance with the law. Thus, a married woman who *did* have inherited land was well protected by the law, but not many women had such property.[31] Land purchased on the market from nonrelatives became the common property of both spouses, of which the woman could claim one-third. In 30 percent of the landholding households, the land had been acquired from the Crown.[32] The decision to sell Crown lands made it considerably easier to get hold of real estate to which one's relatives held no claims, a development that actually turned the reform unintentionally into a woman-friendly measure.[33] For land redeemed from the husband's siblings and relatives, however, women could claim no right to the land as such, not even if she had in fact made the redemption possible through contribution of her own inherited means. It appears that this was generally acknowledged as a problem by local people at the time and that they therefore consciously developed practices with a view to compensating women (and their natal families) for this insecurity.

The most common way of handling the problem in Rystad was to report the surviving spouse's contributions to the men who assessed the dead spouse's estate.[34] When Nils Persson in Västra Torp died in April 1782, his widow Anna Andersdotter summoned two local men of good reputation to have the estate inventoried. Anna was forty-three years old at this time, and she and Nils had five children, all of whom were underage. The children's rights were closely guarded by their relative Sven Nilsson, and the widow was assisted by a brother and a brother-in-law. It was noted in the inventory that the dead husband had inherited one-third of the real estate and redeemed two-sixths from his two sisters. The remaining one-third had belonged to his mother, and he had bought it from her during his marriage. The inventory continued:

As regards the other two-thirds [the mother's and the sisters'], they have been redeemed during the marriage with the widow Anna Andersdotter, so she will have compensation (*vederlag*) for the real estate in the freehold of Fjärdingstad which she has sold.[35]

Nothing in the records from the meeting suggests that Nils and Anna had kept any document testifying to the sale of her estate. It is, of course, possible that such a document did exist, but assessors usually recorded faithfully whether there were any relevant legal documents, such as wills. Therefore, it is more likely that the memory about what had taken place had been kept by Anna herself and by her natal family. Very likely, this was why her brother and brother-in-law were asked to be present at the meeting so that they could vouch that the sale had taken place and support Anna if anyone (that is, Sven Nilsson) should refuse to acknowledge her claims. As it turned out, there were no protests, and Anna received pecuniary compensation for the land she had lost.

Anna Andersdotter's case was not unique; many other cases also show how local people protected the rights of widows. When Stina Nilsdotter was widowed in 1779 at the age of forty-eight, the assessors noted that she had sold her inherited land in Rumkulla during marriage and that the money had accrued to the household. She now wanted to retrieve the value, and "while the exact amount can not be proved," it was still included in the inventory as a claim on her behalf, using a value suggested by her late husband.[36] When Petter Nilsson was widowed a second time in 1803, it was noted in the inventory that his farm had been redeemed during his first marriage and that the second wife, who was now dead, held no claims to it. But it was then added that "the widower concedes that the estate money that he [received] with his now deceased wife . . . should be returned to his little daughter Catharina."[37] Since there was a child, the father had to keep track of what had happened to the wife's inherited means. When Christina Persdotter was widowed in 1804 at the age of forty, it was noted in her husband's probate inventory that he had bought the freehold rights to Gerstad, previously owned by the Crown, during his marriage to Christina. Consequently, the inventory reads, the farm now belonged to her and to their two daughters since "she had let her estate money accrue to the house."[38] In this case, it should not have been necessary to add the information about her pecuniary contribution, since the farm was definitely a pure acquisition and therefore the common property of the spouses. That the wife's estate money was mentioned all the same suggests that it was regarded as very important.

These cases clearly dealt with exactly the same problem that Simon Persson in Vedbo had wrestled with in the seventeenth century: that for some reason, it had proved necessary to sell the wife's inherited land and to invest the capital in other land, to which she had no right under law. In fact almost the same words were used in reference to liquid inherited capital. In the sixteenth and seventeenth centuries, it was called "land money," whereas in the eighteenth and nineteenth centuries it was usually denoted "estate money" (*fastighetspengar*) or "lineage money" (*arvejordsmedel*).[39] Still, the terms all referred to the same phenomenon. Likewise, the strategies deployed over time were similar, although not identical, in the sense that the general objective was to reduce domestic secrecy by making the wife's contributions visible and therefore impossible to ignore. They became visible if described in a will, as Simon Persson had done, or if carefully noted in a probate inventory, as several landowners in Rystad chose to do.

People could use the inventories to describe rather complicated transactions and how the costs for these were to be divided between the spouses. In the inventory set up for Lars Månsson in 1795, it was noted that the estate had been inherited and redeemed by the husband prior to his marriage to Maja Olofsdotter, who was now his widow. Consequently, she had no entitlement to this property. However, the probate inventory went on, "this farm was mortgaged for 707 copper *daler* . . . and the loan was repaid during his last marriage according to a certificate issued by the late husband." Since only the children were entitled to the landed estate, it was stated that "the widow must have some compensation" for the fact that she had paid a part of the debt.[40] In a similar way, when the assessors came to set up the probate inventory for the late Ingrid Olofsdotter, the widower, Måns Månsson, was keen to inform them about some debts he had incurred. He had borrowed money in order to redeem a family estate, but he wanted to take sole responsibility for this debt, and therefore, it was not included in the inventory.[41] In this way, the costs for a property of which he was the sole owner did not fall into his dead wife's estate. Ingrid had been married previously and had three children by her first husband. Unlike their half-siblings, these children would not be entitled to inherit from Måns and had no interest in paying for the redemption of the said farm. Therefore, what Måns did, rather magnanimously, was to protect his stepchildren from himself.

Landowning families, however, were not the only ones to use inventories to make spouses' contributions visible. In some cases, the importance of women's estate money was even noted in inventories of households with no land of their own. When Anna Svensdotter was widowed in 1795 at the age of thirty, the assessors came to a house with nothing but movable property and, what was more, to a house where the inventoried estate did not suffice to cover all debts. It was decided, therefore, that the movable property be disposed of by auction. However, the largest debt was due to the widow herself: "[since] the widow's inheritance from the estate of Månsta [has] accrued to the house and

been consumed in the house during marriage, it will revert to her as all those concerned agree."[42] When the soldier Carl Björkman was widowed in 1806 at the age of forty-four, there were four children at home, three of whom had been born during their mother's first marriage. The stepchildren informed the assembled assessors and relatives that their dead mother had once held inherited land in another parish, "which had been sold, and the money had accrued to the house during her marriage to the stepfather." Björkman confessed this to be true but said that, as far as he could remember, the value of the land had not been more than 800 copper *daler*. His stepchildren agreed that this was the approximate amount but wanted to come back later when they had found the relevant document.[43] When Stina Arvidsdotter was widowed in 1793 at the age of thirty-eight, there was very little in the estate, her husband having been a crofter. But the husband had written a will in which he pointed out that upon marriage Stina had contributed 500 copper *daler* to their common estate and that she wanted him to have them if she died first. Even if this did not eventually happen, the will nevertheless served as evidence of her pecuniary contributions, making them visible and indisputable. The assessors and the relatives had to take them into account. Stina could have kept the entire estate for herself, but "out of tenderness," she decided to give her late husband's clothes to his son from a previous marriage.[44]

Married women's estate money was obviously very important to these nonlandholding households; it constituted their last, meager link to the landholding strata from which they had descended. In this way women's estate money opens a window upon the proletarianization process going on in this period, during which crofters and rural laborers became more numerous, while many farmers grew more affluent. It has been shown that proletarianization was not the effect of more children being born to nonlandholding families but rather was the result of the inability of many farmers' children to remain on the social level of their parents.[45] Although some women with inherited means could marry farmers, others had to accept a crofter or a soldier as their husband. If this happened, it would probably be quite difficult for the new household to reinvest the wife's estate money in new land in view of how expensive land had become. Instead, the capital was likely to be used to cover daily needs. Of course, this could happen to men as well, but since their inheritance shares were larger, this was less likely. Claims for compensation for lost estate money were a means, albeit probably futile, of trying to avoid further proletarianization in the coming generation.

As these examples have shown, people in Rystad obviously kept close track of their own property as well as of that of others. It must have been common knowledge that there was a need to assert one's rights to compensation for inherited means lost during marriage and that this had to be done in conjunction with the death of the spouse. There is nothing to suggest that this practice was recommended "from above" through statutory law. Rather, registering claims for compensation seems to have been a social, and possibly local, practice.[46] Both widows and widowers could benefit from having their claims noted in the probate inventories, but it is probably no coincidence that almost all instances of this practice dealt with the rights of widows. Since women's shares were smaller, they were generally more likely to have to accept payment for their shares in the form of estate money. The clauses about wives' contributions that we find in some inventories and wills can, and should, be read as strategic precautions taken by the husband and wife or by the widow and relatives, with a view to protecting the woman after married life had ceased. They reveal love and consideration as well as a considerable amount of insight into the workings of the law. At the same time, the clauses illustrate how many women depended entirely for their economic well-being upon men, either husbands or male relatives such as fathers, brothers, or brothers-in-law. More than anything else, the need of these women to have special legal arrangements made for them by others succinctly captures the situation of many rural women in the eighteenth century.

The Increasing Use of Contractual and Testamentary Arrangements

There was a general tendency toward regulating the transfer of land between generations with the help of written contracts or wills in eighteenth-century Sweden.[47] Historians have demonstrated that these contracts included detailed instructions about how the young generation was to care for the old generation, with meticulously described conditions about the amounts of food and the number of church visits to which the old people were entitled. The stipulations often became bones of contention, spawning discord and hostility within families and constituting a burden on the landed property, since the contracts were registered as a form of mortgage.[48]

Thus, land was often transferred during a person's lifetime by means of written contracts and always in a way that allowed the older generation to express their wishes (except in the cases when a peasant died young and unexpectedly). The devolution of land to the next generation was rarely mechanical, as it were, guided by the words of the legal code only. Instead, parents' ideas about which child was the most suitable successor often played a crucial part in the process. Consequently, even if all children had a legal right to claim their inheritance (something English children did not have, because of the strong legal position of the father), in practice this right could be considerably modified and subject to negotiation. All children could claim something, but they could not claim to be entitled to take over the family farm.

What were the reasons for these contractual practices, and why did they increase in this period? The accepted view has been to place the contracts within the context of the older generation's need for retirement arrangements. The contracts have been seen as a means by which older peasants could make sure that they would be able to continue to live a decent life, as opposed to other, less advantageous alternatives such as "buying" a place in a monastery, living on poor relief, or begging.[49] Of course, the contracts did fulfill the expected function, yet it is hard to see why they would increase so markedly in the eighteenth and nineteenth centuries if their occurrence was only related to old people's personal needs. Old people had certainly had the same needs in previous centuries. That childless couples made spousal wills in the seventeenth century counters the assumption that written arrangements were an unknown device to ordinary people at that time. Neither lack of need nor lack of knowledge can explain their lower occurrence prior to 1700.

What these contracts did was to give parents a means by which they could continue to control their land by stipulating in detail what children and their spouses should do when they had assumed responsibility. The conditions often emphasized the importance of good and obedient behavior toward the old. Parents also seized the opportunity of explaining in the contract why a particular child had been appointed successor, the reasons often expressed in terms of industriousness, capacity to work, obedience, and reliability.[50] Therefore, it appears that these contracts restored to parents at least some of the influence they had lost when the requirement for relatives' consent was abolished in 1734. Parents were no longer in a position where they could veto a sale of land by their son-in-law; instead, they had to rely on their daughter's ability to say no, if the proposed sale was an unwise one. If one was not satisfied with this solution, if one believed with Claes Rålamb that women were easily persuaded by their husbands, it was necessary to think of new methods of reestablishing control. A retirement contract, with all its conditions and demands, could be one way of doing this. Thus, the older generation compensated itself for what it had lost in terms of power and influence.

If the contractual arrangements were *only* a new way of controlling how sons-in-law used land, it would be incomprehensible why parents used these contracts just as frequently with respect to sons as to daughters. However, these arrangements were also compensating practices in another, and perhaps even more important, sense. They compensated mothers for the insecurity with which they had to live if their inheritance had been invested in their spouse's family farm. As was pointed out above, women were in a precarious situation as widows and depended on the good will of their children or of their husbands' relatives. With the help of retirement contracts and wills, peasant couples could bind their successors (whether children, nephews and nieces, or nonrelatives) to take good care of the spouse who lived longer. Since even then the statistics show that men died younger than women, these contracts de facto catered to the needs of widows in most cases, and widows were the ones who needed these arrangements most.

It is striking to what extent the arrangements not only mentioned the widow but emphatically drew attention to various contributions she had made to the household. In this way, the character of compensation to the wife became even more obvious. In Roslagen, Mats Andersson made a will for his wife Margareta Andersdotter, giving her movable property in acknowledgement of her help in freeing his family farm from all debts. It was explicitly spelled out that, since her investments could not benefit her children, his relatives must agree to compensate her before taking over the farm.[51] Anders Engberg decided that when he and his wife were both dead, his stepdaughter Magdalena should have the farm, since her maternal inheritance had been used to free it from its debts. However, she had to pay off her siblings first.[52] Both husbands candidly acknowledged the property contributions of their wives, making it superfluous to report these facts orally to the assessors when the estate was inventoried. In Jämtland, Anna Wulf and her husband, Simon Björkebom, made a mutual will, mentioning that Anna had used "her own money" to buy off Simon's siblings, the words indicating that they knew well what was his and what was hers.[53] Erik Ersson and Ingeborg

Persdotter also made a mutual will, stating that Ingeborg had given money to Erik to help him buy two farms. In return, she was now given the right to sell or will away the property to whomever she trusted.[54] Being a childless woman, she would have to find a child substitute to care for her in her old age, and with property in her hands, this would probably not have been difficult. In Stora Tuna, Karin Persdotter had given landed property to her (second) husband, Olof Matsson, which caused her son's guardians to protest on his behalf. But the stepfather answered that Karin had given him the land as compensation for Olof's having been obliged to sell some of his lands during marriage.[55] Through arrangements like these, couples made their past contributions of property and capital visible and therefore less easy for children and relatives to ignore. It was a rational and entirely understandable thing for them to do, in view of how little attention the law paid to such contributions, but it also bears witness to an appreciation of the risk that such contributions would otherwise be overlooked. Not everybody may have been aware of these risks, which is probably the reason why not everyone made such arrangements. Of course, those who failed to make such arrangements could resort to having their contributions noted in the probate inventory.

Spouses who were really alert could make a prenuptial agreement, regulating their respective rights and duties in advance. Such agreements were more frequent within the higher echelons of society and indeed distinctly more uncommon among ordinary people until the nineteenth century.[56] Prior to 1734 such agreements had even been illegal.[57] In principle, peasant families could have made use of such contracts too, since they offered a new opportunity for protecting property from the son-in-law. It is likely that they preferred retirement contracts or wills precisely because such documents offered better protection to the mother of the previous generation. However, in 1779 Olof Andersson and Brita Persdotter in Uppland made a prenuptial agreement to the effect that Brita would show Olof "all due love, honor and friendship, and that she in friendliness [would] fulfill all the duties of an honest wife"; if she should fail in these respects, she forfeited her marital rights, according to the agreement. On her side, Brita demanded that Olof should take her into his confidence and let her share happiness and love with him if he wanted to have her inherited property.[58] The words about "her inherited property" probably referred to her estate money and they show, once again, the kinds of property transfers that tended to take place within marriage, despite the intent of the law, simply because it was very difficult to uphold the distinction between his and hers in everyday married life.[59]

Apart from property, spouses also drew attention to contributions such as labor or love and care devoted to children — just as seventeenth-century spouses had done. When Carl Thelin made a will for his wife, Ingeborg Wrangel, giving her the right to keep the estate undivided and to be the children's guardian, he explained his decision by pointing to his wife's toil and labor, her education of the children, and her contributions of property.[60] Ingeborg's surname indicates that, unlike her husband, she was of noble family, and this may explain why special care was devoted to making her contributions visible. In their mutual will, the childless couple Nils Flink and Brita Nilsdotter in Fäviken (in northern Sweden) stated that they wanted to give their entire property to the one who lived longer. They probably anticipated that this might induce their relatives to complain, because they added that they had built their croft and reclaimed the land "from shrubs and roots" (*från ris och rot*),[61] a concrete description of what the place had looked like before they had invested time and labor upon it. In view of the extensive reclamation of land that took place in this period, particularly in the forested parts of the country, it is likely that many people could and did draw attention to this kind of work.

Thus, the value attached to hard agricultural or forest work was often brought to the fore, but so was the importance of taking good care of human beings. In a dispute caused by the will drawn up by Jan Persson in Medstugan that benefited one daughter and son-in-law, another son-in-law claimed that the couple had refused to take the father-in-law to church when he wanted to receive Holy Communion; instead, they had attended a wedding party. Despite the fact that Jan himself had expressed his wish to be taken care of by this particular daughter and her husband, the other son-in-law tried to prove that, objectively speaking, the couple had neglected the old man.[62] Failures to carry out certain tasks were seen as acts that weakened property rights, just as the fulfillment of the same tasks improved property rights. When Johan Ersson and his wife, Karin Olofsdotter, decided to transfer their farm to the widow and children of their dead son, it was emphasized that the son had invested much labor in the farm and that the parents had been supported by him for twenty-seven years.[63]

Arguments about investment of labor and mutual love were not new to the eighteenth century, as has been seen. Rather, they were a continuation of Protestant rhetoric that went back at least one hundred years in time.[64] However, arguments about contributions of property are different, in the sense that they are less easy to refute. While relatives could express doubts as to whether couples had really lived in mutual love and concord, or if one spouse had really worked as hard as was alleged, it was harder to deny that a person had actually sold landed property simply because such claims could be investigated and verified. Therefore, statements of this type could not, and cannot, be ignored and proclaimed mere rhetoric but are rather extremely valuable sources of information on the internal property arrangements of households. Even if it is not possible at this stage to provide quantitative evidence that women's property contributions figured more frequently in eighteenth-century wills and contracts than previously, it is nevertheless striking how often evidence of this comes up once we start reading the documents closely.

Explaining Silence

Husbands had several practical solutions at their disposal if they wanted to compensate their wives for property that had been invested in the husbands' family farms. They could draw up a will or compel the younger generation to take care of the widow through a retirement contract. Male relatives could also assist widows when their dead husbands' estates were inventoried by asserting the woman's right to compensation for lost estate money. In none of the investigated areas were such practices entirely absent, and the closer we look (as in the case of Rystad), the more examples we find. Men compensated women in various ways in the eighteenth century. I do not emphasize this fact to argue that men were generous and just (even if some of them undoubtedly were); I emphasize it because it shows that many women needed to be compensated.

Still, not all women were properly compensated for the loss of their inherited wealth. Consequently, some of them filed complaints with the courts in order to make the judiciary investigate whether the sale had been carried out in accordance with the stipulations of the law. In these cases, the crucial question was whether land had been sold against the wishes of the woman. If this was found to be the case, the court could make amends by ruling that the widow be given other land as a substitute for what had been lost. In a case from 1788 the husband had sold the farm he and his wife had bought from her parents without first having acquired her consent. The wife filed a complaint and in the court of last instance, the judges found in the wife's favor, arguing that one-quarter of the farm was inherited and three-quarters were redeemed land; consequently, the husband had no property rights whatsoever in regard to it.[65] Bertha Åkesdotter, mentioned at the inception of this chapter, was also a woman who took legal action when she felt that her capital had been lost to her dead husband's family.

But even if there are examples of women filing complaints, they are not as numerous as one would expect them to be. One obvious reason for this silence is of course that the legal capacity of early modern women was restricted, unless they were widowed.[66] Therefore, some complaints concerning the loss of women's inherited land were instead brought to court by their male relatives or their heirs. This is hardly surprising, since the heirs were also affected by a sale. For instance, in 1741 the two brothers Göran and Erik Ersson in Svärdsjö, Stora Tuna, claimed restitution of land that their grandfather had given to his second wife and which was now in the possession of their father's half-brother, Hans Hansson. The alleged reason for their claim was that their grandfather had bought the said land with "the value for which the first wife's inherited land had been sold." Clearly, Göran and Erik thought that their grandmother's lineage property, to which they were entitled, had been lost from her family's overall purview. Unfortunately, the court did not share their view of what had happened and ruled that the land should be regarded as the grandfather's acquired property and therefore devisable.[67] In Undersåker Mårten Ranklef had sold his first wife's lineage property and invested the money in his own family estate, Mo, which does not seem to have caused any immediate resentment among his wife's relatives. It was not until Mårten drew up a will that would benefit two of his three daughters that a dispute erupted in 1751 at the instigation of Mårten's sons-in-law, prompting the court to make a closer investigation into how Mårten had come into possession of the Mo estate.[68] His first wife appears never to have lodged a complaint herself.

A more weighty reason for the silence often surrounding sales of married women's inherited land, however, was probably that, in many cases, the couple had decided to sell amicably. The husband and wife had both agreed to the transaction, and neither ever regretted the decision. The main reason for this conclusion is that, if the couple had children, a sale was not really risky for the woman. When her husband died, their children would be entitled to demand an immediate division of his estate, at which her rights only consisted in her third of the common property, her morning gift, and some minor objects (*fördel*). She would have no rights whatsoever to the family farm if it had come through his lineage, even though her own inheritance had been invested in it. Because children did not often evict their mother, there seems little reason to expect complaints in such instances. Indeed, the solution to sell the mother's land may have seemed ideal to the children. Not only had the farm been liberated from debts due to their paternal uncles and aunts; their maternal and paternal inheritance shares also merged, conveniently, within the same object. Instead of making two divisions of landed estates (one after each parent), they now only had to make one. Family economy was vastly simplified.

But simplification can entail risks, and it did so for women who failed to produce offspring.[69] The moment their husbands died, they were at the mercy of his heirs, who were not their common children but rather his siblings, uncles, cousins, or children from previous marriages, all of them eager to assert their rights to the lineage property. Would they be willing to let the widow stay at the farm until her death? Would they be prepared to acknowledge and compensate her for the investment of her inheritance in "their" property? Although some relatives may have been willing to do so, the fact that will making among spouses correlated strongly with childlessness in Sweden does suggest that many spouses feared that their survivor would find it difficult to negotiate favorable terms with the kinsmen of the deceased spouse.

Children could also be exposed to risks. If their maternal inheritance had been invested in the paternal family farm, and if the mother died and the father remarried, fathering new children by his second wife, it would be extremely difficult if not impossible to disentangle the first children's shares of their maternal inheritance from those of their half-siblings. The ultimate effect would be that the children of the second wife would benefit from the fact that the first wife's inheritance had raised the value of the estate. This was not in keeping with the general principle of Swedish real estate law and inheritance law, which taught that lineage property must never be transferred to other kin groups and that, for this reason, a proper division of the estate should always take place before a parent could remarry. However, this principle presupposed that property was static and only took the form of well-defined objects such as land. In eighteenth-century society, where land prices increased, where land changed owners more frequently, and where many people had to accept having their inheritance in the form of money or movable property, it was obviously hard to sustain the principle.

Thus, a woman's rights were strongly affected by her family situation. For many women a sale was no problem at all, whereas for others it could constitute a major threat to their living conditions in old age. The women who had children and whose husbands had made some kind of provisions for them fared much better than did those who lacked off-spring and whose husbands had taken no special precautions. The following example from Rystad illustrates this point. When Maja Larsdotter and Lars Persson were betrothed to be married, they made a "mutual will and agreement" to the effect that, if Maja survived Lars, she should have everything in the estate, including the land. She should have this in return for "the large inheritance and amount of money" which Lars would receive upon consummation of their marriage. If, however, any children were born who survived their parents, the will would be void.[70] Unfortunately, one might say, a son was born before Lars passed away in 1803, and the will was annulled without any new arrangements being made for Maja. When the probate inventory was taken, it was noted that Lars had inherited one-third of the farm and that the residual parts had been redeemed from relatives during marriage. For some reason, however, "the large inheritance" Lars had received from Maja was not noted. This had dire consequences for the young widow (age twenty-seven), who was forced to sell or lease most of the property and live with her young son on a minor part of the estate.[71] This case clearly shows that it was of paramount importance to have all claims to compensation carefully noted in the inventory or in a valid will, precisely because otherwise the law did not acknowledge widows' rights to any share in land their husbands had redeemed from relatives. Maja's situation was aggravated by the fact that, since her son was so young, he was unable to take over the farm and protect his mother.

Silence must also be understood in relation to the complexity of the legal situation. The assumption must be made that, in order to file a complaint, the aggrieved party has to believe that he or she stands a chance of winning. People are less likely to bring complaints to the judiciary if such confidence is lacking. This confidence, in turn, presupposes knowledge of the law. The more people know about how the law operates, the more they are able to judge for themselves whether success is feasible or not. On the other hand, where legal knowledge is restricted, or where the outcome of a legal dispute is hard to predict, people are less likely to file complaints, even if they have good reasons to do so.

The total number of civil cases increased in eighteenth-century Sweden as compared to the previous century, which is not surprising in view of population growth. More importantly, their share of the total caseload in the courts grew.[72] This might suggest that people felt confident about the outcome of their civil suits, or that they were extremely unsatisfied with their situation and willing to take any risk. Unfortunately, it is not known how many of these civil cases concerned real estate law and marital property law. Consequently, it is not possible to say whether such cases waxed or waned over time. However, there is indirect evidence suggesting that the law entailed complications for ordinary people and that both the local courts and common men and women were at a loss when it came to understanding many of the rules concerning lineage property. In particular, the stipulations about redemption of land and surrogate (both highly pertinent to the situation of married women) were looked upon as "convoluted and difficult to handle."[73] Due to these uncertainties, legal practice varied, and the outcome of a dispute was often unpredictable. Therefore, we have good reason to believe that legal complexity dampened some forms of litigation, notably those pertaining to real estate law and marital property law.

In order to illustrate these matters, let us assume that an eighteenth-century woman brought her inheritance of 100 *daler* into marriage. The couple then decided to use the capital to buy off the husband's siblings, that is, to redeem his family farm. The value of the farm subsequently increased (as it often did in the eighteenth century) and then the husband died. According to law, the widow would now be entitled to claim one-third of the common property (which could be considerably less than 100 *daler*, depending on how the assets had been used within the household), while the husband's heirs would take the whole farm. If the widow had brought her inheritance in the form of land instead, and if the land had been kept during marriage, she would have reaped the profit of increasing land values, which is likely to have been much more than 100 *daler*.[74] This interpretation of the law is based on the crucial tenet that land bought from a relative was subject to the same restrictions as inherited land, that is, that the spouse had no rights to it whatsoever, regardless of whether he or she had invested any money in it. But legal practice shows that, on this point, courts did not interpret the law consistently.

For instance, a woman had inherited a tenant farm owned by the Crown and allotted to the support of military forces (*kronorusthåll*).[75] She had then married, and when the option to buy the farm from the Crown became available, the couple decided to exercise it. Later, after the woman died, the husband became embroiled in a dispute with his stepson and son-in-law concerning whether he had any marital rights in the farm thus acquired by the spouses. The court of the first instance (*häradsrätten*) found that, since the wife had "allowed her husband to redeem the farm with her," he must be regarded as owner of two-thirds of it, the farm being "an acquired estate obtained during marriage." The court of the second instance (*lagmansrätten*) agreed with this verdict. By contrast, the court of the third instance (*hovrätten*) found that "the security of inheritance" must not disappear because of the expenditure "made simply for improvement" of the farm. In other words, the farm should be passed on to the next generation, not to the widower, but the heirs should compensate the father for some of his costs. For the most part the court of the last instance (*Kungl. Maj:t*) approved of the previous verdict.[76] It is very clear from this case that the two first courts weighed investments most heavily, whereas the two latter courts focused on lineage and kinship and even expressed some contempt for investments ("simply for improvement").

Thus, it seems as if courts of the first instance interpreted redeemed land as a form of acquired land, which in this case would have given the man two-thirds of the actual farm. By way of contrast, courts higher up in the judicial hierarchy routinely seem to have classified redeemed land as inherited. In a case from 1788 this pattern emerges very clearly. The husband had sold the farm he and his wife had bought from her parents without having first acquired her consent. The court of the first instance said that the farm had been acquired during marriage, and, therefore, two-thirds of it belonged to the husband. He was rebuked for not having asked his wife's permission to sell her one-third; however, since her share was so small, the court decided that she should accept money for it from the new owner. This verdict was approved by the court of the second instance. The court of the third instance argued that the wife had inherited one-quarter of the farm and that the husband had been unauthorized to sell that part without her permission. As for the remaining three-quarters, which the couple had redeemed from her sisters, the court argued that the sale of the husband's two-thirds could not be annulled. Apparently, like the two previous courts, the court of appeal this time regarded redeemed land as a form of acquired land and, consequently, as part of the common property. The court of the final instance ruled that one-third was inherited and two-thirds redeemed; consequently, the husband had no property rights whatsoever.[77] It is clear from the writings of contemporary legal experts, such as David Nehrman, that, like the higher courts, these experts classified redeemed land as a form of inherited land, since the special status of lineage property would otherwise soon founder.[78]

These two cases were complicated, although not at all as complicated as disputes of this type could get. They illustrate how difficult it must have been for the courts to make sense of the law and to balance the value of investments against rights based on lineage and kinship. Problems like these did appear in the seventeenth century too, but the fact that land values were rising in the eighteenth century made them even harder to solve. Two other cases (from Undersåker in northern Sweden) show that ordinary people may have shared the opinion expressed by the primary courts, that is, that redeemed land should be classified as acquired land.[79]

Gunnar Eriksson in Berge and his wife, Brita Andersdotter, lacked offspring and had decided to give their freehold farm to her nephew, Olof Kristensson, in return for a promise of "good behavior" and care and support in their old days. (If these conditions were not fulfilled, the spouses would rescind the agreement, or so they threatened.) Olof was exhorted to try to come to terms with the other heirs after the death of Gunnar and Brita, but if this should prove impossible, he could at least rest assured that he would be able to keep the part of the farm that had been "redeemed and otherwise acquired."[80] The language used here suggests that, to Gunnar and Brita, the term "redeemed land" was more or less synonymous with acquired land. In a similar way, the childless man Kristen Andersson in Överocke made a will for the benefit of his wife, Dordi, and his stepbrother, Anders Larsson, who were each to receive one-half of Kristen's farm. Kristen pointed out that his father had bought the farm long ago "from kinsmen" (*inom börd*), without anyone having as yet filed complaints against the acquisition. Therefore, his relatives had no right to question his will.[81] Kristen's argument was sophisticated. He seems to have meant that his relatives had given their tacit consent to the father's redemption of the land by not filing a complaint in due time. Therefore, they had forfeited their right to make any claims, and the land was now a form of acquired land. Of course, Kristen's intention may also have been simply to intimidate his kinsmen to accept the will.[82]

In the seventeenth century people who made mutual wills invariably mentioned that they had *not* inherited the property in question, but acquired it through their own exertions and "by the sweat of their brow." This gave them the right to use it as they liked, they maintained: even a man of such prominence as Axel Oxenstierna used this argument. It is now clear that in the eighteenth century the same form of reasoning informed ordinary people's ideas about redeemed land. They had not received their land as a mere consequence of belonging to a certain kin group but had had to invest their own money and labor in it. Therefore it was natural and equitable that they should have the right to use it as they preferred. This reasoning often meant that they wanted their spouses to have a share of the land. As such, this argument was not new, but it now acquired a new pertinence since land was so often redeemed at ever higher costs for the purchaser. It is not surprising that people like Gunnar, Brita, and Kristen are found employing this argument; nor is it in any way remarkable that the lower courts reasoned in a similar fashion. After all, the lay judges were ordinary peasants.

Yet, despite the obvious importance of this issue, there was no unambiguous legal definition of redeemed land in eighteenth-century Sweden. Depending on person and court, the outcome of a dispute could vary. This state of affairs cannot have encouraged people of either sex to file complaints, but it is possible that the weaker legal position of women made them particularly susceptible to these uncertainties. The legal intricacies are likely to have been too many and too incomprehensible for ordinary people to grasp.

In some cases the effects of real estate law could even be blatantly absurd. After 1734 a person who had received an inheritance in the form of personal property or money instead of land was required to compensate relatives if the latter were deprived of the opportunity to inherit. This stipulation (often referred to as a "surrogate") was very obscure. It was not at all clear if it applied only when the person concerned wanted to write a will for the benefit of someone outside the kin group, or if it also applied when the person concerned had sold inherited land during his or her lifetime.[83] In any case the rule was rather strange. Instead of offering support to persons who had been unfortunate enough *not* to receive land, or whose land was sold during their lifetime (for example, married women), the law imposed special restrictions and duties upon these persons. The subsequent example illustrates what the implications could be.

Olof Eriksson had received his inheritance in the form of money from his brother Mårten in Edsåsen; in total, he had been given 38 *daler* silver. Olof then became seriously ill, and he drew up a will for the benefit of his wife, Kerstin Persdotter, giving his property to her as a compensation for the care she had bestowed upon him during his illness. Olof also implored his brother to respect the will, and Mårten had answered, according to one witness, that his sister-in-law deserved "one hundred thousand times more" and that he was only glad that she nursed his brother. However, after Olof died, Mårten disputed the will. Referring to what the legal code said about how an owner could not make a will before he had restored his inherited money to his kinsmen, Mårten refused to accept the will. When asked about the comforting words to his dying brother, Mårten answered that he had not wanted to worry his ailing brother, but he would never abstain from claiming his right to "the land money which his brother did not have the authority to will away." The court admitted that, according to the law, the money Olof had received did retain the quality of inherited land. (So, in principle, Mårten was right.) However, the court continued, the estate included so little wealth that there was no way to compensate the widow for her faithful services other than to let her keep what she had received. Should anything be left after her death, though, that property must be returned to Mårten.[84] The court clearly regarded Mårten's claims as inequitable, albeit lawful, and they found a way of circumventing them.[85]

This case may have been unusual, but it was strictly in accordance with the new legal code. It makes very clear the power with which kinsmen were still endowed. In reality, Olof's "inheritance" was little more than a small allowance with which he could, perhaps, support himself, but he was not allowed to decide what should happen to it after his death. In principle, everything that remained in his estate should revert to his heirs, that is, to his brother. The parish of Rystad shows a similar case. When Maja Nilsdotter was widowed in 1805 at the age of forty, her brother-in-law turned up at the meeting with the assessors, informing the latter that his dead brother (who had been a crofter) had contributed more than 166 *riksdaler* of estate money to the household. Since this money came from the family farm in Västra Torp, the brother now claimed a surrogate on behalf of his nephew and niece. But since the estate turned out to be severely debt ridden (which would also affect the children), the brother relinquished his claim. He and the widow managed to reach an amicable solution.[86]

Within the lower social strata, people obviously had to use their inherited means to buy food or to buy care in their old age. With its stipulation about how people had to provide a surrogate for lost estate money, the new legal code created bewilderment as to whether one could really use inherited money to cover daily needs without being liable afterward to pay one's relatives. Moreover, it is clear from both court practice and learned jurisprudence that the concept "surrogate" was used in two different ways.[87] It was one thing to say that a widow must be given a surrogate for the property she had contributed to the household. In this case, the surrogate was given to her as a compensation for what she had done for the household and for the improvement of the other spouse's family farm. It was quite another thing to argue that a household must repay estate money to the lineage from which the money had originally come, even in cases where the family had hardly anything to live on. The latter application of the law could clearly have absurd effects, but these must have been unforeseen, indeed entirely inconceivable, to the men who created the legal code of 1734.

Thus, real estate law was highly confusing.[88] There is every reason to believe that not only peasants and crofters but also judges and lawyers had considerable difficulties understanding how the law should be interpreted and, by extension, what one was allowed to do with one's property. It is likely that some people took advantage of the situation (like Olof Eriksson's brother). Moreover, it is the obscure character of eighteenth-century real estate law and marital law that explains why previous historiography has provided so little insight into the developments in this period.[89] It *is* very difficult to disentangle how various interpretations of law and various practices of compensation interacted and what the effects were on women in general. That these matters are often surrounded by silence in the sources does not help to make the picture more lucid. In the latter half of the eighteenth century, however, a shift in women's property rights and an attendant increased risk of poverty brought these issues to the public interest, clearly indicating a problem in need of solution.

Women and Proletarianization

Many varying forms of evidence suggest that the legal protection of married women's separate property started to wither away in the course of the eighteenth century, partly as a consequence of the abolition of the kin veto in 1734 and partly as a result of increasing commercialization in society. Thus, women's risk of *losing* inherited land during their lifetime grew more serious in this period. What happened then to their chances of *receiving* land through inheritance? The answers to these two questions will illuminate the still incompletely understood process of proletarianization, which affected both men and women. Still, the emphasis on women is justified due to their particularly precarious situation in the period, caused by the fact that their inheritance shares were smaller than those of men and because they were not acknowledged as legal actors in their own right unless they were widows.

The eighteenth century witnessed marked changes in Swedish demographics. After a century when a substantial part of the young male population had been quite literally eradicated as a consequence of the many wars, the sex ratio was at its most extreme around 1720 (table 5). With the return of peace, however, it gradually became more balanced again.[90] As a consequence, rural women's chances of getting married must have improved after 1720. However, there were considerable differences with respect to social estate. Women from the higher echelons of society seem to have found it increasingly difficult to find a suitable spouse. Some noble women resorted to marrying below their own rank, while many remained unmarried. The situation was particularly difficult for daughters of noblemen who did not own land but who supported themselves as civil servants.[91] Widows also became more numerous and, after 1800, older. This was one effect of lower mortality: men died later in life and women were older when widowed, which made them less prone to remarry.

These facts are of obvious importance to women's inheritance rights and to their economic situation in general. When more young men stayed alive and remained at home, daughters' chances of taking over the family farm must have been adversely affected. Even though studies of eighteenth- and nineteenth-century inheritance practices are not numerous, the ones that do exist show that men were consistently favored when it came to identifying successors to the old farmers.[92] For instance, Sofia Holmlund has shown how daughters seldom took over responsibility for the family farm in nineteenth-century Uppland (north of Stockholm), unless there were no brothers at all. She also shows that, for a woman to inherit a farm, being married was close to being a prerequisite.[93] Thus, more women married but their chances of inheriting land probably declined. Women from noble families found it particularly difficult to locate a spouse. Generally, more women lived as widows. Taken together, these trends suggest that, unless women could support themselves through waged work, many of them lived in a precarious economic situation. To the extent that they were affected by the new domesticity ideal (against which Anna Maria Rückerschöld was railing in the 1770s),[94] waged work was perhaps not the ideal solution. In brief, there was a need for some kind of reform.

These matters would come to the fore in the early nineteenth century, as will be shown in chapter 6, but, as early as the middle of the eighteenth century, the new sociodemographic situation was sufficiently obvious to cause concern and disquiet. In fact several men with access to the medium of print used their influence to direct public attention to the economic situation of women and argued for reform. Even if their descriptions cannot be accepted as objective, disinterested statements, it would still be a serious mistake to entirely disregard them. Just as in the case of the member of the law commission, Leijonmarck, the fact that they devoted attention to the matter suggests that there was a more common concern with the lot of women at the time.

One proposal on this theme was presented to the Diet in 1786. Jon

Bengtsson, a member of the peasants' estate from Kronoberg, argued that the nation would be much invigorated if all children could continue to receive their shares of the parental property. With the investment of labor, all small farms would flourish, Jon Bengtsson maintained. In this way, many children would be born, and the Swedish population would increase. Jon Bengtsson linked population increase to property rights, and particularly to women's property rights. His words about how all children should *continue* to receive their land shares is particularly telling, since it displays a concern with the discontinuance of a legal practice of which he approved: that rural women inherited land.[95]

Jon Bengtsson was clearly speaking from the point of view of the small peasant freeholder, advocating widespread but small-scale ownership. That he came from Kronoberg, where women's property rights were stronger than elsewhere, is also important to keep in mind. Another man who was engaged with the question was Eric Schagerborg. Writing in 1765 and also addressing himself to the Diet, Schagerborg's main concern was with what he perceived as growing celibacy among young women of good parentage. As a remedy he proposed to set up a state-financed fund to support young women who lacked the means to get married. Aware of the fact that members of the Diet abhorred everything that might increase the tax burden upon citizens, Schagerborg formulated his case very carefully. First of all, he pointed out, the state already accepted responsibility for the "worthy poor" — those who could not be blamed for their poverty, such as orphans and widows. Secondly and more importantly, the Swedish population was too small, and it would remain so, as long as young women were unable to get married. Instead, these women would choose to emigrate. During his travels abroad Schagerborg had encountered many Swedish women supporting themselves in various ways. Even though they had been brought up in Sweden at the cost of Swedish society, these women did not contribute to the wealth of their native country in the final account. The implicit argument was that, from an economic point of view, the investment was of no avail unless the young women married and had children in Sweden.[96]

It is clear that the only women who may have found it difficult to locate a husband were those from the highest social strata. Therefore, Schagerborg's implicit description of these as the "worthy poor" is ludicrous, and his obsession with marriage rates seems misplaced in a situation where more women could actually marry. But like Jon Bengtsson, Schagerborg may have sensed that something was happening, that it was difficult for women to inherit land or to make ends meet at all.

TABLE 7. Children's claims to inheritance after death of their parent(s) in a sample of eighteenth-century Swedish courts

Place	Time	Population size (1751)	Total number	Female claims	Male claims	Several claims
Central Sweden						
Vendel	1736–37	1,963	5	4	1	0
Stora Tuna	1741–45	6,000	19	8	7	4
Northern Sweden						
Undersåker	1750–64	1,583	4	3	1	0

Sources: *Vendels 1736–37*; Kopparbergs läns häradsrättsarkiv, Domböcker för Stora Tuna 1741–45, Uppsala landsarkiv; Jämtlands läns häradsrättsarkiv, Domböcker för Undersåker 1750–64, Östersunds landsarkiv.

Indeed, his words about women "who lacked the means to get married" are noteworthy in a country where women's rights of inheritance were actually very strong according to the legal code.

Nor was the legal code a dead letter. Court records from various parts of the country convey a strong impression of a judiciary that sought to uphold and protect men's and women's inheritance rights (table 7).[97] Two examples are of particular interest in this respect. In 1741 Per Persson Larf sued his neighbor, Erik Ersson, claiming that Erik had purchased land from Per's sister, Kerstin, who was "feebleminded" (and therefore unable to make commercial deals). The court, however, allowed Kerstin to give testimony. She told the court that her brother withheld her part of the landed property from her, that he had not paid her for the time he had used her farmland, and that he was so careless with his own farmland that he could not even support his own family, much less his sister. For these reasons, she had made a deal with Erik instead, and she did not want to have their agreement annulled.[98] Judging by this testimony, Kerstin does not appear to have been feebleminded at all. In fact, her decision to find another person who could manage her lands seems a highly rational thing to have done. This must also have been what the court concluded. Instead of annulling the agreement between Kerstin and Erik, they appointed two men to investigate how the brother had managed his sister's inherited property. Since Kerstin was an unmarried and, allegedly, feebleminded woman who depended on her brother for her economic well-being, the court took special care to make sure that her inheritance was safe.

Courts were not the only ones who acted in the interest of unmarried women. In 1751 the guardians of Ingrid Månsdotter sued her two brothers-in-law, claiming her part of the parental property. The brothers-in-law argued that, since Ingrid was feebleminded and guilty of fornication, it would be difficult to marry her off and, what was more, she would not be able to serve as the matron of a household. Hearing this evidence, the court emphasized that Ingrid's rights of inheritance were just as strong as those of her two sisters. It was therefore decided to investigate whether the farm could be divided and, if so, into how many parts. In the end the parties reached an amicable solution, which the court endorsed, whereby the two sisters were given two other farms and Ingrid 600 silver *daler* and some clothing.[99]

Both of these cases illustrate that courts and guardians continued to take inheritance rights very seriously and that they regarded sex, civil status, mental health, and crime as irrelevant to the question of whether a person's inheritance should be legally protected or not. This was entirely in accordance with the legal code, which stipulated that all children of legitimate birth were entitled to have their inheritance. There were some restrictions with regard to what form the inheritance should take that were laid down in statutory law,[100] but apart from that, the judiciary seems to have paid close attention to everybody's right to inherit.[101]

However, the attitude displayed by courts was only one part of the problem. There was always the possibility that those who had enough courage to go to court or who had spokesmen who took their cases to court (which makes them visible to the historians) were a lucky but small minority. The more interesting, but also the more difficult, question is what happened to all the others. To what extent were *parents* (as opposed to courts) anxious to respect all children's rights to their shares? To what extent did they want all children to have land? On the one hand, it seems reasonable to assume that parents love all their children and want to make their lives as materially good as possible. This is one important conclusion in Amy L. Erickson's research, and the point has also been made for Sweden.[102] On the other hand, there is a mass of evidence that land is a very particular sort of economic commodity, that people in agrarian societies are guided by a desire to safeguard the future viability and security of their farms, and that these people will not jeopardize land in the interest of gender equality. In short, parents in agrarian societies have a strong interest in keeping the land "within their overall purview" and that includes what happens to land after their own death. Whether these interests can be smoothly reconciled with the interests of providing equally for all children will depend on a number of circumstances. Naturally, the extent to which parents have *both* land *and* other valuable assets is important for the outcome.

Schagerborg, Jon Bengtsson, and other men engaged in this question[103] suggested that in some circles young women were economically less well off in the middle of the eighteenth century. Even if their analyses may not have been correct in all details, it is hard to escape the impression that they had noticed crucial trends both within the nobility and, more importantly, within the peasantry. In some cases, young women received property other than land, while in other cases they received hardly anything at all. In still other cases, young women received small plots of land, while their brothers took over the family farm. Sometimes the plot of land could be sold, sometimes it could be used to set up a small cottage on the outskirts of the hamlet. In both cases, the distance between those who retained the family farms and those who did not probably grew. Gradually, a cleavage appeared within the peasant estate, manifesting itself in a new social terminology: crofters, cottagers, day laborers, and old widows.

While the number of persons who could call themselves freeholders slowly rose during the eighteenth century as a consequence of the decision to sell off Crown land, freehold land nevertheless ceased to be the most central form of property for many people. More importantly, among those who did hold freehold land, a declining minority had received it through inheritance. An increasing number of people bought land on the market from nonrelatives, from the state, or from kinsmen under market-like conditions. As has been seen, women were probably even less likely than men to inherit land. Consequently, the number of women who held inherited land around 1800 can be approximated as quite low. A maximum (and highly unlikely)[104] estimate is that 25 percent of all women held inherited land, while a minimum estimate is 5 percent (table 8). A more reasonable approximation is that between 10 and 15 percent of all married women had inherited land,[105] a figure that conforms well to the shares found in Rystad and Estuna.[106] The residual 85 to 90 percent co-owned acquired land with their husbands, held personal property only, or had no property at all. It is impossible to gauge the relative sizes of the latter three groups.

What these figures definitely do show, however, is that by the turn of the nineteenth century inherited land meant very little to most women — or to many men, for that matter. The long-term societal processes leading up to this situation are obvious. The proletarianization process made landholding less common in society at large (affecting men and women), and the increasingly balanced sex ratios made men

TABLE 8. Approximate number of adult women who had inherited
land, in proportion to whole adult female population

	1620	1718	1800
Maximum number	98,578 (31%)	168,477 (30%)	212,000 (25%)
Minimum number	19,716 (6%)	67,390 (12%)	42,400 (5%)

Sources: For 1620 and 1718, Professor Jan Lindegren's population model (Uppsala University);
for 1800, contemporary statistics (printed in *Emigrationsutredningen* IX).

Assumptions: (i) that the maximum number of adult women who had inherited land was 100
percent of all adult women in the landholding part of the population (see also table 5); (ii) that
the minimum number of adult women who had inherited land was higher in 1718 than in 1620
and 1800 because of the skewed sex ratios following the war period (see table 5); the minimum
number has been calculated as 40 percent in 1718 and as 20 percent in 1620 and 1800. See also
Holmlund, *Jorden vi ärvde*, 85, who found that in 18 percent of all cases a daughter inherited the
farm (between 1810 and 1845).

more likely heirs to farms. Despite strong rights of inheritance and, as
far as we know, a conscientious judiciary, the connection between landholding and the female sex was becoming tenuous.

While men such as Eric Schagerborg feared that young women
would be affected by these developments in the sense that they would
remain unmarried, it is actually more likely that widowed women were
the most vulnerable. Those who lacked inherited land upon the demise
of their husbands (either because they had not inherited any or because
it had been lost during marriage) would only receive the legally required
forms of property: one-third of the common estate (the marital rights),
the morning gift (which varied in size), and some smaller items (*fördel*,
5 percent of the net value of the deceased's estate). When Kerstin
Olofsdotter was widowed in 1794, the net value of the deceased's estate
was 208 *riksdaler*. Of this, Kerstin received approximately eighty-two
riksdaler: sixty-six represented the marital rights, six the morning gift,
and ten the *fördel*.[107]

Consequently, to women who lacked inherited land, the marital
rights were of utmost importance. If only reasonably generous, the marital rights could make the whole difference between a dignified life and
a life in poverty. Women could use these rights in their old age, selling
their entitlement to land to someone else in return for a promise of care
and support until death. Because of the marital rights, wives of previous
Crown tenants who had become freeholders had a much better legal
and economic situation than did a farmer's daughter who had received
some estate money but had subsequently been forced to consume it
during marriage to a crofter or a laborer. Even if the marital rights were

worth less to a crofter's wife, in monetary terms, it was very important to her as well. To claim that the marital rights had gradually become the most important asset for many married women is not to overstate the case. Indeed, from a statistical point of view, it was more important at this time than both the inheritance right and the right to hold land separately during marriage.

The size of the men's marital rights, which was twice as large as the women's, is likely to have appeared more inequitable within those social strata where so much depended on these rights than it did among landowners with inherited wealth. Every time a married person died, the importance of gender became apparent. A widower would retain a larger share of the estate, thanks to his marital rights, than a widow could. Therefore, his chances of keeping the household intact as a unit of production and consumption were better. To men as well as to women, these realities were probably both obvious and disquieting. Moreover, that widows were overrepresented among the poor in the nineteenth century served as tangible evidence of the insufficient economic provisions for women.[108] To all those who did not inherit land, reformed marital rights must have seemed more desirable than anything else. Against this backdrop, the king's decision to follow Leijonmarck's advice in 1807 deserves to be labeled as in some sense enlightened. Recognizing a social and economic problem, the new law shifted its focus from lineage property to the more flexible forms of ownership that many spouses wanted and that were more easily accommodated with a market-oriented society.

Conclusions

Prior to 1734 a woman's natal family had been able to exert control over the land that she had taken with her into marriage, most of all through the right to veto sales by the son-in-law. This possibility may not have been used very often within the peasantry, perhaps because peasant households did not often experience the need to sell the wife's lands to somebody outside the kin group. Still, the right to veto was there, vesting women's relatives with considerable influence, if they wanted to use it, and no doubt affecting husbands' actions. After 1734 by contrast, the right to veto sales was gone, precisely at a time when we have very good reason to believe that peasant households would be increasingly prone to sell the wife's lands. The vitalized land market and the enclosure movement both tended to make separate land holdings for wives appear to be awkward, dysfunctional, and, above all, unnecessarily costly. It is something of a paradox that, as long as the stipulation about relatives'

Female beggar. Drawing by Elias Martin.
(Nationalmuseum, Stockholm, Sweden)

consent was there, it was rarely needed, whereas, when it was needed, it was no longer there.

If the methods rural households used to handle the new situation are placed in focus, it is clear that many people developed strategies that must be understood as compensatory. These methods aimed at increasing the economic security of individual women, while at the same time restoring some of the influence landholding families used to have over their married daughters' property. This was most pertinent in the case of land that husbands had redeemed from their relatives, since married women had no legal rights to such land, not even if their inherited means had made the redemption possible. In this case the law of 1734 actually condoned the swallowing of the woman's inheritance, as it were, by the husband's lineage property. Another way of expressing this metaphorically is to say that the law allowed economic value to "leak" from one lineage to another. This is all the more conspicuous since precisely at this time, the legal code had introduced new and convoluted methods of making sure that no leakage took place, through its injunctions concerning how those who received their inheritance in the form of money had to pay a "surrogate" to their kinsmen.

Married women (and, by extension, their children) were compensated in various ways. Their contributions of property to the marital estate could be acknowledged in wills or in probate inventories, and they could benefit from the increasingly formalized retirement contracts that were set up in the eighteenth century. Such arrangements could also benefit men, but they were definitely more commonly used for the sake of women. Sometimes, the arrangements were instigated by the husbands, whereas in other cases, the woman's kinsmen were probably instrumental. When probate inventories were set up, kinsmen would be there to protect the woman's rights, but indirectly they were also protecting their own rights. If the woman received compensation for lost estate money, that compensation might come back to the kin group in one form or another, but if compensation was never granted, the economic value could not be retrieved, as it was definitively incorporated into the other family's land. Thus, that families were deprived of their traditional means of controlling women's property did not in itself affect women's chances of inheriting land, because many families invented new ones.

By way of contrast, shifting sex ratios and an incipient process of proletarianization definitely had an impact on how the inheritance system worked. As 1800 approached, it became increasingly clear to many observers that women's chances of inheriting entire farms were diminishing, both because more men survived than in the previous century and because an increasing share of the population had to support itself as rural laborers or outside the agrarian sector. The fate of women's inherited money serves as an example that gives sharper contours to the process of proletarianization than what previous research has been able to do. If the estate money inherited by daughters could not be retrieved and restored in any of the ways described above, for the simple reason that it had been consumed by the household, this meant that the daughter and her offspring were no longer members of the landholding class. The unwillingness of farmers to split up farmland among many heirs or their interest in retrieving the surrogate for themselves may be viewed as expressions of a growing cultural distance within families or, at least, within kin groups. In the early nineteenth century, these tendencies translated into left-wing reproaches against the wealthy for dissociating themselves from the laboring classes.[109]

In the first half of the nineteenth century, then, many Swedish women were likely to have been more dependent upon individual arrangements made for them by other people or upon their one-third of the common marital estate than upon their rights of inheritance. This was the upshot of a century of increasing commercialization and social stratification, which had left a large share of the population as either middle-class citizens or landless rural workers. English research has also shown the growing importance of individual arrangements, where the propensity of husbands to draw up wills for their wives has been seen as of great consequence to widows. English research has also demonstrated how individual arrangements (jointures or trusts) were gradually substituted for the wife's legally regulated right to dower (set at one-third of the husband's estate). Jointures and trusts had many advantages for women: for example, trusts counted as debts and were therefore given priority before claims to inheritance. Still, they were not given to all women, as a universal gift of law (like dower was), but depended upon decisions that had to be taken by individual men. In a different but at the same time similar way, Swedish eighteenth- and nineteenth-century women were increasingly dependent upon men to make wills for their benefit, or for men to acknowledge in writing the contribution their wives had made. There were always women for whom no such arrangements or acknowledgements were made.

Women's property rights were crucial components of what was to be known as "the social question" in the first half of the nineteenth century. They played a central role in political debate for a period of thirty years. Yet social problems, however burning, do not translate automatically into politics or policies. They must be perceived as problems and be put on the political agenda. How did this happen? In this context, it is important to note that Ulrica Helena Funck (whom we met at the beginning of this chapter) not only appealed to the Svea Hovrätt to seek redress for her daughter's grievances. She also published her plea, making it accessible to the reading public. In this way, she exposed the evil deeds of her son-in-law to the judgment of public opinion. As the following chapter will show, intelligent uses of the public sphere provide a clue to the process of politicization.

BANKRUPTCY & THE EMERGENCE
OF A NEW PUBLIC SPHERE

A small publication circulated in the taverns and coffeehouses of Stockholm in 1765. To those who were interested, the publication told the story of the disputed will of the late Gotthard Hildebrand. Being childless, Hildebrand had drawn up the will for the benefit of his alleged wife, Magdalena De Wallé, but his relatives disapproved of the arrangement and sued the widow, claiming a surrogate and suggesting that she was not really the lawful wife of their dead kinsman. Magdalena admitted that their marriage had not been confirmed through an ecclesiastical ceremony, but she still maintained that she and Hildebrand had regarded each other as husband and wife and that mutual consent is what makes a marriage valid. The relatives resorted to stronger tactics. They produced the written testimony of a former servant of Hildebrand, who had traveled with his master to Venice. There they had taken lodgings with a man by the name of Battista Bosetti, who ran a barbershop and had three daughters. The two elder ones each had an "amoroso," whereas the youngest, whose name was Magdalena, had none. She presently started visiting Hildebrand's lodgings, telling the servant that she would very much like to become his master's "amorosa." In the end, the servant claimed, Magdalena left Venice dressed in men's clothes, and he was later to encounter her in the house of his master in Stockholm. She now called herself Magdalena De Wallé.[1]

There was little that was unusual about this case. As has been seen above, these wills made by one spouse for the benefit of the other often caused protests from relatives, who claimed that the will was illegal. In cases involving wills the spouses invariably stressed their mutual love, and relatives attempted to refute this argument by showing that the surviving spouse had been quarrelsome, lazy, and, in general, unworthy of any special favors from their dead relative. Gotthard Hildebrand's relatives may have applied particularly underhanded means, using the story of the servant to insinuate that Magdalena was a fortune hunter and, perhaps, not entirely respectable. The meeting at the barbershop and the flight in borrowed clothes were both intended to cast doubt upon her honor. These relatives were working, however, within a well-established genre.

What was new was the way in which a case involving a woman of lowly origins was made into a public matter. First, the case was referred to the Diet, where the will was approved.[2] It was not unusual for noblewomen to petition the Diet for help; for example, this was what a Miss Stenbock did in 1734, when she found out that her guardian had dissipated her paternal inheritance through debts.[3] But ordinary women were normally confined to using only the primary courts and, possibly, the courts of appeal. Second, and more importantly, when the legal documents were printed, the case was also "referred" to public opinion. It was exposed to everyone who could read or, more correctly, to all those who knew someone who could read to them. Magdalena used this opportunity to try to enlist public support and to influence its view of what was true. She had been "tenderly moved," she said, when she realized how many "demeaning circumstances" had been brought to the attention of the public. Having the legal documents published was a way for her to correct the impression created by the opposite party and to state her side of the dispute.

Magdalena De Wallé's recourse was not unique. In the eighteenth century, and particularly in the period 1765 to 1775, hundreds of legal cases were brought to public attention as a consequence of somebody's decision to have his or her legal documents published.[4] It became something of a fashion to have one's dirty linen washed in public. But, as will be seen, people had rational grounds for doing this. Even if many of these cases simply air sordid domestic disputes, they are nevertheless an important part of the story of women and property rights in Sweden. First, they show how the topic was gradually politicized, in the sense that private and political issues merged in the small publications and in the debates they caused. The publications built a bridge to the major parliamentary debates about property rights that erupted in the early nineteenth century. Second, they clarify how the debate was democratized, allowing a broader spectrum of the population to take part and even giving women a public voice. In the late seventeenth century, only statesmen and highly placed lawyers could have a say as to how property law should work, but now almost anyone could present his or her grievances, some of which did have wider implications. Finally, these cases illustrate how complex and paradoxical the subject of women's property rights was. Precisely at the time when in some senses spouses' property arrangements were coming to be more private than ever before, these documents turned some property arrangements into intensely public affairs, challenging again the idea that family matters ought to remain domestic secrets.

Freedom and Publicity

The publication of legal documents started in the period 1718 to 1772, an era commonly known as the "Age of Liberty" in Swedish history. The term suggests that absolutism and autocracy had come to an end with the death of Karl XII and that the Diet of the four estates was now free to rule the country according to its own precepts. Since the early seventeenth century, the Diet had been in charge of taxation (sometimes referred to as "the immemorial right of Swedes to tax themselves"), and, to some extent, legislation. The Diet's powers came to be substantially increased at the cost of the monarch and his government. Political life was vitalized with the emergence of rudimentary "political parties."[5] This new political life also entailed a new form of social life. During the protracted sessions of the Diet members of the different estates had to stay in Stockholm, where they started meeting each other at coffee-houses and in wine cellars. Old allegiances to one's estate or to one's constituency withered away as members were instead united by common interests and political goals.[6] In this atmosphere even ordinary Swedes started taking part in public debates about freedom or more mundane matters.

Emphasizing freedom was not something entirely new, however. Freedom had been an important part of the Swedish identity in the absolutist era as well. Ever since the days of Gustaf I, Swedes were taught that they had been freed from the yoke of the Danes and that they should be grateful to the kings for this freedom. What was more, freedom was also a crucial component of what it meant to be a Protestant. Protestants lived in the freedom given by God, the church taught, and while they were certainly subject to man-made laws, Protestant rhetoric nevertheless insisted that Catholics were the ones who were bound by artificial rules.[7] Yet, there was something decisively different about the way in which the concept of freedom operated in the eighteenth century. It was combined with a great appreciation of openness, suggesting that if all information is openly available and if everybody is free to use that information, everybody will then understand what the truth is and society will benefit from this truth. This complex of ideas was by no means straightforward or uncontested. It is only necessary to consider that some state issues were regarded as too important and too delicate for the peasant estate to know anything about and that these matters were thus referred to the special secret committee of the Diet (*sekreta utskottet*) — much to the annoyance of peasants, of course. Still, the ideal of openness did play a very important role in society in general,[8] including in the field of law.

An illuminating example is provided by the new pietistic religious movements, which stressed that each individual must read and contemplate the Bible on his or her own. Only in this way would the soul arrive at a true understanding of the message of God. This idea was expressed in an especially radical form by the Moravian brothers, who inspired the vicar Anders Rutström in Stockholm to argue that man becomes righteous through faith alone and that interpretations and instructions by the clergy are of little consequence. Because of his political affiliations, Rutström was embroiled in a number of legal disputes, and his theological ideas made him even more suspect. His antiauthoritarian standpoint made him unpopular within the clergy and caused him to be accused of heresy.

Rutström's case caused an anonymous author to publish a booklet, the professed objective of which was to provide the public with all relevant information so that it could reach an independent conclusion as to whether or not Rutström was guilty of the charges leveled against him. Rumors were circulating about him, the author said, but "if only this case can be scrutinized by many, then the public will be able to question these rumors." The author went on to argue that "one of the most urgent buttresses" of a well-functioning society was complete enlightenment about the nature of all legal cases. He was a firm believer in the idea that everybody would realize the truth, the *same* truth, if they only had access to the relevant documents. But here, the author expressed an interesting ambiguity. When he wrote that "every soul, who wants to be blessed, must search the writings[9] himself, thus acquiring certainty, without listening to the interpretations of the teachers," he was clearly talking about Rutström's theology, the "writings" referring to the Bible as a vessel of truth. But in view of what he had said previously, the sentence could also be understood to be about the legal documents in Rutström's case. The same idea (the importance of openness and the belief in people's capacity to draw conclusions) was expressed both within a religious and a secular discourse.[10]

If only people could have access to the word given by God or pronounced by a court, they would also be able to draw their own conclusions about the truth. The problem was, of course, that people could draw *different* conclusions, depending on whose version they were reading. People could also read newspapers or hear rumors circulating in the streets. If they listened to what Gotthard Hildebrand's relatives said, they would reach a different conclusion than they would if they paid attention to what Magdalena De Wallé claimed to be true.

This created a highly competitive situation where many people had a strong interest in spreading their versions of the truth and canvassing support for their cases. This was the reason why they wanted to have their legal documents published, because, ultimately, what other people believed to be true was important. This was also the reason why many published documents included explicit appeals to the public.[11] Inserted in headings, in preambles, or in footnotes added to the text, whose main content was simply a copy of the court records, was an abundance of appeals and addresses to the public. People addressed themselves to "the public" or to "the honorable public," they exposed their grievances to "the eyes of the public," they presented facts "to the enlightenment of the public," or they appealed to "the court of public opinion." Magdalena De Wallé was far from alone in wanting to clear herself in the eyes of the public, and Rutström's defender was not the only one to express confidence in the public's ability to see what was right. Nor was this phenomenon unique to Sweden; in France, for example, it was also apparent.[12]

What made this publishing activity possible was access to printers. During the eighteenth century, some sixty printing houses were at work in Stockholm, although not all at the same time. Smaller cities and towns had fewer, with Gothenburg boasting eleven, Linköping ten, and Uppsala seven. But even in very small towns with only one printing house (like Hälsingborg, Härnösand, Karlshamn, Mariefred, Turku, and Vasa), this type of legal document was published and distributed.[13] Thus, publishing was not limited to the capital but was a more widespread phenomenon; still, there is no denying that the majority of these documents were printed in Stockholm. Often, one case resulted in several publications, as the parties started quarrelling in print; it was not uncommon for these protracted disputes to start with a publication printed in a provincial town but to end with publications printed in the capital. This may say something about how the population and the government offices in Stockholm were, after all, regarded as the most important audience to address.

Publishing also presupposes that printing is legal, which cannot be taken for granted in the early modern world. In England and France the fad to publish one's legal cases had started already in the late seventeenth century. In Sweden, it had been declared legal for parties to print their own legal documents in 1735, but these documents were subject to censorship. From 1766 onward Sweden had almost complete freedom of the press, and all legal documents could be published without prior censorship.[14] When Gustav III reintroduced autocracy in 1772, he put a temporary stop to this freedom, which is reflected in the decline in publishing activity in the 1780s, but it increased again in the early part of the nineteenth century.[15]

The print medium and the freedom to print were thus important prerequisites of the recourse to publicity that is found in the eighteenth and early nineteenth centuries. However, the technical and legal possibilities to make one's case known to the public do not suffice to explain why many people seized this opportunity so avidly. There was something else that accounted for the keen desire to clear oneself and to defend one's honor in front of the public, and that was credit legislation in general and bankruptcy law in particular.

Bankruptcy Law

Credit was a matter of deep public concern in the eighteenth century. The national debt was a much-debated issue in the Diet in the 1760s,[16] and the question of private debt was under almost constant scrutiny in the press. Some contemporary observers convey the impression that the country abounded in squanderers and profligates and that they even held a privileged position. The young nobleman Axel Reuterholm wrote in his diary that it was utterly wrong for an indebted nobleman to be temporarily protected against his creditors' claims just because the Diet had convened. "It is unfair that a profligate shall be allowed to . . . wriggle out of the claims of his creditors by merely flaunting a certificate saying that he has to go to Stockholm," Reuterholm wrote in 1738.[17] Statutory law often mentioned the problem of debtors going abroad to escape from their creditors and tried to find ways of preventing this.[18] In 1772 the situation was particularly bad: it was said that bankruptcies had of late "flooded the country."[19]

Like freedom of the press, credit was accorded a fundamental role in a free society in eighteenth-century Sweden. Free nations, it was argued in 1772, had always taken care to protect credit as being "a buttress of freedom." Credit was the fountain of wealth upon which freedom depended, and, therefore, credit should be "a sanctuary to the people." The best constitution and the best laws were of little avail in a country based on weak finances and "abounding in private debt." If foreign creditors discovered that they could not recover their money from Swedish debtors, Sweden's international reputation would be seriously damaged. What was more, if men working as civil servants were found to be notorious for their bankruptcies, the Swedish public would be filled with disgust. Consequently, for both international and domestic reasons it was necessary to create bankruptcy legislation that made the situation of creditors and debtors more secure, while at the same time giving stability to the Swedish constitution. After all, what was it that had prevented the total extinction of the Swedes after Karl XII's fatal defeat and subsequent death in 1718? It was the fact that credit and honor had remained intact among ordinary men.[20]

Late seventeenth-century lawyers had not been unaware of the need for bankruptcy legislation. They used the Roman legal term *cessio bonorum* in legal practice, and bankruptcy was also mentioned, although very briefly, in some statutory law.[21] Still, bankruptcy remained largely unregulated, and this was true even in the legal code of 1734. The section of the code dealing with matters of trade included a chapter on "how a debtor may all at once cede his goods to his creditor,"[22] but it was concise and obviously insufficient, as constant complaints and the incessant proposal of new statutory laws show. For example, the legal code said little about what rights one spouse might have to claim separation of property in the event of the insolvency of the other spouse, which was a crucial issue if a married man went bankrupt. The first more elaborate Swedish bankruptcy act (which included the regulation of separation of property) was not passed until 1767 and was later amended three times.[23] A completely new bankruptcy act was introduced in 1818, which was amended in 1830.[24] The intense legislative activity in the field indicates the continuing and growing importance of credit in Swedish society.[25]

Bankruptcy was defined as the possibility to cede one's entire property to creditors in an ordered manner in return for which the slate was wiped clean. It offered the opportunity of a new start in life, with one's good name intact, and appears to have been available to most men.[26] Consequently, being granted an honorable bankruptcy was seen as a great privilege or, in Latin, as *beneficium cessionis bonorum*. The privilege presupposed, however, that the debtor acted entirely honorably and that he cooperated with the judge in charge of the case, with the creditors, and with the executors they had appointed. He was required to stay at home and always to be prepared to answer any questions they might have. By way of contrast, debtors who tried to defraud their creditors could not hope for lenient treatment or an honorable bankruptcy. Judging by bankruptcy law's detailed enumerations of ways in which a debtor could deceive his creditors, there was no end to debtors' inventiveness in this respect. They could conceal assets or neglect to have the entire estate properly inventoried. They could make fictive sales of property or manipulate their bookkeeping. They could act in collusion with their wives or with some of their creditors in order to deceive the others. Failing any other option, they could simply flee, which — according to statutory law — was not an uncommon solution.[27]

To prevent such misdemeanors, bankruptcy law emphasized two things more than anything else: speed and openness. The debtor's assets had to be inventoried without delay, the law consulted, and all debts had to be ascertained as soon as possible, so that the case could be resolved quickly. It was primarily in the interest of the creditors that the case not be unduly drawn out, as they were the ones who suffered, since they had to wait for their money. In order to assert their rights, they had to act speedily and vigilantly. A creditor who failed to report his claims before the stipulated deadline had forfeited them.[28] Thus, while still very preoccupied with improving the position of creditors, the law expected a special sort of behavior from them. "The law [only] assists those who are awake" was a frequently repeated expression at the time.

The emphasis on openness was equally important and even more revealing from our point of view. The law taught that debtors had to be candid and open about all their private affairs in order to receive the *beneficium cessionis bonorum*. Some debtors were indeed innocent victims of forces beyond human control or incidents that could not be foreseen. Such debtors should be protected by law, but the law could only do so if the judiciary had access to complete information about what had happened. Thus, the debtor had to be completely candid with the judge and the creditors and conceal no information, however compromising. Openness was promoted in other ways as well. In order to contact all creditors, the case had to be publicly announced. In the first half of the eighteenth century, such announcements were communicated to the public either from the pulpits or in the streets, where drummers caught the attention of passersby.[29] But in 1767 it was suggested that bankruptcies should be published in the newspapers, and in 1772 a proposal was made that announcements of bankruptcies from the pulpits should cease.[30] From that time on every bankruptcy case had to be publicized in the newspapers on a number of occasions. First, a general call for all creditors was made. Then, the time for the creditors' meetings would be announced. Finally, the outcome of the case was made known to the public through the newspapers.[31] Since it had become possible to follow the cases in detail in the newspapers, bankruptcy cases were no longer only matters of local concern.

Active behavior by the creditor, candid behavior by the debtor, and a high degree of publicity in the course of the legal procedure promoted speed, openness, and transparency in bankruptcy cases. It was believed that candor would not be a problem to an honorable man, since he would always act in a way that could stand up under public scrutiny.

In the same way, publication of legal matters could not hurt an honest man. As for those who were dishonest, it was a service to the public (including creditors) that their dishonesty became widely known. Whether or not one could stand up to public scrutiny turned into a sort of litmus test of whether or not one was honorable. With its focus upon openness and publicity, bankruptcy law exposed debtors and their economic matters to the public in a way that did not at all dovetail with the notion of domestic privacy. In fact, it was completely impossible to go bankrupt in secret. Moreover, it was impossible for a person who was bankrupt to prevent this tarnishing of his honor from being made known throughout the country. Everybody who could read and who had access to newspapers could obtain information about the bankruptcy.

This put enormous pressure upon debtors to reduce the damage to their good names by trying to affect readers' opinions of the case. Before the final verdict was announced (and bankruptcy cases could be drawn-out affairs), it was entirely rational for debtors to publish their views of the case and to implore the public to side with them. If the newspapers had given one version of the case, a person might feel the need to correct that version. In this way, the publication of one view triggered the publication of the other. Similarly, the creditors were under pressure to act fast. This created a competitive situation, and very likely this was the main reason why the publication of legal documents peaked around 1770. This was not primarily because of the Freedom of the Press Act of 1766 but rather because the Bankruptcy Act of 1767 stipulated that bankruptcy cases should be announced in the newspapers.

Several cases illustrate the mechanisms at work in bankruptcy suits. In the early 1820s a legal dispute erupted in a Stockholm family. The case was soon brought to the attention of a startled public through the publication of the legal documents. Not only were the two combatants father and son-in-law, they were also judges on the Svea Hovrätt. The public thought the case was a disgrace to the legal profession, but the father, Justice Dufwa, claimed (in one of the publications) that it had been necessary for him to go public in order to calm down the creditors who believed bankruptcy to be imminent. Obviously, Dufwa feared these men who were, he believed, prone to interpret everything as a sign of insolvency.[32]

Dufwa's fears may have been well-founded. Rumors traveled fast in Stockholm, and a person's creditworthiness could quickly be adversely affected. This was brought out very clearly in a similar dispute caused by the bankruptcy of the famous Stockholm merchant Anders Plomgren in 1781. A broker was summoned to court to give testimony about when the Plomgren company had ceased to be creditworthy. The broker told the court how the company had been regarded as solid before the weekend of April 17 and 18. On Monday the broker stayed at home, as he had felt unwell, and thus had no access to information. When he did go out again, on Tuesday, April 20, "somebody in the street had told him about the requested mortgage on the Plomgren estates, and then at noon and in the afternoon people in general had started talking about this mortgage *and the insolvency they believed to be connected with it.*"[33] Clearly, rumors of this kind could be devastating to someone who had large debts or who needed new credit. That the creditors took precautions to register a mortgage on their debtor's estate was interpreted as a clear sign of the latter's insolvency. For a merchant, being shut off from access to credit meant that he could not continue with his business. What was more, since limited liability was not practiced at that time, owners were personally responsible for all debts. Consequently, fear of what creditors might believe was a force propelling debtors to publish their legal documents in order to influence both creditors and public opinion. Alternatively, they could try to use the newspapers as a channel though which their own version might reach the public.

Bankruptcy law promoted transparency and publicity in other ways as well. A successful settling of a bankruptcy case presupposed a correct and comprehensive inventory of the debtor's estate. It also presupposed accurate bookkeeping, if the debtor ran a company. Inventories and account books were both excellent means by which an outsider could gain insight into the private economic matters of the debtor. It should not cause surprise that Swedish bankruptcy law rigorously demanded that account books be correctly kept and that inventories be confirmed by oath. It also demanded that prenuptial agreements be publicly registered in order for them to be valid against the claims of the husband's creditors.[34] In this way, bankruptcy law contributed to the creation of a public sphere for economic matters. It made it legal and natural to unveil through publication facts and arguments related to the economic affairs of private persons. Even if many disputes were not related to bankruptcy (like the dispute about Gotthard Hildebrand's will), they were nevertheless drawn into this new public sphere. Not only persons who had declared bankruptcy but all honest citizens had to be able to stand up to public scrutiny.

Apart from its effects upon the public sphere and on the behavior expected of citizens, bankruptcy law was also instrumental in putting the wife's situation and property rights on the agenda through its explicit treatment of spouses' separation of property. By doing this, and by doing this in public, bankruptcy law contributed to an increasing public awareness of the situation of wives. In the long run this awareness would translate into the politicization of the matter.

The right of one spouse to separate her property from that of the other spouse (*separatio bonorum*) had been known to late seventeenth-century lawyers.[35] However, it was not until the early eighteenth century that the term was translated into Swedish, which suggests that it began to have a broader relevance.[36] Separation of property was mentioned briefly in the legal code of 1734, but it was not until the Bankruptcy Act of 1773 that it was given a more exhaustive treatment. That treatment, however, built on principles established in 1734. The granting of separation of property was dependent upon whether the person applying for separation had consented to the loans and whether she could be said to have profited personally from the loans. If the answers to these two questions were no, then the wife could "take out her share," as it was phrased.[37]

It is very important to understand that the right to separate one's property from that of one's husband referred to the common marital estate, that to which wives could claim one-third and husbands two-thirds. If the wife had inherited landed property, that property was already, by definition, separate and was better protected. Thus, the right to claim separation of property meant most to those married women who had no inherited land at all. As we have seen, this group of women was increasing apace in the late eighteenth century, and by 1815 they must have represented a very large majority of the female population. That separation of property was accorded scant interest at the beginning of the eighteenth century and more profound interest toward the end provides yet another indication of social changes taking place in society at large. When more women lacked inherited land, the need to regulate their right to the common marital property intensified.

Christina Furuträd's 1783 case illustrates how the emphasis shifted from land to movables in many households, and how women could navigate to protect their property. Christina was one of the rather few women who had brought inherited land into the marital estate. However, she had also brought a considerable amount of movables. When her husband went bankrupt and sold her land behind her back, she petitioned for separation of her part of the common estate. At this stage, she was too poor to pay for a copy of the court verdict.[38]

In a country where trusts for married women did not exist, the new right to have property separated from the common estate challenged old conceptions about marriage and marital rights. This was something of which the widow Biljer, in 1830, became painfully aware. In connection with her late husband's bankruptcy, she had asked for and been granted separation of property. She used her separate means to buy merchandise, whereupon she then carried on the same sort of business as her husband. In this way she was able to support not only herself and her children but also her husband. But upon his death his creditors demanded that his part of the common marital estate be included in his inventory and, thus, made available to them. The widow argued that the common marital estate no longer existed, while the creditors argued that, as long as the spouses lived together, the marital rights were a reality and any incomes from the wife's separate estate had to accrue to the common estate. In other words, the day after the bankruptcy, the husband had immediately acquired a right to his wife's income, even though she had received that income as a consequence of her property being separated from his! This line of argument failed to impress the courts, which sided with the widow Biljer. She particularly pointed to the inequity that would ensue if the court found in favor of the creditors; this would mean, she argued, that her late husband's creditors could enjoy a stronger claim to her property than did her own creditors.[39]

The introduction of separation of property was a small revolution in Swedish property law. While it had always been possible, indeed mandatory, to keep inherited land separate, it now became an option for spouses to hold purchased movable property as their separate estate. The longstanding equating of "movable" and "common" was significantly affected by spouses' needs in cases of bankruptcy, just as the equating of "land" and "separate" was turned upside down in some mutual wills.[40] Sometimes people wanted to make land into common marital property, and sometimes they wanted to separate movable property from the marital estate. These obstinate efforts to create arrangements that best suited the individual case tugged the whole property system in new directions. Seen within a long perspective, it was a sort of ebb and flow that shifted the emphasis from separateness in one context (landholding) to separateness in another (to protect families from debtors). Thus, bankruptcy law introduced a crucially new idea into property law.

While no doubt very useful to wives of men who had declared bankruptcy, the quantitative importance of separation of property should not be exaggerated. This legal device was not available to all those women whose husbands had sound economic affairs. It could not be used to give the woman power over her economy. It was not a means by which she could attain emancipation. It was a medicine to be used in a crisis situation, not in ordinary economic life.

Similarly, bankruptcy law did not in any significant way improve women's rights to surrogates. Women who had never held any claims to inherit land were not entitled to surrogates, and women who had received and maintained their inherited land intact did not need surrogates. The surrogate was for women who had, willingly or not, received their inherited land in the form of money or who had consented to selling their inherited land. The local case of Rystad showed how the right to surrogate worked: women were compensated from out of their deceased husbands' estates. But the law was disturbingly unclear about wives' rights to surrogate if the husband had gone bankrupt. The bankruptcy commission of 1772 argued that it was impossible to claim a surrogate in this situation.[41] This was a realistic appreciation of the situation, no doubt, but an alternative could have been to say that the wife had a preferential claim. However, the new Bankruptcy Act of 1818 explicitly said that wives' claims to a surrogate should *not* be regarded as preferential claims.[42] It is unclear how the issue had been treated prior to this date, but the standpoint adopted in 1818 suggests that nonlandowning wives of men who went bankrupt had a very weak position.

Property and Debt Exposed in the New Public Sphere

The zeal to publish legal documents, and particularly so in matters of economic importance,[43] meant that cases of the type we have been discussing were brought to the attention of everybody who was interested enough to read the publications. Disputes about inherited property, separation of property, redemption of land, right to surrogate, spouses' contributions to the common estate, and debts could be followed in the various publications. Some of these disputes were so protracted and the parties so eager to have their say that the publications almost turned into a serial story.[44] Often, they displayed matters that were in some sense scandalous.

The dispute between Justice Dufwa and his son-in-law provides an excellent example. Dufwa's late wife had inherited a landed estate from her parents, the Kosta glassworks. The estate had not been encumbered with debt when she received it, but now, after her death, it definitely was. Her son-in-law (Judge Heerman) was apparently getting nervous about these debts; he suspected that his father-in-law would not be able to pay with what was his and feared that his wife's inheritance would have to be used. Consequently, Heerman had decided to use the possibility of demanding separation of property on behalf of his wife. He claimed one-half of the landed estate (obviously, his wife had a sister) and one-half of his mother-in-law's part of the common property. This would have meant that Justice Dufwa had only his part of the common property (two-thirds) at his disposal when facing his creditors.

Heerman claimed that his mother-in-law had never benefited from the loans her husband had incurred. This argument was crucial, since the law only released a spouse from responsibility if the loan had been of no use to him or her. Dufwa argued that his wife had not received Kosta until they had been married for several years. During the initial phase of marriage, Dufwa had had to pay large sums of money for "the setting up of a house, five childbeds, illness and funerals." These costs, he emphasized, had been partly covered by his own inherited money; still, his inheritance had not been sufficient, which was why he had had to incur debts. The incomes he had later received from Kosta had in no way compensated him for what he had thus lost. No, his "new fortune" had been acquired simply through his own "assiduity, prudence, and a better salary." Dufwa's argument was that, contrary to what the son-in-law claimed, his wife had indeed benefited from the loans, since they had covered some of their common costs. The wife was, in a sense, even indebted to her husband, since he had paid much more during their first years together. Being a lawyer, Dufwa must have realized that it was completely impossible for him to claim a share in the landed estate of Kosta. He did underline, though, that all movable property at Kosta was part of the common estate. Stressing his own work and efforts was also a way of proving that he had not benefited unduly from his wife's property. He was a self-made man.

Dufwa suffered from the fact that, while the law protected inherited land, it paid very scant attention to investments that spouses had made. As we have already seen, the law did not normally ask where the money had come from. The royal statute of 1807 was an improvement in this respect, but it did not help Dufwa, since he had used his money to cover daily needs and not to invest in his wife's lands. Printing his legal documents, Dufwa exposed his case to judges and to the public, imploring them both to see what was right and to restore his honor. In fact, his action seems to have backfired, since Dufwa both lost the case and became the target of much scorn.

A similarly convoluted case was brought to the attention of the public in 1767, involving rights of inheritance, redemption of land, and claims to a surrogate. Daniel Burén had lost his first wife, Hedvig Althin, in 1754, and apparently he had not divided the estate among his children immediately, as the law required. He later married Catharina Margaretha Adlerklo, and during their marriage he bought some land from his previous brothers-in-law. The contested issues involved what kind of purchase this had been and where the children's maternal inheritance had gone. The brothers-in-law claimed that they thought Burén had redeemed the land on behalf of his children; they would never have consented to selling it so cheaply, they said, if they had not believed that the estate would finally become the property of their nephews. Burén's second wife claimed that the land had not been redeemed but that it was a simple acquisition made with money. What was more, she had contributed no less than 9,000 copper *daler* — money she had received for estates she had sold. There was no doubt but that she must be given a surrogate for this money, she argued. Burén himself courted ambiguity throughout the legal process, trying to appease both his children and his new wife. His son, Carl Daniel, who was an auditor (*auskultant*) in one of the courts of appeal and who was the one to have the records printed, appealed to his father's "natural parental love" and asked if the father really wanted "a hostile public to think badly of him?"[45]

The complicated character of this case becomes obvious from the differing opinions expressed by the courts involved. In the primary court the legally trained chairman argued that the estate had been acquired by the father, while the majority of lay judges said it must be regarded as redeemed on behalf of the children. The court of the second instance agreed with the chairman of the primary court, annulling the first verdict. The court of the third instance (the Göta Hovrätt) found in favor of Burén's son, arguing that the land had been redeemed for him and that his stepmother had no right to it. The rules about redemption of landed property were difficult to understand and, often, hard to reconcile with other rules, such as wives' right to compensation for invested land money. However, like other, similar cases, Burén's dispute suggests that lower courts perceived redemption of land as a form of acquisition and that they paid attention to who had paid, whereas higher courts were reluctant to equate redemption of land with pure acquisition.[46]

Several cases that reached the public dealt with household indebtedness and its consequences. This remained a highly problematic field, despite the changes and clarifications that had been made in the legal code of 1734, after almost a century of debate. The new legal code regarded two circumstances as important for the question as to whether or not a spouse was responsible for the other spouse's debts: whether she had benefited from the loans and whether she had signed the credit instrument. If she had signed it, this was taken as a token of consent and acceptance of responsibility. But even with a clear signature, it would often prove difficult to settle the case.

In Anders Plomgren's bankruptcy, an important question was whether or not his widow, Margareta Björkman, had deceived the creditors. The question was highly pertinent in this case, which was rife with fraud. The widow's new companion, Fredrik Lundin, had infringed on almost every section of the bankruptcy law. The widow herself, on hearing that bankruptcy could not be avoided, had hastened to pack up all her silver knives and candlesticks and had them transported to the landed estate of her son in an attempt to hide them from the assessors and, hence, the creditors. The servants witnessed that "Mrs. Plomgren," as she was called,[47] used to have twelve silver tea spoons but that no more than four of these had been inventoried. The creditors had also complained about the way in which she had been running around in the city, whereas, according to the law, she should have stayed within her own doors. Some even argued that she should be arrested. The whole case was clearly scandalous.

There was little doubt, then, that Margareta Björkman was suspected of defrauding the creditors, together with Fredrik Lundin. Still, it was difficult to prove that she had been jointly responsible for the loans of her husband. The handwriting on the credit instruments looked "remarkably similar to that of Mrs. Plomgren," but she denied having signed them. Moreover, she claimed not to understand French, which was the language used in the credit instruments; hence, it was difficult to fairly hold her responsible for paying the debts. In the final instance, she was acquitted and the whole blame was laid on Fredrik Lundin.

Another case also focused on married women's written consent. In 1718 Ingela Gathenhielm had paid the debts of a man by the name of Billberg. As a security for her claim upon him, Ingela had registered a mortgage on his wife's inherited estate. (Presumably, Billberg had no property of his own.) But long afterward, in 1760, a dispute broke out between the heirs of Billberg and Gathenhielm, which focused upon whether or not Billberg's wife (M. E. von Hofdal) had really signed the credit instrument voluntarily. Before this question was settled, her inherited estate could not be used to cover her husband's debts. A vicar testified that, on her deathbed, the wife had sworn never to have signed any credit instruments, and the court devoted some attention to the wife's signature. She was said to normally sign her name as "M. E. von Hofdal," but the bond was signed by "M. E. von Hoffdal," which might suggest that someone else had signed for her behind her back. However, the court concluded that this difference was of little importance: "since she is a woman, one cannot expect her to spell consistently."[48]

One wife who had undoubtedly signed the credit instruments, and who was consequently hit very hard when her husband went bankrupt, was Countess Beata Sparre, who was married to the county governor, Adam Otto Lagerberg. When she learned how serious his financial situation was, she petitioned the Göta Hovrätt to grant separation of property. However, it turned out to be very difficult to disentangle all competing claims to the estate. In the end, all creditors and relatives had to strike a deal, in which everybody conceded some of their rights. Beata Sparre had to accept the fact that her separate property could not be spared. However, an installment plan was set up for her and her children, with the objective of making them free from all claims after a period of ten years.[49] Obviously, Lagerberg's bankruptcy was a great scandal. County governors had special responsibility for the prompt execution of debts. What was more, Lagerberg was one of the men who had been especially appointed by the Diet in 1772 to investigate the causes behind and remedies for the frequent bankruptcies. That a man in his position used credit so recklessly that he would be bound to his creditors for the foreseeable future could only cause disgust. The effects upon his family did not endear him further to creditors or to the public.

In all these cases, the notion of truth was crucial. Things had taken place and words had been uttered in the private or even intimate sphere, and they were therefore inscrutable domestic secrets. Because they turned out to be legally relevant, it was necessary to divulge them to the formal courts and also to the informal court of public opinion. It was necessary to convince these two types of courts of the truthful character of one's own version: that Dufwa had indeed used a fortune on his family, that Plomgren's widow had hidden her spoons, and that Gotthard Hildebrand had regarded Magdalena De Wallé as his lawful wife. Of course, many of these expositions were extremely biased, stressing the aspects that spoke in favor of the publisher and remaining silent on others. The statements could also be outright rude, and they were often charged with personal feelings. But these circumstances only show, emphatically, how extremely anxious people were to establish their own version of the truth. And in this public competition about truth, women did have a stake.

Women's Use of the New Public Sphere

A small publication with the meaningless title "Narration and Documents in a Dispute over Inheritance" came out in 1792. It recounted how the late bricklayer Friese had been married twice and had made a mutual will together with each of his two wives. Since the estate had never been properly divided after the death of the first wife, a dispute had erupted between her heirs and the second wife. There was nothing particularly spectacular about this dispute. Readers who cared to study the reprinted wills would find the standard arrangements and the standard arguments about how the property had been acquired "by the sweat of our brows." More interesting was the eloquent exposition on the value of freedom with which the publication started. The objective of freedom of the press is, it said, enlightenment and improvement. Therefore, all legal documents must be published, so that everybody can see that the judiciary adheres to the law. "It is the finest token of freedom only to be judged according to the written law"; this freedom, the text went on, "has always been possessed and held sacred in England."[50]

The author of the publication had appropriated a language of freedom and enlightenment, just as members of the Diet and participants in the new religious movements had. England and its legal principles were also known to the author, who made explicit references to this role model. In this way, lofty ideals were brought to bear on the rather mundane issue of a contested will. The case was not unique in this respect; ordinary Swedes seem to have been well aware of what happened in Europe. At this time, France was of course most likely to exert an inspiring or frightening influence.[51]

It is not entirely clear who had taken the initiative to publish this case. As the publication does speak for the rights of the widow Schlecht, it is likely that she took part in the decision to have the legal documents published, although we cannot know for certain if she had formulated every word herself. It is not impossible that she had, and in some cases, it seems obvious that it is the voice of the woman herself that we can hear. As early as the seventeenth century, a majority of the Swedish population was able to read, and this included women as well.[52] The ability to write may have been less well developed, but less is known about this. However, it is clear that both women and men in the eighteenth century should be considered as part of a literate culture, as people who could definitely read and who were also aware of the advantages (in terms of influence) offered by the written word.[53] Anna Maria Rückerschöld, mentioned in the first chapter, provides a striking example. Therefore, it should come as no surprise that in some cases women were demonstrably the ones who had taken the initiative to publish the legal records.[54]

A case in which the initiative was unquestionably taken by a woman was Ingrid Baas's dispute with the burgher Eklin about a manor her husband had turned over to Eklin for a period of fifty years in return for a large sum of money. The husband had done this prior to his marriage, probably because he lacked liquid means. Later, he had been fortunate enough to meet and marry Ingrid Baas, who was a wealthy widow and who soon bore him a son. The couple wanted the estate back, and Ingrid, who had money, tried to force Eklin to return the manor in advance. But Eklin had, in turn, sold his right to the manor to Justice Falkengren, who was not inclined to oblige her. Eklin and Falkengren joined forces to prove that Ingrid Baas had no right to this manor. Her husband had alienated it to his creditor prior to his marriage, which meant that Ingrid had no marital rights and her son no rights of inheritance. Ingrid Baas chose to have the legal documents published, which must mean that she wanted to elicit support from the public. However, she did not explicitly appeal to public opinion or to God; instead she implored the king for redress.[55]

Another case presented to the public by a woman concerned rights of inheritance and the sale of women's separate property. Ebba Christina von Becker petitioned the Diet in 1771 to support her in her dispute with her distant relatives, the Gagge family, who, according to Becker, withheld her lawful inheritance. The dispute went back to the early years of the century and to Becker's maternal grandfather's mother. In the detailed legal documents presented to the Diet and to the public, readers could also find other information about the family's economic transactions — information the family may have preferred not to see in print. For example, a Lieutenant Svinhufvud, who had married into the family, had first mortgaged and then sold the inherited estates of his wife, despite not having any rights to that property.[56] While not being outrageously scandalous, the case nevertheless divulged domestic secrets and alerted the readers to the fact that some married men used their wife's property in unlawful ways.

Elisabeth Larsson was another woman who petitioned the highest level of the judiciary for help and who also exposed her case to the public. The small publication, which only comprised one and a half quarto pages, told the sad story of how her previous husband, the tobacco planter Ekman, had deceived her. Elisabeth had brought a house in Stockholm into the marital estate, and the couple had later acquired yet another house in the same city. But then Ekman committed adultery, which led Elisabeth to divorce him. She received a court verdict in her favor, giving her right to three-fourths of the entire estate,[57] but when she asked the local governor to help her take out her share, Ekman submitted a petition for bankruptcy. However, as Elisabeth pointed out, this was all a fraud: Ekman was not indebted or, at least, his debts had not been incurred during marriage but possibly after the divorce. Ekman had used the ruse of asking his friends to register false claims to his estate and, apparently, he had succeeded, even though this was illegal,[58] possibly because the mayor had assisted him by appointing executors who were partial and favored Ekman. When Ekman won the case in the court of the first instance, he had, according to Elisabeth, "darted around, telling everybody how he had won, [and] that his friends had helped him to protect the property against his former wife, and that the false credit instruments were sewn into the back of his coat, which he never takes off." Invoking her responsibility as a mother as well as the tears of her children, Elisabeth Larsson begged for redress.[59]

One of the most spectacular publications of all was initiated by Elisabeth Reenstierna in the 1760s. Reenstierna's eager commitment to having the legal documents immediately published can be gauged from the complaints she filed when the court did not hasten to let her have copies of the documents. The story finally divulged to the public stretched back to Elisabeth's mother, and it continued after Elisabeth's death. It told the public about a family whose life seems to have been wrecked by incessant quarrels over property and money. Elisabeth was the daughter of Abel Reenstierna and Anna Björn, both wealthy members of the nobility. She married a man by the name of Hästesko-Fortuna, a marriage that turned out to be both unhappy and unfortunate. The husband was convicted for, among other things, using damning words about the constitution, and he had to spend several years in jail. Elisabeth divorced him, but the former spouses were subsequently embroiled in a dispute in which he accused her of not having taken proper care of his property while he was absent.

Of the couple's three daughters, Anna Helena also married a man (Yxkull) who turned out not to be an asset to the family, and she finally divorced him. This divorce seems to have caused considerable strain in the relations between Anna Helena, her mother, and her grandmother. Apparently, the latter two would have preferred for Anna Helena to apply for separation of property instead. It seems as if the grandmother had paid Anna Helena's husband's debts. Consequently, the grandmother was not inclined to let her inherit anything, and Anna Helena and Elisabeth were both aware of this risk. In a misguided (it later turned out) effort to help Anna Helena, Elisabeth promised in writing that if she should die before her mother, Anna Helena would be guaranteed a sum of 200,000 to 300,000 copper *daler*. However, the grandmother died first, leaving her two houses in Stockholm to her two other granddaughters, as was anticipated. Anna Helena expressed dissatisfaction with this outcome, and her mother tried to soothe her. But when Anna Helena proceeded to sell her mother's written note, cashing the full amount immediately, the mother took the case to court. Elisabeth argued that what she had written was not a promissory note but a plan for the future settlement of inheritance claims, in the event that Anna Björn survived Elisabeth Reenstierna. When it was clear that Elisabeth had survived her mother, the paper was worthless, she maintained. The problem was only that Elisabeth had not written that she would, under certain conditions, pay her daughter a certain amount of money. She had written that she would pay to *the holder of the note* that same amount of money. Consequently, the legal dispute dealt both with the character of the note and with whether Anna Björn had intended to make a will that would have benefited Anna Helena.[60]

Characteristic of this case was its quasi-literary qualities. It was filled with sentimental phrases expressing heated emotions, as well as lively and sometimes startling dialogue. Elisabeth Reenstierna told the court and the public how she was unable "to express how hard it is to meet at court someone whom I have carried under my heart, and on whom I have devoted all my motherly tenderness." She explained that she wanted to divulge certain circumstances, and once these had in print "faced the court of public opinion, they will show a terrible example of how a child has treated her mother." These attacks cannot have failed to draw attention and cause amusement or disgust among readers. Similarly, some of the printed testimonies allowed readers to picture concrete scenes that had taken place within the Reenstierna family. One witness told the court how he had personally tried to persuade the grandmother to think of Anna Helena in her will. The grandmother had replied, "What do you want me to give her?" When he suggested some rural estates, the grandmother retorted, in a bad temper, "Go to hell!" Another witness told the court how the grandmother had complained, "People come running in and out of my house, asking me to give [something] to Mrs. Yxkull, and that gossipmonger Mrs. Witte wants me to give her a farm, but what can I give her, I have not more than what I need myself. A farm will not do her much good, and her mother has [already] given her, from what she has been able to pinch and scrape." A third testimony conveyed a more conciliatory portrait of the two older women. The grandmother had asked her daughter, "What will you do about your daughter Lena?" The mother answered, "God knows that I want her to have the same as her sisters." The grandmother concluded, "This is well done of you."[61]

The Impact of the Published Legal Documents

Reading publications of this sort, ordinary men and women gained insight into two different but closely intertwined fields. The publications allowed them to "snoop" into other people's private lives, to listen to heated family debates, and to be amazed by the depths to which people could sink. The publications disclosed domestic secrets but at the same time taught people something about the law, although the information was fragmented and possibly gave distorted versions. People who read the publications could not fail to acquire some insight into will making, redemption of property, credit instruments, and inheritance law. They also became accustomed to debates on constitutional matters or at least to a rhetoric inspired by ideas about the value of freedom and about how freedom and law formed the pillars of society. In the words of Arlette Farge, who has analyzed similar phenomena in France, "Knowledge of public affairs began with a knowledge of other people's business."[62]

It is likely that the often private character of these cases made them tantalizing and tempting to read. Thus, curiosity may account for why people chose to read them, but once they were reading they received other things in the bargain. Many publications were considerably briefer and less spectacular than the Reenstierna case, but even in these other cases, legally relevant facts and legal arguments were imparted to readers in almost furtive ways. In one case, it was mentioned in passing how a man had committed a number of reprehensible actions, one of which was that he had sold the property he had received with his wife.[63] In another case it was mentioned, also in passing, how a woman had never contributed anything to the household and that, therefore, she should not be given anything from her late husband's estate.[64] These pieces of information reached readers and affected their ideas of what was right and reasonable. Or maybe they did not need to be affected? Maybe most people already considered it a reprehensible action for a husband to sell his wife's property? Maybe most people already thought it unreasonable if a woman, who had contributed nothing, was to receive means from her dead husband's estate? Maybe it was precisely because there was consensus about these fundamental values that those who published their grievances chose to emphasize these sorts of facts?

Many publications showed specific people in an unfavorable light. The picture of Anna Helena Hästesko was deliberately unflattering, as was that of Magdalena De Wallé. There were more men than women, however, who were exposed in an unfavorable way in the new public sphere, and for a very simple reason. Adult men were legally capable of doing things that unmarried or married women were not allowed to do. If one were to adhere strictly to the law, these categories of women were not permitted to make any contracts on their own and, even if we know that exceptions were made in daily life, it was still a fact that men were less restrained in their economic activities. Someone who is allowed to do more will also fail more often than someone who is allowed to do less. Thus, there is an almost statistical explanation as to why men set negative examples in the new public sphere more often than women.

It is a matter of some importance that it was often negative examples of male behavior that were spread in society by means of the new medium of print. In late seventeenth-century society, property law and credit law had also been in focus. At that time, it was not uncommon for debaters — who constituted a small and socially restricted circle without access to a broader public — to claim that women were prone to lavish consumption. As a consequence, women ought to take a larger responsibility for household debt, they had argued. Whether it was true that women did cause debt more often than men was of course very difficult to prove. Claes Rålamb never tried to refute the argument but built his defense of women's rights on other foundations. Modern research suggests, however, that in fact men were as prone to lavish consumption as women and that it is probably a myth that wealthy women had no other task than to "consume and display what men produced."[65] Be that as it may, what seems important in the Swedish case is that in the late eighteenth century the public was often confronted with vivid examples of *men* who had incurred large debts for various reasons or who had tried to defraud their creditors, their business partners, or their family members. Women were prone to lavish consumption and often had too large stores of linen, it was argued in 1762, but men doted on their large libraries and were as infatuated by fashion as women were.[66] The message was that men, no less than women, needed to reform their behavior. In this perspective, Fredrik Lundin, who became the new partner in the Plomgren company, was a terrible warning, and so, for that matter, was the politically influential Fredrik Gyllenborg, whose wealthy wife found it necessary to apply for separation of property when his debts soared. It was much more difficult to claim that only women caused debt when so many examples to the contrary were presented to the public.

While such examples of male irresponsibility were often held up to the public, men's responsibility to care for their own families continued to be an important part of the cultural script (Paul's first letter to Timothy, in which he described men who did not provide for their household members as worse than infidels, was still a favorite biblical text), making the contrast between the ideal and real life all the more striking. Moreover, the contrast could be exploited directly by women now that they had access to an arena that had not existed a hundred years before. Even if they were few, some women did take advantage of the possibility of acquiring a voice and addressing the public, spreading their word not only to others of their station but perhaps also to those less well off.

Conclusions

Public opinion was a formidable force. Nobody could ignore its presence and power, not even well-established state institutions like the Bank of Sweden. In 1771 one of its employees published a small document concerning a dispute in which the bank had become embroiled. Just like so many ordinary men and women, the bank employee appealed to the public, asking it to judge for itself as to who had behaved dishonorably and unlawfully, the bank or its opponent. The decision to print the text had been triggered by a short article published in one of the major Stockholm newspapers. Since the bank felt the article gave a false version of what had happened, it had no other option but to enter a verbal duel.[67]

The importance of public opinion for political life is commonly accepted for the nineteenth century, with its "bürgerliche Öffentlichkeit." A recent study has shown that public opinion was a vital factor in Swedish political life as early as the 1760s.[68] But even before this decade, public opinion had acquired a crucial role in the economic and legal spheres. People who were dissatisfied with the outcome of litigation turned to the public as a sort of appeals court, asking it to listen to their version and to find in their favor. Although the zeal to publish one's legal documents reached a peak in the 1770s, legal documents were published and spread as early as in the 1740s. With their combined focus on private matters and legal principles, the publications created a new form of public discourse. It was precisely this combined focus which allowed this public discourse subsequently to be used and developed for political purposes. The publications created a virtual arena for both gossip mongering and the spreading of fragmentary legal knowledge. In a society where literacy was high (although of uneven quality) this arena allowed ordinary people to relate to and talk about legal cases and to draw their own conclusions. That the bankruptcy law both demanded publicity and problematized the common marital property of spouses served to bring women's property rights into this arena in a way that facilitated their subsequent politicization.

Studies of other parts of the world show that similar mechanisms were at work in other countries at the same time. When an American creditor announced in the newspapers that he would auction his debtor's promissory note in 1798, it triggered the debtor to publish his views of the creditor's mean intentions.[69] Clearly, the debtor's action was a way of trying to protect his good name; many Swedes used the same strategy. Similarly, in England a previous mistress of one of the princes had all his love letters printed and then sold the whole edition to the royal family for a fortune.[70] This was a scandal, just as some of the Swedish cases retold here, but it was also an ingenious way of using the massive force of public opinion for one's own ends. In France, finally, through skillful adaptation by lawyers, printed *mémoires judiciaires* were offered to the public, exposing the inner life of prominent families. Gradually, they acquired a political subtext which made them highly relevant to the later outbreak of the Revolution.[71] In a similar way, a new public sphere was created around Swedish legal cases, and the notion that the public could "see the truth" better than anyone else gave to some of these cases a political flavor, particularly when they employed a constitutional rhetoric about law and freedom.

The published legal documents present us with a world reminiscent of the worlds created by Balzac, Eliot, and Bremer. It was a world where family, property, and indebtedness were crucial themes. This is important because it proves that there must have been a public awareness about these matters in late eighteenth- and early nineteenth-century European society and because more lowly placed persons did have a voice in this context. It is particularly important that at least some of these persons were women.

However, even if the results presented here have much in common with what we know about other countries at the same time, or with famous novels, it is essential to see that they also have a good deal in common with the situation in the sixteenth and early seventeenth centuries. At that time, everyone was rooted in a local community with a court at its center. In order to settle conflicts and to mete out justice, the courts depended on local knowledge harbored by the lay judges or by other old and knowledgeable persons in the local community. These people had acquired their knowledge by living in the same place and by keeping their eyes open. Thus, they turned into an authority to which individuals could, and did, appeal for justice and support. What lay judges and the majority of the assembled men thought was true would also be accepted as the truth. In this sense "public opinion" existed long before the eighteenth century, and in the eighteenth century people were still members of local communities. Therefore, it was not entirely correct to describe households as domestic secrets, as legislators had done in the late seventeenth century: they were only secrets to outsiders, not to the people within the local community. It was the reforms carried through around 1700 that made households more private and secretive.

The emergence of a new public sphere, however, changed the balance again. It made it possible to open up the household with its internal problems to a public that was no longer local and personal but national and impersonal. Through the printed medium it became possible to divulge household matters to onlookers who were anonymous to those whose lives were exposed. In principle, the new public sphere was infinite, and, in this respect, it differed from the old, local public sphere. It was also its infinity that accounted for its formidable force and for the effects it would have in the upcoming era of reform.

((6))

DRASTIC CHANGES

In the early nineteenth century, the members of the Swedish Diet spent much time and energy on discussing large-scale legal reform. In particular, they were engaged in family law and in whether or not an egalitarian inheritance system ought to be introduced. Such a proposal had come up as early as 1809, but it was still on the list of unresolved issues in 1844. Consequently, equal rights of inheritance still applied only in urban areas and among the clergy. The vast majority of the population, the peasantry, accorded women smaller shares than men, as did the nobility. At one point during the deliberations the nobleman von Troil attacked those opposed to the reform, arguing that there was no rational ground for withholding equal inheritance rights from women. That rural women had inherited only half as much as men since the Middle Ages had nothing to do with justice or what was deserved — it was, he argued, merely the disgraceful result of men having monopolized the legislature and having taken advantage of the situation to improve their own position.[1]

The nobleman von Troil was not the only one to strike this chord. A French woman petitioning the National Convention in 1795 used almost exactly the same words: if the Convention were to repeal the new inheritance law, all women would say "with good reason that you are unjust and that you have taken advantage of the fact that we are not represented at the Convention. . . . They will say to you that men have made the laws and they have made them for themselves."[2] When John Stuart Mill wrote *The Subjection of Women*, a tract outspoken for its day, he made a similar analysis: the age-old wrongs inflicted upon the female sex should be understood as the result of the rule of the strongest, he wrote. Women's historical absence from all legislative assemblies accounted for their less well-developed legal rights.[3]

These three voices suggest that the situation of women was regarded as equally problematic in many countries and that the rhetoric circulating around the issue was international. As we will see, many Swedish arguments referred to Enlightenment ideals or to ideas well-rehearsed in other countries. Equally important, though, is that Swedish arguments and analyses must also be understood against the backdrop of the national experience. Without a clear view of what eighteenth-century social and economic developments meant to women and without a proper appreciation of the concomitant process of politicization taking place in the public sphere, we run the risk of seriously misunderstanding both the debates and their results.

The proposal to extend women's rights of inheritance met with both support and opposition in all four estates, but, as time wore on, there was a certain tendency for the nobility to perceive the proposal as an attack on its traditional rights and privileges. A few noblemen even saw the proposal as a conspiracy on behalf of the other three estates and as inspired by the writings of Alexis de Tocqueville. In his book *Democracy in America* (1835–40) Tocqueville suggested that one of the best ways of promoting a democratic constitution was to reform the inheritance system. It was particularly vital, according to Tocqueville, to abolish primogeniture, since this was the means by which traditional landholding classes maintained their positions of power in society.[4]

Sweden did not have a system of primogeniture, but it is true that the law distinctly favored sons and disfavored daughters of peasants and noblemen. If noblewomen were to inherit more land and if they were to subsequently marry non-noblemen, the effect would be that the wealth of the nobility would seep out to new social groups, which would then take over the nobility's position in society — a line of reasoning in line with Tocqueville's ideas. The theory presupposed that husbands had complete control over their wives' inherited property, which was, of course, far from self-evident. In spite of this obviously restricting factor, a *few* noblemen argued as if they actually believed that the three other estates wanted to undermine their position through a reform of inheritance law.[5]

Strangely enough, this has become the standard interpretation of the reform of 1845, one that was first proposed by Gunnar Qvist, the doyen of women's history in Sweden. Historians who have written about the reform era since 1960 have repeated this interpretation, stating that the Inheritance Act had nothing to do with the situation of women but must be interpreted along lines of class conflict or, perhaps, conflict among the estates. They have done so, despite the fact that Qvist did not really present any convincing evidence for his claim. His main concern was the reform of women's rights to trade in 1846. What he said about the previous reform built mainly on a brief analysis of the newspaper debate in the 1840s in which Tocqueville was mentioned.[6] But whether Tocqueville's ideas had any real bearing on the deliberations in the Diet and on the positions adopted by the estates is another question which Qvist never pursued. That the idea to reform women's rights of inheritance had been broached in 1809, long before Tocqueville's book was written, is of course a strong argument against this standard interpretation. But there are other arguments as well that suggest that the standard interpretation is simply incorrect.

At the meetings of the Diet, a member of the peasant estate repeatedly made a proposal that was later to be called "Petter Persson's compromise." Petter Persson[7] proposed that, if the nobility did not want to amend marital law and inheritance law, they should be allowed to keep the old rules for themselves but that the other estate that had traditionally applied unequal rights — the peasantry — should be allowed to adopt the new rules because they needed them.[8] This proposal met with acclaim, to some extent even among members of the noble estate.[9] The biggest drawback was, of course, that this proposal would not create legal uniformity, but it would provide a swift and simple solution to a problem the Diet had wrestled with for more than two decades. It is thus clear that Petter Persson's compromise is highly pertinent to the overall interpretation of the reform. He argued, first, that the peasantry cared little for what the nobility did with what was theirs. This view was expressed by members of the other estates as well — people who we would expect to covet the lands of the nobility. As Fries, a member of the clergy, expressed it, "What do the inheritance laws of the nobility matter to us?" Many of his colleagues agreed.[10]

The reform of 1845 was not simply an expression of antagonism between the estates, nor was it irrelevant to women's situation in society. What Qvist failed to observe was the way in which the inheritance reform was closely interlinked with the reform of women's marital rights.[11] He also overlooked the almost unanimous support for the latter in the Diet. A closer analysis of the debates leading up to these reforms divulges patterns that have little to do with constitutional issues and class conflict. Instead, they must be understood as reflections of broad social problems that were seen at the time from the vantage point of Enlightenment ideals. The debates suggest, emphatically, that the reforms had very much to do with women's situation in society.

The Reform Era

The first half of the nineteenth century was a period of reform in many parts of Europe. In the wake of the Revolution, France embarked on a wide-reaching project of legal reform, resulting in the Code Napoléon. In Britain, the Reform Era brought Catholic emancipation, parliamentary reform, and the abolition of slavery. In the Nordic countries, national borders were redrawn as Sweden lost Finland to Russia but entered into a union with Norway, formerly under Danish control. Sweden's second, short period of autocracy (initiated in 1772) came to a close with the coup against King Gustav IV Adolf in 1809. A new constitution was promulgated the same year, and a year later one of Napoleon's field marshals was chosen to become the new king. However, the ambition to write a more modern and democratic constitution built on principles of the division of power was only partly successful. On paper the power of the state was divided between the king, the Diet and the judiciary, but the latter never became a force on a par with the other two.[12] The attempts at substituting a two-chamber parliament for the previous four-estate Diet were obviously premature. Sweden remained a constitutional monarchy with a severely restricted franchise, but the nobility consented to the repeal of some of their traditional prerogatives.

From the start the project to rewrite the Swedish constitution was closely connected with the endeavor to modernize civil and criminal law, with a view to replacing the code of 1734 with a completely new code. Just as in the seventeenth century, there was recurring criticism of the bewildering and contradictory character of the existing legal code, which legislators claimed was "not a book for the people."[13] This argument suggested that law ought to be intelligible to ordinary Swedes and that its interpretation should not be the sole prerogative of professional lawyers. Since ordinary Swedes still served as lay judges in the primary courts and as assessors of estates of deceased persons, this opinion is understandable. The efficiency and uniformity of the law (ideals that were becoming more commonly acclaimed) did presuppose fairly good legal knowledge on the part of the population at large. The grandiose ambition of completely overhauling the legal code, however, never met with success. Instead, the areas of law in most urgent need of adjustment were amended through what contemporaries called "partial reform." Symptomatically, these areas were deeply relevant to women's economic situation. Most well-known are the reform of inheritance law and marital law (reformed through the Act of 1845), and the reform of women's right to trade (reformed through the Act of 1846). Less scholarly attention has been devoted to the new testamentary law (reformed through the Act of 1857), although it was through this act that the medieval system of lineage property was finally brought to an end. Somewhat earlier, in 1807, the king had introduced new statutory law to the effect that spouses could co-own redeemed land, and already in eighteenth-century bankruptcy law the legal device of separation of property had been introduced. Through these five reforms the legislature acknowledged not only that economic life had changed drastically but also that these developments called for a complete reconstruction of women's property rights. Arguably, the most burning issue was the reform of marital rights.

The Need to Reform Marital Rights

When a member of the peasant estate representing Örebro *län* summed up the most important reasons for giving men and women equal marital rights, he focused upon the situation of widows. Marital rights do not become important until one of the spouses has died, he said, "and who will not acknowledge for a fact that, if the surviving spouse is a woman and a mother, she will have the same (if not even greater) needs for the upkeep and prosperity of the household, as would her husband have had." Why then should she be deprived of a larger share of the common estate, and what does it matter if the estate consists of inherited property or means acquired through the spouses' common concerns, efforts, and household skills? One cannot assume, he continued, that a woman will squander or spoil (assets) more than a man. Is it not rather the case, he asked rhetorically, that we see more examples of men who are guilty of these lapses than women? And if the widow is childless, why should we take for granted that she can support herself more easily than a man? Moreover, what evidence is there to prove that a widow ought to be entitled to a smaller share of the common estate? In fact, a larger share of that estate may have come from her side than from that of her late husband.[14]

The honorable representative from Örebro employed a wide range of arguments to sustain his point. Yet they all sound familiar. It is almost as though he had read this book. The probate inventories from Rystad show how little a widow might receive when her husband died, especially if she had no inherited land of her own, and these records also made very clear how important marital rights were to such women. Increasing the size of the inheritance available through marital rights would mean very much to them, and these women were probably in the majority in the first half of the nineteenth century. Furthermore, the legal records published in the eighteenth and early nineteenth century presented many examples of married men who had failed as managers of the marital estate, implicitly countering the view that women have a particularly poor aptitude for economics. Women's needs, efforts, and property contributions suggested that it was high time to reform marital rights.

The peasant representative from Örebro in central Sweden was not alone in his concern for widows. In addition to Petter Persson from Jönköping in southern Sweden, Olof Nilsson and Lars Bygdén from Västerbotten (northern Sweden) and Tuve Månsson from Malmöhus (southern Sweden) struck the same note. The latter three focused particularly on the problem of the spouses' contributions of movable property to the household. It often happened in their constituencies, they said, that one spouse contributed movable property that was worth just as much as the immovable property of the other spouse. It was also common for the immovable property to be burdened by debt. But as time wore on and the assets of the estate diminished for various reasons, it frequently turned out that very little remained at death. After the payment of debts and perhaps even the mortgage, nothing remained

> but the landed property, inherited or acquired before marriage
> by the deceased spouse, in which the widowed party does not
> have any marital rights, and the obvious consequence is that the
> widowed spouse, who owned some small fortune upon marriage,
> is now at the death of the other spouse left with almost nothing.[15]

Olof Nilsson and Lars Bygdén phrased their argument in gender-neutral terms, which was correct in the sense that both men and women could be afflicted by the law's silence on this point. This was exactly what Justice Dufwa had experienced. Tuve Månsson described a situation where a man "with a fortune consisting of money" married a woman who owned nothing but a debt-ridden farm. The couple used his money to redeem the farm from the claims of her siblings, but when the wife subsequently died the husband had to leave everything, "even though it should rightfully be his property since it was paid for with his money." Evidently, the statute of 1807 had not been implemented according to the intentions of the monarch.[16] In order to remedy this unfortunate situation, Tuve Månsson recommended that husband and wife have the same marital rights — a proposal which would not solve the entire problem but which would ameliorate it considerably.[17] The basic problem was that the law allowed movable property to be "swallowed" by immovable property, and this could have adverse effects for anyone who married.

It was, of course, more likely that women would be adversely affected. This was a point made in the burgher's estate by the representative Hörnstein, who stressed how much contemporary society differed from that of 1734, when law was codified. He pointed out that almost all landed property was encumbered with mortgages and other types of debts. Yet the law was based on the premise that land was a static unit, unaffected by human actions, and applied accordingly in legal processes. Hörnstein was appalled by the way the law allowed a husband to pay off all debts with means his wife had brought into the estate. If the husband died without any heirs, then his relatives would immediately take possession of the inheritance, including his marital rights, "so that his wife will suffer badly and unfairly." The honorable representative expressed the thought that, in the new law that was being contemplated, legislators ought to do something about this unfortunate state of affairs. Moreover, he considered it necessary to take a broader view of the problem and to acknowledge that landed property was no longer the only and most important type of capital. Chattels, money, shares, and bonds should also be taken into account when marital law was under reconstruction and classified as separate property, Hörnstein argued, and restrictions should be placed upon the claims to such property from the relatives of the dead spouse.[18]

With its emphasis on the importance of new and more dynamic forms of property, this was a lucid and highly informed analysis. Other members of the Diet also dwelt, approvingly or disapprovingly, on the changing nature of property. When one of them described how landed property was now a form of "immovable chattels" (*orörlig lösegendom*), it was obvious he did not like this new state of affairs. Land ought to remain in the hands of the family that had held it by tradition and should not be sold willfully when the owner happened to need cash. But others wanted the law to promote economic modernization and to facilitate the transformation of land into liquid capital. Public opinion was opposed to the antediluvian institute of *bördsrätt*, it was said, because *bördsrätt* caused much discord, hassle, and disgraceful lawsuits.[19]

It is obvious that many members of the Diet possessed a very accurate picture of how contemporary family law worked. They also made explicit references to the source of their knowledge: their long-standing experience as lay judges in the primary courts or as assessors of the estates of deceased persons.[20] For instance, Niklas Nilsson from Kalmar *län* described families, whose inventories he had drawn up, where adult daughters had done all the work on the family farm during their brothers' childhood without receiving any compensation after their parents' death.[21] These men had also seen many examples of how widows who lacked inherited land of their own found themselves in dire straits when their husbands died. They must also have been aware (as were assessors in Rystad) that women often made important contributions of property to the estates, but that these contributions were poorly protected unless somebody assisted the widow by asserting her rights when the inventory was drawn up.

Representatives of the clergy also made references to the situation in their constituencies, to what people "at home" did and wanted. The vicar Sandberg, who represented the clergy in Kalmar *län*, said that it had become increasingly common for ordinary people to be of the opinion that men and women should have equal marital rights. He referred to his own constituency, where the majority of all couples who came to him to announce their intention of getting married had set up prenuptial agreements or similar contracts with the intent of making it possible for them to equally share the marital estate. Given that this was what people preferred, Sandberg said, it would be best if this was also what the law stipulated.[22] Members of the Diet were also well-informed about how wills were used and of the pros and cons of such arrangements. Wills were used to improve the situation of widows, but it was claimed that these documents were insufficient in this respect because they often included formal errors making them legally invalid and because inherited land was not devisable. Therefore, a man who held only inherited land could not improve his wife's lot through a will, no matter how much he wanted to.[23]

It is difficult to find any member of any estate who was explicitly opposed to an expansion of married women's rights to the common estate, and among those who had firsthand knowledge about conditions among the rural population — that is, members of the peasant estate and of the clergy — there were even some ardent advocates of the reform. Some peasants disapproved of equal rights of inheritance, while at the same time supporting the proposal to increase the marital rights for women, which suggests that the latter reform was much less controversial than the former.[24] Indeed, the need for an immediate reform of marital rights was seen as urgent, particularly for peasant women.

The Diet's legal committee was positively disposed to a change in marital law as early as 1828, when it made the explicit statement that such change was particularly called for with regard to peasant women.[25]

It was also well known that the Law Commission in charge of the complete overhaul of the legal code was going to suggest equal marital rights, claiming the old law to be inequitable.[26] Using many of the arguments already presented by other actors, the committee particularly emphasized that marriage was a form of cooperation in which spouses joined forces with a view to working together for their common good. This was particularly pertinent for the peasantry, the committee pointed out. Not only did a peasant wife have to take care of the children and all domestic chores, "she must also take part in outdoor work, and with her labor contribute to what the household needs." When women from the estates of the burghers and the clergy had the same marital rights as their husbands without ever having to perform outdoor work, with what right could legislators then refuse peasant women these claims? Drawing on notions of equity and equality of rights, the committee started to address the issue of women's labor contributions in a way legislators had not previously done.[27]

The committee also drew attention to how married women were at the mercy of their husbands, who could make decisions of far-reaching consequence to their wives and children. This subject included many sensitive aspects, since it touched upon the very heart of patriarchal marriage relations: that the husband was regarded as the head and mouthpiece for the entire household. It is not surprising to find that the committee chose to avoid most of the delicate questions, but it did actually describe the dependent situation of women as a problem. A man who married in a city would become entitled to one-half of the property his wife brought into the estate, the committee pointed out, but if he then decided to move to the countryside, his marital claim would automatically increase, and hers decrease. This state of affairs was inequitable, the committee concluded. One partner must not be allowed to change the premises on which the partnership was established. Likewise, if the husband used the property his wife had brought into the estate to buy a landed estate in the countryside, his share of that estate would automatically be twice as big as hers. Or if he became indebted because of the transaction, his wife would become coresponsible for the debt, "since it is often difficult to prove who caused the debt."

The examples all highlight how predictability was low in property transactions within the household. They also show that the husband could take advantage of his privileged position in marriage to act in ways that could have detrimental effects upon his wife. In both cases, it was the opaqueness of the household that accounted for the problems. Outsiders could not know which spouse had caused the debt or which spouse had contributed what to the marital estate, making it difficult for the law to help the wife. Making marital rights uniform throughout the country was one way of shifting the balance in favor of married women.

Most members of the peasant estate argued that, if the marital rights of women were increased, as they ought to be, there was little reason to retain the custom of presenting morning gifts to women. In fact, it was not equitable, since widowers never received this type of property. The choice to improve one form of women's property instead of another is telling, since it probably reflects the composition of household property at the time. Widows who had no inherited land of their own and who had not acquired anything jointly with their husbands would not gain much from a larger share of the common estate. To such women, the right to a morning gift may have been a more valuable asset, and its abolition would probably have affected them adversely. By way of contrast, women who lacked inherited land of their own but who had bought land or other forms of capital with their husbands would gain considerably if their share of the common estate grew. (To the minority of women who had inherited land of their own, neither the marital rights nor the morning gift mattered much.) Thus, the unanimous support of reformed marital rights, accompanied by the abolition of the morning gift, suggests once again that, on the whole, inherited landed property was less important in many rural households, while ownership of acquired property was widespread. That this was indeed the case was also stated in explicit terms in the subsequent debate about wills in 1857.[28] The economy was gradually shifting focus, becoming less based on static landed property and more directed toward more volatile forms of economic endeavors. A more active land market was one of the main effects of these developments.

However, inherited landed property was still crucial on a symbolic and political level, which accounts for the opposition to equal rights of inheritance that existed both within the nobility and the peasantry. Excessive fragmentation of land was perceived by some as a threat to these two estates, the members of which had of old been the pillars of society. Thus, there were certain connections between the issue of inheritance and the ideological concerns about the sort of society one wanted to see in the future, as we shall presently see. But the question of the increase of the wife's marital rights was a much more down-to-earth issue, linked to the concrete situation of women and to concerns about growing costs for poor relief. The issue of marital rights was a prominent part of the set of problems known as "the social question," rather than "the constitutional question." To reform marital rights was definitely a "woman's question," and the reform had been called for since at least the eighteenth century, when the property rights of women had begun to deteriorate.

A New Relationship between the Sexes?

While the reform of marital rights was caused by practical problems extant among large parts of the rural population, the background of the inheritance reform was more complex, and opinions were split. Some noblemen were strongly opposed to such a reform, and in the peasant estate opinions were divided along geographical lines.[29] This reform did offer remedies to practical problems, just as the other one had done, but at the same time, the inheritance issue was rife with emotional and ideological tensions which were almost entirely absent in the case of marital law. Even if the final bill, resulting in the Act of 1845, presented a package solution for both the marital rights and the rights of inheritance, it is important to see the two issues and the accompanying arguments as separate.

Some debaters, particularly noblemen, linked the reform of inheritance rights to the demographic situation, which was perceived as highly problematic. Many young women did not get married, they claimed, and the reason was that they could not bring enough property into marriage. Increasing women's inheritance shares would be a way of making them more attractive on the marriage market. This description of the problem has a familiar ring; in fact, it was not unlike the one employed by Eric Schagerborg in the 1760s in a pamphlet presented to the Diet.[30] Now, it was reiterated within the estates of the nobility and the clergy, but accompanied by a different solution. A reform of inheritance rights, it was argued, would provide a counterincentive to choosing "a bachelor's life," and it would reduce celibacy in society.[31] "In our egoistic times," the nobleman von Troil declared, "no marriages are arranged where attention is not paid to the woman's fortune." This was why marriage rates were dipping, and morality was in peril. Increased inheritance shares for women would make it more attractive for men to get properly married, and this would have positive effects upon morality, that is, reduce the number of illegitimate children.[32]

The fear of male bachelorhood was not limited to the Diet but was more widespread in Swedish society,[33] and it was also expressed in other countries around 1800.[34] Something needed to be done about the bachelors, it was argued, and legal reform was one way of inducing young men to get married. Yet the instrumental attitude with regard to marriage struck other debaters as extremely cynical. Marriage was not a contract like any other, and young men should not be encouraged to look upon their future spouses as sources of income. What good does it do to society, the nobleman Ribbing asked, if young men act as if guided by a divining rod? And what good does it do to a daughter if her parents "gild" her (by letting her inherit more) in order to make her more attractive to a man? Men whose behavior is merely governed by a desire for material goods are not the sort of sons-in-law parents would wish for, he continued. Instead, parents should help their daughters to develop and refine their natural endowments, so that the girl is worthy of the man, and the man equally worthy of her.[35] Thus, while some debaters saw reformed inheritance rights as an appropriate means of coming to terms with the demographic and moral situation in society, others were strongly opposed to the idea, not because they denied that celibacy was increasing, but because they thought it a sacrilege to use marriage in this way.

It is clear that debaters had sharply varying perceptions of what kind of union a marriage was. Some thought of it as a partnership and argued that the partners should be placed on an entirely equal footing, including their rights and duties — just as influential lawyers had argued around 1700. Others were vehemently opposed to this view of marriage and emphatically stressed its emotional and moral sides. According to the latter, the husband and wife chose each other solely on grounds of affection and mutual respect. To insert sordid considerations (like wealth) into the matter was to degrade the most basic institution in society. A wife should not be chosen because of her material assets, nor should she in any way assert her separate material interests against those of her husband. Although seldom made explicit, the conclusion of this line of argumentation was that the economic aspects of marriage were better kept in the dark. These ideas, envisioning marriage in a somewhat sentimental light, were expressed particularly clearly when the Law Commission discussed indebtedness and separation of property.

Separation of property was very important in cases of bankruptcy, as we have seen, and particularly so to women who had no inherited land of their own. That separation of property became increasingly well-defined in the latter half of the eighteenth century strongly indicates that indebtedness was a frequent problem, that more women lacked inherited land, or both. But when separation of property was discussed among early nineteenth-century legislators, an interesting shift seems to have occurred. Even if legislators unanimously conceded that separation of property was sometimes necessary to protect the wife, they were still at pains to restrict its applicability as much as possible, arguing that separation of property was in itself "an evil."[36]

This position reflected a particular view of marriage, unmistakable in the proposal written by Johan Gabriel Richert, the best-known member of the commission and one of the most famous proponents of liberalism at the time.[37] Richert strongly stressed the spouses' common interests. The general objective of law was to let the marital estate, governed by "one of the spouses" (a convoluted way of referring to the husband), "merge to complete unity." This objective could not be reached, Richert argued, if the spouses entered marriage "with distrust," each suspecting the other of having brought secret debts, and each fearing that their separate properties might be confounded during marriage in a way that made them impossible to disentangle later. A complete separation of assets and debts presupposed that detailed inventories were set up prior to marriage, but such a practice would only be conducive to increasing distrust between the spouses. Instead, it was much better to give the manager of the estate (the husband) complete freedom to use the common estate as he liked and, consequently, to give the husband's creditors unlimited access to the property.[38] Therefore, separation of property must be used as sparingly as possible.[39] Richert placed his proposal in an internationally and historically comparative perspective. French and Prussian marital laws were "repugnant," he thought, and should not be used as examples for Swedish law; he was particularly disgusted by the way French law gave wives "an independent position." English marital law was better, he argued, because "it is much closer to what Swedish law has always presupposed," stipulating "the complete merging of spouses' property under the unrestricted governance of the husband."[40] What Richert had in mind here was coverture.

Richert's proposal and its professed motives are startling. His historical description was fundamentally incorrect. With its strong emphasis on spouses' separate ownership of land, medieval Swedish property law had never aimed at "the complete merging of spouses' property," and the many restrictions that law placed upon a husband's scope of action clearly refuted the idea of his "unrestricted governance." Even the legal code of 1734 retained separate property rights to inherited land. The power invested in the woman's family to restrict the actions of the husband had in 1734 been replaced by the power of the courts. Richert was wrong, but his views are reminiscent of ideas that had been put forward in the late seventeenth century, when some reformers had invoked the biblical words about spouses being "one flesh" to argue for a similar view. Moreover, Richert's arguments can be read as a form of "invention of tradition," put forward to reinforce tendencies that he saw, and liked, in nineteenth-century society. Movable property was becoming a more important form of capital, and women's movable property *was* poorly protected during marriage; another way of expressing this development was to say that the spouses' property tended to merge. Seen in this light, Richert's use of history dovetailed neatly with simultaneous tendencies in Denmark where legislators reinterpreted women's legal position in the past to make it fit into a new society based on liberal ideals and a capitalist economy.[41]

Other members of the commission concurred with Richert with respect to his view of marriage. Marriage was a very special institution and should not be treated "like a contract on property," they said. Marriage presupposed mutual trust and respect between the spouses and, therefore, law should not demand that spouses make an inventory of all their assets and debts prior to marriage. Such an inventory would be pointless unless it was made public, but publication would doubtless hurt the delicate nature of marriage. Privacy and love made it unwise to draw up and publish an inventory, but without an inventory, it would be impossible to let the wife separate her share of the community property and to save it from her husband's creditors. However, this was not a great problem, legislators thought, precisely because marriage was not comparable to ordinary companies. While rights and duties must be equally distributed among shareholders in a company, it was incumbent upon spouses not to assert their individual rights but to be prepared to sacrifice them out of love for each other.[42] In taking this view, the debaters may have been thinking of the public exposure of family matters through printed legal documents and newspapers, which happened almost daily, causing scandal and indignation. Richert was probably appalled by the public disgrace of Justice Dufwa.

From another standpoint opinion held that, while it was an invalid argument to claim that women needed larger inheritances to increase their chances of getting married, it was equally invalid to argue that women should inherit more because it was fair. Fairness and equality had nothing to do with matters of inheritance, according to opinions put forward by some debaters. It should come as no surprise that many noblemen took this stance. The French Revolution, with its attack on the ancient monarchy and privileges, had reduced the enthusiasm of Europe's noblemen for the rhetoric of equality. "Equality is a form of disease that stalks the world, infecting all minds and causing, despite its honorable intentions, much inconvenience," one nobleman declared in 1845.[43] Fairness was a less problematic concept, being essentially synonymous with equity, a term which had long been in use in the legal sphere, but as an argument for equal rights of inheritance, it caused much protest. "Justice and natural fairness" have nothing to do with inheritance laws, the ultraconservative von Hartmansdorff argued. If inheritance law were built on fairness, then Swedes, Englishmen, and Austrians would be less morally perfect than Germans and Frenchmen, von Hartmansdorff pointed out. But obviously, this could not be the case, and the reason was simple: the laws of inheritance were political constructions, to be chosen by each people as they liked.[44] One of his estate fellows, Löwenhielm, argued that one would be mistaken to apply "the principle of equality" everywhere, since it was false. Equality did not exist in the natural world where every species had been created in its own way by God, "the great aristocrat."[45] C. R. Cederström read aloud a memorial written by Professor Schlyter, where it was proved (probably "beyond all doubt") that the institution of marriage was based not on equality but on naturally given differences between the sexes. On the basis of this, Cederström attacked the bill and particularly "artificial legal concepts" such as equality.[46]

If there was one group who argued that fairness and equality were irrelevant arguments and that the relationship between the spouses was sentimental in character, there was another that truly wanted to adduce fairness and thought that "there was a new relationship between the sexes" that demanded a number of legal reforms, including the reform of inheritance rights.[47] This group had sympathizers in all four estates, all of whom based their arguments on the concept of equity and on the discourse of the Enlightenment. The first report from the Diet's legal committee in 1828 stated the reasons for advocating equal rights of inheritance for women in this spirit. As of old, the report said, men have been favored and woman disfavored in terms of inheritance rights. This difference was probably attributable to the more extensive education men received, which they needed in order to serve the state. (Here, the report must have had noblemen in mind.)[48] However, the report went on, political ideals were different today. Consequently, because of "natural equality" and "convinced that this is what citizens want, following the new manners and ways of thinking that prevail within all estates," the report proposed to give to all children equal rights of inheritance. In fact, when women had been accorded half a share in the thirteenth century, the first step toward this reform had already been taken. Now, justice and natural equality demanded that the next step be taken.[49]

Natural equality and general opinion demanded that women be given the same rights of inheritance as men, according to these debaters. This way of thinking was a reference to what other debaters explicitly termed enlightenment. Thus, the nobleman Gustaf Hjerta argued that equal rights of inheritance were "a fruit of enlightenment," and the peasant Petter Persson said that "old law is now like a stranger amongst us, whom we ask whence and why it has come," now that enlightenment and education have proceeded so far. The peasant Johannes Andersson described the opponents of the reform as "enemies of the light," and the clergyman Poppius argued that society had changed since the inheritance laws were first formulated and that "widespread enlightenment, legal equality and a more equitable distribution of wealth" was what most people wanted.[50] The references to enlightenment were strikingly common, as were the concerns with justice. The nobleman von Troil said that it "becomes our enlightened times" to remedy old injustices. That injustices were old did not make them more appealing or less unjust.[51] This nobleman was not alone in his concern for justice and fairness. In fact, many peasant advocates of reform described the legal situation of women in just this way, as unfair. "Law has thus far been unjust," a representative from Östergötland said, and so did the speaker for the peasant estate, Anders Danielsson from Älvsborg.[52] Professor Hasselrot of the clergy declared that he did not share the views of his fellow estate member, the famous poet and historian Geijer, who worried about the risk of excessive fragmentation of land: equity and natural justice were more important than political and economic gains.[53]

Two perceptions of marriage were pitted against each other in the debates. One portrayed marriage as a union based on love but also on authority and subordination. According to this view, marriage was primarily a private union in which neither law nor the public had the right to intervene. Marriage was an end in itself and could not be manipulated for other, societal ends. The other view depicted marriage as a union based on love but also as an economic partnership where equal rights and duties were a must, both to make the partnership work well but also to meet the demands of justice and equity. Spokesmen for the latter view argued from a perspective of enlightenment and improvement. The old laws were "barbarian" and bore the imprint of feudalism, they claimed, but now mankind had arrived at a stage in historical development where it was simply wrong not to accord the same rights to women as to men. Whether women did enjoy the same rights as men was seen as a litmus test of the degree of civilization which Swedish society had reached.[54]

Advocates of reform thus identified themselves with modernity and progress and saw their view of marriage as a new and correct one. They depicted their opponents as misinformed reactionaries who tried to perpetuate a medieval system. But this was a gross oversimplification. Their opponents' view was arguably just as new as theirs. Even if Richert tried to attribute historical roots to his (and others') view of marriage, the attempt was not very convincing. The kind of marital union Richert wanted to promote was a blueprint of English coverture, and there is very little to suggest that such a system had ever existed in Sweden. (A study of Rålamb's writings would have shown this, if nothing else.) The kind of sentimental and at the same time authoritarian model that Richert advocated was the bourgeois marriage model, and this was just as new as was the progressive one.

The claim that the enlightened model of marriage was completely new was an overstatement of the case. As we have seen, early modern Swedish couples often stressed that their married lives had been based on love, on jointly performed labor, and on jointly acquired property. Mutual wills from the early seventeenth century to the nineteenth century show that these were the arguments that ordinary men and women used and that they appealed to notions of equity when they implored relatives and courts to respect their arrangements for the surviving spouse.[55] Attacking arguments about spouses' investment of labor was also a standard strategy for those who felt that their rights were infringed upon by the will. Therefore, even if the rhetoric was new, the model that the advocates of reform presented rested on old domestic practices. By way of contrast, Richert's model was grounded on newer domestic developments that had made movable property more important in many households. Put simply, paradoxically the model of marriage that reformers described as new was in fact at least in part very old, while the model Richert depicted as old was, in fact, rather new.

Men's and Women's Contributions to Society

While some advocates of reform argued that women should have equal rights of inheritance simply because they were human beings, others pursued a line of argument that emphasized women's contributions to society. Women should have the same rights as men, not primarily because they were equally human, but because their contributions were equally valuable. In this way, the previous silence on women's contributions was broken in an unprecedented way. Women's efforts, which had previously been concealed within the household, were now put on the political agenda.

It was the hard work of peasant women that was highlighted most in these debates. That women's work was physically less demanding was a view put forward by some debaters, but it was emphatically refuted by others. Peasant women used the plough and the scythe, just as male peasants did, and their industriousness and attention to economics were important assets for the households, the clergyman Gumaelius pointed out. His fellow member of the estate Hardin praised women as mothers and workers: "From the minute the linseed is sown until the clothes are put on her husband, children, and servants, the woman is constantly at work."[56] The nobleman af Malmborg referred to his long-standing experience as a judge when he stated that a peasant's wealth was mainly to be attributed to the work of his wife.[57] Lars Olsson of the peasant estate said that he was convinced that his daughters contributed just as much to the household as did his sons, and his fellow estate member Johannes Andersson agreed.[58] Göran Jonasson told his fellow colleagues how women in his constituency in Kronobergs *län* used to work outdoors, even in the winter.[59] Clearly, it was hard rural work, mainly outdoors, that these men had in mind.

Women's domestic and maternal contributions were also important, however, to a well-functioning society. The clergyman Almquist deplored the way the value of women was denigrated in society. The only thing a woman received in acknowledgment of her contributions to the household was her husband's love, he said, while the husband was abundantly praised for his various achievements in society. This was inequitable, since the well-being of the state rested particularly on the shoulders of women, who were responsible for bearing and bringing up the new generation.[60] Similar arguments were put forward by representatives of the peasant estate, who compared the risk a young man took when going to war with the risk a young woman took at childbirth.[61] The picture painted by these arguments was that women contributed just as much, and maybe even more, to society than men did.

These contentions encountered intense opposition. Young men worked considerably harder than young women, many representatives at the Diet claimed, and while women's contributions were no doubt important, they were still not as important as men's. Peasant representatives from the northern parts of Sweden described how young boys had to go out every day with their fathers, regardless of weather and temperature, while their sisters were allowed to indulge themselves at the household hearth. That young male servants were paid higher wages than young female servants was taken as proof of the greater value of men's work (and not of previous injustices, cemented into custom). Even more important was the argument that young men defended the country and that they needed special compensation for the risks they took in this context. Bengt Nilsson of Örebro *län* described how their ancestors had given them "the rights of freedom," which included larger inheritance shares for boys. This rule, which applied to the peasantry and the nobility, was justified by the fact that the men from these two estates assumed special military responsibilities. "Depriving the man of this right is tantamount to depriving the soldier of his courage, and in this way the security of the nation will be jeopardized."[62]

These voices may say less about men's actual capacity to work and more about a fear that young men would no longer be wholeheartedly committed to defending Sweden. Who would want to risk his life for a nation that repaid its soldiers so poorly, the argument ran. There was a feeling at that time that the Diet had to create incentives to make men continue to work hard and defend the country. Apparently, it was not regarded as self-evident that men would make that commitment unless they were specially remunerated for their services. In other words, men had to be *made patriotic*, and the laws of inheritance had to be used to achieve this end. To be infused by patriotic feeling was seen as one of the most valuable qualities in a male citizen.[63]

Many speakers explicitly referred to the need to create positive incentives for young men. Young men had to be enticed into keeping their farms and tilling the land. Girls married early and left their homes, while boys stayed and faithfully cared for their elderly parents. If they ceased doing this because they were not properly rewarded for their work, it would create great problems for the country, it was argued. Agriculture would degenerate, old people would suffer, and, in case of war, there would be no soldiers to defend the country.[64] Thus, speakers often linked the structure of incentives to men's patriotic feelings, describing the proposed reform as "an insult to men's rights as citizens," as "a threat to patriotism," and as "a loss of moral power." To promote patriotic feeling among men, there was nothing that compared with providing them with land of their own. Nothing threatened national security as much as proletarianization.[65]

However, it was the peasant daughters who were the ones most in danger of proletarianization. Studies of the early nineteenth century show that by this time women seldom inherited land.[66] Therefore, women were the ones legislators should have worried about most, if avoiding proletarianization was the most pressing objective of inheritance law. In spite of these realities, there was a feeling in early nineteenth-century society that there was a shortage of men, particularly in agriculture.[67] Clearly, some members of the Diet paid more attention to this problem, which suggests that they saw men as more important members of society, both for their roles as farmers and as soldiers. Both the health and the wealth of the nation were connected with the economic situation of young men.

Some advocates of reform expressly put women and their property rights within the patriotic framework. Does not a country need the commitment of its women as well as that of its men? was the rhetorical question they posed. Johannes Andersson asked with what right Sweden required "patriotic feelings and a strictly moral behavior" (*stränghet i seder*) from persons who were "condemned to domestic thralldom." Sweden should not take for granted that women would continue performing their indispensable tasks even without incentives and remuneration. Hessle, who was a representative of the burghers, pointed out that patriotic loyalty also depended on what "the other sex" thought of its situation in society. The clergyman Sidner argued that daughters became more committed to taking care of the home if they received a larger inheritance share; in the present situation, daughters were said to leave their parents and to move elsewhere to find better paying jobs.[68] Here, as elsewhere in the debates, some members of the Diet used arguments and statements that were strikingly similar to the ones employed in France during the Revolution. In both countries there was a feeling that one needed to do something for women in order to gain their support for the new state.[69]

In the debates about rights of inheritance men were construed as free individuals who could not be ordered to defend the country or to take over responsibility for a farm. They needed to be enticed and rewarded. To a more limited extent, the same was true for women. It was at least suggested by some debaters that women were also susceptible to various incentives and that the country needed to use the incentives at hand — inheritance rights — in the wisest way possible. Perhaps the allegiance of young people to their native country could not be taken for granted. This fear may have been what accounted for the heated feelings that permeated the inheritance debate and that were largely absent from the debates on marital rights. The latter were part of the social question, and almost everybody agreed that the situation of widows needed improving. The inheritance reform was more multifaceted and ambiguous, but to a significant extent, it was also linked to a new nationalistic project, which set out to make free men into trustworthy patriots. Could one rely on noblemen to accept the responsibility of being officers and civil servants, and on peasants to risk their lives as soldiers, if their rights of inheritance were reduced?

Many members of the Diet believed that an inheritance reform would lead to an immediate fragmentation of farms, and, by extension, to proletarianization. Others tried to refute this conviction as illogical. Surely farms were *more* fragmented in the present situation when female children received smaller shares, the peasant Anders Danielsson argued. Moreover, if a son and a daughter received shares of the same size, the farm would not be more fragmented than if there had been two brothers. The only system that could prevent farms from being split up was "the English system," that is, primogeniture, and few were ready to accept this form as a solution.[70] However, those who feared fragmentation took for granted that daughters did not receive their shares in the form of land but rather in cash. A small share was cheaper and easier for a brother to buy than a larger share would be. If brothers had to pay more, they would inevitably become indebted, and in the end the land would fall into the hands of "capitalists."[71] These fears may not have been entirely unfounded. As early as the eighteenth century complaints were made about men becoming heavily indebted because they bought off their sisters and younger brothers. Moreover, there were regional economic differences that made it difficult to come to an agreement as to what inheritance system was best. Peasants from areas in southern and western Sweden were often strongly committed to giving daughters larger shares (such as Petter Persson and Anders Danielsson), whereas peasants from northern Sweden objected vociferously to these plans. The quality of the local soil and the access to protoindustries are likely to have affected their standpoints. To many peasants from northern Sweden, it seemed difficult to make ends meet if the farmer was burdened with even larger debts, whereas peasants from southern Sweden knew that one could live well on a small farm if it was combined with trade or ancillary crafts.

In fact, several debaters even regarded land fragmentation as desirable because it provided people with the incentive to work harder. A peasant representative from Älvsborg (in southwestern Sweden) argued that farmers often took better care of small shares of land. The clergyman Fries from Småland (in southern Sweden) believed that equal inheritance rights promoted industriousness and thrift in the male population, and his estate fellow Säve argued that large inherited estates only made owners lazy and extravagant. By way of contrast, experience showed how many poor peasants managed to work their way up to affluence through their diligence and thrift.[72] According to these debaters, land fragmentation and a certain degree of poverty were almost to be regarded as assets to the country. This view did not reflect a desire among wealthy landholders to keep down wages for rural laborers. Instead, it suggested that there was a great potential in small-scale farming and that noble estate owners contributed little to the wealth of the nation. These ideas were succinctly and eloquently summarized by the radical writer Carl J. L. Almqvist. In 1838 he published an essay called "On the Importance of Swedish Poverty," in which he accused the nobility and gentry of being unpatriotic because they had distanced themselves from the frugal lifestyle of the Swedish people. The true national character, Almqvist claimed, consisted in a combination of poverty and indomitable mirth; humorously but at the same time sincerely Almqvist argued that the Swede was never as happy as when he went bankrupt and had to part with his possessions.[73] From this perspective, women would do men, and the country, a favor by accepting larger inheritance shares.

When discussing whether farms should be large or small, debaters could draw on regional examples, as did many peasants, but they could also rely on foreign experiences. This was what noblemen often did. Those who were against the inheritance reform pointed to Ireland and asked, rhetorically, whether this was the sort of society Sweden should emulate. Would it not be better, von Hartmansdorff asked, to take England as a role model? "In what other country do civic virtues so flourish as in England?" Another country von Hartmansdorff admired was Norway, because Norway also practiced a form of primogeniture (through the *åsetesret*). There was no other country where it was so difficult for capitalists to buy land from the peasants, he declared peremptorily. Debaters did not agree, however, what conclusions should be drawn from the English and Norwegian examples. Cederschjöld thought England was a country replete with contradictions. It could be said to be an excellent country despite, not because of, its inheritance system. As for Norway, Cederschjöld reminded his estate fellows of the high levels of Norwegian emigration. Their colleague among the nobility, Dalman, argued that Ireland's problems had more to do with the endurance of the feudal system than with the rules of inheritance. France was a better example of the way that land fragmentation could be conducive to economic development. Lars Hierta agreed that economic growth had been quite remarkable in France since the Revolution, while poverty was widespread in England. He referred to stories he had read in the newspapers about evicted English tenants who had been driven by desperation to commit arson.[74]

Those members of the Diet who worried about land fragmentation and its possible effects envisioned the proletarianization of Swedish peasants and farmers as a result of indebtedness and the emergence of unidentified "capitalists" who would take over the Swedish soil. They feared that the economy would suffer and that the patriotism of men would be adversely affected. What they saw happening around them in Europe fueled their anxieties, but it also inspired their visions for the future of their own country. Would landed property continue to be the basis of economic life, or would other forms of economic activities gain the upper hand? What would the roles of men and women be? Gradually, it became increasingly clear to everybody that the Diet could not avoid addressing the most fundamental question of all: whether or not lineage property should be retained.

The Abolition of Lineage Property

A proposal to allow owners of property a wider scope of opportunities for devising property was first proposed by members of the burghers' estate in 1828. They were dissatisfied with the rules that applied in towns and cities, both because the law was a patchwork of obscure and contradictory rules and because in many cases the freedom to will land was actually greater in the rural areas, since many peasants held large amounts of purchased land. This was seen as unfair: all citizens should have the same rights, the burghers claimed, as a consequence of the principle of legal uniformity.[75]

Gradually, the focus shifted to the precarious situation of widows and widowers and to the usefulness of wills in improving their lot. Some peasants proposed that the law consider spouses as one another's heirs, regardless of whether arrangements had been made in a will or not. This was totally incompatible with the system of lineage property. (In fact, the right of spouses to inherit from one another was only introduced into Swedish law in 1987-88.) The proposal, however, made legislators interested in exploring the possibilities of instead giving spouses the right to devise inherited land to each other — something spouses had tried to do, albeit illegally, since at least the seventeenth century. The nobleman Adlercreutz was opposed to the abolition of lineage property, but he approved of the idea of extending the use of spousal wills. Such wills would be a way of caring for the surviving spouse, while at the same time providing an incentive for spouses to invest in the inherited lands of the other spouse, Adlercreutz pointed out. His fellow member of the estate, Dalman, saw the proposal as a way of letting the wife keep the estate of the deceased undivided, which would make it easier to consolidate capital and, by extension, to avoid bankruptcies. Not surprisingly, the peasantry was all for the idea of spousal wills. They were intensely aware of the problematic situation of many widows.[76]

It was not until after the inheritance reform in 1845, however, that the will issue really became a burning question. The reason was simple. Those who had been opposed to the reform saw an extended right to make wills as a useful means of correcting the negative effects of the new inheritance law. A reformed will law was perceived as a "balm on the wound caused by the inheritance reform," as a way of preventing excessive fragmentation of land and as a means of restoring the position of sons. On the other hand, those who were enthusiastic about the new inheritance law feared the effects of a reformed will law. They reproached their opponents for wanting to undermine the law of 1845, and the opponents candidly admitted that this was exactly the point! In other words, the will reform should be seen as a direct sequel to the inheritance reform.[77]

Whether fragmentation of land in fact reached a peak after 1845 is uncertain. How could the effects be gauged after only a couple of years? But the claim that fragmentation peaked was frequently made, and that daughters inherited more was repeatedly given as the reason. If parents were allowed to endow one child with more property than the others, this person (and it was taken for granted that it was a son) would be able to retain the farm undivided, and land fragmentation would slow down. But since the old rules did not permit an owner to devise inherited land, legal change was called for. The proposal suggested that an owner should be able to devise such land but only within a very restricted group of close relatives, while the freedom to devise acquired land remained unrestricted. Thus, the distinction between inherited and acquired land was still retained in the original proposal.

A peasant representative from Älvsborg made an astute analysis of the current situation in the country. Because of population growth and land fragmentation, the old "kinship right" was disappearing, he said. Peasants had many children and little land these days. It was impossible for them all to stay "on the land," since every share was so small. Moreover, not all children possessed the aptitude for taking good care of the land. Subsequently, farms were broken up, and in the end the land went to someone (the ubiquitous "capitalist") who had struck a deal with the ill-advised children. However, parents would be able to prevent this kind of development, if only they were allowed to select their successor. In fact, the representative said, the system of lineage property now worked contrary to its own purpose. While intended to safeguard the land and its possessors, the fact that lineage property was not devisable actually undercut the position of landholding families.[78] The nobleman Sparre agreed and pointed to the situation in Dalarna (a little north of central Sweden) where a radical version of partible inheritance was practiced, giving each heir the right to take possession of a plot of land no matter how small it was. It was the intense love of land that caused its excessive fragmentation, Sparre argued.[79]

The four estates were at a crossroads that offered several alternatives among which to choose. While some wanted to modify inheritance law by means of the extension of testamentary freedom, others thought one should accept the situation as it was. Petter Jönsson from Jönköpings *län* (southern Sweden) believed that it was too late to stop land fragmentation. Population growth made it impossible to effectively uphold the prerogative of the kinship group. Therefore, the Diet should leave everything as it now stood, including women's right to inherit equally with their brothers. A third alternative would be to retreat and to adhere strictly to the principles of lineage property and to repeal the law of 1845. Would it not be better to reduce the shares of daughters once again, if that was the objective one hoped to attain through a reformed will law, von Hartmansdorff asked caustically. Or why not let the nobility create entailed estates? His fellow estate member, Rudolf Cederström, contended that lineage property was still a bulwark protecting kin groups and making them invulnerable to the caprices of individuals. He feared that the right to make wills, which had been created to favor the church, would now be used by individualistic egoists. Once again, the examples of the English and Norwegian systems were held up and praised.[80]

A thought-provoking argument used to prove the drawbacks of the current system was that in everyday life it was impossible to make the distinction between acquired and inherited property. Two peasants from northern Sweden (Nils Larsson from Jämtland and Paul Hedström from Västerbotten) both argued that the distinction was useless in a society built on money transactions and credit. These two peasants were not alone in their skepticism. The legal committee made the same point, and so did the Law Commission. It was deemed impossible to make the distinction between acquired and inherited chattels, just as it was impossible to keep track of what was his debt and what hers.[81] In small-scale local communities where everybody knew everybody, it had been feasible to make these distinctions, but how could this be done in a society where economic transactions took place among strangers? It was easiest (if not necessarily best) to regard these things as opaque, unknowable, and therefore legally irrelevant. This view stands out in sharp contrast to the infinitely more optimistic attitude displayed by

Erik Lovisin in the late seventeenth century. Lovisin believed that all problems of low transparency in the domestic sphere could be solved by using the probate inventory. By way of contrast, nineteenth-century men thought that the problems were insurmountable — probably because property *did* change form much more often than 150 years before but also because nineteenth-century men were more prone to look on the property arrangements of families as private matters.

The fundamental principle of Swedish real estate law had long been the distinction between inherited and acquired property, but this distinction was now questioned on the grounds that it was too difficult to apply. Debaters started looking to other countries to find inspiration for a new fundamental principle. The principle had to be easy to use, and, more importantly, it had to balance the rights of owners against those of their children. The obvious alternative was a system built on reasonable parts (*laglott*). If all owners could dispose of 50 percent of their property by will and had to leave the residual 50 percent to their children (or close relatives), most of the problems under discussion could be dealt with. Land fragmentation could be prevented and spouses could make wills for the benefit of one another. This system was said to be used "in all European countries except England."[82]

A reform that introduced reasonable parts would be tantamount to abolishing the notion of lineage property. The Diet's legal committee hesitated to take this step, in spite of the fact that everybody knew that this was what the Law Commission was contemplating. But the legal committee feared that the proposal was not timely. While conceding that a system of reasonable parts would be simpler, it nevertheless argued that "public opinion" was still in favor of lineage property and that legislators should listen to the opinion of common men.[83] The burgher Indebetou expressed what many seem to have believed: that rural people loved lineage property and would be very disgruntled if this principle, used since time immemorial, was suddenly done away with.[84]

However, the discussions in the peasant estate show that the legal committee was wrong. Many representatives voiced criticism of the proposal but not because it abolished the special status of inherited land. Instead, it was the infringement upon the owners' rights to use their acquired property as they liked that caused opposition. Gustaf Glad from Västerbotten argued that the bill was a step backward and a violation of the right of ownership. Apparently in a heated temper, he continued, "I care little about the inherited land, but as for the property that I have acquired through my own labor, I want to be allowed to use it as I like, regardless of whether it is movable or immovable."[85]

Many other peasants felt the same. According to one argument, the unrestricted right of owners to transfer acquired property to whomever they liked encouraged children to treat their parents well. Knowing that they could not count on receiving this sort of property, children had to discipline themselves and think first of their parents' needs. It would be humiliating for a father, Nils Svensson claimed, to have to give 50 percent of his acquired property to an undeserving profligate son, and Nils Hansson contended that "the more we legislate with the objective of restricting the natural right of ownership, the worse the outcome will be."[86] Anders Bäckström found the proposal "curious" in its imposition of new restrictions on owners in a time when most felt that the owners' freedom of disposition should be increased.[87] Like other evidence, these reactions suggest that many peasant estates consisted more of purchased than inherited land. Only if more than 50 percent of one's property was acquired could the proposal be perceived as a reduction of one's freedom and room to maneuver. Obviously, many peasants were in this situation. What they wanted was to retain their freedom to do what they liked with their acquired land while at the same time being allowed to devise inherited land to their widows or their sons. In short, they wanted complete freedom of disposition. Many noblemen agreed. Just like the peasantry, they wanted the freedom to dispose of their lands so that they could be assured that their estates would not be fragmented after their deaths.

The legal committee conceded that the freedom to do as one saw fit with one's own property was an essential part of ownership. At the same time, it was always necessary to modify freedom to make it conducive to the general objectives of civil society. Unfortunately, the committee went on, one consequence of the old system of inheritance was that "he who does not have any inherited property, can deprive his children of all his [noninherited] property, while he who has nothing but inherited property, does not have any freedom of disposition at all, but must accept leaving the property to a distant, anonymous relative [if he does not have children]."[88] Obviously, there was an undeniable need to do something about testamentary law because otherwise inheritance law became almost meaningless. The developments in the land market had slowly changed the system in a way that no one had foreseen around 1700. It was necessary to repeal the old law, which had aimed at protecting landholding families against the caprices of individuals, in order to protect landholding families against the caprices of individuals! Per Erik Andersson from Västmanland summed it up well: it was incumbent upon legislators to prevent the insolvency of family members, particularly since "landed property has become a commodity circulating in the market." In the noble estate, Lagerbielke also argued for the proposed reform. It would have some drawbacks for the nobility, he admitted, but the nobility had to be prepared to make some sacrifices in order to achieve the general objective: unified law.[89]

The Final Result

The reform of 1845 improved the legal and economic situation of widows who did not have any inherited land of their own and who depended entirely on what they could receive from the common marital estate. Without any doubt, this was the most important part of the reform, since it affected the lives of a large part of the female population. It was also an urgent reform, since these women often had considerable problems supporting themselves and were overrepresented among the poor. As for inheritance rights, the immediate effects of the reform must have been modest, despite vociferous complaints after just a few years suggesting that the reform had caused havoc within agriculture. Many rural households (perhaps most) held little inherited land, and this fact reduced the applicability and relevance of the inheritance law. Thus, many young men and women could not count on any inheritance at all but were dependent upon their fathers' good will. If the father wanted to will away his property to someone else, he was free to do so, and the children did not have any legal means of stopping him. In this respect, late eighteenth- and early nineteenth-century Swedish youngsters were in a position resembling that of British youngsters, who could not claim a reasonable part and whose fathers could "cut them off with a shilling."[90]

Through commercialization of the land market, the Swedish inheritance system had become largely unregulated, leaving many owners with a wide-ranging scope of action and making individual arrangements like wills necessary and more common. Some thought that this was exactly the way it should be. Everything must not be regulated by law, it was argued; some areas of life were better left to individuals to arrange by means of contracts. One proponent of this view was the judge Lars Fr. Lind from northern Sweden. In his legal commentary from 1799, Lind asked, rhetorically, why so many statutory laws were passed after 1734. Did this prove that the law code had been deficient? Lind's answer was in the negative. The code as such was not deficient, but the Swedish population had never liked arbitrariness. Swedes had an unfailing abhorrence of oppression, and for this reason they had always demanded to have everything regulated by law. But this was nothing but prejudice, Lind remarked. Some things in life should not be regulated by law but through "the free agreements of citizens." Not law but common sense and conscience should govern parts of human society. Lind wanted less regulation and more freedom, accompanied by high moral standards.[91]

There were others who thought as Lind did. In the Diet, some speakers argued for the greater freedom of owners, while at the same time criticizing the idea that the law needed to regulate inheritance in order to protect children from callous and inhuman parents. The existence of such exceptional parents did not warrant legal regulation. Others reasoned like, what Lind would have described as, typical Swedes: they argued for the need for legal regulation. When discussing the will law, Cederström declared his preference for a system built on general inheritance rights. It was better for the law to prescribe how property be divided than for fathers to make painful decisions, Cederström argued. Law speaks on behalf of society, which makes individuals more willing to accept its words than those of an allegedly partial father. His colleague in the estate, Rehbinder, reiterated the common statement that law was not made for the just and equitable, because they carry the law in their hearts. Rather society needs legal regulation precisely because some people are *not* just and equitable. Staaf, who was a member of the Law Commission, argued against the idea that spouses' property rights should be regulated only through individual agreement. When in love, people could rarely conceive of any sacrifice that they would not be prepared to make for their beloved, and they seldom took necessary precautions, he pointed out. Therefore, it was incumbent on the wise legislator to take precautions on their behalf.[92]

These men, and many others, spoke for legal regulation. They were opposed to a system built on individual solutions and preferred a "general welfare system." The term is slightly anachronistic, I must admit, but at the same time apt. Nineteenth-century reformers wanted everybody to be able to count on certain material assets, even if the assets would not be the same for everybody, and they wanted the law to create the desired predictability. In this respect, the reformers pursued an agenda similar to that of twentieth-century welfare-state politicians, but — and this is important — they were also acting within a very old tradition. The rationale of the lineage property system had been to let everybody have his or her share of the material assets upon which a decent life depended. When this system decayed, because of the increasing commercialization of the land market, a new system had to be constructed, but a majority of the Diet wanted the objectives of the new system to remain consistent with those of the old one.

Consequently, the will reform of 1857 was carried through, establishing the principle of reasonable parts and the idea of equality of rights. It was only after this reform that women's equal rights of inheritance meant anything to the broad majority. From then on, daughters and sons were entitled to equal shares of the nondevisable part of their parents' property. In a family with one daughter and one son, the two children could count on having 25 percent of the estate each and, if their father did not make a will, they would each receive 50 percent. By way of contrast, if we assume that the average seventeenth-century peasant family had nothing but inherited land, the son would have been able to count on 66 percent and his sister on 33 percent. Their father would not have been allowed to make any testament at all. Thus, sons were the ones who lost most from the new law, whereas fathers gained most.

Yet, for all their enthusiasm for equality and justice (which we have no reason to doubt), the proponents of the inheritance reform almost invariably argued for sons' right to buy their sisters' shares of the family land. Very few debaters, if any, counted on women actually taking possession of the land of their ancestors. What the proponents of reform wanted was a system more like the Norwegian one, where one son took over the farm, and the siblings received monetary compensation. The difference between the proponents and the opponents (like von Hartmansdorff) was not as considerable as it would seem at first. The latter wanted to make it easier for sons by keeping down the price of the siblings' shares, whereas the former believed that young farmers could afford to pay a slightly larger sum to their sisters. Consequently, the inheritance reform confirmed and consolidated a tendency which meant that land drifted away from women and only rarely stayed in their hands.

It was precisely because of this strong tendency that it was crucially important to regulate women's rights to the common marital estate (1845), to protect their investments in husbands' redeemed land (1807), and to provide them with the possibility of separating their part of the common marital estate in case the husband became seriously indebted (contemplated since the eighteenth century). Even though some nineteenth-century women were great landowners, for example within the nobility, they were far from representative. The nobility comprised no more than between 0.4 and 0.3 percent of the entire population in the first half of the century.[93] Moreover, female landowners seldom owned land as a result of inheriting it from their family of origin. Instead, they acquired land jointly with their husbands or received it by will. Many women had no land at all but were rich all the same, their wealth consisting of movable property. And very many women had little or no property at all. To all these women, the reforms I have just mentioned were at least as important as the introduction of equal rights of inheritance — probably more.

Conclusions

Nineteenth-century legislators may have disagreed about the direction that the law should take, but they never hesitated about the need to amend it. They were aware of the increasing socioeconomic problems in society and wanted to do something. Many of them were also committed to the ideals of legal clarity and legal uniformity. The law was a patchwork of contradictory and obscure rules, which differed depending on a person's social estate, sex, civil status, age, and so forth. When it came to real estate law, rules even differed depending on where the owner lived (in town or in the countryside) and on how he had acquired his land. Many politically influential men believed that the resulting legal bewilderment hampered economic life, and they also felt that it was practically impossible to keep track of the pedigree of each plot of land, which the system of lineage property presupposed.

These developments have not previously been analyzed against the backdrop of eighteenth-century developments. When seen in this perspective, it is clear that the reform era was the end point of developments that stretched as far back as 1700. At that time, the protection of married women's property rights had been reconstructed as part of a legal reform initiated to improve the situation of creditors. When this reform was combined with unforeseen economic change in the form of rapid commercialization of the land market, women's property rights were gradually undermined. They were compensated to some extent, though, through bankruptcy law (where separation of property was first developed) and through the creation of a new public sphere where women's grievances could be put before the court of public opinion. Even more importantly, they were compensated through a vast array of individual property arrangements. Just as in many other countries, men and women did not simply stand by and accept the deterioration of the economic situation of women, and these grassroots practices go a long way toward explaining the new reforms that were carried out in the nineteenth century. Codified law was adapted to the ways in which many people used their property: they wanted daughters to inherit equal shares and widows to retain a larger share of the marital estate. It was not incidental that members of the Diet often referred to what people in their constituencies did, said, and wanted.

In order to understand the reforms, the roots have to be followed even further back in time. A fundamental problem of medieval and early modern property law was that it did not "see" movable property. It was intensely preoccupied with safeguarding lineage property, including women's lineage property, but it had no means of dealing with the fact that lineage property might be transformed into money and invested in someone else's lineage property. Nor did it normally admit that married women might need to convert their movable property into separate property (something British and French law had accomplished through the trust for married women's separate estate and *séparation des biens*) — separation of property was only available in cases of bankruptcy. This was, I think, the most vulnerable spot in Swedish women's property rights, and it became increasingly problematic as time wore on. However, it was not acknowledged as a problem in need of urgent solution until the quantitative importance of women's movable property and their lack of inherited land was staring everybody in the face.

Legal uniformity had become a key concept in nineteenth-century discourse and could not be ignored. Many felt that if legal uniformity was to be consistently implemented, one had to make a choice: either to give women the same rights of inheritance as men or to deprive them of all such rights. This was how the nobleman von Troil saw the situation: "Give to her the same share or nothing at all; in this way, we would at least be acting consistently."[94] Marylynn Salmon has argued that the existence of "half rights" and other special rules for women was an enduring problem in early modern law and that the tendency everywhere was to curtail women's rights, simply because it made the law easier to apply.[95] Amy L. Erickson's description of how English women's property rights deteriorated in the early modern period fits into this picture, and so do the results presented here. Through a combination of legal and economic change, Swedish women's property rights did deteriorate in the eighteenth century. Women received land less often than men and had to accept money instead — money that was poorly protected by law. In the early nineteenth century, it is likely that women constituted a larger part of the proletarianized population than men. And yet, instead of curtailing women's rights the Diet opted for creating legal uniformity by means of increasing women's shares. Something made it politically impossible to simplify the law to the point where women had no rights at all.

What this "something" was is a complicated issue. It seems too easy to just attribute it to ubiquitous Enlightenment ideals and notions about "natural rights," even if such arguments were frequently used and, for all we know, with sincerity. It is possible, however, that the explicit discussion about women's contributions to society was critical to the choice taken by the Diet. The fact that peasant women's hard manual work and all women's reproductive duties were invoked in the legislative debates is noteworthy. As we have seen, seventeenth- and eighteenth-century Swedish peasants often referred to investment of labor when they argued for their property rights. Without having read John Locke, they articulated a view according to which labor improved property rights. The origins of this view are complex. It partly reflected property law, which drew a strict line of demarcation between inherited land and acquired land, suggesting that owners' freedom to do what they liked with the latter had to do with the exertions made to acquire such property. It may have also reflected the value Protestantism attributed to work "by the sweat of one's brow" and the fact that most ordinary Swedes were hard-working peasants. Finally, it may have been strengthened and sharpened by similar arguments that were part of Enlightenment discourse.[96] Whatever the precise causes, the link between labor and property was a significant feature of early modern Swedish society. The existence of this link made the silence regarding some people's work glaring and increasingly problematic. It was hard to praise the value of labor without in the long run acknowledging all kinds of labor. It is telling that both in Sweden and in its neighboring country Norway women's work was used as an argument to improve their property rights in the nineteenth century.[97] It is hardly surprising that members of the peasant estate used the argument, but so did members of other estates, which suggests that there was a broader consensus about the value of labor.

I am not suggesting that women's work affected the outcome of the legislative process in an uncomplicated manner. The negotiations were protracted and included fierce attacks on the claims made on behalf of women. As always in political debates, there was uncertainty and ambiguity until the very end. Nor do I suggest that the reform in 1845 meant that women's work was acknowledged and upgraded in a more general and permanent way. To a large extent, much of women's work remained secluded inside households, seen and appreciated by very few. The bourgeois marriage ideal made women's contributions to society less, not more, visible. Still, it was important that women's work was mentioned in the Swedish debate, and it should be understood in the perspective of property rights.

Right to "compensation" was a crucial component of Swedish property law. When kinsmen vetoed a land sale to a nonrelative, they had to give him monetary compensation instead. When kinsmen were deprived of their inheritance, they were entitled to a form of compensation, a surrogate. When a married woman invested her estate money in the land of her spouse, she could be given compensation for this, if she asserted her rights when the probate inventory was drawn up for the husband or if the husband made a will for her. When siblings had to leave the family farm to their brother, they were given compensation. When noblemen had improved their landed estates, they were entitled to compensation (melioration) if they subsequently lost the land because someone else had a better claim. In other words, the whole system was based on payment of compensation and on the acknowledgment of the fact that many persons could hold different sorts of rights to the same object.[98] This may have fostered a legalistic attitude, where the right to compensation for both investments and lost benefits was regarded as self-evident. It is possible that this attitude — which was not merely a passing whim but rather a central tenet of property law — helped make the argument about women's work impossible to ignore, especially at a time when there was a growing awareness of the way women were an integral part of the social question and the poverty problem. Just as it was difficult to talk about all human beings having equal rights without in the long run acknowledging the rights of women, it was difficult to praise the value of labor without in the long run applying this precept consistently. The rhetoric engendered a logic of its own, which was hard to ignore.

THE RESTRICTED VISION
OF THE LAW

In response to a reader's query submitted to a major Swedish newspaper in 2007, a lawyer advised a couple to write a will to the effect that when they were both dead, their property would become their child's separate property. The ultimate aim of the proposed will was unmistakable: to make sure that their child's spouse would not become part owner of the property.[1] This small and inconspicuous feature succinctly sums up some of the continuities and ruptures in the story of marital property law in Sweden.

On the one hand, it shows that today, just as in the Middle Ages, legal experts take for granted that parents are hesitant about letting their property come into the hands of sons-in-law and daughters-in-law. The lawyer's advice even suggests suspicion on the part of the in-laws, a suspicion that is likely to be bolstered by high divorce rates in modern society. Parents are assumed to want their children and grandchildren to inherit their property and to not allow parts of that property to be lost to in-laws who will eventually divorce, remarry, and thus transfer the property into other families. The concern with keeping property within one's "overall purview" seems to be an enduring part of the story. Maybe modern parents would like to be able to veto unwise use of property by the younger generation, as their ancestors did hundreds of years ago!

On the other hand, the response also makes very clear that modern marital property law differs radically from the law that existed in the medieval and early modern periods. Contemporary law automatically makes spouses co-owners of each other's property, which is precisely why special legal arrangements have to be made to avoid this outcome.

By way of contrast, medieval and early modern law emphatically denied spouses such rights, even though, as we have seen, some spouses tried to circumvent these rules by drawing up mutual wills. Thus, the fundamental assumption of Swedish law has changed, from a supposition of (partly) separate property during marriage to a supposition of common property. Moreover, the relationship between the sexes is also conceived of in a new light. While medieval and early modern law depicted sons-in-law as the ones who might take advantage of the situation, there is none of this concern in the lawyer's reply, and on good grounds. It was the patriarchal power of the early modern son-in-law which entailed risks for women and their natal families; in a society where neither spouse is endowed with such powers, there is no reason to be more (or less) suspicious of one spouse than of the other.

In order to understand how the view of these matters was gradually reversed, it is necessary to comprehend the legal interpretations made and the roads taken in nineteenth- and early twentieth-century society. However, before embracing this task, a clear and comprehensive picture must be drawn of what had happened to marital property law in the preceding period, namely from 1600 to 1800. It is especially important to grasp what happened in the eighteenth century, a period of time about which knowledge has been particularly scanty and the evidence contradictory.

Three Ways of Looking at Long-Term Developments

In the eighteenth century, Swedish women's chances of getting married must have increased, since there were more men. At the same time, and for the same reason, a growing number of women must have received their inheritance in the form of movable property rather than in the form of land. Movable property was normally looked upon as common to both spouses, but it was the husband who had the right to use it for the common good of the household. Even if new and convoluted legal devices were introduced to protect inherited movable property (the surrogate), there is still reason to suspect that such resources could more easily slip into the "black hole" of the everyday economy than could a piece of land. For households with very small means, the need to have food on the table may have been what prompted them to sell the woman's inherited property, thus pushing them over the brink into a state of proletarianization. In some cases, of course, the wife inherited land from her natal family. But for various reasons, such land was in particular danger of subsequently being sold by spouses. The value would then be invested in the lineage property of the husband, to which the wife held no claims. The increasing importance of forms of property other than land and the insufficient legal protection of such property both suggest that Swedish women's legal and economic situation deteriorated in the eighteenth century.[2] If this interpretation is correct, then the Swedish case was more similar to that of England than has previously been acknowledged, with the exception that Swedish law did not develop the instrument of the trust to protect married women's movable property.

This interpretation is corroborated by the many compensatory practices that were developed and deployed in the eighteenth and early nineteenth century. Married men could set up wills for the benefit of their wives, these men could make retirement arrangements with the next generation including favorable terms for their wives, they could register their wives as co-owners of the family farm (after 1807), and they could protect the rights of other men's widows when a probate inventory was set up. These practices clearly show that many women needed to have such special arrangements made for them, and they also show that many men realized this. If no special arrangement was made, the woman would have little to fall back upon and her position was thus often weak. Medieval law had provided people with a sort of "general welfare," as it were, giving all children of legitimate birth entitlement to land, but this system failed to provide for everybody when land became increasingly scarce and increasingly expensive. A system in which individual arrangements were necessary was gradually substituted for the previous system that had been built on general rights.[3]

To claim that a process of deterioration took place implies that, in some sense, the situation had once been better. To some extent, I do think this argument can be made without being accused of romanticizing the past. Daughters no doubt had a better chance of receiving their inheritance in the form of land in the seventeenth century than would later be the case. Since the law accorded better protection to land than to other forms of property, it was generally better to inherit land. Moreover, medieval law explicitly acknowledged that husband and wife could have different interests and laid down certain rules that served as a check on husbands who might abuse their patriarchal power. It is true that the law did not recognize that the woman's male kinsmen could also abuse their power over her, which may also have been likely. Medieval law was mainly concerned with preserving lineage property and less concerned with protecting women as such. Still, if we have to choose between a form of patriarchy that openly admits that the power of husbands needs to be controlled and sometimes annulled and a form that takes for granted that husband and wife always have identical interests, the choice is quite simple.

On the other hand, a case can be made for a more optimistic interpretation. It is possible to see the developments I have described here as expressions of an amelioration of women's legal and economic position. The supply of land for sale grew in the eighteenth century, partly because of the state's decision to sell out large parts of its land to its tenants (*skatteköp*). When a tenant and his wife during their marriage bought a farm previously owned by the state, the land was classified as acquired and, consequently, as part of the common property of which the wife owned one-third. In view of the way land values increased during the century, this entitlement to land was extremely valuable to the wife of a former tenant. Her legal and economic position was considerably better than that of a woman who had invested her inherited means in the lineage property of her husband. What the latter could hope for was, at best, to be given pecuniary compensation for what she had lost. The wife of a former tenant could barter her share of the farm for care and support during her old age — just as wealthy freeholders had always done. The transformation of state-owned farms into freeholds had substantial impact on the overall structure of ownership in society. By 1850, no less than 60 percent of all farms were freeholds, as compared to approximately 33 percent around 1700. If most of the new freeholds were co-owned by husband and wife (which is not an implausible assumption), an increasing share of all women became co-owners of land as early as the eighteenth century. Through the expansion of the land market, the old restrictions concerning lineage property could be circumvented in a way that offered better opportunities to women. It is important to note that this happened as a result of new statutory law and not of privately made arrangements. In other words, it was a development that did not presuppose the good will of individual men. Seen in this light, the market had liberating and beneficial effects. The model that appeared through these developments — of husband and wife co-owning their farm — was also the one that was in effect recommended through the reforms of 1807, 1845, and 1857. Henceforward, women seldom inherited land from their natal families, but their inheritance shares became larger. When women married and these shares were invested in the family farms, the wives could be registered as co-owners.

Finally, a strong case can be made for an interpretation stressing continuity and lack of change, rather than deterioration or amelioration. This interpretation emphasizes that from the Middle Ages and up to the nineteenth century, Swedish women were deeply dependent upon their natal families for their economic well-being. It is very clear that prior to 1734 the law took for granted that families and broader kin groups had an interest in and a responsibility for women's property. It is probable that families sought to ensure that sons-in-law did not use their wives' land unwisely. In particular, they had a keen interest in ensuring that the wife's land was not relinquished to creditors and that her land money was not invested in the lineage property of the son-in-law. Some families may have closely guarded these matters, and, if the son-in-law failed to live up to expectations, they could sue him, invoking the medieval stipulations about what a husband could and could not do. Other families may not have bothered at all. The relatives may have left the woman to herself, and they may even have abused their role as her guardian. Thus, whether the woman's property rights were upheld or not depended to a large extent upon the actions taken by her family, even if, in the last instance, a woman could turn to the courts to seek redress.

However, this picture may fit equally well for the period after 1734. Although the sources seldom reveal any details about these issues, it is entirely possible that women's families continued to give advice and support, even when their formal right to veto sales by the son-in-law had been abrogated. It is possible that it was the woman's close relatives who urged the husband to make a will for her benefit or to make a proper retirement contract. We definitely know that relatives were the ones who helped widows assert their claims to compensation when their estate money had been lost. Thus, the role of kinsmen and relatives may have continued to be extremely important,[4] and the women who fared less well in the eighteenth and nineteenth centuries may have been the ones who, for some reason, lacked this kind of family support. The family may have been dispersed, or uninterested; they may also have lacked the knowledge necessary to realize that a certain legal arrangement was required. But subtle psychological mechanisms may also have played their part, as when the family revered the son-in-law too much to dare to claim a will for the woman. This scenario, which may have applied mainly to middle- and upper-class families, was captured by George Eliot when she had Mr. Gascoigne of *Daniel Deronda* regret his trust in his niece's husband: "I had shown my reliance on Mr. Grandcourt's apparent liberality in money matters by making no claims for her beforehand. That seemed to me due to him under the circumstances. Probably you think me blamable."[5]

These three interpretations are not mutually exclusive. Instead, there are very strong reasons to believe that they each provide an accurate description of one aspect of the very complicated processes that were at play when European societies were transformed into the sort of world we now take for granted. The three interpretations also help us understand the ways in which women's legal and economic position was conceived of in the nineteenth century. They explain how and why women's situation in society, which had not been an issue in the seventeenth century, gradually came to have a place on the Swedish political agenda.

Fredrika Bremer and the Birth of Women's Rights

When *Hertha* was published in 1856, Fredrika Bremer was already an internationally renowned author. Several of her previous books had been translated into German and English, and she corresponded widely with intellectuals sharing her interests in arts and society. Shortly before the publication of *Hertha*, Bremer made a tour of the United States, for which she had held an interest since her childhood when she had read Tocqueville and Harriet Martineau. Socializing with famous Americans like Longfellow and Emerson, she also visited prisons in the north and slave plantations in the southern states and in Cuba. She was deeply affected by what she saw; had it not been for the publication of Harriet Beecher Stowe's book *Uncle Tom's Cabin* a few years earlier, Bremer declared, she would have written a similar book of indignation herself.[6]

Consequently, when Bremer compared the situation of Hertha Falk and her sisters to that of slaves, it was very potent imagery coming from someone who had actually witnessed the lives of those who were forever bound to a master. It showed her strong commitment to improving the living conditions of Swedish women, and at the end of her life, she was proud to think that her novel had indeed contributed to this end.[7] It is no coincidence that the first Swedish organization devoted to the emancipation of women bears the name of Fredrika Bremer.

What Bremer was most concerned with, however, was freedom: the freedom of unmarried adult women. Freedom is what Hertha covets and what Fredrika herself had longed for as a young woman. Freedom, in the sense of full legal capacity for spinsters, was also a hotly debated issue in the middle of the nineteenth century, and it resulted in a number of bills (in 1858, 1863, and 1884) relaxing and finally removing the restraints previously imposed on these women.[8] Giving full legal capacity to spinsters was tantamount to abrogating the patriarchal power of their fathers or, in the absence of fathers, their guardians. It meant that unmarried adult women were free to pursue the economic activities they preferred. In this way, the reforms offered new opportunities to women of the middle and upper classes, who would often find it difficult (or unappealing) to get married. Often, these women worked as teachers;

it is no coincidence that Hertha ends her life as headmistress of no less than two schools. Teaching was seen as a respectable job for middle-class women and as a mission that would give them an outlet for their "natural" inclination to mother.

These belated reforms made Swedish spinsters more like their British sisters who had been looked upon as legally competent economic actors during the entire early modern period. The reforms diminished the dependence of unmarried women upon their families, which may have been one of the long-lasting continuities in previous times, as has been suggested. Indirectly, they are also likely to have made markets grow, as more women were authorized to participate as producers and consumers.[9]

Still, without downplaying the importance of these reforms, this book suggests that the story of the Falk family should perhaps have been written from the point of view of Hertha's mother, because to a large extent the socioeconomic problems identified in the early nineteenth century concerned the legal situation of married women (and particularly of peasant widows). Moreover, along with suffrage and the right to higher education, the improvement of married women's legal situation remained one of the chief objectives of the early women's movement in Scandinavia.[10] In this period, the reform giving wives the right to make decisions about their own incomes (1874) was important, as was the abolition of the husband's patriarchal power over his wife,[11] in conjunction with the extension of suffrage to all Swedish women in 1921.[12] In the preceding period, namely the first half of the nineteenth century, reforms to improve married women's property rights were of crucial importance but, as we have seen here, the much-touted inheritance reform probably had less impact on the majority of women than has previously been acknowledged. Instead, the reform allowing spouses to co-own property redeemed from relatives (1807), the reform giving married women an equal share of the common marital estate (1845), and the reform abolishing lineage property (1857) had more far-reaching implications, precisely because they sought to come to terms with domestic secrecy: the problem that what married women contributed to the common estate always ran the risk of being overlooked and ignored. The emergence of women's hard manual work within the household in the political debates both in the first half of the nineteenth century and around 1920 is probably indicative of the fact that, when radical improvement was called for, arguments about labor contributions were correctly identified as particularly forceful ones.[13]

Against this backdrop, there is reason not to downplay the importance of Fredrika Bremer and also to reappraise the role played by those men and women who unassumingly but doggedly emphasized the importance of married women's contributions of labor and property. These included some of the male deputies of the Diet as well as women such as Anna Maria Rückerschöld, who appealed to public opinion in her quest to raise awareness of the value of women's labor. But they also included a number of often anonymous Swedes, who helped to make this question into a political issue by simply taking active part in the new public sphere established in the late eighteenth century. By not fearing publicity but instead using it for their own ends, these persons acted within the tradition of an old legal culture in which all problems had been settled in the public arena and with the help of locally held knowledge.

Women's Property Rights and the Credit Nexus

Although this has been a story of Swedish women's property rights, it is also a story with broader relevance. Throughout early modern Europe there were many differing legal systems, but many of them included rules and devices designed specifically to defend women's economic rights. These systems were based on, or at least justified with reference to, the idea that women were vulnerable and therefore in need of special protection, even against their own husbands.

For instance, early modern German law provided married women with a special "guardian of the sex" (*Geschlechtsvormund*), who had to be male but who should emphatically not be the husband. Consequently, while being the manager of the household, the German husband was nevertheless barred from using his wife's property if she did not explicitly and voluntarily give her consent to do so, and the guardian was there to make sure that he did not use persuasion or violence to force her to give it. Moreover, the husband's property served as a tacit pledge for his wife's marriage portion, but her property was not pledged in return. Thus, the husband's power was patently circumscribed, and the fact that the wife had property of her own (even though she could not use it freely) was manifest to everyone.[14] This system is reminiscent of both the Swedish kin veto (prior to 1734) and of the medieval Venetian system of registering the receipt of the dowry as a mortgage on the husband's property.[15]

The theory that women were vulnerable and therefore in need of special legal protection harked back to Roman law but was rediscovered in early modern Europe. It was often phrased as *imbecillitas sexus* and figured prominently both in French and German law. In the process of rediscovery jurists often seem to have forgotten that both at the time of Justinian and in the late Middle Ages, the legal restrictions imposed on women — conceived of as protection — had actually been rather lenient.[16] In the absence of such awareness jurists reinvented and reinforced both protection and restriction from the sixteenth century onward, and in this context, special attention was invariably devoted to the menace creditors were believed to constitute. A recurring legal tenet was that a married woman could under no circumstances provide economic security for her husband's debts. This was exactly the line of argument Claes Rålamb pursued in Sweden, when he too employed the notion of *imbecillitas sexus.*

Disregarding details, then, there is much to suggest that there was a common European system set up both to protect women's economic interests and to restrict women as independent economic actors. Strong evidence also sustains the claim that this largely common system was put under great pressure by new commercial forces in the early modern period. The core of the matter was that people who provided credit for commerce believed that the system was abused by couples who let the wife "shield" the husband against creditors' demands. Against this backdrop, new forms of contractual arrangement evolved. In France, for example, we find clauses which annulled the rule that a wife could not provide economic security for her husband's debts. These developments subsequently resulted in an edict abolishing the rule; however, this edict was never accepted in Normandy or the Midi — areas where there was a strong tradition of lineage property and of separate estates in marriage.[17] In German cities, similar processes were at play. In the words of Robert Beachy, it was the increased use of credit instruments "that created tensions because creditors could not easily take women merchants to court," since they were protected by the *Geschlechtsvormundschaft.* Not surprisingly, many creditors argued that "if women were allowed to enter exchange contracts, then they should be considered legally competent and therefore held liable for their debts."[18] Because of their close family contacts with merchants, German jurists often shared the outlook of merchants and thus advocated legal change.[19] There are striking similarities between the arguments used by these jurists and those employed by Swedish seventeenth-century lawyers who also argued for the need to improve the situation of creditors.

British common law was conspicuous for its scant interest in married women's property rights, but this was partly made up for through equity law and the establishment of separate estates for married women.[20] Thus, even if the origin of this system was different, it nevertheless created structures that did have some traits in common with what we find in many other European countries. However, the English system was also put under strong pressure by commercialization. In the early American colonies, creditors argued that separate estates for wives could be used to defraud creditors; for example, a husband who was indebted could resort to setting up such an estate for his wife, thereby depriving his creditors of their security for loans. In order to prevent the creation of such fraudulent arrangements, the legislatures started to demand public registration of all settlements and trusts. In this way, the technical problem of knowing who owned what was solved, replacing secrecy with openness and legibility.[21] In a similar vein, creditors' interests occasioned the use of probate inventories and the public registration of debts in Sweden.

An image emerges that casts the credit nexus as the villain of the story, or at least as the prime mover. Credit brought about change, and change did have some negative consequences for women's property rights. This was precisely what staunch conservative defenders of the patriarchal system, like Claes Rålamb, had predicted would happen. This is also the picture conveyed by many nineteenth- and even twentieth-century novelists. George Eliot was not alone in depicting credit as the force that threatened to wring the livelihood out of the hands of ordinary families. Balzac hinted as much in some of his stories.[22] Recent historiography also suggests that indebtedness, and fear of what it would bring about, had a profound impact on the mindset and everyday practices of early modern people, particularly among those known as the "middling sort."[23]

Yet it would be a serious mistake to assume that credit and debt were new to the early modern period. People have always needed and will always need help and mutual support in difficult situations, and this is after all what credit is all about.[24] What was new, then, was perhaps not the pervasive importance of credit but that credit relations tended to transgress the borders of small local communities whose inhabitants were well-known and started to link stranger to stranger, creating anonymous and impersonal patterns of dependence. Even more important, what was new was the introduction of a logic which dictated that debts be honored at any cost and that this should take precedence over all other interests, such as protecting allegedly vulnerable women or retaining good relations within the kin group. The Swedish novelist Hjalmar Bergman captured this in one of his novels, where a poor soldier's handsome daughter is married into one of the wealthiest middle-class families in town. While first awed by the splendor and affluence in her new surroundings, she soon finds out that her meek husband is too generous in providing credit to his relatives. In an effort to create order and clarity in the account books, she forecloses all debts, bringing about a chain of bankruptcies throughout the adjacent countryside and, of course, alienating herself and her poor husband from all these unfortunate kinsmen. In a spate of candor, one of them tells her how the relatives had often helped her husband from his childhood onward, adding that "we had our own little system and it was not that bad. And it was simple. We stuck together, that was all." A system of mutual support worked well, as long as it was not misconstrued and discarded by an outsider who was in too much of a hurry to wait until she had understood it.[25]

The Restricted Vision of the Law

The law plays a crucial role in this story. Therefore, it is vital to reflect upon its character. Law is not, and has never been, a painting representing society in a detailed and realistic manner. Instead, what law does is to identify certain relations in human society as worthy of its attention, to point to certain facts that it defines as relevant to the understanding of these relations, and to establish certain norms that should govern them. It also lays down certain procedures, or methods, that will allow problems that may occur in these relations to be dealt with. In brief, law is a social technique.

It follows from this that law is, and has to be, selective. In fact, one of the main characteristics of law is that it defines some things as legally interesting and others as legally uninteresting. A more metaphoric way of expressing this is to say that the law does not see everything, or, more correctly, that it *chooses* not to see everything, in society. Law has a restricted vision. When people come to court to present their cases, the judiciary is flooded by words, descriptions, and details of everyday experience. But in the course of decision-making, this plethora of social facts is reduced to what the law defines as relevant to the question. The reason for this selectivity is that it simplifies decision making, making it swifter and, possibly, more consistent, but with the concomitant risk that vital aspects are left out. A very good example of this tendency toward simplification is, I think, the English coverture system. Here, the wife was regarded as "covered" by her husband, in a legal sense, and therefore invisible to law. By contrast, the husband was constituted as the legally relevant person of the household. Interestingly, the term coverture relates to our vision, to the way in which the moon is covered by the sun so that we cannot see it. English law simplified its vision of the couple by restricting its view to the husband.[26] Research has shown how the woman's invisibility created problems, both for herself and for the legal system as a whole.

In a similar way, medieval Swedish law restricted and simplified its view of ownership. It was mainly interested in ownership of land, and it took for granted that land could only be inherited or acquired, without elaborating on the exact meaning of this distinction. Moreover, it paid very little or no attention to the actions through which human beings can affect the value of land. In the seventeenth century, this restricted vision of the law became particularly pertinent in three contexts: the effects of credit, the effects of investment of money, and the effects of investment of labor upon real estate. Swedish law was not entirely clear about whether or not the need to honor debts was more important than the wish to keep spouses' property separate. The law paid no attention at all to where the money came from when land was redeemed from relatives, and, finally, it often accepted the claim that labor improves property but did not apply this principle consistently.

The restricted vision of early modern law becomes comprehensible if we think of its longevity. The legal code used at the turn of the seventeenth century was about three hundred years old, and on some points it was clearly out of step with society. Still, the restricted vision of the law was not merely a legacy from the past. The inclination to reduce complicating factors was very much present in the early modern period as well. The best example of this is perhaps the attempts at simplifying credit law by making the wife's property available for seizure by her husband's creditors. Even if these ideas never came to full fruition, they nevertheless illustrate the temptation to simplify legal problems in a way that might prove highly detrimental to some of those concerned.

This example reveals the way in which the restricted vision of the law could have obvious implications for gender relations; however, this does not mean that women were always disfavored in a simple and direct fashion. For instance, it is evident that the Swedish law's lack of interest in who had provided the money for the redemption of land could affect both men and women. The fact that women were more likely to be affected was not only the result of the law's disinterest in forms of property other than land but was also an effect of the smaller shares of inheritance that women had. Put otherwise, the protection of women's property rights would have increased considerably if early modern law had paid greater attention to contributions of money or if it had increased women's shares of inheritance. If the former alternative had been chosen, men's property rights would in some instances have been improved as well. The basic problem was the law's inability to "see" property other than land.

On the other hand, courts often seem to have accorded great importance to investment of labor despite the fact that nothing was said about this in the legal code. Possibly, the role played by this argument may be explained with the reference to Protestant ideology. However, this principle was applied highly selectively, and women's work, inside and outside the household, does not seem to have been seen at all until the early nineteenth century. In this case, the restricted vision of law translated more directly into a disfavoring of women.

In view of the importance of the law's restricted vision, it is enlightening to reflect upon how three influential lawyers conceptualized domestic secrecy. In the late seventeenth century, Claes Rålamb thought that it was little more than rubbish to talk about domestic secrets. According to him, the law was more or less crystal clear with respect to who owned what within the household: the spouses held their inherited land separately, and they each had a well-defined share of the common property. In one sense, he was probably right; the legal code was quite unambiguous, so long as one did not complicate the issue by recognizing that land was frequently transformed into liquid capital, which was then reinvested in other forms of property. Rålamb argued for a sort of visibility, or legibility, that was closely tied to land and to local control of land. As long as most property took the form of land, it could easily be perceived in the landscape, and it was relatively simple to keep track of who owned what.

By way of contrast, his colleague Erik Lovisin was much more aware of the increasing importance of forms of property other than land. He was eager to find ways of making these new forms visible to the judiciary (and to creditors), and he was an enthusiastic advocate of new techniques, such as probate inventories, and of the public registration of mortgages. While Rålamb argued that the judiciary knew everything it needed to know about these matters, Lovisin was keen to explore the technical means by which new knowledge about a household's property could be stored and retrieved for the benefit of those outside the household. He does not seem to have worried about whether these new methods might be misused so that domestic privacy could be encroached upon. (Had he lived today, he would probably have been intrigued by the possibilities offered by the computer.)

Richert, a much later colleague of Rålamb and Lovisin, took yet another view of the household and its inner affairs. Living more than a century later, he was fully aware of the importance of movable property. It is revealing that he and his colleagues paid such great attention to the spouses' separation of property, which was an issue of relevance mainly for movable property. But their attitude was radically different from the one expressed by Lovisin. Richert and his colleagues explicitly said that it would be perfectly possible to make an inventory of everything that spouses owned prior to marriage so that one could later decide exactly what had been added to and deducted from the estate and who was responsible for the debts. In this way, transparency and legibility would be total. But Richert did not want to do this. If such an inventory were to have any meaning, it had to be made public, and Richert found this unacceptable. The public advertising of inventories would disclose sensitive household matters in a way that would be highly detrimental to married life. Since marriage was more important than the complete elimination of domestic secrecy, Richert consciously chose a restricted legal view of the household, a view according to which everything in the estate was presupposed to be at the complete disposal of the husband. The extreme exposure of private life that had taken place in some scandalous cases from the late eighteenth century on may well have influenced his standpoint, as did of course the bourgeois family ideal. In fact, Richert adopted exactly the same standpoint as the protagonist of *Hertha*, who could not bear to have her father publicly disgraced, no matter what injustices he had inflicted upon her.

Thus, the restricted vision of the law depended on both technical and ideological factors. It had to be technically possible for outsiders to obtain verifiable knowledge about the property relations inside a household if law were to take it into account, but it was equally important that ideological perceptions about the household and married life did not bar the law from taking such knowledge into consideration. The interest of openness had to be balanced against the interest of privacy. This balance was struck differently in the early nineteenth century than around 1700. In sixteenth- and seventeenth-century local communities, the balance was struck in yet another way. Here, the distinction between private and public had hardly been meaningful since "private" matters were continuously surveyed and discussed in the local public sphere. It is an intriguing paradox in this story that privacy and new and more extensive forms of publicity started appearing at the same time, attracting and repelling each other in ways that were probably new to human society.

The law had greater impact on Swedish women's property rights through what it did not see than through what it saw. Still, it is important what the law actually said, or implied, about husband and wife and their property rights. Here, there is reason to stress change over time. Male authority over women was a constant factor throughout the period, but it was constructed very differently in the early nineteenth century as compared to the seventeenth century. Male authority had been considerably circumscribed in the seventeenth century, not least with regard to wives' inherited land. The medieval legal code smacked of a view according to which husbands needed to be controlled by their in-laws and the broader kin group, so that they did not misuse their wives' landed property. This view was challenged both by legislators, who wanted to increase husbands' (and indirectly creditors') power over the marital estate, and by spouses, who described themselves as united by love and common interests. What emerged in the early eighteenth century was a new and more positive view of the husband, who was accorded greater leeway in several respects. Even if this view was subsequently challenged by pictures displayed in the public view of male spendthrifts and bankrupts, there was no way back. It is telling that nobody proposed to solve nineteenth-century women's economic problems by reintroducing the veto, which had once been the means by which a woman's natal family could guard her rights. In a society where men's rights to do what they pleased with their property were much lauded, it was impossible to place men officially under the inspection of their fathers-in-law. But it was equally impossible entirely to disregard women's, and particularly widowed women's, needs and rights.

The difficulty of entirely ignoring social facts and consequences is a crucial part of this story, and it also has broader, theoretical implications. While early modern law had a restricted vision of property and labor (and of other matters), early modern lawyers, judges, and ordinary people were often aware of these shortcomings. Vociferously or unobtrusively, they pointed to the legal relevance of social facts that lay outside the vision of the law. Throughout this book, we have encountered several examples of litigants, lay judges, or parliamentarians who have argued for the need to pay attention to women's investments of property or labor. We saw how the court in Undersåker found a way of protecting the will of the ailing Olof Eriksson for the benefit of his wife, in spite of the fact that his brother claimed that it was illegal.[27] The court apparently did this because they regarded any other solution as inequitable. Higher up in the legal hierarchy but in a similar vein, a member of the Law Commission, Leijonmarck, questioned the fairness in not allowing a spouse to become co-owner of the other spouse's redeemed land.[28] And in the reform era, the nobleman von Troil expressed doubts as to whether the old inheritance law was founded on justice and equity rather than on male selfishness.[29]

Considerations of equity, or fairness, proceed from a simple acknowledgment of the fact that social reality is always more complex than the law ever manages to take into account at any given point in time and that judges must be aware of this in order to return just verdicts. Whether we call this equity or not, and whether it is institutionalized or not, is of little consequence. What is important is that this more flexible way of looking at and applying law is likely to exist in most legal traditions.[30] Should it be entirely absent, the law courts the risk of becoming illegitimate in the eyes of the people, as E. P. Thompson once argued.[31] The restricted vision of the law may lead to absurd consequences (and it sometimes does), but it seems as if considerations of equity and fairness are a counteracting and correcting force. When legal problems are considered from the point of view of fairness, the law becomes more malleable and, hence, more useful for solving new sorts of problems. Therefore, the ways in which equity and fairness work in periods of social and economic transformation may help to explain historical change. Equity provides a vantage point from which we can observe how socioeconomic developments and cultural processes of interpretation and mobilization have interacted.

However, we should not equate "fairness" with the good part and "law" with the evil part in the story. Precisely because of their malleability and permeability, considerations of equity are likely to be influenced by various social groups and actors with different and possibly irreconcilable interests. It is clear that the creditor's interest exerted a strong influence upon late seventeenth-century understandings of the law and upon the subsequent abrogation of the kin veto. It is also clear that this caused a reconstruction of married women's property rights that was not entirely beneficial to women. Considerations of what was necessary and equitable switched the perspective of the law in a way that many are likely to have found inequitable; indeed, this was just what Rålamb claimed when he wanted to hold on to the old law. Likewise, when the law was changed in another direction around and after 1800, giving women larger and more secure property rights, there were those who explicitly said that the new law was inequitable.

Considerations of equity and fairness will have varying consequences for different social groups. What is important to observe is what groups have access to the arenas where arguments based on equity become important. Who describes "social reality," who defines "fairness," and who deems it necessary to take action to achieve fairness? In this context, the emergence of a burgeoning, nationwide public sphere in Sweden should not be neglected. Even if it was by no means totally democratic — one needed knowledge, social contacts, and money to be able to enter — this public sphere still opened up an arena where entirely new voices could be heard. Once heard, they were hard to ignore for those who had the power to describe and define social reality. It is no coincidence that the Revolution in France tapped into ideas and opinions that were first put forward in the public sphere, nor should it surprise us that arguments about fairness and unfairness figured prominently in that context.[32] While not as boisterous and violent as in France, the Swedish developments in the late eighteenth and early nineteenth centuries still provide a parallel in that they show the importance of the public sphere, of considerations of fairness, and of the ideal of giving everybody the same rights.

CHRONOLOGY

c. 1350   Promulgation of *Magnus Eriksson's Landslag* (the national legal code pertaining to the rural parts of Sweden) and *Magnus Eriksson's Stadslag* (the national legal code pertaining to the urban parts of Sweden); central tenets of the former were lineage property and kinsmen's right to redeem such property (*bördsrätt*)

1442   Promulgation of *Kristoffer's Landslag* (slightly revised version of *Magnus Eriksson's Landslag*)

1682–1718   Period of royal autocracy

1686   Great Legal Commission instituted

1718–72   Age of Liberty

1720   *Bördsrätt* reformed and restricted

1730   Public registration of mortgages made compulsory

1735   Permission to print legal documents

1736   National Legal Code of 1734 put into practice (included demand for probate inventories)

1757   Parliamentary enclosures (*skiften*) start

1766   Freedom of print introduced

1767   Bankruptcy law introduced (amended in 1770, 1773, and 1798)

1772–1809   Period of royal autocracy

1807 Statute law giving a spouse the right to become co-owner of land redeemed by the other spouse

1818 New bankruptcy law introduced (amended in 1830)

1845 Men and women accorded equal rights of inheritance and equal marital rights

1846 Women accorded the right to trade

1856 *Hertha* published

1857 New testamentary law introduced, which abolished the distinction between lineage land and nonlineage land

GLOSSARY OF SWEDISH WORDS

arve[jord]: lineage property, acquired by owner through inheritance; usually
    used about land only
auskultant: auditor, trainee (at court)
avlinge[jord]: property acquired by owner in other ways than through
    inheritance; usually used about land only
avlingepengar: an unusual word meaning money not received through inheritance
äktenskapsförord: prenuptial marriage agreement
ärva: inherit (see also *köpa, lösa*)
ärvdabalken: section of the legal code pertaining to inheritance
billig, skälig: equitable
bodräkt: embezzlement of property in marital estate by one spouse
boskillnad: separation of spouses' common property
bouppteckning: probate inventory
bördlöst jord: land redeemed from a relative (see also *lösa*)
bördsrätt: right of first refusal (in Latin referred to as *ius retractus*); kin's
    prerogative to take over farm so that it remains within the lineage
daler: coin/monetary unit of changing value
fastighetspengar: inherited money received in lieu of land (compare *jordapengar*)
fördel: widow's or widower's right to take out some small property from the estate
    before division
giftermålsbalken: section of the legal code pertaining to marriage
giftorätt: marital rights; the part of the common property a spouse could claim
    after the dissolution of the marriage
häradsrätt: rural primary court, in charge of all legal matters
hemman: farm and, at the same time, the main cadastral unit
hovrätt: royal appeals court; in the seventeenth century, there were four such
    courts (in Stockholm, Jönköping, Turku, and Tartu)
inom börd: within the kin group; locution often used in conjunction with *lösa*
inteckning: public registration of a mortgage

jord: land, soil, real estate

jordabalken: section of the legal code pertaining to real estate

jordapengar: inherited money received in lieu of land (compare *fastighetspengar*)

köpa: purchase (see also *lösa*, *ärva*)

kronorusthåll: a farm, the rents of which have been allotted to cover certain military needs

kunglig förordning: statute law

Kungl. Maj:t: the king, not as a person but as an institution invested with state powers; the concept often refers to those who execute the king's powers on his behalf or in his absence

kyrkobalken: section of the legal code pertaining to ecclesiastical matters

lagkommittén: nineteenth-century extraparliamentary commission in charge of revising the whole legal code

laglott: guaranteed share of the net value of a deceased's estate (compare Latin *legitima*, English "reasonable part")

lagmansrätt: second-level court, between *häradsrätt* and *hovrätt*

lagutskottet: special committee of the nineteenth-century Diet, in charge of matters of legislation

län: province under leadership of provincial governor (who is the king's representative)

lösa [jord]: to redeem land; to acquire a right to land from a relative by paying a certain amount of money, usually on more favorable terms than would have been the case if the seller had been a nonrelative (see also *köpa*, *ärva*)

lös egendom: movable property, chattels

morgongåva: morning gift; groom's gift to bride on the morning after the wedding day

nämnd: collective noun denoting the twelve lay judges of the local primary court

ömsesidigt testamente: mutual will, spousal will

örtug: unit of land measurement, used for cadastral purposes

Reduktionen: the repossession of Crown lands from the 1680s onward; since similar repossessions had taken place earlier, this action is often referred to as the Great Repossession of Crown lands ("den Stora Reduktionen")

Riksskattmästare: chancellor of the exchequer

sekreta utskottet: special committee of the eighteenth-century Diet, in charge of politically sensitive matters

skatte[jord]: real estate on which state taxes were levied, usually owned by freeholder peasants; in principle, all farms were categorized as either *skatte*, *frälse* (held by nobility, taxed less heavily or not at all), or *krono* (state property)

skatteköp: sale of previously Crown-owned farms, often to tenants

skattevrak: a farm for which no taxes had been paid for three consecutive years; it was at least in theory forfeit to the Crown

surrogat: a special form of compensation (compare *vederlag*), provided either by

a person to his or her kinsmen before he or she could make a will or by one
spouse to the other

testamente: will

undantag: a retirement arrangement: the part of a farm that was kept by the
elder generation when the major part of the farm was transferred to the
younger generation; usually included a house, some land, and the right to
certain benefits; more or less synonymous with *födoråd*

vederlag: compensation (compare *surrogat*)

NOTES

CHAPTER ONE

1 Renoverade domböcker, Svea Hovrätts arkiv, Åkerbo härad vol. 12, fol. 373 (1659), 396 (1658), Riksarkivet; Åkerbo härads domböcker, vol. A I:2 (1 Jan. 1673), A I:4 (14 Oct. 1687), A I:7 (8 June 1696), Uppsala Landsarkiv. I am grateful to Jonas Lindström for drawing my attention to this case.

2 Helmius, *"Olyckliga swenska fruentimret."*

3 For a concise overview of the field of women's work, see Simonton, *European Women's Work*. A particularly interesting case study of women's work in the early modern period is provided by Ogilvie, *Bitter Living*. For the role of woman investors, see Green and Owens, "Gentlewomanly Capitalism."

4 Eliot, *Mill on the Floss*.

5 Bremer, *Hertha*.

6 Guzzetti, "Dowries in Fourteenth-Century Venice."

7 Hardwick, *Practice of Patriarchy*, 53–55, 62, 73–74, 112, 114–15, 142.

8 Erickson, *Women and Property*. See also Salmon, *Women and the Law of Property*.

9 Erickson, *Women and Property*, 103; Salmon, *Women and the Law of Property*, 81, 90; Staves, *Married Women's Separate Property*.

10 Compare introduction of Ågren and Erickson, *Marital Economy*, 16: "Given that poor relief records in England show that the system supported primarily women, mostly widows and abandoned wives, we should consider the possibility that poor relief developed at least partly as a consequence of England's extraordinary marital property laws." For a similar conclusion about the early American colonies, see Salmon, *Women and the Law of Property*, 183–84.

11 University Library of Uppsala, B 133 c: 178, 189, 194.

12 Salmon, *Women and the Law of Property*, 188–89.

13 Scott, *Seeing Like a State*, 366n79 : "It is worth noticing that, like the modern tax system, the modern credit system requires a legible property regime for its functioning."

14 Roberts, "Recovering a Lost Inheritance."

15 Howell, *Marriage Exchange*.

16 This is, roughly, the argument put forward in Scott, *Seeing Like a State*.

17 Agarwal, *Field of One's Own*, 82.

18 Erickson suggests that separate estates for wives were "the means of removing marital property from liability for the husband's debt" and that they allowed "a woman's natal family to secure its property descent through her and her children." Erickson, *Women and Property*, 107. See also Salmon, *Women and the Law of Property*, 85–86: "As fathers began to favor daughters and younger sons in their wills, they came to realize the inadequacies of the laws on women's property. Why give a daughter an estate, only to see it fall into the hands of husbands?" See also Goody, "Dowry and the Rights of Women."

19 Palm, *Folkmängden*, 49. These figures only refer to the area comprising Sweden today, that is, they do not include Finland, which was part of the Swedish realm until 1809.

20 Ibid., 86–87.

21 Myrdal, *Jordbruket under feodalismen*, 334–35.

22 Ibid., 214.

23 Palm, *Folkmängden*, 88.

24 A substantial part of the taxes paid by the peasantry was calculated on the production capacity of their farms. This means that, even though acreage was of course very important, other factors (such as soil quality and access to woods and fishing waters) were also taken into account when the farm was assessed for tax purposes. In principle, these assessments were made in the course of the sixteenth century, and the state administration was often slow or reluctant to make any changes to the system. Therefore, we quite often find confusing discrepancies between farm size and tax duties, as well as complaints about these matters.

25 It has been assumed that the idea of differentiating between inherited and noninherited land dates back to the introduction of Christianity. Before this time, all land is believed to have been looked upon as belonging to the kin group. However, the Catholic Church wanted individuals to be free to donate land to the Church. Consequently, the system that emerged can be seen as a compromise between kin interests and church interests (see Palme, *Studier i sturetidens*). It is difficult to know anything about how medieval people understood the legal distinction between inherited and acquired land. In the seventeenth century, however, the distinction seems to have been linked to differences in terms of what the owner had done to become owner. Inherited land had been received without any effort, as a mere consequence of one's membership in the kin group. Therefore, such land had to be returned to where it had come from. By way of contrast, the fact that one had exerted oneself to purchase the land justified a greater freedom of disposition. See for example Rålamb, *Observationes*, 293, which argued that investment of labor was what turned acquired land into the common property of the spouses.

26 "Right of first refusal" or, in Latin, *ius retractus*. It would not be entirely mis-

leading to translate the term as birthright, since the right derived from the fact that one was born within a certain family.

27 *Lagläsaren Per Larssons*, 126.

28 The effects of *bördsrätt* upon the land market depended upon three factors. First, who could adduce this right, or, in other words, how large was the relevant kin group? Christer Winberg has shown that, in the seventeenth century, the relevant kin group was usually defined very broadly and that this was of particular interest to the aristocracy. With a broad definition, virtually all sales of land could be vetoed and no land would leave the kin group. Second, what price would the kinsman adducing this right have to pay? According to the law, the price should be decided by impartial assessors and did not necessarily have to correspond to what the first buyer had paid, although in Lars's case it appears he was able to retrieve all his money. Third, how long would a new owner have to wait until he could feel certain that no claims of this sort could be raised against his purchase? Here the scope for variation was stunningly large, and the conclusion must be that, in principle, a seventeenth-century owner could never feel entirely secure. Winberg, *Grenverket*; compare *Magnus Erikssons Landslag*, Jordabalken 3.

29 The crisis was set off by the Black Death and led to a massive decline in population. The effects of the crisis can be gauged from the decline in number of farms.

30 On the effects of the 1560–67 war, see Österberg, *Gränsbygd under krig*.

31 Lindegren, "Men, Money, and Means."

32 Perlestam, *Rotfaste bonden.*

33 Lindegren, *Utskrivning och utsugning.*

34 Palm, *Folkmängden*, appendix C. This means that, on average, each local court catered to the needs of 5,400 persons in 1700.

35 Tamm, Johansen, Næss, and Johansson, "Law and the Judicial System," 48–52; Österberg, Lennartsson, and Næss, "Social Control," 251–52.

36 Tamm, Johansen, Næss, and Johansson, "Law and the Judicial System," 48–52.

37 Liliequist, "Kostnadsansvar för rättegångar," 16–26. Liliequist shows that costs for executions and corporal punishments were covered by the Crown, the local peasant community, or both, irrespective of whether the charge was brought by a bailiff or by a private person. Costs for the apprehension, trial, and support of incarcerated criminals were covered by the aggrieved party (*målsägaren*) if one brought the charge, but this party could then request a reimbursement from the guilty party. When the charge was brought by the bailiff, all costs were covered by the Crown (and to some extent by the local peasant community). Liliequist also shows that there was statute law (1661) stressing that poor people did not have to pay anything, since "one has a duty to assist such persons for free and without compensation." Liliequist summarizes that, early on, the Swedish state accepted economic responsibility (or demanded that local communities do this) for legal costs related to the apprehension, incarceration, and support of serious criminals, when the guilt of the criminal was regarded as obvious. The legal code of 1734 enforced these principles even more. Naturally, in the case of litigation, costs had to

be borne by the involved parties, and the one who lost would have to pay a larger share.

38 Sogner, Lindstedt Cronberg, and Sandvik, "Women in Court," 174–75.

39 Lindmark, *Reading, Writing and Schooling*, chapter 11.

40 See for example Erickson, *Women and Property*.

41 In Britain, a distinction was made between probate inventories and probate accounts. One of the most important differences between these two sources seems to have been that the latter included information on credit and debt, which the former did not. See Erickson, *Women and Property*, 33–34. Swedish probate inventories always included information on credit and debt and would therefore appear to combine the qualities of these two types of British sources.

42 To a large extent, property relations within the seventeenth-century nobility have been omitted, partly because the nobility constituted a very small part of the population (and cannot be said to represent "ordinary people") and partly because their property arrangements were often particularly complex and call for a study of their own.

43 Ågren, "Lösa ekonomiska tvister." The primary court material has still not been extensively explored for questions concerning everyday economic matters instead of crime, and much more could be gleaned from the records. For instance, they allow us to study land transactions in a way that is not possible for Britain. Compare Erickson, *Women and Property*, 67.

44 For more information on these court records, see Table 1.

45 Larsson, "Borgrätt och adelsjurisdiktion"; Johansson, "Herrar och bönder."

46 What this meant to criminal law is analyzed in Thunander, *Hovrätt i funktion*, 52–67. More scholarly attention should be devoted to the role played by equity in civil law.

CHAPTER TWO

1 Stadin, *Stånd och genus*, 49–50, 68.

2 Crusius, "Vår äldsta kommentar till landslagen," commentary on Giftermåls-balken 5: "Ubi notandum, quod uxor post mortem mariti non sit domina omnium bonorum sed tertiam saltem partem accipiat ex bonis mobilibus" ("Where it is noted that the wife may not be [regarded as] the owner of all property after the demise of her husband, but she should in any case receive one third of the movable property"); and 14: "Cur maritus iure non potest divendere bona immobilia uxoris, haec est ratio, quia non fit dominus bonorum immobilium." ("Why the husband may not alienate his wife's lands according to the law, the reason is this, that he is not the owner of [her] lands").

3 *Magnus Erikssons Landslag*, Ärvdabalken 1. In the region of Uppland, there was a rule stipulating that sons should receive their shares of land in the center of the hamlet, whereas daughters should have their shares on the outskirts. This rule went back to the regional legal code, ratified in 1296, but it was still referred to in late sixteenth-century sources. See *Upplands Lagmansdombok 1581 och 1586*, 113–14, 164.

4 *Magnus Erikssons Landslag*, Giftermålsbalken 19.

5 Petersson, *Morgongåvoinstitutet*.

6 *Upplands Lagmansdombok 1578–1579*, 44–45.

7 Mathematically, $1/3 + (3/7 \times 2/3) = 13/21$ or 61.9 percent.

8 Ågren, *Hävda sin rätt*, 185–86.

9 *Lagläsaren Per Larssons*, 84.

10 *Magnus Erikssons Landslag*, Jordabalken 32.

11 *Magnus Erikssons Landslag*, Jordabalken 5.

12 *Magnus Erikssons Landslag*, Giftermålsbalken 20. Giftermålsbalken 20 dealt specifically with the interests of heirs and consequently used the word *arvingar*. In Jordabalken 5, the woman's relatives were called *fränder*, designating a broader kin group. People from the broader kin group would not necessarily be entitled to inherit the land, but they would have the right to adduce *bördsrätt*. Thus, the stipulations in Jordabalken 5 can be seen as a reminder of the fact that the *bördsrätt* always applied.

13 Desan, *Family on Trial*, 65.

14 Compare Rålamb, *Observationes*, 173–74. Rålamb thought Jordabalken 32 and 5 referred to one sort of situation, whereas Giftermålsbalken 20 referred to a different sort of situation.

15 *Magnus Erikssons Landslag*, Giftermålsbalken 1 and 3.

16 Sandén, *Stadsgemenskapens resurser*, 100; Hansen, *Ordnade hushåll*, 151. In a detailed study of the late medieval period, the result was the same: the stipulations were adduced but not very frequently. Bjarne Larsson, "Kvinnor, manlighet," 97–98.

17 Sjöberg, *Kvinnors jord*, 92, 142. Sjöberg points out that more research is needed to clarify the limits on the husband's power.

18 Ibid., 110–11.

19 That is to say, regions like Bohuslän and Jämtland.

20 See for example Österberg, "Land Transactions."

21 Land transactions within families do not seem to have been recorded as rigorously as sales to nonrelatives. Christer Winberg argues, and I agree, that it is almost meaningless to compare the number of land transactions made at different points in time, since we do not know what we are measuring before c. 1700. Winberg, *Grenverket*, 211.

22 *Vendels 1615–1645*, 36–37, 43–44, 53.

23 Ibid., 54.

24 Ibid., 154.

25 Ibid., 63, 147; *Upplands Lagmansdombok 1581 och 1586*, 4, 17, 79, 112, 119, 122–23, 125, 158, 160, 163, 167, 180, 189–90. See in particular 53: when a man had used his wife's separate property to pay his own debts, his heirs had to compensate the wife's heirs. See also Bjarne Larsson, "Kvinnor, manlighet," 92.

26 *Tingsprotokoll för Njurunda*, 108 (1635:18). See also 109 (1635:24).

27 *Domboksutdrag rörande Fryksdals härad*, 1:73.

28 *Upplands Lagmansdombok 1578–1579*, 47.

29 Almquist, *Frälsegodsen*, for example, 534 (Alby, Ytter Grans socken), 541 (Aspvik, Näs socken), 548 (Berga, Brännkyrka socken), 573–74 (Byrsta, Grödinge socken).

30 The Swedish expressions are *arvfallen till* and *till arvs med sin hustru*. See for example *Tingsprotokoll för Njurunda*, 107 (1635:14) and 46–47 (1620:25). See also Almquist, *Frälsegodsen*, 540 (Askarbäck, Järlåsa socken).

31 *Tingsprotokoll för Njurunda*, 164 (1646:39).

32 Almquist, *Frälsegodsen*, 537.

33 Österberg, Lennartsson, and Næss, "Social Control," 241.

34 *Upplands Lagmansdombok 1578–1579*, 19.

35 *Tingsprotokoll för Njurunda*, 23–24 (1614:13) and 27–28 (1617:4).

36 There was no requirement to register that one had received land through inheritance.

37 *Upplands Lagmansdombok 1578–1579*, 51–52.

38 It turned out that Jöns had not sold his wife's land at his own instigation but because another family had claimed to have *bördsrätt* to it. Members of this family appeared before the court, saying that they hoped to be able to keep the land. They knew that Jöns would never have let it go if he had not been forced by law, because Jöns was "an affluent man who would not willingly have alienated any of his lands" (ibid., 52).

39 Svea Hovrätts arkiv, Becchius-Palmcrantz Juridiska Samlingar, vol. 17, chap. 16, 518, Riksarkivet.

40 For instance, court records do not always make clear whether the wife's land was inherited from her natal family (in which case the three stipulations applied) or acquired in other ways (in which case they did not). See for example *Upplands Lagmansdombok 1581 och 1586*, 169: A man had died, leaving his land to his child. Then the child died, leaving the land to the mother. The mother remarried and her new husband offered her land for sale. The court records say nothing about her relatives' consent. In this case, this was clearly correct, considering the fact that the land had come from the first husband's lineage and not from hers. But in other cases, it may be very difficult to know whether consent was legally required or not.

Moreover, we do not know what the absence of information on consent means: that she/they had not given their consent? That the consent had been given but a long time ago, many years before the spouses appeared in front of court? The last alternative is not unlikely. Information about sales often comes up en passant in cases dealing with other matters.

41 Swedish women's legal capacity was restricted. Unmarried women had to have guardians (in principle for the duration of their lives), and married women were supposed to be represented by their husbands, unless the case concerned inherited land, in which case they were, prior to 1734, represented by their relatives. Only as widows did adult women have approximately the same legal capacity as adult men. However, the apparently widespread use of legal representatives among widows suggests that it was difficult, although legally accepted, for widows to take legal action on their own. Andersson argues, on good grounds, that the legal capacity of women was most restricted in cases concerning property and other economic matters. There are some cases of married women appearing on their own in such court cases, but they are often difficult to interpret. Andersson, *Tingets kvinnor och män*, 54–59, 238, 293–302. Jansson has also shown that accusations of rape

were taken very seriously by seventeenth-century local courts, even when the victim was a lonely woman without much social support. Jansson, *Kvinnofrid*. Husbands' control of the movables in the marital estate is not a well-researched topic. Chapters 4 and 5 present what is known about these matters.

42 *Lagläsaren Per Larssons*, 84.

43 Renoverade domböcker: Vedbo 1668 (no pagination). Göta Hovrätts arkiv. Summarized in *Ur Vedbo härads domböcker*, 81.

44 Lahtinen, "Könspecifika maktpositioner," 226.

45 The same observation is made in Andersson, *Tingets kvinnor och män*, 107. Her evidence suggests that husbands spoke more frequently on behalf of their wives in the early eighteenth century than in the previous century.

46 *Lagläsaren Per Larssons*, 9, and *Tingsprotokoll för Njurunda*, 270 (1662:13). See also Hansen, *Ordnade hushåll*, 151–52, for further examples.

47 Ågren, "Domestic Secret."

48 *Magnus Erikssons Landslag*, Jordabalken 11; Winberg, *Grenverket*, 144.

49 See for example *Vendels 1615–1645*, 37; *Upplands Lagmansdombok 1581 och 1586*, 156.

50 Such land could be called, for example, *bytesjord*. See *Upplands Lagmansdombok 1581 och 1586*, 73.

51 By way of contrast, money that did not originate from the sale of inherited land could be used freely, and it was sometimes called acquired money (*aflingepengar*), a parallel to the word for acquired land. That the distinction of inherited/acquired was to be applied to money is not very clearly outlined in the medieval legal code, but sixteenth- and seventeenth-century legal practice suggests that this is how it worked at the time. See for example *Upplands Lagmansdombok 1578–1579*, 69.

52 *Magnus Erikssons Landslag*, Jordabalken 11: land bought from a relative should not be regarded as acquired land.

53 Sjöberg, *Kvinnors jord*, 131, rightly points out that lineage property was flexible. But she adds that "in principle, lineage property never ceased to be lineage property."

54 Renoverade domböcker: Vedbo 1666 (no pagination). Göta Hovrätts arkiv. Summarized in *Ur Vedbo härads domböcker*, 78. The dispute focused on where Simon had obtained the money he had used to buy Åsen from his grandmother. His relatives argued that he had used his own land money from Högen (another farm to which he, and they, held inheritance claims) while Per said that it was Simon's wife's land money.

55 *Tingsprotokoll för Njurunda*, 1651:17. The court record actually reads "without being troubled by them," but my conjecture is that this refers to her relatives.

56 Renoverade domböcker: Vedbo 1669 (no pagination). Göta Hovrätts arkiv. Summarized in *Ur Vedbo härads domböcker*, 86.

57 *Tingsprotokoll för Njurunda*, 1619:39.

58 *Domboksutdrag rörande Fryksdals härad*, 1:21.

59 *Lösa* can also be translated as "liberate" or "release." However, I think the relevant analogy in this context is "to redeem a pledge," which is why I choose to translate *lösa* as "redeem." I am aware, of course, of the English

legal concept "equity of redemption," the meaning of which is not identical with, yet still similar to, the Swedish procedure.

60 Sjöberg, *Kvinnors jord*, 115–28, 143. Sjöberg shows that most land transactions carried out within the kin group were between siblings. She also shows that people mainly exchanged smaller pieces of land and seldom entire farms.

61 What sort of entitlements noble families had to land that originated from the state was the main bone of contention in the protracted legal procedures associated with the repossession of state lands (*Reduktionen*) from the 1680s and onward.

62 One might call the morning gift marital property, one commentator suggested. University Library of Uppsala, B 124, 376–391, "Om morgongåva, en undervisning."

63 *Upplands Lagmansdombok 1581 och 1586*, 175: "Her brother's *purchased land* ... which he had lawfully *redeemed* from his maternal lineage" (emphasis added). See also *Domboksutdrag rörande Fryksdals härad*, 2:133, 146, 149: Ingeborg Nilsdotter could only will away her *acquired property*, that is, the three-twelfths she and her husband had *redeemed* from her sisters.

64 Agarwal, *Field of One's Own*, 82.

65 Bergman, "Testamentet," 14.

66 Medieval ecclesiastical law taught that 10 percent of one's inherited land could be devised at will; more than 10 percent required the consent of one's relatives (*Magnus Erikssons Landslag*, Jordabalken 11; *Upplandslagen*, Kyrkobalken 14). The Statute on Wills (*Kongl. May:tz Stadga och Förordning angående Testamenten 3 July 1686*) stipulated that owners who had no acquired land could devise 10 percent of the inherited land, provided that it was used *ad pios usus*. The statute explicitly stated that movable property should count as acquired property. It also stipulated that parents who had small children and no lineage property at all could not will away all their acquired property.

   Urban law did not draw a sharp distinction between inherited and acquired land. Here, the main principle was that persons who had children could only give away 10 percent of their property through a will. If they had no children but other relatives within the country, they could will away one third. If their relatives lived abroad, they could will away one half of their property. *Magnus Erikssons Stadslag*, Ärvdabalken 19.

67 *Ölme härads dombok 1629–1650*, 47, 82. See also Bjarne Larsson, "Kvinnor, manlighet," 87, who suggests that few families held noninherited land in the period 1350–1500.

68 Erickson, *Women and Property*, 115.

69 Winberg, *Grenverket*. For similar tendencies in the rest of Europe, see Thirsk, "European Debate."

70 Löfstrand, "Högadlig ideologi," 25–26.

71 Ågren, "Contracts for the Old"; Sjöberg, *Kvinnors jord*, 108–9; Bergman, "Testamentet," 31–34.

72 Andersson, *Tingets kvinnor och män*, 264; Ågren, "Contracts for the Old"; Hansen, *Ordnade hushåll*, 156–58.

73 Swedish *ömsesidigt testamente*.

74 Wahlberg, *Åtgärder för lagförbättring*, 69.

75 Stiernhöök, "Förslag till ärvdabalk," 29; Lovisinus, "Materiam successionis," University Library of Uppsala.

76 See for example Svea Hovrätts arkiv, Huvudarkivet, Liber causarum, vol. 161, no. 18, Riksarkivet.

77 Bergman, "Testamentet," section 5.

78 Here, and in other cases, the parties used the expression *ifrånärfva* (or *ärfva ifrån*). This expression is not in use in modern Swedish, and it should not be translated as "disinherit." Hans Kirs did not want to say that his relatives threatened to cut off his inheritance; what he meant was that through their inheritance claims (or claims of *bördsrätt*) the relatives wanted to take his current possessions from him.

79 Svea Hovrätts arkiv, Huvudarkivet, Liber causarum, vol. 105, no. 1:4, Riksarkivet.

80 See also Bergman, "Testamentet," 15.

81 If it was correct that the property in question had not been obtained through inheritance, the will was entirely legal. However, we can seldom tell whether or not such statements were true.

82 Svea Hovrätts arkiv, Huvudarkivet, Liber causarum, vol. 107, no. 2:5, Riksarkivet. For a similar argument, see *Uppländska häradsrättsdomböcker från 1500-talet*, 227.

83 Svea Hovrätts arkiv, Huvudarkivet, Liber causarum, vol. 112, no. 9:13, vol. 123, no. 7:11, Riksarkivet.

84 See also *Långhundra härads dombok 1545–1570*, 137: "by the sweat of their brow."

85 Svea Hovrätts arkiv, Huvudarkivet, Liber causarum, vol. 161, no. 18, Riksarkivet.

86 Svea Hovrätts arkiv, Huvudarkivet, Liber causarum, vol. 106, no.2:11, Riksarkivet.

87 Svea Hovrätts arkiv, Huvudarkivet, Liber causarum, vol. 127, no. 5:11, Riksarkivet.

88 Stadin, *Stånd och genus*, 53–55, on the importance of marital love; see also Stadin, "Vara god eller att göra sin plikt," on industriousness as a very important quality in men.

89 Howell, *Marriage Exchange*, 172: a contract mentioned "properties acquired in the course of their marriage through their common labor, industry, and assets, for this reason and for the conjugal love and affection they hold for one another"; Hardwick, *Practice of Patriarchy*, 116: a donation mentioned "the reciprocal love and affection they feel for each other," and donations frequently acknowledged "the role of the couple's own efforts (rather than kin contributions) in any success that they had enjoyed"; Ewan, "'To the Longer Liver,'" 199: a notary recorded that a man had acquired "his goods and lands by industry and conquest" and that he "lovingly bestowed the same" on his wife. Another man gave property to his spouse "for the affection and love" he bore for her; Desan, *Family on Trial*, 162–63: mutual gifts were justified with reference to "reciprocal affection" and a "desire to share the results of their joint labor."

90 The reason for this is that seventeenth-century wills were registered in the

court records, along with all other types of cases, which makes it extremely time-consuming to locate and analyze them.

91 *Lagläsaren Per Larssons*, 55.

92 *Tingsprotokoll för Njurunda*, 216 (1656:6).

93 Löfstrand, "Högadlig ideologi," 15.

94 Winberg, *Grenverket*.

95 Howell, *Marriage Exchange*, 143; Sjöberg, "Kvinnans sociala underordning," 178.

96 *Upplands Lagmansdombok 1581 och 1586*, 50, 87.

97 Johansen, "Widowhood in Scandinavia," 183.

98 Scott, *Seeing Like a State*.

99 Ågren, *Hävda sin rätt*.

100 Nilsson, "Militärstaten i funktion," shows how increasing pressure was exerted on the tax-paying peasantry in the early seventeenth century and how some taxes were even calculated on the basis of men rather than farms.

101 The technical term was, in Swedish, *skattefall* or *skattevrak*.

102 *Upplands Lagmansdombok 1578–1579*, 40.

103 *Vendels 1615–1645*, 84.

104 Ågren, *Hävda sin rätt*.

105 For example, *Lagläsaren Per Larssons*, 126; *Upplands Lagmansdombok 1581 och 1586*, 72.

106 *Upplands Lagmansdombok 1581 och 1586*, 155–56. The sister-in-law did not only base her claims on investment of labor; she could also claim compensation for her morning gift and for the land that she had inherited from her dead child.

107 *Tingsprotokoll för Njurunda*, 1639:13.

108 *Upplands Lagmansdombok 1581 och 1586*, 42, 51. See similar observations in Sjöberg, *Kvinnors jord*, 116–17; Ågren, "'Hon skall ha min stickmaskin'"; Bjarne Larsson, "Kvinnor, manlighet," 108.

109 Andersson, *Tingets kvinnor och män*, 239, 268; Franzén, *Sturetidens monetära system*, 149; Sjöberg, *Kvinnors jord*, 111; Bjarne Larsson, "Kvinnor, manlighet," 97.

110 *Upplands Lagmansdombok 1578–1579*, 44–45.

111 *Tingsprotokoll för Njurunda 1640:14*.

112 *Upplands Lagmansdombok 1581 och 1586*, 176.

113 Lass's words are a pun, since Swedish uses the same word for soil and land.

114 *Upplands Lagmansdomsbok 1581 och 1586*, 56.

115 *Upplands Lagmansdombok 1578–1579*, 71–72.

116 The use of "oath helpers" as a means of disproving guilt is another example of how local knowledge and local support played an important part in early modern legal practice. See Sogner, Lindstedt Cronberg, and Sandvik, "Women in Court," 172.

117 *Tingsprotokoll för Njurunda*, 180 (1651:15). If the parents were betrothed, their children counted as if born within wedlock.

118 *Upplands Lagmansdombok 1581 och 1586*, 190–91.

119 *Upplands Lagmansdombok 1581 och 1586*, 115–16.

120 For both cases, see Ågren, *Hävda sin rätt*, 164–65, 176.

121 The recent literature on local courts and communities in Sweden is vast. The main results and tendencies are summarized and interpreted in Österberg, "Social Arena," and Österberg, "Local Political Culture." For a local case study, see Simonson, *Den lokala scenen*.

122 See also Winberg, *Grenverket*, 91, on the often surprisingly detailed genealogical knowledge displayed by seventeenth-century people.

123 See also, for Norway, Sogner and Sandvik, "Ulik i lov og lære."

124 Scott, *Seeing Like a State*, 22–24.

125 This point is elaborated in Ågren, *Hävda sin rätt*.

CHAPTER THREE

1 Johan Skytte (1577–1645). *Svenskt Biografiskt Lexikon*, vol. 32.

2 *Riksrådet Johan Skyttes kommentar*, 124–25.

3 The code of 1734 was a comprehensive legal code, the first one to be valid for both town and countryside. The Law Commission continued to exist as an advisory board until 1808 (with the exception of 1785–91).

4 University Library of Uppsala, B 133: c 162.

5 Holmbäck, *1686 års testamentsstadga*, 59–70.

6 *Magnus Erikssons Landslag*, Ärvdabalken 20.

7 University Library of Uppsala, B 123 (Rålamb), B 133: c 159–61 (the Svea Hovrätt), B 133: c 175–76 (Rålamb), B 133: c 186–87 (three judges of the Göta Hovrätt).

8 See also University Library of Uppsala, B 123, where Claes Rålamb argues that the wife should not be regarded as her husband's heir. What Rålamb wished to say here, is that the wife had a *more* privileged position than an heir had, that is, that her claims were more similar to those of creditors. Compare Erickson, *Women and Property*, 132: English settlements for wives were looked upon as the husbands' debts, and, consequently, they conveyed a stronger right to the wives than did reasonable parts.

9 Bergman, "Testamentet," 89.

10 Johan Stiernhöök (1596–1675).

11 Stiernhöök, "Gifftermåhlsbalken," 124.

12 Hildebrand, *Svenskt Järn*, 17–19, 25, 147–48.

13 Revera, "1600-talsbönderna," 40–41.

14 Löfstrand, "Högadlig ideologi"; Janzon, "Överdåd på kredit," 216, 220, 222.

15 Nilsson, "Kontinentala krigens finansiering," 194; Lindegren, "Men, Money, and Means," 153–54; Janzon, "Överdåd på kredit."

16 Ågren, *Jord och gäld*, 46.

17 See, for example, the court records of the Svea Hovrätt in the years 1651 and 1686, where debt cases abound. Svea Hovrätts arkiv, Huvudarkivet, Domböcker, Riksarkivet.

18 Melkersson, *Staten, ordningen och friheten*, 234.

19 One example is the statute of 28 May 1687, which declared that all yields from a wife's lineage land could be taken to cover debts her husband had made for his sole benefit. The legal inconsistencies with respect to spouses' responsibility for each other's debts are clearly brought out in Thyrén, *Makes gäld*, 95–111, particularly 109.

20 Quoted in Ågren, *Jord och gäld*, 45.

21 In the 1660s the debate focused on whether or not the wife's share of the common property could be used to cover debts her husband had made prior to the marriage. In the 1680s the debate concerned whether or not the wife's lineage lands could be used to cover debts the husband had incurred during marriage. In previous research, only Holmbäck, *1686 års testamentsstadga*, and Bergman, "Testamentet," touch upon aspects of these debates.

22 University Library of Uppsala, B 133:c 193. These debates are analyzed in greater detail in Ågren, "Domestic Secret."

23 University Library of Uppsala, B 133: c 178, 189, 194.

24 See the statement by Schüttehielm, quoted in Bergman, "Testamentet," 22n1.

25 University Library of Uppsala, B 123; B 133: c 159–209. See also Ågren, "Domestic Secret."

26 Claes Rålamb (1622–1698). *Svenskt Biografiskt Lexikon*, vol. 31.

27 University Library of Uppsala, B 123: 102–21, particularly 103–4.

28 University Library of Uppsala, B 123; B 133: c 167–79, particularly 175. See also Ågren, "Domestic Secret."

29 University Library of Uppsala, B 123; B 133: c 167–79.

30 Salmon, *Women and the Law of Property*, 62.

31 A valuable analysis of gender aspects in these debates is Andersson Lennström, "Makt och myndighet."

32 Sjögren, *Förarbetena*, 1:76.

33 Ibid., 58.

34 Ibid., 7:45. Some of its judges maintained that the Statute on Wills (1686) compelled a husband to compensate his wife if he sold or mortgaged her land, whereas others simply thought that the relatives' consent was a dead letter by this time and that it would suffice if the husband showed the court that his wife did not object to the sale.

35 Ibid., 89.

36 Ibid., 3:158.

37 Gustaf Cronhielm (1664–1737). Appointed chairman of the commission in 1710. *Svenskt Biografiskt Lexikon*, vol. 9.

38 Sjögren, *Förarbetena*, 3:159.

39 Ibid., 102: when discussing a draft set up in 1713, the commission wanted to add "with the advice and consent of the closest relatives," but after this, relatives' consent does not seem to have been discussed any further.

40 Ibid., 4: 49, 61; 5:11–12.

41 Such as England, America, and (prior to 1687) Norway.

42 Sandvik, *"Umyndige" kvinner*, 20, 172, argues convincingly that early modern law did not think of legal capacity and legal incapacity as sharply divided, dichotomous categories.

43 Sjögren, *Förarbetena*, 1:212.

44 Ibid., 3:169.

45 "Qui commodum sentit, incommodum etiam sentire debet."

46 "To the extent that she participates in *lucrativis*, she must also participate in *damno*." Notice that Swedish lawyers and appeals court judges frequently

mixed Latin (and sometimes German) with Swedish in this way. Sjögren, *Förarbetena*, 1:303. See also Sjögren, *Förarbetena*, 3:169.

47 Sjögren, *Förarbetena*, 3:159 (emphasis added).

48 Ibid., 170 (emphasis added): "It is commonly known that it is in the interest of the state that no one uses his property unwisely." (interest reipublicae, ne quis re sua male utatur.)

49 *1734 års lag*, Giftermålsbalken 11 §§ 1, 2.

50 *1734 års lag*, Giftermålsbalken 11 § 1.

51 *1734 års lag*, Giftermålsbalken 11 § 8 (emphasis added). See also Giftermåls-balken 11 § 3.

52 See also Andersson Lennström, "Makt och myndighet," 61. The author concludes that, at this time, adult unmarried women were increasingly accepted as legally responsible actors.

53 *1734 års lag*, Giftermålsbalken 11 § 7.

54 See chapter 2. See also Rålamb, *Observationes*, 173, where Rålamb emphasizes the importance of the stipulation that the husband has to sell twice as much of his own land.

55 Sjögren, *Förarbetena*, 8:13 (emphasis added). See also *Sveriges ridderskaps och adels riksdags-protokoll* 6 (1731): 75.

56 Bror Rålamb (1668–1734). *Svenskt Biografiskt Lexikon*, vol. 31.

57 Rålamb, *Observationes*, 173–74, 295–315. When Rålamb wrote this book, the question was whether the wife's property could be used to cover debts her husband had incurred prior to their marriage; debts incurred during marriage did not come on the agenda until the 1680s. Rålamb's treatment of the subject takes the form of *pro et contra* arguments. His final conclusion can be found on 315.

58 Andersson Lennström, "Makt och myndighet," 46, notices that some legislators mentioned wives' contributions to the family (for example, their role as mothers and keepers of property) and depicted these as just as important as contributions by husbands. However, their productive labor never seems to have been on the agenda in the way that was the case in the early nineteenth century.

59 Compare Staves, *Married Women's Separate Property*, especially chapter 7, on how the principle of inalienability was applied selectively in English law, and what this meant for women.

60 But women from the higher echelons of society did sometimes lodge complaints about the loss of their lineage property. See for example Svea Hovrätts arkiv, Huvudarkivet, Dombok 1686, Carl Bååt/Christina Leijon-sköld, Riksarkivet. Christina's late husband had sold the contested estate to Carl's father in 1663. In 1681 the Crown had taken possession of the estate (as a consequence of the *Reduktion*), and Carl sued Christina as being responsible for his eviction. Christina argued that the sale had taken place prior to the marriage and that she had not benefited from it. What was more, she had had to sell her lineage landed property to cover her husband's debts. Christina won the case.

61 These trends correspond to a similar tendency in English law. Staves, *Married Women's Separate Property*, 228.

62 Winberg, *Grenverket*, 56–62.

63 Odén, "Relationer mellan generationerna," 88, 92. See also chapter 4.

64 Ighe, *I faderns ställe*, 61–62.

65 Sjögren, *Förarbetena*, 2:73.

66 Ibid.

67 Ibid., 1:59.

68 Liliequist, "Mannens våld och välde," 107–9.

69 *Magnus Erikssons Landslag*, Jordabalken 11 (equals *Kristoffers landslag*, Jordabalken 9).

70 Holmbäck, *1686 års testamentsstadga*, 56–70; Bergman, "Testamentet," 81–82.

71 *1734 års lag*, Jordabalken 5:3.

72 Sjögren, *Förarbetena*, 8:28.

73 Hällström, "Arvejordsinstitutet," 264.

74 Ibid., 261.

75 *Lagutskottets betänkande*, no. 13 (1856–58), statement made by Hasselrot.

76 *1734 års lag*, Ärvdabalken 17:2. Compare *Magnus Erikssons Landslag*, Jorda-balken 11 (which does not speak in terms of an obligation); Holmbäck, *1686 års testamentsstadga*, 62–63.

77 See *Theses Juridicae de Surrogato*, thesis 6 and 9, and *1734 års lag*, Giftermåls-balken 11 § 7. In a way, this usage of the term "surrogate" could be seen as a modified version of the medieval stipulation that husbands had to compen-sate wives with new land.

78 Bergman, "Testamentet," 108, 114–15. Bergman argues that the strong legal position of kinsmen and the weak authority of courts explain why executors were rarely used.

79 Sjögren, *Förarbetena*, 1:36–37.

80 Ibid., 218–20, 319–22, 329–34.

81 Ibid., 320.

82 That is to say, it was possible but not compulsory to register a mortgage before 1730. Jägerskiöld, *Handelsbalkens utländska källor*, 195.

83 Johansson, "Godsförvärv och likviditetsproblem," 119.

84 Bergman, "Testamentet," 33. See also *Kongl. Maj:ts Förnyade Nådiga Stadga, angående afträdes- och förmons- samt boskilnads- och urarfwa mål*, §§ 1, 18, which argues for the need to make prenuptial agreements public.

85 Sjögren, *Förarbetena*, 1:333.

86 Jägerskiöld, *Handelsbalkens utländska källor*, 197; Ågren, *Jord och gäld*, 50.

87 Svea Hovrätts arkiv, Huvudarkivet, Dombok 1687, Riksarkivet.

88 Magalotti, *Sverige under år 1674*, 101–2.

89 Svea Hovrätts arkiv, Huvudarkivet, Dombok 1687, Riksarkivet (the creditors included, for example, Abraham Persson, Didrik Wittfogel, Johan Scheur-man, and Christian Heraeus). See also Dombok 1686, where the heirs of the tailor Jean Sedan sued Gustaf Rosenhane's heirs for wages and goods that were due since 1640.

90 Johansson, "Godsförvärv och likviditetsproblem," 60, 174.

91 Erik Lovisin was also a member of the so-called Likvidationskommission, which was in charge of parts of the *Reduktion*.

92 See chapter 2 and Ågren, *Hävda sin rätt*.

93 Johansson, "Godsförvärv och likviditetsproblem," 119–21, shows that even the Bank of Sweden relied on personal guarantees in the late seventeenth century.

94 Erickson, *Women and Property*, 111, 123; Howell, *Marriage Exchange*, 162.

95 Compare Mann, *Republic of Debtors*, 47–48.

96 Scott, *Seeing Like a State*, 366n79: "It is worth noting that, like the modern tax system, the modern credit system requires a legible property regime for its functioning."

97 The concept of *imbecillitas sexus* harks back to a decision in Rome in 46 A.D., which made it illegal for a wife to provide a personal guarantee for her husband. Beauvalet-Boutouyrie, *Être veuve*, 186.

98 Rålamb, *Observationes*, 143.

99 University Library of Uppsala, B 133 c: 202–3.

100 ". . . dominibus inclusae et per connatum simulandi et dissimulandi artificium." Quoted in Bergman, "Testamentet," 22n1.

101 Claes Rålamb agreed that husband and wife should share good times and bad times or, in his own words, that they should share "the unexpected things and accidents that may befall them" (Rålamb, *Observationes*, 291). But debts were not unexpected or accidental, Rålamb added, they were the result of conscious actions. Therefore, the words about sharing good times and bad times were not applicable to the case of indebtedness. See his discussion in University Library of Uppsala, B 133: c 169.

102 Sjögren, *Förarbetena*, 1:59.

103 Scott, "Gender," 48: "The terms of . . . discourse were not explicitly about gender, but they were strengthened by references to it."

104 Sogner, Lindstedt Cronberg, and Sandvik, "Women in Court," 182, 186. See also Jansson, *Kvinnofrid*.

105 Eliot, *Mill on the Floss*.

CHAPTER FOUR

1 *Till Kongl. Swea hof-rätt.*

2 *Juridiskt Arkif*, 11:307–20.

3 Compare Winberg, *Grenverket*, 211.

4 Agarwal, *Field of One's Own*; Goody, "Dowry and the Rights of Women."

5 The concept "Kungl. Maj:t" does not denote the king's person but the king as being invested with state power. It often refers to those state offices that execute the king's powers, on his behalf or in his absence.

6 Gustaf Adolph Leijonmarck (1734–1815). Member of the Law Commission in 1792. *Svenskt Biografiskt Lexikon*, vol. 22.

7 Utdrag af Protocollet, hållet uti Kongl. Lag-Commissionen d. 29 November 1806. Reprinted in extenso in Olivecrona, *Om makars giftorätt*, Bilaga.

8 *Kongl. Maj:ts Nådiga Förklaring öfwer Allmänna Lagens Stadganden i åtskilliga rum 23 March 1807*, § 1.

9 Holmlund, "Arvejord och äktenskap."

10 See chapter 2 on Simon Persson's will for the benefit of his stepson.

11 Herlitz, *Jordegendom och ränta*; Backlund, *Rusthållarna i Fellingsbro*.

12 Herlitz, *Jordegendom och ränta*, 322, 344–45.

13 Bengtsson, *Ödmjukt anförande til protocollet*.

14 Herlitz, *Jordegendom och ränta*, chapter 9.

15 See for example Nygren, *Svensk kreditmarknad*; Perlinge, *Sockenbankirerna*.

16 Ahlberger and Mörner, "Betydelsen av några latinamerikanska produkter," 83.

17 Isacson, *Ekonomisk tillväxt*; Ahlberger, *Vävarfolket*, 24.

18 Thisner, *Militärstatens arvegods*.

19 Carlsson, *Fröknar, mamseller, jungfrur och pigor*, 36–37, table 13.

20 Rydeberg, *Skatteköpen i Örebro*; Gadd, *Den agrara revolutionen*, 198–202.

21 See for example *Vendels 1736–1737*, 25; Svea Hovrätts arkiv, Renoverade småprotokoll, Frösåker 1750 (Mats Mikaelsson's and his wife's retirement contract), Frösåker 1752 (Brita Ersdotter's will), Riksarkivet.

22 Andersson, *Tingets kvinnor och män*, 266.

23 Hoppe, "Svenska jordskiften"; Granér, *Samhävd och rågång*.

24 In Norwegian law, the eldest son would always have the right to take possession of the farm according to the *åsetesret*.

25 See table 4.

26 Norell, *Sjette Samlingen*, 96–100. The references were to Giftermålsbalken 11 § 1 and Jordabalken 10.

27 Åkerbo häradsrättsarkiv, Rystad F II 14, 795, Vadstena Landsarkiv.

28 Åkerbo häradsrättsarkiv, Rystad F II 15, 1325, Vadstena Landsarkiv. The quotation is from 1339.

29 Åkerbo häradsrättsarkiv, Rystad F II 10, 543, Vadstena Landsarkiv.

30 The following analysis is based upon a study of all married persons who died in Rystad in the period 1779 to 1810 leaving a probate inventory. The number of such persons was 130, seventy-eight of whom were men and fifty-two women. Forty-two of these were part of a household that owned land, and eighty-eight belonged to nonlandowning households.

31 Four cases out of forty-two.

32 Fifteen cases out of forty-two.

33 See also *Juridiskt Arkif* 7:440–41. The reported case shows that land purchased from the state was regarded as acquired and, consequently, devisable.

34 This method was used in thirteen cases out of forty-two but also in three cases where the household was landless, that is, in three cases out of eighty-eight.

35 Åkerbo häradsrättsarkiv, Rystad F II 12, 33, 435, Vadstena Landsarkiv. The quotation is from 436.

36 Åkerbo häradsrättsarkiv, Rystad F II 11, 353, Vadstena Landsarkiv. The quotation is from 365.

37 Åkerbo häradsrättsarkiv, Rystad F II 16, 803, Vadstena Landsarkiv. The quotation is from 810.

38 Åkerbo häradsrättsarkiv, Rystad F II 17, 111, Vadstena Landsarkiv. The quotation is from 126.

39 Holmlund, *Jorden vi ärvde*, 122–23.

40 Åkerbo häradsrättsarkiv, Rystad F II 10, 947, Vadstena Landsarkiv. The quotation is from 952.

41 Åkerbo häradsrättsarkiv, Rystad F II 12, 323, Vadstena Landsarkiv.

42 Åkerbo häradsrättsarkiv, Rystad F II 10, 1067, Vadstena Landsarkiv. The quotation is from 1069.

43 Åkerbo häradsrättsarkiv, Rystad F II 18, 339, Vadstena Landsarkiv. The quotation is from 684.

44 Åkerbo häradsrättsarkiv, Rystad F II 10 and A II a 5, 39, Vadstena Landsarkiv.

45 Winberg, *Folkökning och proletarisering*.

46 Another practice, designed to achieve the same ends, was used in Estuna (central Sweden). Here, spouses registered the woman's contribution as a form of mortgage. Holmlund, *Jorden vi ärvde*, 122–23. Compare Fiebranz, *Jord, linne eller träkol*, 346–47, for Bjuråker (northern Sweden), where the practice seems to have been more similar to the one in Rystad.

47 I want to point out that in this period it is hard to draw any clear demarcation lines between different types of contracts and between contracts and wills. What I have in mind here are retirement contracts, wills, prenuptial agreements, and service contracts, all of which became more common in this period. But often, people combined in the same deed regulations that we think of as belonging to different types of contracts.

Seventeenth-century lawyers discussed whether or not mutual wills were to be regarded as contracts. This shows that to them, too, the distinction was hard to sustain. See Ågren, "Caring for the Widowed Spouse," 53–54.

48 Högnäs, *Sytning och arvslösen*; Winberg, "Familj och jord"; Gaunt, "Property and Kin Relationships"; Odén, "Relationer mellan generationerna"; Rosén, *Himlajord och handelsvara*; Perlestam, *Rotfaste bonden*; Fiebranz, *Jord, linne eller träkol*.

49 Taussi Sjöberg, "Mellan far och make," 63; Odén, "Planering inför ålderdomen."

50 See for example the contract made by Erik Appelman and his wife, in which they explained that their daughter had always been recalcitrant and that they dared not hope for any help from her. See also the will made by Erik Andersson in Gåsvik, in which it was said that the daughter must accept that which her brother was willing to give her, since she had married against the wishes of her parents. Svea Hovrätts arkiv, Renoverade småprotokoll, Väddö och Häverö 1751, Riksarkivet.

51 Svea Hovrätts arkiv, Renoverade småprotokoll, Frösåker 1753, Riksarkivet.

52 Svea Hovrätts arkiv, Renoverade småprotokoll, Frötuna och Länna 1752, Riksarkivet.

53 Undersåkers häradsrättsarkiv, Dombok 1763, Östersunds Landsarkiv.

54 Undersåkers häradsrättsarkiv, Dombok 1786, Östersunds Landsarkiv.

55 Kopparbergs läns häradsrättsarkiv, Dombok Stora Tuna 1744, 24 September, Uppsala Landsarkiv.

56 *Statistik och redogörelse*, 519–20. Compare Salmon, *Women and the Law of Property*, 88, which observes that marriage settlements were uncommon in seventeenth-century America because society lacked the wealth and class structure that was required. In South Carolina in the period 1790 to 1810, only 1 to 2 percent of all marrying couples wrote marriage settlements. Desan, *Family on Trial*, 385n25, makes a similar point for Normandy.

57 Inger, *Svensk rättshistoria*, 92.

58 Håbo häradsrätts arkiv, Småprotokoll 1779, 8 May, Uppsala Landsarkiv.

59 Compare Howell, *Marriage Exchange*, 161.

60 Svea Hovrätts arkiv, Renoverade småprotokoll, Frösåker 1753, Riksarkivet.

61 Undersåkers häradsrättsarkiv, Dombok 1763 vårting § 8, Östersunds Landsarkiv.

62 Undersåkers häradsrättsarkiv, Dombok 1755 höstting § 32, Östersunds Landsarkiv.

63 Svea Hovrätts arkiv, Renoverade småprotokoll, Frösåker 1752, Riksarkivet.

64 Compare chapter 2.

65 Norell, *Sjette Samlingen*, 96–100. For another example, see Kopparbergs läns häradsrättsarkiv, Dombok Stora Tuna 1741, 16 April, Uppsala Landsarkiv.

66 Like married women, unmarried women were not regarded as legally capable. Only as a widow did a Swedish woman have approximately the same legal capacity as an adult man. See also chapter 2.

67 Kopparbergs läns häradsrättsarkiv, Dombok Stora Tuna 1741, 13 April, Uppsala Landsarkiv.

68 Undersåkers häradsrättsarkiv, Dombok 1751 vårting § 30, Östersunds Landarkiv.

69 See also Scott, *Seeing Like a State*, for an analysis of the risks inherent in schemes of simplification.

70 Åkerbo häradsrättsarkiv, Rystad A II a 5, 589f, Vadstena Landsarkiv.

71 Swedish *undantag*. Åkerbo häradsrättsarkiv, Rystad F II 16, 1043, Vadstena Landsarkiv.

72 Ågren, "Lösa ekonomiska tvister"; Österberg, "Bönder och centralmakt." Ågren and Österberg both show that civil cases amounted to a little more than 50 percent of all cases in the eighteenth century. By way of contrast, civil cases constituted only 37 percent of all cases in Vendel 1615–24, according to Österberg.

73 Hällström, "Arvejordsinstitutet," 267, 277.

74 Olivecrona, *Om makars giftorätt*, 292–328.

75 Tenants of these farms had very strong rights and, according to royal statute law, children of tenants had the right to take over possession after their parents. The reason given for this is interesting: the statute said that the tenant and his children should be accorded this right because of the *toil and labor* they had invested in the farm. *Kongl. Maj:ts Nådige Förordning angående Crono-Rusthåll 22 February 1749.*

76 Norell, *Sjette Samlingen*, 181–86.

77 Ibid., 96–100.

78 Nehrman, *Föreläsningar öfwer Giftermåls Balken*, 147–46; Calonius, *Om äktenskapsförord*, 21 (§ 4n7). See also Olivecrona, *Om makars giftorätt*, 292–94, which clearly argues that redeemed land was not part of the common property according to the legal code of 1734.

79 This was also a view put forward, unsuccessfully, by one speaker when the Diet had discussed the new legal code. See chapter 3.

80 Undersåkers häradsrättsarkiv, Dombok 1757 vårting § 16, Östersunds Landsarkiv.

81 Undersåkers häradsrättsarkiv, Dombok 1764 höstting § 5, Östersunds Landsarkiv.

82 See also Hällström, "Arvejordsinstitutet," 263, which points out, correctly, that even inherited land could be willed away, as long as relatives did not complain.

83 Ibid., 267.

84 Undersåkers häradsrättsarkiv, Dombok 1750 höstting § 8, Östersunds Landsarkiv.

85 The court referred to Jordabalken 8 § 1, which admitted that inherited property could be given away for the duration of a lifetime, to someone who had rendered considerable services to the owner.

86 Åkerbo häradsrättsarkiv, Rystad F II 17, 897, Vadstena Landsarkiv.

87 See for example *Theses Juridicae de Surrogato*, theses 6 and 9.

88 That seventeenth- and eighteenth-century economic legislation was both obscure and, for the same reason, flexible is a point made in Gadd, "Varför är äldre näringslagstiftning så oklar?"

89 See also Staves, *Married Women's Seprate Property*, 196; Erickson, "Introduction," 13, which argues that English law was extremely convoluted, which had negative effects for women.

90 Palm, *Befolkningen*, 64–66; Lundh, "Remarriages."

91 Carlsson, *Fröknar, mamseller, jungfrur och pigor*, 27, 36–37, 116, table 6.

92 Winberg, "Familj och jord"; Rosén, *Himlajord och handelsvara*, 68–71, 195, 197, 225; Perlestam, *Rotfaste bonden*.

93 Holmlund, "Arvejord och äktenskap," 247–48; Holmlund, *Jorden vi ärvde*, 85, 112, 180–81.

94 See chapter 1.

95 Bengtsson, *Ödmjukt anförande til protocollet*.

96 Schagerborg, *Förslag til en utgiftnings-fond*. The proposal was finally dismissed by the Diet as being too costly.

97 Compare chapter 2; Holmlund, "Arvejord och äktenskap"; Ighe, *I faderns ställe*, 215.

98 Kopparbergs läns häradsrättsarkiv, Dombok Stora Tuna 1741, 16 September, Uppsala Landsarkiv.

99 Undersåkers häradsrättsarkiv, Dombok 1751 höstting § 10, Dombok 1752 höstting § 44, Östersunds Landsarkiv. The parental farm was sold, and the money used to purchase two other farms.

100 Statutory law said that a person who did not intend to get married could not claim to have a part of the parental farm but would have to accept to have his or her inheritance in another form. See *Kongl. Maj:ts Nådige Förordning angående Hemmans Klyfning 30 June 1747*.

101 Holmlund, *Jorden vi ärvde*, 119–20, makes the same point.

102 Erickson, *Women and Property*; Winberg, "Familj och jord."

103 Among these were Abraham Magnus Sahlstedt, who wrote *Project til en inrättning af pupill-medels förwaltning, och hemgift för flickor* (1756), and Carl Wilhelm Cederhielm, who set up the proposal to start Vadstena Jungfrustift (founded in 1739).

104 The reason why this is an unlikely level is that unmarried women (who are

included in table 8) seem to have had very slim chances of inheriting land. See also Holmlund, *Jorden vi ärvde*, 180–81.

105 For another set of data, yielding similar results, see *Historisk statistik för Sverige. Del 1. Befolkning 1720–1967*, table 22. In 1815, a total of 952,082 women were registered by estate or occupation (approximately 300,000 were not registered by estate or occupation, according to table 17). If we assume that one-fourth of all women who were married to peasants, crofters, officers, and civil servants had inherited land of their own, and that the same was true for one-fourth of all widows, we arrive at a sum of 93,250 women, which is approximately 10 percent of all women registered by occupation. The reason why we should use one-fourth is that daughters seldom inherited land unless there were no brothers. It is often assumed in demographics that one-fifth of all families have only daughters. Thus, calculating with one-fourth means that we arrive at a conservative estimate. If the share is wrong, it is too large, not too small. The fact that the calculation is only based on those whose occupation was registered rather than on all women is also likely to exaggerate the number of women with inherited land. Compare Erickson, *Women and Property*, 5.

106 Compare footnote 31 above; Holmlund, *Jorden vi ärvde*, 85; Lindström, *Distribution*, 211.

107 Åkerbo häradsrättsarkiv, Rystad F II 10, 383, Vadstena Landsarkiv. The quotation is from 393.

108 Skoglund, *Fattigvården*. See also Rosén, *Himlajord och handelsvara*, 225; Jordansson, *Den goda människan*, 149–50; Rosén, *Gamla plikter och nya krav*, 188; Ighe, *I faderns ställe*, 166.

109 Aspelin, *Europeiska missnöjet*, 185–96.

CHAPTER FIVE

1 *Handlingar angående afledne Gotthard Hildebrands testamente.*

2 Elgenstierna, *Introducerade svenska adeln* 3:601.

3 *Sveriges ridderskaps och adels riksdags-protokoll från och med år 1719*, vol. 7 (1734): 393–94, 441.

4 In the period 1700 to 1829, a total of 1253 legal cases were made public in this way. In many of these, several documents were published (in one case as many as 117). Some of the titles are exceedingly long; strictly speaking, they are not real titles but the first sentences of the court records. Sometimes in what follows, I will abbreviate the titles, following Bring, *Svenskt Boklexikon 1700–1829. Rättegångshandlingar.*

5 There has been some debate as to when the four-estates Diet came into being, but most historians would say some time during the sixteenth century. During the seventeenth-century, the Diet was deeply involved in the war efforts through its right to accept, or deny, extra taxes. Whether or not it is correct to talk about a party system during the eighteenth century is discussed in Winton, *Frihetstidens politiska praktik.*

6 Sennefelt, "Stockholmsliv."

7 Ågren, "Domestic Secret." For the role played by freedom and Protestantism in eighteenth-century British culture, see Colley, *Britons*, chapter 1.

8 See also Alm, *Kungsord i elfte timmen*, 130–53.

9 The Swedish word *skrifterna* can be understood to mean both "the holy scriptures" and "the documents."

10 *Wälmente tankar och anmärkningar öfwer den widtbekanta Rutströmska religions- och rättegångs-saken til allmänhetens närmare granskning. Framgifne af En Owäldug Swensk.* According to Bring, *Svenskt Boklexikon 1700–1829. Rättegångshandlingar*, the author was Isac Faggot.

11 See also Hallberg, *Ages of Liberty*, chapter 3. Hallberg shows that the publications gradually became smaller and cheaper. In this way, Hallberg argues, the medium was made available to the people.

12 Farge, *Subversive Words*.

13 Bring, *Svenskt Boklexikon 1700–1829. Rättegångshandlingar*, ix–xi; Ågren, "Inför allmänhetens oväldiga domstol."

14 Boberg, *Gustav III och tryckfriheten*, 4–6.

15 Ågren, "Hemligt eller offentligt," 30.

16 Winton, *Frihetstidens politiska praktik*, chapter 5.

17 *Axel Reuterholms dagboksanteckningar*, 33.

18 *Kongl. Maj:tz Stadga och Förordning huru med debitorer, som för giäld rymma uhr rijket förhållas skall . . . 6 July 1730; Kongl. Maj:ts Nådige Förordning, angående rymmande för gäld 11 December 1766.*

19 *Betänkande til riksens ständers justitiä deputation angående allmänna creditens uphjelpande genom lagarnes förbättring uti concurs- och executionsmål*, 26.

20 Ibid., 4–9.

21 See for example *Svea Hofrätts bref, huruwijda i de sterbhus, der cessio bonorum skier . . . 27 April 1699.*

22 *1734 års lag*, Handelsbalken 16.

23 In 1770, 1773, and 1798.

24 *Kongl. Maj:ts Nådige Förklaring, om hwad wid fallissementer samt cessions och concours-twister hädanefter bör i akttagas 8 May 1767; Kongl. Maj:ts Nådige Förklaring, om hwad wid fallissemens- samt cessions- och concours-twister hädanefter bör i akt tagas 23 March 1770; Kongl. Maj:ts Förnyade Nådiga Stadga, angående afträdes- och förmons- samt boskilnads- och urarfwa mål 26 August 1773; Kongl. Maj:ts Förnyade Nådiga Stadga, angående afträdes- och förmons- samt boskilnads- och urarfwa-mål 28 June 1798; Concurs-Lag, gifwen Stockholms Slott å Rikssalen 13 July 1818; Concurs-Lag, gifwen Stockholms Slott å Rikssalen 12 March 1830.* On nineteenth-century bankruptcy law, see Adamson, *Järnavsättning och bruksfinansiering*, 158–61.

25 See also Beachy, "Women without Gender," 207–8, on how new bankruptcy legislation was developed in the German area in the eighteenth century.

26 Eighteenth-century legislation is somewhat unclear on this point. On the one hand, bankruptcy rules were included in the part of the code which dealt with trade, and bankruptcy law consistently stressed the importance of bookkeeping, all of which suggests that tradesmen were the ones eligible to declare bankruptcy. On the other hand, the law argued as if both urban and rural courts were in charge of bankruptcies, which suggests a broader social spectrum of bankrupts. *Kongl. Maj:ts Nådige Förklaring om hwad wid*

fallissementer samt cessions och concours-twister hädanefter bör i akttagas 8 May 1767, § 11.

27 See for example *Kongl. Maj:ts Förnyade Nådiga Stadga, angående afträdes- och förmons- samt boskilnads- och urarfwa-mål 28 June 1798.* For an analysis of eighteenth-century bankruptcy law in America, see Mann, *Republic of Debtors.*

28 On the importance of speed, see for example *Kongl. Maj:ts Nådige Förklaring, om hwad wid fallissemens- samt cessions- och concours-twister hädanefter bör i akt tagas 23 March 1770, § 2; Kongl. Maj:ts Förnyade Nådiga Stadga, angående afträdes- och förmons- samt boskilnads- och urarfwa mål 26 August 1773, § 7; Kongl. Maj:ts Förnyade Nådiga Stadga, angående afträdes- och förmons- samt boskilnads- och urarfwa-mål 28 June 1798, § 6.*

29 *Kongl. Maj:tz Stadga och Förordning huru med debitorer, som för giäld rymma uhr rijket förhållas skall 6 July 1730.*

30 *Kongl. Maj:ts Nådige Förklaring om hwad wid fallissementer samt cessions och concours-twister hädanefter bör i akttagas 8 May 1767, § 2; Betänkande til riksens ständers justitiä deputation angående allmänna creditens uphjelpande genom lagarnes förbättring uti concurs- och executions-mål,* 20.

31 On the importance of openness, see for example *Kongl. Maj:ts Nådige Förklaring, om hwad wid fallissemens- samt cessions- och concours-twister hädanefter bör i akt tagas 23 March 1770, § 5; Kongl. Maj:ts Förnyade Nådiga Stadga, angående afträdes- och förmons- samt boskilnads- och urarfwa mål 26 August 1773, §§ 6, 12, 15; Kongl. Maj:ts Förnyade Nådiga Stadga, angående afträdes- och förmons- samt boskilnads- och urarfwa-mål 28 June 1798, § 6.*

32 Dufwa, *Till Stockholms vällofl. rådhus-rätt;* Dufwa, *Warning åt förmögna föräldrar, hvilka bortgifta sina döttrar, eller de till Kongl. Svea hof-rätt ingifna besvär ... om arfwingars rättighet att söka boskillnad; Fortsättning af handlingar ... jemväl Kongl. Svea hof-rätts utslag af den 15 martii 1822; Ytterligare fortsättning af rättegångshandlingar emellan hof-rätts-assessoren M. Heerman samt hans svärfader hofrättsrådet J. F. Dufwa.*

33 *Handlingar rörande afträdes och förmons twisten emellan handelshuset i Stockholm under namn af Anders Plomgrens enka & compagnie och samtelige des borgenärer, samt emellan borgenärerne och afledne Anders Plomgrens arfwingar,* 55–56; *Ytterligare handlingar hörande til Plomgrenska concours-saken* (emphasis added).

34 See for example *Kongl. Maj:ts Förnyade Nådiga Stadga, angående afträdes- och förmons- samt boskilnads- och urarfwa mål 26 August 1773, §§ 1, 18; Kongl. Maj:ts Förnyade Nådiga Stadga, angående afträdes- och förmons- samt boskilnads- och urarfwa-mål 28 June 1798, §§ 5, 14:3.*

35 It is not surprising that Claes Rålamb and his third wife used this legal device.

36 The first registered example of the word is from 1723. *Svenska Akademiens Ordbok,* B 4071, "boskillnad."

37 *Kongl. Maj:ts Förnyade Nådiga Stadga, angående afträdes- och förmons- samt boskilnads- och urarfwa mål 26 August 1773, § 18.*

38 Svea Hovrätts arkiv, Huvudarkivet B III a, Civila resolutioner 1783, fol. 731, Riksarkivet.

39 *Juridiskt Arkif*, 13:257 (emphasis added): "Jag kan ej föreställa mig detta . . . att nämnde kreditorer med någon anledning af lag, jag vill ej säga sken af *billighet*, kunna göra anspråk på hvad jag möjligen kan hafva förvärfat genom boskillnadsmedlens användande i lagligt tillåten och lagligt beskattad handel och köpenskap" (I cannot envisage . . . that the said creditors can lawfully, much less *equitably*, claim what I may have earned by using the separated property for lawful and lawfully taxed trade and commerce).

40 See chapter 2.

41 *Betänkande til riksens ständers justitiä deputation angående allmänna creditens uphjelpande genom lagarnes förbättring uti concurs- och executions-mål*, 43.

42 *Concurs-Lag, 13 July 1818*, 7 § 11.

43 Very few of the publications dealt with criminal cases.

44 The best example of this was the 1807–13 bankruptcy of John Hall, resulting in 117 publications by Hall himself and the curators of his estate.

45 *Rättegång emellan bruks-patronerne Claes och Peter Altjn och håf-rätts auscultanten Carl Daniel Burén samt bruks-patronen Daniel Burén och dess fru, Catharina Margareta Adlerklo, ömsom kärande och swarande, angående förment aflinge och äskad förmyndare-räkning och redogörelse för bröst-arf, sidoarf och bördköpt egendom; Fortgång af Burénska rättegången.*

46 See also chapter 4.

47 The reader will have noticed that Swedish women normally kept their maiden names during marriage. Consequently, the correct way of referring to this woman was Margareta Björkman. Calling her by the name of her late husband may have been a subtle way of associating her with him and of implying that she was an accomplice.

48 *Handlingar hörande til rättegångs-saken emellan framledne öfwerstens Brovalls respective arfwingar och afledne ryttmästaren Billbergs respective arfwingar.*

49 *Hos Kongl. Hof-rätten hafwer; Sedan samtelige landshöfdingens Adam Otto Lagerbergs och des fru Beata Sparres samtelige borgenärer kommit i tillstånd at . . . göra en almän utredning, så hafwa . . . de heldre welat ingå en almän öfwerenskommelse.*

50 *Berättelse och handlingar i en arfs-twist emellan victualie-skrifwaren Schlechts enka och murarmästaren Frieses enka.*

51 Alm, *Kungsord i elfte timmen.*

52 Johansson, *History of Literacy in Sweden*; Lindmark, *Pennan, plikten.*

53 The importance attached to reading, and women's role in teaching, is illustrated by a probate inventory from Rystad. Stina Nilsdotter was widowed at the age of forty-one, having one son, nine years old. The household was poor and indebted. The inventory concludes that the widow was allowed to keep the estate, on condition that she would feed and clothe the son, *and teach him to read*. Similar formulations can be found in other probate inventories. Åkerbo häradsrättsarkiv, Rystad F II 14, 719, Vadstena Landsarkiv.

54 Compare Hallberg, *Ages of Liberty*, 123, 133, on women's participation in the public sphere.

55 *Rättegångs-handlingar emellan fru Ingrid Baas, hofrättsråd Falkengren och borgaren Eklin rörande inlösen af Aneboda säterie med derunder lydande lägenheter mot pantskillingens betalande.*

56 Becker, *Underdån-ödmjukt memorial*.

57 The verdict was correct. Elisabeth Larsson was the sole owner of the house she had brought into marriage, that is, two-fourths of the estate. She was also entitled to one-half of the other house since this was in Stockholm and urban law gave husband and wife equal shares of the common estate.

58 Bankruptcy law stipulated that all creditors had to swear an oath to the effect that their claims were accurate.

59 *Till justitie-canzlers-embetet.*

60 *Handlingar och protocoll rörande den besynnerliga process, som af friherrinnan Anna Hel. Hästesko emot sin moder fru Elisab. Charl. Reenstierna blifwit orsakad och anstäld, dels om testamente uti egit namn, dels om twå hundrade tusen dal. kmt.*

61 Ibid. Quotations are from court sessions held 23 January 1768, 3 March 1768, 17 March 1768, and 18 March 1768.

62 Farge, *Subversive Words*, 197.

63 Weidling, *Til allmänheten*.

64 *Arfs- och testaments-twist emellan lärftskrämaren Carl Saebom och kryddkrämaren Anders Gladhem.*

65 Vickery, *Gentleman's Daughter*, 161–94, quotation from 162.

66 *Det riksfördärfweliga swenska öfwerflödet, uti några wissa rum och ställen, samt nödiga botemedel deremot, utmärkt och angifwit under riksdagen i Stockholm år 1762.* Carl Leuhusen was said to be the author.

67 *På det allmänheten måtte få et rätt begrep om den sak, som stads-mäklaren Gustaf Rahm Eriksson uti Dagligt allehanda n:r 258 allenast i generelle termer upgifwit, har jag trodt mig böra följande til uplysning meddela.*

68 Winton, *Frihetstidens politiska praktik*.

69 Mann, *Republic of Debtors*, 8.

70 Colley, *Britons*, 217–18.

71 Maza, *Private Lives and Public Affairs*.

CHAPTER SIX

1 *Ridderskapets och adelns riksdagsprotokoll, 1840–41*, 13:95.

2 Desan, *Family on Trial*, 141.

3 Mill, *Subjection of Women*, 431–40.

4 Tocqueville, *Democracy in America*, 23–25.

5 Very few representatives argued along these lines. One of them was Magnus Björnstjerna, who made explicit reference to Tocqueville (*Ridderskapets och adelns riksdagsprotokoll, 1844–45*, 5:249). Another one, Wolrath Tham, argued along lines Tocqueville was to argue a few years later (*Ridderskapets och adelns riksdagsprotokoll, 1828–30*, 29:64).

6 Qvist, *Kvinnofrågan i Sverige*.

7 The most correct way of referring to this person, and to other peasants with a "surname" ending with -son (or -dotter), is to use the full name: Petter Persson. The reason is that at this time, stable surnames or family names did not exist. A person had one Christian name only (Petter) and then added who his or her father was: I am Petter, son of Per, or I am Maja, daughter of Per. It was not until the end of the nineteenth century that these patronym-

ics "froze" into stable family names that were kept through generations. From this time on, a man or a woman can have Persson as his or her family name, even when the father is not called Per. Note that Icelandic still retains the old naming principle.

8 *Bondeståndets riksdagsprotokoll*, 1844–45, 2:275. Petter Persson had put forward his proposal early, in 1829 and 1834; see *Lagutskottets betänkande*, no. 68, 1 (1829) and no. 122, 10 (1835).

9 Noblemen who supported the compromise included Palmstierna and Günther.

10 *Prästeståndets riksdagsprotokoll*, 1844–45, 6:157–58. See also *Prästeståndets riksdagsprotokoll*, 1840–41, 7:443, 445, 448, 451.

11 In fact, these reforms were introduced through the same act.

12 Hirschfeldt, "Domstolarna som statsmakt."

13 *Lagutskottets betänkande*, no. 82, 12 (1845).

14 *Bondeståndets riksdagsprotokoll*, 1844–45, 2:270–75.

15 *Bondeståndets riksdagsprotokoll*, 1844–45, 1:232–33.

16 See chapter 4.

17 *Lagutskottets betänkande*, no. 122, 11 (1835).

18 *Borgarståndets riksdagsprotokoll*, 1844–45, 2:497–98.

19 *Prästeståndets riksdagsprotokoll*, 1847–48, 5:157 (Broman); *Lagutskottets betänkande*, no. 123, 1 (1835) (Dalman).

20 *Bondeståndets riksdagsprotokoll*, 1828–30, 9:293, 295, 309.

21 *Bondeståndets riksdagsprotokoll*, 1844–45, 2:171.

22 *Prästeståndets riksdagsprotokoll*, 1840–41, 7:435–36; *Prästeståndets riksdagsprotokoll*, 1844–45, 6:218–19.

23 For example *Lagutskottets betänkande*, no. 99, 8 (1841). A frequent argument that appears as early as the eighteenth century was that wills often included formal errors. See for example Sahlstedt, *Project til en inrättning af pupillmedels förwaltning, och hemgift för flickor*.

24 For example Olof Nilsson from Västerbotten. See *Bondeståndets riksdagsprotokoll*, 1844–45, 6:80.

25 See for example *Lagutskottets betänkande*, no. 68, 6 (1829).

26 The commission's proposal for a new marital law was published in 1815 as *Förslag till Giftermåls Balk*. To avoid confusion, I have translated *Lagcomitén* as "the Law Commission" and *lagutskottet* as "the legal committee (of the Diet)."

27 *Lagutskottets betänkande*, no. 122, 15–16 (1835). Almost identical versions of this proposal were presented in 1840–41 and 1844–45.

28 *Lagutskottets betänkande*, no. 13, 7 (1858).

29 Many peasants from southern and western Sweden advocated the reform, while many from northern Sweden opposed it. The peasantry from central Sweden, around the lake Mälaren, tended to be opposed during the first phase of the debate but subsequently changed their minds. See Ågren, "Fadern, systern och brodern."

30 See chapter 4.

31 See for example *Ridderskapets och adelns riksdagsprotokoll*, 1828–30, 29:71 (P. G. Cederschjöld); *Ridderskapets och adelns riksdagsprotokoll*, 1834–35,

14:18 (J. Cederström); *Ridderskapets och adelns riksdagsprotokoll*, 1840–41, 13:76 (P. G. Cederschjöld); *Prästeståndets riksdagsprotokoll*, 1840–41, 7:442 (Agrell).

32 *Ridderskapets och adelns riksdagsprotokoll*, 1844–45, 5:271 (S. G. von Troil).

33 Larsson, *Moraliska kroppen*, 138–42.

34 Desan, *Family on Trial*, 55–56.

35 *Ridderskapets och adelns riksdagsprotokoll*, 1828–30, 29:109 (A. Ribbing); similar arguments in 29:87–88 (von Hartmansdorff).

36 *Förslag till Giftermåls Balk*, 69 (Richert).

37 Johan Gabriel Richert (1784–1864).

38 *Förslag till Giftermåls Balk*, 55.

39 The main difference between Richert and the other members of the commission was that Richert wanted the husband's marital rights, which were cancelled through separation of property, to be resuscitated should the period of separation come to an end.

40 *Förslag till Giftermåls Balk*, 59.

41 Dübeck, *Købekoner og konkurrence*.

42 *Förslag till Giftermåls Balk*, 14–16.

43 *Ridderskapets och adelns riksdagsprotokoll*, 1844–45, 5:267 (C. A. Löwenhielm).

44 *Ridderskapets och adelns riksdagsprotokoll*, 1828–30, 29:81.

45 *Ridderskapets och adelns riksdagsprotokoll*, 1828–30, 29:96–97.

46 *Ridderskapets och adelns riksdagsprotokoll*, 1844–45, 5:252–56.

47 The existence of a new relationship between the sexes was a claim made in *Lagutskottets betänkande*, no. 122, 9 (1835), and in *Lagutskottets betänkande*, no. 99, 6 (1841).

48 It was the privilege, and duty, of the nobility to serve the state as officers or civil servants. Since men were the only ones who were allowed to fulfill these duties, it was argued that they should inherit more, since a university education was expensive.

49 *Lagutskottets betänkande*, no. 68, 1–2 (1829).

50 *Ridderskapets och adelns riksdagsprotokoll*, 1828–30, 29:66–67; *Bondeståndets riksdagsprotokoll*, 1828–30, 6:704; *Prästeståndets riksdagsprotokoll*, 1828–30, 6:288; *Bondeståndets riksdagsprotokoll*, 1844–45, 2:173.

51 *Ridderskapets och adelns riksdagsprotokoll*, 1844–45, 5:270.

52 *Bondeståndets riksdagsprotokoll*, 1828–30, 6:663 (Jacob Peter Andersson), 669 (Anders Danielsson).

53 *Prästeståndets riksdagsprotokoll*, 1828–30, 6:303–5. In 1840, Geijer had changed his mind and supported the reform. *Prästeståndets riksdagsprotokoll*, 1840–41, 7:448.

54 See for example *Ridderskapets och adelns riksdagsprotokoll*, 1844–45, 5:256–57 (L. Hierta); *Bondeståndets riksdagsprotokoll*, 1844–45, 2:174–75 (J. Andersson).

55 For a long-term study stretching into the early twentieth century, see Ågren, "'Hon skall ha min stickmaskin.'"

56 *Prästeståndets riksdagsprotokoll*, 1844–45, 6:163, 204.

57 *Ridderskapets och adelns riksdagsprotokoll*, 1828–30, 29:115.

58 Bondeståndets riksdagsprotokoll, 1828–30, 6:677; Bondeståndets riksdagsprotokoll, 1844–45, 2:177.

59 Bondeståndets riksdagsprotokoll, 1844–45, 6:92.

60 Prästeståndets riksdagsprotokoll, 1844–45, 6:177–80.

61 Bondeståndets riksdagsprotokoll, 1828–30, 6:708 (L. Larsson); Bondeståndets riksdagsprotokoll, 1840–41, 1:479 (M. Persson); Bondeståndets riksdagsprotokoll, 1844–45, 2:177 (J. Andersson).

62 Bondeståndets riksdagsprotokoll, 1828–30, 6:658–59, 674 (B. Nilsson, N. Persson); Bondeståndets riksdagsprotokoll, 1834–35, 2:91–100 (Insulin, Wiklund); Bondeståndets riksdagsprotokoll, 1844–45, 6:53–55, 101 (O. Johansson, N. P. Pettersson); Lagutskottets utlåtande, no. 122 (1829), reservations registered by Printzensköld and Lundström.

63 Enefalk, Patriotisk drömvärld; Sundin, 1809. Statskuppen och regeringsformen, 242.

64 Bondeståndets riksdagsprotokoll, 1844–45, 6:53–60 (O. Johansson, L. Gezelius, L. Olsson).

65 Bondeståndets riksdagsprotokoll, 1834–35, 2:90 (A. Andersson); Prästeståndets riksdagsprotokoll, 1834–35, 11:55 (af Wingård); Ridderskapets och adelns riksdagsprotokoll, 1834–35, 14:8–9 (Klingspor).

66 See chapter 4.

67 Qvist, Kvinnofrågan i Sverige, 71–72, 85, 98, 129, 134, 155, 164.

68 Bondeståndets riksdagsprotokoll, 1840–41, 1:466; Borgarståndets riksdagsprotokoll, 1834–35, 6:21; Prästeståndets riksdagsprotokoll, 1840–41, 7:447.

69 Compare Desan, Family on Trial, 44–45.

70 Bondeståndets riksdagsprotokoll, 1828–30, 6:669.

71 Borgarståndets riksdagsprotokoll, 1844–45, 7:500 (Lagergren); Prästeståndets riksdagsprotokoll, 1844–45, 6:175 (Osterman).

72 Bondeståndets riksdagsprotokoll, 1844–45, 6:72 (J. P. Dahllöf); Prästeståndets riksdagsprotokoll, 1844–45, 6:154–55, 181–182. See also Ridderskapets och adelns riksdagsprotokoll, 1828–30, 29:113 (af Malmborg).

73 Almqvist, "Svenska fattigdomens betydelse," 330. Kurt Aspelin calls this work an "ingenious paradox" and points out that the focus on poverty should not only be understood as political radicalism but also as an expression of Christian ideals. Aspelin, Europeiska missnöjet, 197.

74 Prästeståndets riksdagsprotokoll, 1834–35, 6:284 (af Wingård on Ireland); Ridderskapets och adelns riksdagsprotokoll, 1828–30, 29:88, 105 (von Hartmansdorff and Cederschjöld on England), 49:124 (Björnstierna on Ireland); Ridderskapets och adelns riksdagsprotokoll, 1834–35, 14:26–27 (Dalman on Ireland and France); Ridderskapets och adelns riksdagsprotokoll, 1840–41, 13:84, 86 (Cederschjöld and von Hartmansdorff on Norway); Ridderskapets och adelns riksdagsprotokoll, 1844–45, 5:250–51, 257–58 (Björnstierna on France, L. Hierta on France and England).

75 Lagutskottets betänkande, no. 72 (1829).

76 Lagutskottets betänkande, no. 13 (1858), reservation by Adlercreutz; Lagutskottets betänkande, no. 82 (1845); Bondeståndets riksdagsprotokoll, 1856–1858, 4:221, 224–26.

77 For example Prästeståndets riksdagsprotokoll, 1847–48, 9:429 (Broman).

78 *Bondeståndets riksdagsprotokoll, 1847–48*, 4:320 (L. Larsson).

79 *Ridderskapets och adelns riksdagsprotokoll, 1853–54*, 8:68.

80 *Bondeståndets riksdagsprotokoll, 1847–48*, 4:320–26; *Ridderskapets och adelns riksdagsprotokoll, 1853–54*, 15:245, 3:88–91.

81 *Bondeståndets riksdagsprotokoll, 1856–1858*, 4:232, 5:355–56; *Lagutskottets betänkande*, no. 82, 13 (1845); *Förslag till Giftermåls Balk*, 11, 36–37.

82 *Lagutskottets betänkande*, no. 32, 16 (1857).

83 *Lagutskottets betänkande*, no. 82 (1845), no. 36 (1848), no. 63 (1851), no. 29 (1854), no. 13 (1858).

84 *Borgarståndets riksdagsprotokoll, 1847–1848*, 2:608.

85 *Bondeståndets riksdagsprotokoll, 1856–1858*, 4:222–23.

86 *Bondeståndets riksdagsprotokoll, 1856–1858*, 4:233, 5:350–51.

87 *Bondeståndets riksdagsprotokoll, 1856–1858*, 4:221–22.

88 *Lagutskottets betänkande*, no. 13, 7 (1858).

89 *Ridderskapets och adelns riksdagsprotokoll, 1853–1854*, 8:73. On the nobility's professed willingness to make sacrifices, see Sundin, *1809. Statskuppen och regeringsformen*, 149–50.

90 Compare Erickson, *Women and Property*.

91 Lind, *Domarens pröfning efter Sweriges lag*, chapter 1.

92 *Ridderskapets och adelns riksdagsprotokoll, 1853–54*, 3:90, 15:244; *Förslag till Giftermåls Balk*, 21.

93 Carlsson, "Ståndsriksdagens slutskede," 196.

94 *Ridderskapets och adelns riksdagsprotokoll, 1844–45*, 5:270.

95 Salmon, *Women and the Law of Property*, 188–89.

96 Desan, *Family on Trial*, 139 ("it would not be just for a wife . . . to lose her recompense . . . the just compensation for their common work"), 147 ("Work is the first title of property.")

97 Fløystad, "Innføring av lik arv," 550–51.

98 Compare Winberg, *Grenverket*, 145, who discusses the importance of prescription to a property system that acknowledges many simultaneous claims to the same object.

CHAPTER SEVEN

1 *Dagens Nyheter*, Fråga Juristen (reply by Håkan Fälth).

2 See Erickson, *Women and Property*, 6, 230–31, for the argument that English women's legal and economic situation deteriorated in the course of the early modern period.

3 For a discussion about how the concept of welfare can be used for premodern societies, see Green and Owens, *Family Welfare*.

4 Through a skillful and meticulous analysis, Catherine Frances has been able to show that the role of families and friends was much more pronounced in England than has previously been assumed. Frances, "Making Marriages."

5 Eliot, *Daniel Deronda*, 758.

6 Burman, *Bremer*.

7 Ibid., 322, 325, 501.

8 Blom, "Veien til juridisk likestilling," 68.

9 Compare Ogilvie, *Bitter Living*; Erickson, "Coverture and Capitalism."

10 Blom, "Veien til juridisk likestilling," 65.

11 Niskanen, "Marriage and Economic Rights." Niskanen emphasizes that Scandinavian family law in the 1920s was progressive by international standards. Still, transitional rules applied into the 1950s, which meant that even after 1921 there continued to be some women who lived under the patriarchal rules of 1734.

12 This was late by Scandinavian standards. Finland extended the right to vote to women in 1906, Norway in 1913, and Iceland and Denmark in 1915.

13 Niskanen, "Marriage and Economic Rights," 253.

14 Beachy, "Women without Gender."

15 See chapter 1.

16 Petot, *Histoire du droit privé français*, 119–20, 453–55. For Germany, see Holthöfer, "Geschlechtsvormundschaft," 403–5, 412–13, and in particular 415: "der Zeitgeist der Frühen Neuzeit, den an 'Finsternis' dem in vieler Hinsicht toleranteren Mittelalter jedenfalls nicht nachstand, nahm nun gewisse geradezu frauenfeindliche Züge an und verfestigte die Vorherrschaft des Mannes sowohl im Haus als auch in der Öffentlichkeit" (While never really less "dark" than the in many ways tolerant Middle Ages, the early modern period now even acquired some outright misogynist aspects and consolidated male power both at home and in the public sphere).

17 Beauvalet-Boutouyrie, *Être veuve*, 186–187.

18 Beachy, "Women without Gender," 196. On the abolition of the Geschlechtsvormundschaft, see Sabean, "Allianzen und Listen."

19 Beachy, "Women without Gender," 199.

20 See chapter 1.

21 Salmon, *Women and the Law of Property*, 93–97.

22 See for instance *Le père Goriot*, where the misery of Goriot's younger daughter has to do with the fact that if she claims her separate property, her husband will go bankrupt (or so he tells her).

23 Hunt, *Middling Sort*.

24 On this, see Finn, *Character of Credit*.

25 Bergman, *Farmor och Vår Herre*, 192–93.

26 Of course, coverture may have been supported by other values as well and was perhaps not only a construction that allowed for legal simplification.

27 See chapter 4.

28 See chapter 4.

29 See chapter 6.

30 Sweden did not have special equity courts in this period, but the insight that law should not be applied mechanically but with sensitivity to fairness and social consequences was well-established. Ågren, "Domestic Secret."

31 Thompson, *Whigs and Hunters*, 258–69.

32 Desan, *Family on Trial*.

BIBLIOGRAPHY

Note: Swedish Å and Ä appear at the end of the letter A, and Swedish Ö appears at the end of the letter O.

MANUSCRIPT SOURCES
Jönköping, Sweden
  Göta Hovrätts arkiv
    Renoverade domböcker: Vedbo
Östersund, Sweden
  Östersunds Landsarkiv
    Undersåkers härad, Domböcker
Stockholm, Sweden
  Riksarkivet
    Svea Hovrätts arkiv, Huvudarkivet
    Svea Hovrätts arkiv, Renoverade domböcker och småprotokoll: Frötuna
      och Länna, Frösåker, Väddö och Häverö, Åkerbo (in Västmanland)
    Svea Hovrätts arkiv, Becchius-Palmcrantz Juridiska Samlingar
Uppsala, Sweden
  Uppsala Landsarkiv
    Åkerbo härad (in Västmanland), Domböcker
    Håbo härad, Småprotokoll
    Kopparbergs läns häradsrättsarkiv, Domböcker: Stora Tuna
  University Library of Uppsala
    Palmskiöldska samlingen, vol. 149: Lovisinus, Ericus. Materiam successionis
      seu haereditatis ab intestato quodammodo adumbrans
    B-samlingen
Vadstena, Sweden
  Vadstena Landsarkiv
    Åkerbo härad (in Östergötland), Småprotokoll

Legislation and Legal Treatises

1734 års lag = Sveriges Rikes Lag gillad och antagen på Riksdagen 1734 [1780]. Stockholm: Nordiska Bokhandeln, 1984.

Betänkande til riksens ständers justitiä deputation angående allmänna creditens up-hjelpande genom lagarnes förbättring uti concurs- och executions-mål. Stockholm: Johan Georg Lange, 1772.

Calonius, Matthias. *Om äktenskapsförord. 8:e capitlet Giftermålsbalken* (trans. into Swedish). Lund: no publisher, 1834.

Concurs-Lag, gifwen Stockholms Slott å Rikssalen 13 July 1818. Stockholm: Kongl. Tryckeriet, 1818.

Concurs-Lag, gifwen Stockholms Slott å Rikssalen 12 March 1830. Stockholm: Kongl. Boktryckeriet, 1830.

Crusius, Benedictus Olai. "Vår äldsta kommentar till landslagen: juris professor B. Crusius' föreläsningar vid Uppsala universitet hösten 1630." *Uppsala universitets årsskrift.* Uppsala: no publisher, 1927.

Förslag till Giftermåls Balk. Stockholm: Fr. Cederborgh & Comp., 1815.

Juridiskt Arkif. 34 vols. Christianstad: no publisher, 1830–62.

Kongl. Maj:ts Förnyade Nådiga Stadga, angående afträdes- och förmons- samt boskil-nads- och urarfwa mål 26 August 1773. Stockholm: Kongl. Tryckeriet, 1773.

Kongl. Maj:ts Förnyade Nådiga Stadga, angående afträdes- och förmons- samt boskil-nads- och urarfwa-mål 28 June 1798. Stockholm: Kongl. Tryckeriet, 1798.

Kongl. Maj:ts Nådiga Förklaring öfwer Allmänna Lagens Stadganden i åtskilliga rum, 23 March 1807. Stockholm: Kongl. Tryckeriet, 1807.

Kongl. Maj:ts Nådige Förklaring, om hwad wid fallissemens- samt cessions- och concours-twister hädanefter bör i akt tagas 23 March 1770. Stockholm: Kongl. Tryckeriet, 1770.

Kongl. Maj:ts Nådige Förklaring, om hwad wid fallissementer samt cessions och concours-twister hädanefter bör i akttagas 8 May 1767. Stockholm: Kongl. Tryckeriet, 1767.

Kongl. Maj:ts Nådige Förordning angående Crono-Rusthåll 22 February 1749. Stockholm: Kongl. Tryckeriet, 1749.

Kongl. Maj:ts Nådige Förordning angående Hemmans Klyfning 30 June 1747. Stockholm: Kongl. Tryckeriet, 1747.

Kongl. Maj:ts Nådige Förordning, angående rymmande för gäld 11 December 1766. Stockholm: Kongl. Tryckeriet, 1766.

Kongl. Maj:tz Stadga och Förordning huru med debitorer, som för giäld rymma uhr rijket förhållas skall . . . 6 July 1730. Stockholm: Kongl. Boktryckeriet, 1730.

Kongl. May:tz Stadga och Förordning angående Testamenten 3 July 1686. Stockholm: Kongl. Booktrychare, 1686.

Kristoffers landslag = Corpus iuris sueo-gotorum antiqui. Samling af Sweriges gamla lagar, på kongl. maj:ts nådigste befallning utgifven af d. C. J. Schlyter. Vol. 12. Lund: Berlingska boktryckeriet, 1869.

Lind, Lars Fr. *Domarens pröfning efter Sweriges lag, eller Sättet, at utröna lagens rätta förstånd, mening och grund.* Stockholm: Carl Fred. Marquard, 1799.

Magnus Erikssons Landslag i nusvensk tolkning av Åke Holmbäck och Elias Wessén(MELL). Stockholm: Nordiska Bokhandeln, 1962.

Magnus Erikssons Stadslag i nusvensk tolkning av Åke Holmbäck och Elias Wessén(MESL). Stockholm: Nordiska Bokhandeln, 1966.

Nehrman, David = Ehrenstråhle, David. *Föreläsningar öfwer Giftermåls Balken*. Stockholm: no publisher, 1747.

Rålamb, Claes. *Observationes Juris Practicae*. Stockholm: no publisher, 1679.

Riksrådet Johan Skyttes kommentar till stadslagen [1608], edited by Emil Wolff. Göteborg: no publisher, 1905.

Sjögren, Wilhelm, ed. *Förarbetena till Sveriges rikes lag 1686–1736*. 8 vols. Uppsala: no publisher, 1900–1909.

Stiernhöök, Johan. "Erffdabalcker heller den swenska arffzrätt." *Uppsala universitets årsskrift 1933*. Vol. 2. Juridik. Uppsala: Almqvist & Wiksell, 1933.

———. "Gifftermåhlsbalken." *Uppsala universitets årsskrift 1933*. Vol. 2. Juridik. Uppsala: Almqvist & Wiksell, 1933.

Svea Hofrätts bref, huruwijda i de sterbhus, der cessio bonorum skier . . . 27 April 1699. Stockholm: no publisher, 1699.

Theses Juridicae de Surrogato. Praeses Daniel Solander, respondit Erland Wall. Uppsala: no publisher, 1765.

Upplandslagen = Svenska landskapslagar tolkade och förklarade för nutidens svenskar av Åke Holmbäck och Elias Wessén. Vol. 1. Stockholm: Gebers, 1933.

Printed Court Records

Domboksutdrag rörande Fryksdals härad, part I, 1610–78, edited by Gunnar Almqvist. Sunne: no publisher, 1969.

Domboksutdrag rörande Fryksdals härad, part II, 1679–95, edited by Gunnar Almqvist. Sunne: no publisher, 1970.

Lagläsaren Per Larssons Dombok 1638. Vol. IV of *Uppländska Domböcker*, edited by Nils Edling. Uppsala: Kungl. Humanistiska Vetenskapssamfundet i Uppsala, 1937.

Långhundra härads dombok 1545–1570. Vol. VII of *Uppländska Domböcker*, edited by Nils Edling. Uppsala: Kungl. Humanistiska Vetenskapssamfundet i Uppsala, 1946.

Ölme härads dombok 1629–1650, jämte andra handlingar, edited by Axel Emanuel Löf. Kristinehamn: no publisher, 1921.

Tingsprotokoll för Njurunda. Ur Medelpads domböcker 1609–1672, Vol. 1, edited by Algot Hellbom. Sundsvall: Medelpads fornminnesförening i samarbete med Njurunda hembygdsförening, 1982.

Upplands Lagmansdombok 1578–1579. Vol. II of *Uppländska Domböcker*, edited by Nils Edling. Uppsala: Kungl. Humanistiska Vetenskapssamfundet i Uppsala, 1929.

Upplands Lagmansdombok 1581 och 1586. Vol. VIII of *Uppländska Domböcker*, edited by Nils Edling. Uppsala: Kungl. Humanistiska Vetenskapssamfundet i Uppsala, 1950.

Uppländska häradsrättsdomböcker från 1500-talet. Vol. V of *Uppländska Domböcker*, edited by Nils Edling. Uppsala: Kungl. Humanistiska Vetenskapssamfundet i Uppsala, 1941.

Ur Vedbo härads domböcker 1613–1732, edited by Anders Edestam. Ed: C. Zakariasson, 1977.

Vendels sockens dombok 1615–1645. Vol. I of *Uppländska Domböcker*, edited by Nils
Edling. Uppsala: Kungl. Humanistiska Vetenskapssamfundet i Uppsala, 1925.
Vendels sockens domböcker 1736–1737. Vol. IX of *Uppländska Domböcker*, edited
by Nils Edling and Walter Ljusterdal. Uppsala: Kungl. Humanistiska Veten-
skapssamfundet i Uppsala, 1956.
Wahlberg, C. J. *Åtgärder för lagförbättring 1633–1665*. Uppsala: no publisher, 1878.

Other Printed Primary Sources

Almqvist, Carl Jonas Love. "Den svenska fattigdomens betydelse." In *Carl Jonas
Love Almquist*, Svalans svenska klassikerserie. Stockholm: Albert Bonniers
förlag AB, 1958.
*Arfs- och testaments-twist emellan lärftskrämaren Carl Saebom och kryddkrämaren
Anders Gladhem*. Stockholm: Peter Hasselberg, 1772.
Axel Reuterholms dagboksanteckningar under riksdagen i Stockholm 1738–1739. Ed-
ited by Göran Nilzén. Kungl. Samfundet för utgivande av handskrifter rörande
Skandinaviens historia. Handlingar del 29: Stockholm, 2006.
Becker, Ebba Christina von. *Underdån-ödmjukt memorial!* Stockholm: Lorentz
Ludvig Grefing, 1771.
Bengtsson, Jon. *Ödmjukt anförande til protocollet*. Stockholm: Per Andreas Brodin,
1786.
*Berättelse och handlingar i en arfs-twist emellan victualie-skrifwaren Schlechts enka
och murarmästaren Frieses enka*. Stockholm: Anders Zetterberg, 1792.
Bondeståndets riksdagsprotokoll. 1828–30, 1834–35, 1840–41, 1844–45, 1847–48,
1856–58.
Borgarståndets riksdagsprotokoll. 1834–35, 1844–45, 1847–48.
Bring, Samuel E. *Svenskt Boklexikon 1700–1829. Rättegångshandlingar*. Uppsala:
Svenska Litteratursällskapet, 1958.
Dagens Nyheter, Fråga Juristen.
Dufwa, Johan Fredric. *Fortsättning af handlingar . . . jemväl Kongl. Svea hof-rätts
utslag af den 15 martii 1822*. Stockholm: Olof Grahn, 1822.
———. *Till Stockholms vällofl. rådhus-rätt!* Stockholm: Olof Grahn, 1821.
———. *Warning åt förmögna föräldrar, hvilka bortgifta sina döttrar, eller de till
Kongl. Svea hof-rätt ingifna besvär . . . om arfwingars rättighet att söka boskillnad*.
Stockholm: Olof Grahn, 1822.
———. *Ytterligare fortsättning af rättegångshandlingar emellan hof-rätts-assessoren
M. Heerman samt hans svärfader hofrättsrådet J. F. Dufwa*. Stockholm: Olof
Grahn, 1822.
Elgenstierna, Gustaf. *Den introducerade svenska adelns ättartavlor med tillägg och
rättelser*. 9 vols. Stockholm: Norstedts, 1925–36.
Fortgång af Burénska rättegången. Norrköping: Johan Benjamin Blume, 1767.
Handlingar angående afledne Gotthard Hildebrands testamente. Stockholm: Kungl.
Tryckeriet, 1765.
*Handlingar hörande til rättegångs-saken emellan framledne öfwerstens Brovalls respec-
tive arfwingar och afledne ryttmästaren Billbergs respective arfwingar*. Stockholm:
Wennberg & Nordström, 1772.
*Handlingar och protocoll rörande den besynnerliga process, som af friherrinnan Anna
Hel. Hästesko emot sin moder fru Elisab. Charl. Reenstierna blifwit orsakad och*

anstäld, dels om testamente uti egit namn, dels om twå hundrade tusen dal. kmt.
Stockholm: Peter Hasselberg, 1768.

Handlingar rörande afträdes och förmons twisten emellan handelshuset i Stockholm under namn af Anders Plomgrens enka & compagnie och samtelige des borgenärer, samt emellan borgenärerne och afledne Anders Plomgrens arfwingar. Stockholm: Kungl. Tryckeriet, 1781.

Historisk statistik för Sverige. Del 1. Befolkning 1720–1967. 2nd ed. Örebro, Stockholm: Statistiska Centralbyrån, 1969.

Hos Kongl. Hof-rätten hafwer . . . No place, publisher, or date [identified by Samuel E. Bring as the verdict of 11 May 1773 in the case concerning Beata Sparre's application for separation of property].

Lagutskottets betänkande no. 68. Bihang till Samtlige Riks-Ståndens Protocoll, vid Lagtima Riksdagen i Stockholm. Sjunde samlingen, Första Avdelningen. Stockholm: Elméns & Granbergs tryckeri, 1829.

Lagutskottets betänkande no. 72. Bihang till Samtlige Riks-Ståndens Protocoll, vid Lagtima Riksdagen i Stockholm. Sjunde samlingen, Första Avdelningen. Stockholm: Elméns & Granbergs tryckeri, 1829.

Lagutskottets betänkande no. 122. Bihang till Samtlige Riks-Ståndens Protocoll, vid Lagtima Riksdagen i Stockholm. Sjunde samlingen, Första Avdelningen. Stockholm: Elméns & Granbergs tryckeri, 1829.

Lagutskottets betänkande no. 122. Bihang till Samtlige Riks-Ståndens Protocoll vid Urtima Riksdagen i Stockholm. Sjunde samlingen, Första Avdelningen. Stockholm: J. A. Walldén, 1835.

Lagutskottets betänkande no. 123. Bihang till Samtlige Riks-Ståndens Protocoll vid Urtima Riksdagen i Stockholm. Sjunde samlingen, Första Avdelningen. Stockholm: J. A. Walldén, 1835.

Lagutskottets betänkande no. 99. Bihang till Samtlige Riks-Ståndens Protocoll vid Lagtima Riksdagen i Stockholm. Sjunde samlingen, Första Avdelningen. Stockholm: Kongl. Ordens-Boktryckeriet, 1841.

Lagutskottets betänkande no. 82. Bihang till Samtlige Riks-Ståndens Protocoll vid Urtima Riksdagen i Stockholm. Sjunde samlingen, Första Avdelningen. Stockholm: W. F. Dalman, 1845.

Lagutskottets betänkande no. 36. Bihang till Samtlige Riks-Ståndens Protocoll vid Lagtima Riksdagen i Stockholm. Sjunde samlingen, Första Avdelningen. Stockholm: f.d. Schultze's Boktryckeri, 1848.

Lagutskottets betänkande no. 63. Bihang till Samtlige Riks-Ståndens Protocoll vid Lagtima Riksdagen i Stockholm. Sjunde samlingen, Första Avdelningen. Stockholm: Isac Marcus, 1851.

Lagutskottets betänkande no. 29. Bihang till Samtlige Riks-Ståndens Protocoll vid Lagtima Riksdagen i Stockholm. Sjunde samlingen, Första Avdelningen. Stockholm: f.d. Schultze's Boktryckeri, 1854.

Lagutskottets betänkande no. 13. Bihang till Samtlige Riks-Ståndens Protocoll vid Lagtima Riksdagen i Stockholm. Sjunde samlingen, Första Avdelningen. Stockholm: N. Marcus, 1858.

Lagutskottets betänkande no. 16. Bihang till Samtlige Riks-Ståndens Protocoll vid Lagtima Riksdagen i Stockholm. Sjunde samlingen, Första Avdelningen. Stockholm: N. Marcus, 1858.

Lagutskottets betänkande no. 32. Bihang till Samtlige Riks-Ståndens Protocoll vid Lagtima Riksdagen i Stockholm. Sjunde samlingen, Första Avdelningen. Stockholm: N. Marcus, 1858.

Lagutskottets utlåtande no. 122. Bihang till Samtlige Riks-Ståndens Protokoll, vid Lagtima Riksdagen i Stockholm. Sjunde samlingen, Första Avdelningen. Stockholm: Elméns & Granbergs tryckeri, 1829.

Magalotti, Lorenzo. *Sverige under år 1674.* Stockholm: Rediviva, 1986.

Mill, John Stuart. *The Subjection of Women.* 1869. World's Classics No. 170. Oxford: Oxford University Press, 1969.

Norell, Carl Johan, ed. *Sjette Samlingen af Kongl. Maj:ts Bref, Rescripter och Förklaringar, 1792–1798.* Stockholm: Kgl. Ordens-Boktryckeriet, 1800.

På det allmänheten måtte få et rätt begrep om den sak, som stads-mäklaren Gustaf Rahm Eriksson uti Dagligt allehanda n:r 258 allenast i generelle termer upgifwit, har jag trodt mig böra följande til uplysning meddela. Stockholm: Peter Hasselberg, 1771.

Prästeståndets riksdagsprotokoll. 1828–30, 1834–35, 1840–41, 1844–45, 1847–48

Rättegång emellan bruks-patronerne Claes och Peter Altjn och håf-rätts auscultanten Carl Daniel Burén samt bruks-patronen Daniel Burén och dess fru, Catharina Margareta Adlerklo, ömsom kärande och swarande, angående förment aflinge och äskad förmyndare-räkning och redogörelse för bröst-arf, sidoarf och bördköpt egendom. Linköping: Gabriel Björckegren and widow, no year.

Rättegångs-handlingar emellan fru Ingrid Baas, hofrättsråd Falkengren och borgaren Eklin rörande inlösen af Aneboda säterie med derunder lydande lägenheter mot pantskillingens betalande . . . Stockholm: Peter Hasselberg, 1761.

Ridderskapets och adelns riksdagsprotokoll. 1828–30, 1834–35, 1840–41, 1844–45, 1853–54.

Det riksfördärfweliga swenska öfwerflödet, uti några wissa rum och ställen, samt nödiga botemedel deremot, utmärkt och angifwit under riksdagen i Stockholm år 1762. [Author identified as Carl Leuhusen by Samuel E. Bring.] Stockholm: Nyström & Stolpe, 1762.

Sahlstedt, Abraham Magnus. *Project til en inrättning af pupill-medels förwaltning, och hemgift för flickor.* Stockholm: Kongl. Tryckeriet, 1756.

Schagerborg, Eric. *Förslag til en utgiftnings-fond för fattiga flickor, ingifwit til riksens ständer under riksdagen år 1765.* Stockholm: K. Finska boktryckeriet, 1769.

Sedan samtelige landshöfdingens Adam Otto Lagerbergs och des fru Beata Sparres samtelige borgenärer kommit i tillstånd at . . . göra en almän utredning, så hafwa . . . de heldre welat ingå en almän öfwerenskommelse . . . Stockholm: Henric Fougt, 1774.

"Statistik och redogörelse för de under åren 1912–1914 till domstolarna ingivna äktenskapsförorden." Appendix to *Bihang till riksdagens protokoll vid lagtima riksdagen i Stockholm, 2 samlingen, 2 avdelningen, 1 bandet.* Stockholm: Kungl. Boktryckeriet. P. A. Nordstedt & Söner, 1918.

Svenska Akademiens Ordbok = Ordbok över svenska språket, utgiven av Svenska Akademien. Lund: Gleerups, 1893–.

Svenskt Biografiskt Lexikon (SBL). Stockholm: Svenskt Biografiskt Lexikon, 1918–.

Sveriges ridderskaps och adels riksdags-protokoll från och med år 1719. 32 vols. Stockholm: various publishers, 1875–1982.

Till justitie-canzlers-embetet. Stockholm: Johan Petter Lindh, 1820.

Till Kongl. Swea hof-rätt. Stockholm: Carl Delén & Carl Deleen, 1815.

Tocqueville, Alexis de. *Democracy in America.* 1835-40. Wordsworth Classics of World Literature. Ware: Wordsworth Editions Limited, 1998.

Wälmente tankar och anmärkningar öfwer den widtbekanta Rutströmska religions- och rättegångs-saken til allmänhetens närmare granskning. Framgifne af En Owäl- dug Swensk. [author identified by Samuel E. Bring as Isac Faggot] Stockholm: Peter Hasselberg, 1768.

Weidling, Michaël. *Til allmänheten.* Linköping: Kongl. Gymnasie Boktryckeriet, 1800.

Ytterligare handlingar hörande til Plomgrenska concours-saken. Stockholm: Johan Christofer Holmberg, 1781.

BOOKS AND ARTICLES

Adamson, Rolf. *Järnavsättning och bruksfinansiering 1800–1860.* Göteborg: Elander, 1966.

Agarwal, Bina. *A Field of One's Own: Gender and Land Rights in South Asia.* Cambridge: Cambridge University Press, 1994.

Ahlberger, Christer. *Vävarfolket: hemindustrin i Mark 1790–1850.* Göteborg and Borås: Institutet för lokalhistorisk forskning and De sju häradernas kulturhistoriska förening, 1988.

Ahlberger, Christer, and Magnus Mörner. "Betydelsen av några latinamerikanska produkter för Sverige före 1810." *Historisk Tidskrift* (Stockholm) 1 (1993): 80–104.

Alm, Mikael. *Kungsord i elfte timmen: Språk och självbild i det gustavianska enväldets legitimitetskamp 1772–1809.* Stockholm: Atlantis, 2002.

Almquist, Johan Axel. *Frälsegodsen i Sverige under storhetstiden: med särskild hänsyn till proveniens och säteribildning.* 9 vols. Stockholm: Liber Förlag/Allmänna förlag, 1931–76.

Andersson, Gudrun. *Tingets kvinnor och män: Genus som norm och strategi under 1600- och 1700-tal.* Uppsala: Univ., 1998.

Andersson Lennström, Gudrun. "Makt och myndighet. Kring 1686 års lagkommission och kvinnans vardagsmakt." In *Sprickor i muren: Funktion och dysfunktion i det stormaktstida rättssystemet,* edited by Gudrun Andersson Lennström and Marie Lennersand, 1–87. Uppsala: Historiska institutionen, Univ., 1994.

Aspelin, Kurt. "*Det europeiska missnöjet.*" *Samhällsanalys och historiespekulation.* Vol. 1 of *Studier i C. J. L. Almqvists författarskap åren kring 1840.* Stockholm: Norstedt, 1979.

Ågren, Maria. "Caring for the Widowed Spouse: The Use of Wills in Northern Sweden during the Eighteenth and Nineteenth Centuries." *Continuity and Change* 19 (2004): 45–71.

———. "Contracts for the Old or Gifts for the Young?: On the Use of Wills in Early Modern Sweden." *Scandinavian Journal of History* 25 (2000): 197–218.

———. "A Domestic Secret: Marriage, Religion and Legal Change in Late Seventeenth-Century Sweden." *Past and Present* 194 (2007): 75–106.

———. "Fadern, systern och brodern: Makt- och rättsförskjutningar genom 1800-talets egendomsreformer." *Historisk Tidskrift* (Stockholm) 119 (1999): 683–708.

———. *Att hävda sin rätt: Synen på jordägandet i 1600-talets Sverige, speglad i institutet urminnes hävd.* Stockholm: Institutet för rättshistorisk forskning: Nerenius & Santérus, 1997.

———. "Hemligt eller offentligt?: Om kön, egendom och offentlighet i 1700-talets Sverige." *Historisk Tidskrift* (Stockholm) 126 (2006): 23–45.

———. "'Hon skall ha min stickmaskin': bruket av testamenten i en region i omvandling." In *Tid och tillit: En vänbok till Eva Österberg*, edited by Irene Andersson, Kenneth Johansson, and Marie Lindstedt Cronberg, 419–23. Stockholm: Atlantis, 2002.

———. "Inför allmänhetens oväldiga domstol." *Kungl. Humanistiska Vetenskaps-Samfundet i Uppsala Årsbok* (2005): 71–90.

———. *Jord och gäld: Social skiktning och rättslig konflikt i södra Dalarna ca 1650–1850.* Uppsala and Stockholm: Univ. and Almqvist & Wiksell International, 1992.

———. "Att lösa ekonomiska tvister — domstolarnas främsta sysselsättning på 1700-talet?" *Historisk tidskrift* (Stockholm) 108 (1988): 481–511.

Ågren, Maria, and Amy L. Erickson, eds. *The Marital Economy in Scandinavia and Britain, 1400–1900.* Aldershot, Hants, England; Burlington, Vt.: Ashgate, 2005.

Backlund, Janne. *Rusthållarna i Fellingsbro 1684–1748: Indelningsverket och den sociala differentieringen av det svenska agrarsamhället.* Uppsala and Stockholm: Univ. and Almqvist & Wiksell international, 1993.

Balzac, Honoré de. *Oeuvres complètes. Scènes de la vie parisienne. Le Père Goriot.* Paris: Société d'Éditions Littéraires et Artistiques, 1900.

Beachy, Robert. "Women without Gender: Commerce, Exchange Codes, and the Erosion of German Gender Guardianship, 1680–1830." In *Family Welfare: Gender, Property, and Inheritance since the Seventeenth Century*, edited by David R. Green and Alasdair Owens, 195–215. Westport, Conn.: Praeger, 2004.

Beauvalet-Boutouyrie, Scarlett. *Être veuve sous l'Ancien Régime: mythes et réalités.* Paris: Belin, 2001.

Bergman, C. Gunnar. "Testamentet i 1600-talets rättsbildning." *Lunds universitets årsskrift.* Ny följd. 8. Lund: Gleerup, 1918.

Bergman, Hjalmar. *Farmor och Vår Herre.* 1921. Reprint, Stockholm: Wahlström & Widstrand, 1987.

Bjarne Larsson, Gabriela. "Kvinnor, manlighet och hushåll 1350–1500." In *Hans och Hennes: Genus och egendom i Sverige från vikingatid till nutid*, edited by Maria Ågren, 81–111. Uppsala: Historiska institutionen, Univ.: Swedish Science Press, 2003.

Blom, Ida. "Veien til juridisk likestilling: Hovedtrekkene i arbejds-, ekteskaps-, og familielovgivningen i de nordiske land fra midten av 1800-tallet til ca. 1970." In *Historica. 4, Föredrag vid det XVIII Nordiska historikermötet, Jyväskylä 1981*, edited by Mauno Jokipii and Ilkka Nummela, 57–74. Jyväskylä: Jyväskylä Univ., 1983.

Boberg, Stig. *Gustav III och tryckfriheten 1774–1787.* Stockholm: Natur och Kultur, 1951.

Bremer, Fredrika. *Hertha eller "En själs historia": teckning ur det verkliga livet.* Göteborg: Minerva, 1986.

Burman, Carina. *Bremer: En biografi.* Stockholm: Bonnier, 2001.

Carlsson, Sten. *Fröknar, mamseller, jungfrur och pigor: Ogifta kvinnor i det svenska ståndssamhället.* Uppsala and Stockholm: Univ. and Almqvist & Wiksell International, 1977.

———. "Ståndsriksdagens slutskede (1809–1866)." In *Riksdagen genom tiderna,* edited by Herman Schück, Ingemund Bengtsson, and Nils Stjernquist, 181–210. Stockholm: Sveriges riksdag: Riksbankens jubileumsfond: Almqvist & Wiksell International, 1985.

Colley, Linda. *Britons: Forging the Nation, 1707–1837.* New Haven, Conn.: Yale University Press, 2005.

Desan, Suzanne. *The Family on Trial in Revolutionary France.* Berkeley and Los Angeles and London: University of California Press, 2004.

Dübeck, Inger. *Købekoner og konkurrence: Studier over myndigheds- og erhvervrettens udvikling med stadigt henblik på kvinders historiske retsstilling.* København: Juristforbundets forl., 1978.

Eliot, George. *Daniel Deronda.* 1860. London: Penguin Books, 2003.

———. *The Mill on the Floss.* 1860. Oxford: Clarendon, 1980.

Enefalk, Hanna. *En patriotisk drömvärld. Musik, nationalism och genus under det långa 1800-talet.* Uppsala: Acta Universitatis Upsaliensis, 2008.

Erickson, Amy Louise "Coverture and Capitalism." *History Workshop Journal* 59 (2005): 1–16.

———. "Introduction: The Marital Economy in Comparative Perspective." In *The Marital Economy in Scandinavia and Britain, 1400–1900,* edited by Maria Ågren and Amy L. Erickson, 3–20. Aldershot, Hants, England; Burlington, Vt.: Ashgate, 2005.

———. *Women and Property in Early Modern England.* London: Routledge, 1993.

Ewan, Elizabeth. "'To the Longer Liver': Provisions for the Dissolution of the Marital Economy in Scotland, 1470–1550." In *The Marital Economy in Scandinavia and Britain, 1400–1900,* edited by Maria Ågren and Amy Louise Erickson, 191–206. Aldershot, Hants, England; Burlington, Vt.: Ashgate, 2005.

Farge, Arlette. *Subversive Words: Public Opinion in Eighteenth-Century France.* London: Polity Press, 1994.

Fiebranz, Rosemarie. *Jord, linne eller träkol?: Genusordning och hushållsstrategier, Bjuråker 1750–1850.* Uppsala: Acta Universitatis Upsaliensis, 2002.

Finn, Margot C. *The Character of Credit: Personal Debt in English Culture, 1740–1914.* Cambridge: Cambridge University Press, 2003.

Fløystad, Ingeborg. "Innføring av lik arv for kvinner og menn: Lov av 31/7 1854." *Historisk Tidsskrift* (Oslo) no. 4 (1990): 537–57.

Frances, Catherine. "Making Marriages in Early Modern England: Rethinking the Role of Family and Friends." In *The Marital Economy in Scandinavia and Britain, 1400–1900,* edited by Maria Ågren and Amy Louise Erickson, 39–56. Aldershot, Hants, England; Burlington, Vt.: Ashgate, 2005.

Franzén, Bo. *Sturetidens monetära system: Pant eller penningar som information i köpstaden Arboga.* Stockholm: Almqvist & Wiksell International, 1998.

Gadd, Carl-Johan. *Det svenska jordbrukets historia.* Vol. 3, *Den agrara revolutionen 1700–1870.* Stockholm: Natur och Kultur/LT i samarbete med Nordiska museet och Stift. Lagersberg, 2000.

————. "Varför är äldre näringslagstiftning så oklar?: Kring ekonomisk lagstiftning, lagefterlevnad och sedvana, ca 1680–1850." In *Historia: Vänbok till Christer Winberg 5 juni 2007*, edited by Lennart Andersson Palm and Maria Sjöberg, 87–103. Göteborg: Historiska institutionen, Göteborgs universitet, 2007.

Gaunt, David. "The Property and Kin Relationships of Retired Farmers in Northern and Central Europe." In *Family Forms in Historic Europe*, edited by Richard Wall, 249–79. Cambridge: Cambridge University Press, 1983.

Goody, Jack. "Dowry and the Rights of Women to Property." In *Property Relations: Renewing the Anthropological Tradition*, edited by C. M. Hann, 201–13. Cambridge: Cambridge University Press, 1998.

Granér, Staffan. *Samhävd och rågång: Om egendomsrelationer, ägoskiften och marknadsintegration i en värmländsk skogsbygd 1630–1750*. Göteborg: Ekonomiskhistoriska institutionen, Univ., 2002.

Green, David R., and Alasdair Owens, eds. *Family Welfare. Gender, Property, and Inheritance since the Seventeenth Century*. Westport, Conn.: Praeger, 2004.

Green, David R., and Alasdair Owens. "Gentlewomanly Capitalism? Spinsters, Widows and Wealth Holding in England and Wales, c. 1800–1860." *Economic History Review* 56 (2003): 510–36.

Guzzetti, Linda. "Dowries in Fourteenth-Century Venice." *Renaissance Studies* 16 (2002): 430–73.

Hallberg, Peter. *Ages of Liberty: Social Upheaval, History Writing, and the New Public Sphere in Sweden*. Stockholm: Statsvetenskapliga institutionen, Univ., 2003.

Hansen, Anna. *Ordnade hushåll: Genus och kontroll i Jämtland under 1600-talet*. Uppsala: Acta Universitatis Upsaliensis, 2006.

Hardwick, Julie. *The Practice of Patriarchy: Gender and the Politics of Household Authority in Early Modern France*. University Park: Pennsylvania State University Press, 1998.

Hällström, Erik af. "Arvejordsinstitutet." In *Minnesskrift ägnad 1734 års lag av jurister i Sverige och Finland den 13 december 1934, 200-årsdagen av riksens ständers beslut*. Vol. 2. Stockholm: Svensk juristtidning: Marcus, 1934.

Helmius, Agneta. *"Det olyckliga swenska fruentimret": om kokboksförfattarinnan Anna Maria Rückerschöld och kvinnors villkor på 1700-talet*. Stjärnsund: Polhemsstift., 1993.

Herlitz, Lars. *Jordegendom och ränta: Omfördelningen av jordbrukets merprodukt i Skaraborgs län under frihetstiden*. Göteborg: Ekonomisk-historiska institutionen, Univ., 1974.

Hildebrand, Karl-Gustaf. *Svenskt Järn: Sexton- och sjuttonhundratal. Exportindustri före industrialismen*. Stockholm: Jernkontoret, 1987.

Hirschfeldt, Johan. "Domstolarna som statsmakt: några utvecklingslinjer." In *Kungl. Vitterhets historie och antikvitetsakademiens årsbok*, 131–50. Stockholm: Kungl. Vitterhets historie och antikvitetsakademien, 2007.

Holmbäck, Åke. *Om 1686 års testamentsstadga: Föreläsningar vid Uppsala universitet*. Stockholm: Norstedt, 1916.

Holmlund, Sofia. "Arvejord och äktenskap på den uppländska landsbygden under 1800-talet." In *Hans och Hennes: Genus och egendom i Sverige från vikingatid till nutid*, edited by Maria Ågren, 241–66. Uppsala: Historiska institutionen, Univ.: Swedish Science Press, 2003.

————. *Jorden vi ärvde: Arvsöverlåtelser och familjestrategier på den uppländska landsbygden 1810–1930*. Stockholm: Historiska institutionen, Stockholms universitet: Almqvist & Wiksell International, 2007.

Holthöfer, Ernst. "Die Geschlechtsvormundschaft: Ein Überblick von der Antike bis ins 19. Jahrhundert." In *Frauen in der Geschichte des Rechts: Von der Frühen Neuzeit bis zur Gegenwart*, edited by Ute Gerhard, 390–451. München: Beck, 1997.

Hoppe, Göran. "Svenska jordskiften och samhällsutvecklingen." In *Statens jordbrukspolitik under 200 år*, edited by Janken Myrdal, 45–54. Stockholm: Nordiska museet, 1991.

Howell, Martha C. *The Marriage Exchange: Property, Social Place, and Gender in Cities of the Low Countries, 1300–1550*. Chicago: University of Chicago Press, 1998.

Högnäs, Hugo. *Sytning och arvslösen: den folkliga sedvänjan uti Pedersöre- och Nykarlebybygden 1810–1914*. Åbo: Åbo akademi, 1938.

Hunt, Margaret R. *The Middling Sort: Commerce, Gender, and the Family in England, 1680–1780*. Berkeley: University of California Press, 1996.

Ighe, Ann. *I faderns ställe: Genus, ekonomisk förändring och den svenska förmyndarinstitutionen ca 1700–1860*. Göteborg: Ekonomisk-historiska institutionen, Univ., 2007.

Inger, Göran. *Svensk rättshistoria*. 4th ed. Malmö: Liber ekonomi, 1997.

Isacson, Maths. *Ekonomisk tillväxt och social differentiering 1680–1860: Bondeklassen i By socken, Kopparbergs län*. Uppsala and Stockholm: Univ. and Almqvist & Wiksell International, 1979.

Jansson, Karin Hassan. *Kvinnofrid: Synen på våldtäkt och konstruktionen av kön i Sverige 1600–1800*. Uppsala: Acta Universitatis Upsaliensis, 2002.

Janzon, Kaj. "Överdåd på kredit — ett rationellt val?: Några problem kring högadelns ekonomiska verksamhet i Sverige under 1600-talets första hälft." *Historisk tidskrift* (Stockholm) 119 (1999): 197–226.

Jägerskiöld, Stig. *Handelsbalkens utländska källor*. Lund: Blom, 1967.

Johansen, Hanne Marie. "Widowhood in Scandinavia: An Introduction." *Scandinavian Journal of History* 29 (2004): 171–91.

Johansson, Egil. *The History of Literacy in Sweden: In Comparison with Some Other Countries*. Umeå: Univ. and School of Education, 1977.

Johansson, Kenneth. "Herrar och bönder: Om jurisdiktionen i några småländska friherrskap på 1600-talet." *Scandia* (Lund) 56 (1990): 161–91.

Jordansson, Birgitta. *Den goda människan från Göteborg: Genus och fattigvårdspolitik i det borgerliga samhällets framväxt*. Lund: Arkiv, 1998.

Lahtinen, Anu. "Könspecifika maktpositioner inom ätten Flemings familjekrets under 1500-talet." In *Kön, Makt, Våld. Konferensrapport från det sjunde nordiska kvinnohistorikermötet 8–11 augusti 2002*, edited by Eva Helen Ulvros, 220–227. Göteborg: Historiska institutionen; Stockholms universitet, 2003.

Larsson, Lars-Olof. "Borgrätt och adelsjurisdiktion i medeltidens och 1600-talets Sverige." In *Historia och samhälle: Studier tillägnade Jerker Rosén*, edited by Anders Grönvall, 49–67. Lund: Studentlitteratur, 1975.

Larsson, Maja. *Den moraliska kroppen: tolkningar av kön och individualitet i 1800-talets populärmedicin*. Hedemora: Gidlund, 2002.

Liliequist, Jonas. "Kostnadsansvar för rättegångar, fängslande och bestraffningar i 1600- och 1700-talens Sverige." *Rettspraksis*. Oslo: Tingbokprosjektet, 1994.

———. "Mannens våld och välde inom äktenskapet: En studie av kulturella stereotyper från reformationstiden till 1800-talets början." In *Mord, misshandel och sexuella övergrepp: historiska och kulturella perspektiv på kön och våld*, edited by Inger Lövkrona, 88–123. Lund: Nordic Academic Press, 2001.

Lindegren, Jan. "Men, Money, and Means." In *War and Competition between States*, edited by Philippe Contamine, 129–62. Oxford: Clarendon, 2000.

———. *Utskrivning och utsugning: produktion och reproduktion i Bygdeå 1620–1640*. Uppsala and Stockholm: Univ. and Almqvist & Wiksell International, 1980.

Lindmark, Daniel. *Pennan, plikten, prestigen och plogen: den folkliga skrivkunnighetens spridning och funktion före folkskolan*. Umeå: Institutionen för religionsvetenskap, Univ., 1994.

———. *Reading, Writing and Schooling: Swedish Practices of Education and Literacy, 1650–1880*. Umeå: Institutionen för litteraturvetenskap och nordiska språk, 2004.

Lindström, Jonas. *Distribution and Differences. Stratification and the System of Reproduction in a Swedish Peasant Community, 1620–1820*. Uppsala: Acta Universitatis Upsaliensis, 2008.

Lundh, Christer. "Remarriages in Sweden in the 18th and 19th Centuries." *History of the Family* 7 (2002): 423–49.

Mann, Bruce H. *Republic of Debtors: Bankruptcy in the Age of American Independence*. Cambridge, Mass.: Harvard University Press, 2002.

Maza, Sarah C. *Private Lives and Public Affairs: The Causes Célèbres of Prerevolutionary France*. Berkeley: University of California Press, 1993.

Melkersson, Martin. *Staten, ordningen och friheten: En studie av den styrande elitens syn på statens roll mellan stormaktstiden och 1800-talet*. Uppsala: Univ., 1997.

Myrdal, Janken. *Jordbruket under feodalismen 1000–1700*. Vol. 2 of *Det svenska jordbrukets historia*. Stockholm: Natur och Kultur/LT i samarbete med Nordiska museet och Stift. Lagersberg, 1999.

Nilsson, Sven A. "De kontinentala krigens finansiering." In *De stora krigens tid: Om Sverige som militärstat och bondesamhälle*, 178–96. Uppsala: Univ., 1990.

———. "Militärstaten i funktion." In *De stora krigens tid: Om Sverige som militärstat och bondesamhälle*, 226–44. Uppsala: Univ., 1990.

Niskanen, Kirsti. "Marriage and Economic Rights: Women, Men, and Property in Sweden during the First Half of the Twentieth Century." In *Family Welfare: Gender, Property, and Inheritance since the Seventeenth Century*, edited by David R. Green and Alasdair Owens, 243–67. Westport, Conn.: Praeger, 2004.

Nygren, Ingemar. *Svensk kreditmarknad 1820–1875: Översikt av det institutionella kreditväsendets utveckling*. Göteborg: Ekonomisk-historiska inst., Univ., 1981.

Odén, Birgitta. "Planering inför ålderdomen i senmedeltidens Stockholm." In *Manliga strukturer och kvinnliga strategier. En bok till Gunhild Kyle, december 1987*, edited by Birgit Sawyer and Anita Göransson, 91–107. Göteborg: Historiska institutionen, Univ., 1987.

———. "Relationer mellan generationerna: Rättsläget 1300–1900." In *Maktpolitik och husfrid: studier i internationell och svensk historia tillägnade Göran Rystad*, edited by Bengt Ankarloo, 85–116. Lund: Lund Univ. Press, 1991.

Ogilvie, Sheilagh C. *A Bitter Living: Women, Markets, and Social Capital in Early Modern Germany.* Oxford: Oxford University Press, 2003.

Olivecrona, S. R. D. Knut. *Om makars giftorätt i bo och om boets förvaltning.* 5th ed. Uppsala: Schultz, 1882.

Österberg, Eva. "Bönder och centralmakt i det tidigmoderna Sverige: Konflikt — kompromiss — politisk kultur." *Scandia* (Lund) 55 (1989): 73–95.

———. *Gränsbygd under krig: ekonomiska, demografiska och administrativa förhållanden i sydvästra Sverige under och efter nordiska sjuårskriget.* Lund: Gleerups, 1971.

———. "Land Transactions: Symptoms of Crisis or the Emergence of Capitalism in Swedish Peasant Society?" In *Plov og Pen: Festskrift til Svend Gissel: 4. januar 1991,* edited by Svend Gissel, Eva Österberg, and Sölve Göransson. Copenhagen: Det konglige Bibliotek: Landbohistorisk Selskab, 1991.

———. "Local Political Culture versus the State: Patterns of Interaction in Pre-industrial Sweden." In *Mentalities and Other Realities: Essays in Medieval and Early Modern Scandinavian History,* 176–91. Lund: Lund Univ. Press; Bromley: Chartwell-Bratt, 1991.

———. "Social Arena or Theatre of Power?: The Courts, Crime and the Early Modern State in Sweden." In *Maktpolitik och husfrid: Studier i internationell och svensk historia tillägnade Göran Rystad,* edited by Bengt Ankarloo, 55–75. Lund: Lund Univ. Press, 1991.

Österberg, Eva, Malin Lennartsson, and Hans Eyvind Næss. "Social Control Outside or Combined with the Secular Judicial Arena." In *People Meet the Law: Control and Conflict-Handling in the Courts. The Nordic Countries in the Post-Reformation and Pre-Industrial Period,* edited by Eva Österberg and Sølvi Bauge Sogner, 237–66. Oslo: Universitetsforlaget, 2000.

Österberg, Eva, and Sølvi Bauge Sogner, eds. *People Meet the Law: Control and Conflict-Handling in the Courts: The Nordic Countries in the Post-Reformation and Pre-Industrial Period.* Oslo: Universitetsforlaget, 2000.

Palm, Lennart Andersson. *Folkmängden i Sveriges socknar och kommuner 1571–1997: Med särskild hänsyn till perioden 1571–1751.* Göteborg and Visby: L. A. Palm and Books-on-demand, 2000.

Palme, Sven Ulric. *Studier i sturetidens statsrättshistoria.* Uppsala: Lundequistska, 1951..

Perlestam, Magnus. *Den rotfaste bonden — myt eller verklighet?: Brukaransvar i Ramkvilla socken 1620–1820.* Lund: privately printed, 1998.

Perlinge, Anders. *Sockenbankirerna: kreditrelationer och tidig bankverksamhet: Vånga socken i Skåne 1840–1900.* Stockholm: Nordiska museets förlag, 2005.

Petersson, Hans. *Morgongåvoinstitutet i Sverige under tiden fram till omkring 1734 års lag.* Stockholm: Nordiska Bokhandeln, 1973.

Petot, P. *La famille.* Vol. 1 of *Histoire du droit privé français.* Paris: Loysel, 1992.

Qvist, Gunnar. *Kvinnofrågan i Sverige 1809–1846: Studier rörande kvinnans näringsfrihet inom de borgerliga yrkena.* Göteborg: Elander, 1960.

Revera, Margareta. "1600-talsbönderna och deras herrar: Om jordägande, skatter och samhällsförändring i ljuset av nyare forskning." *Rättshistoriska Studier* (serien II), Band IX, edited by Göran Inger, 13–45. Stockholm: Nerenius & Santérus, 1984.

Roberts, Michael. "Recovering a Lost Inheritance: The Marital Economy and Its Absence from the Prehistory of Economics in Britain." In *The Marital Economy in Scandinavia and Britain, 1400–1900*, edited by Maria Ågren and Amy L. Erickson, 239–56. Aldershot, Hants, England; Burlington, Vt.: Ashgate, 2005.

Rosén, Ulla. *Gamla plikter och nya krav: En studie om egendom, kvinnosyn och äldreomsorg i det svenska agrarsamhället 1815–1939*. Växjö: Växjö University Press, 2004.

———. *Himlajord och handelsvara: ägobyten av egendom i Kumla socken 1780–1880*. Lund: Lund Univ. Press, 1994.

Rydeberg, Göran. *Skatteköpen i Örebro län 1701–1809*. Uppsala and Stockholm: Univ. and Almqvist & Wiksell International, 1985.

Sabean, David. "Allianzen und Listen: Die Geschlechtsvormundschaft im 18. und 19. Jahrhundert." In *Frauen in der Geschichte des Rechts: Von der Frühen Neuzeit bis zur Gegenwart*, edited by Ute Gerhard, 461–79. München: Beck, 1997.

Salmon, Marylynn. *Women and the Law of Property in Early America*. Chapel Hill: University of North Carolina Press, 1986.

Sandén, Annika. *Stadsgemenskapens resurser och villkor: samhällssyn och välfärdsstrategier i Linköping 1600–1620*. Linköping: ISAK; Enheten för historia, Linköpings universitet, 2005.

Sandvik, Hilde. *"Umyndige" kvinner i handel og håndverk: Kvinner i bynæringer i Christiania i siste halvdel av 1700-tallet*. Oslo: Tingbokprosjektet, 1992.

Scott, James C. *Seeing Like a State: How Certain Schemes to Improve the Human Condition Have Failed*. New Haven, Conn.: Yale University Press, 1998.

Scott, Joan W. "Gender: A Useful Category of Historical Analysis." In *Gender and the Politics of History*, 28–50. New York: Columbia University Press, 1988.

Sennefelt, Karin. "Stockholmsliv. Riksdagsumgänge och identitetsformering under frihetstiden." *Historisk Tidskrift* (Stockholm) 125 (2005): 399–420.

Simonson, Örjan. *Den lokala scenen: Torstuna härad som lokalsamhälle under 1600-talet*. Uppsala: Acta Universitatis Upsaliensis, 1999.

Simonton, Deborah. *A History of European Women's Work: 1700 to the Present*. London: Routledge, 1998.

Sjöberg, Maria. "Kvinnans sociala underordning — en problematisk historia." *Scandia* 63 (1997): 165–92.

———. *Kvinnors jord, manlig rätt: äktenskap, egendom och makt i äldre tid*. Hedemora: Gidlund, 2001.

Skoglund, Anna-Maria. *Fattigvården på den svenska landsbygden år 1829*. Stockholm: Univ., 1992.

Sogner, Sølvi, Marie Lindstedt Cronberg, and Hilde Sandvik. "Women in Court." In *People Meet the Law: Control and Conflict-Handling in the Courts: The Nordic Countries in the Post-Reformation and Pre-Industrial Period*, edited by Eva Österberg and Sølvi Bauge Sogner, 167–201. Oslo: Universitetsforlaget, 2000.

Sogner, Sølvi, and Hilde Sandvik. "Ulik i lov og lære; lik i virke og verd?: Kvinner i norsk økonomi i by og på land ca 1500–1800." *Historisk Tidsskrift* (Oslo) 68 (1989): 434–62.

Stadin, Kekke. *Stånd och genus i stormaktstidens Sverige*. Lund: Nordic Academic Press, 2004.

————."Att vara god eller att göra sin plikt?: Dygd och genus i 1600-talets Sverige." In *Historiska etyder. En vänbok till Stellan Dahlgren,* edited by Janne Backlund et al., 223–35. Uppsala: Historiska institutionen, Univ., 1997.

Staves, Susan. *Married Women's Separate Property in England, 1660–1833.* Cambridge, Mass.: Harvard University Press, 1990.

Sundin, Anders. *1809. Statskuppen och regeringsformens tillkomst som tolkningsprocess.* Uppsala: Acta Universitatis Upsaliensis, 2006.

Tamm, Ditlev, Jens Christian V. Johansen, Hans Eyvind Næss, and Kenneth Johansson. "The Law and the Judicial System." In *People Meet the Law: Control and Conflict-Handling in the Courts: The Nordic Countries in the Post-Reformation and Pre-Industrial Period,* edited by Eva Österberg and Sølvi Bauge Sogner, 27–56. Oslo: Universitetsforlaget, 2000.

Taussi Sjöberg, Marja. "Mellan far och make: Ägandet, arvet och kvinnorna." In *Bryta, bygga, bo.* Vol. 2 of *Svensk historia underifrån,* edited by Gunnar Broberg, Ulla Wikander, and Klas Åmark, 51–71. Stockholm: Ordfront, 1994.

Thirsk, Joan. "The European Debate on Customs of Inheritance, 1500–1700." In *Family and Inheritance: Rural Society in Western Europe, 1200–1800,* edited by Jack Goody, Joan Thirsk, and E. P. Thompson, 177–91. Cambridge: Cambridge University Press, 1976.

Thisner, Fredrik. *Militärstatens arvegods: officerstjänstens socialreproduktiva funktion i Sverige och Danmark, ca 1720–1800.* Uppsala: Acta Universitatis Upsaliensis, 2007.

Thompson, E. P. *Whigs and Hunters: The Origin of the Black Act.* Harmondsworth: Penguin Books, 1977.

Thunander, Rudolf. *Hovrätt i funktion: Göta Hovrätt och brottmålen: 1635–1699.* Stockholm: Institutet för rättshistorisk forskning: Nerenius & Santérus, 1993.

Thyrén, Johan C. W. *Makes gäld enligt svensk rättsutveckling: med hufvudsakligt afseende på makes före äktenskapet gjorda gäld.* Lund: Univ., 1893.

Vickery, Amanda. *The Gentleman's Daughter: Women's Lives in Georgian England.* New Haven, Conn.: Yale University Press, 1998.

Winberg, Christer. "Familj och jord i tre västgötasocknar: Generationsskiften bland självägande bönder." *Historisk Tidskrift* (Stockholm) 101 (1981): 278–310.

————. *Folkökning och proletarisering: Kring den sociala strukturomvandlingen på Sveriges landsbygd under den agrara revolutionen.* Göteborg: Univ., 1975.

————. *Grenverket: Studier rörande jord, släktskapssystem och ståndsprivilegier.* Stockholm: Institutet för rättshistorisk forskning: Nordiska Bokhandeln, 1985.

Winton, Patrik. *Frihetstidens politiska praktik: Nätverk och offentlighet 1746–1766.* Uppsala: Acta Universitatis Upsaliensis, 2006.

UNPUBLISHED THESES AND PAPERS

Johansson, Bernt. "Godsförvärv och likviditetsproblem. Köpe- och låneverksamheten på säterikomplex i Södermanlands och Uppsala län 1680–1720." Licentiat-thesis, Uppsala University, 1969.

Löfstrand, Jeanette. "Högadlig ideologi. Axel Oxenstiernas, Jacob De la Gardies och Ebba Brahes individuella respektive kollektiva ideologi som den kommer till uttryck i deras testamenten." C-level thesis, Uppsala University, 1998.

INDEX

Note: The Swedish Ö appears at the end of the letter O.

resources, 88; and transparency, 90–91; and public registration of mortgages, 93; and social hierarchy, 93, 139; and women's access to property, 102; and land market, 193, 194–95, 196, 203; and credit law, 208–9

Common men, and local courts, 60

Consent of kinsmen. *See* Kin groups

Contracts: and land transfers, 115–20, 239 (n. 50). *See also* Prenuptial agreements; Retirement contracts

Cooperation: and internal disputes, 21–22; marriage as form of, 174

Courts of appeal: and legal uniformity, 22–23; and equity, 25; and proof of land titles, 30; and noble women's dispute of wills, 48; and wills, 48, 50; and written land records, 63; and melioration, 68; and debts, 73, 74; and creditors' rights, 74–76, 78; and spouses' legal responsibility for debts, 74–76, 81; and kin group consent, 79, 234 (n. 34); and attitudes toward women, 94–95; and redeemed land, 125; women's complaints filed in, 141; use of Latin and Swedish terms, 234–35 (n. 46)

Coverture, and married women's property rights, 11, 14, 76, 178, 182, 210–11, 251 (n. 26)

Credit access, 72, 73, 145–46

Credit law: and transparency, 14; and statutory law, 26, 73, 233 (n. 19); and real estate law, 68; and kin groups' consent, 71, 74, 76, 79, 80, 82, 85, 234 (n. 39); and creditors' rights, 74, 92, 208, 215; public debate on, 74, 234 (n. 21); poor development of, 92; and bankruptcy law, 145–52; and commercialized economy, 208–9; and probate inventories, 209, 226 (n. 41); and legal simplification, 211

Credit market: lineage property clashing with, 71; and state, 73; and spouses' responsibilities for debts, 81; and legibility, 99

Creditors' claims: and family law, 12; and domestic secrecy, 13, 14; and married women's property rights, 37, 74, 208, 234 (n. 21)

Creditors' rights: and marital estates, 13, 75, 78, 80–81, 97, 178, 209, 214; precedence over inheritance rights, 70, 71–72; and credit law, 74, 92, 208, 215; and legibility, 75, 209; and responsibilities of creditors, 81–82; and public registration of debts, 92, 97; and bankruptcy law, 146, 147, 148, 149, 151; and equity, 151, 245 (n. 39)

Credit system: and legible property regime, 93, 223 (n. 13), 237 (n. 96); importance of, 145–46

Creditworthiness: and married women's property rights, 10–11; and debt payment, 73; and public registration of debts, 92; and honorable bankruptcy, 146–48; and rumors, 149

Crime, cooperation in combating, 21

Criminal law, modernization of, 169

Cronhielm, Gustaf, 79, 80, 81–82, 96

Crown-owned farms: and land market expansion, 107; as acquired lands, 111, 112, 203, 238 (n. 33); and tenants' property rights, 124, 135, 203, 240 (n. 75); as freehold land, 134, 203

Danielsson, Anders, 181, 186

Debt bondage, in iron industry, 72

Debtors' rights, creditors' rights favored over, 74

Debt payment, and creditworthiness, 73

Debts: and medieval legal code, 68, 69–70, 81; definition of, 70; and marital estates, 71, 72, 74, 82, 99; and married women's property rights, 71, 74, 78–79, 80, 100, 155, 177, 209, 233 (n. 19), 234 (n. 21); international chains of, 72; in iron industry, 72; spouses' legal responsibility for, 73–81, 82, 85, 94, 155–56, 162, 174, 211, 233 (n. 19), 237 (n. 101); and lineage property, 74, 85, 234 (n. 21),

sale of landed property, 82–83, 85, 96; and redeemed land, 88, 107, 110; and legal code of 1734, 88–89, 90, 100–102, 106–7, 204; and sale of inherited lands, 104–10; and enclosure movement, 109, 136; and land market, 108–9; and compensating practices, 111–15, 117, 137–38, 154; and silence surrounding sale of inherited land, 121–23, 127, 129; effect of family situation on, 122–23, 204; and reforms of nineteenth century, 206; and equity, 215; and acquired money, 229 (n. 51)

Martineau, Harriet, 205

Medieval legal code: principles of, 8; and married women's property rights, 10, 11, 32, 42, 76, 204; history of, 26; Ten Commandments included in, 28; and inherited land, 28, 71, 226 (n. 3); and stipulations on husband's scope of action, 31–34, 36–38, 40–41, 42, 59, 64, 66–67, 70, 78, 79, 83, 95, 178, 202, 204, 214, 227 (n. 17), 228 (n. 40); demands for revision of, 45; and dichotomy of inherited/noninherited land, 45–46; and wills, 48–49; and conception of husbands, 53; and fragmentation of farms, 57, 58; complaints about, 67; lack of credit law in, 68; and debts, 68, 69–70, 81; on redeemed land, 87; and sexual crime, 96; and movable property, 197; and general welfare, 202; and legal simplification of ownership, 211; and restricted view of law, 211

Melioration, and courts of appeal, 68

Memory-based information, 59, 60–61, 112

Men's economic contribution to marriage, 4, 16

Men's property rights: and kin groups, 54; and compensation with money, 4, 58–59, 153–54

Men's work, economic importance of, 183–84

Middle-class citizens: passive life of women, 7; and privacy, 16, 17; growth of, 139; and reforms offering options for women, 205–6; and debts, 209

Mill, John Stuart, 166–67

Modernity: and legal methods, 18; and credit law, 74–75; and constitution, 169; and reform of inheritance rights, 181–82

Moneylenders: and entitlements, 72; responsibilities of, 81–82; and trustworthiness, 93. See also Creditors' claims; Creditors' rights

Money transactions, and commercialized economy, 88

Morality, and reform of inheritance rights, 176, 177

Moravian brothers, 143

Morning gift: and married women's property rights, 29, 121, 135, 175; as inherited or acquired, 46, 230 (n. 62); as form of debt, 70

Mortgages: public registration of, 91, 92, 93, 97, 149, 212, 236 (n. 82); land transfer contracts registered as, 116; and married women's inherited assets, 155–56; women's economic contribution to marriage as, 239 (n. 46)

Movable property: protection of, 8, 179; and nobility, 46; legal action concerning, 86; in marital estates, 86, 99, 151; and inheritance claims, 88, 122, 201; and probate inventories, 113–14; in wills, 117; and married women's common property shares, 151; and separation of property, 151–52, 153, 213; and women's economic contribution to marriage, 171; as swallowed by immovable property, 172, 197; as capital, 179; importance of, 182, 197, 213; women's wealth in, 196; and married women's property rights, 202; as acquired property, 230 (n. 66)

(n. 29); and women's contributions
to society, 182–83, 198

Perlestam, Magnus, 21

Personal guarantees, 93

Personal property: and married wom-
en's property rights, 11; protection
of, 42–43, 65; and inherited assets,
57, 91, 127; for settling inheritance
claims, 57, 58–59; land transformed
into, 68; and probate inventories,
91, 93; use within households, 99;
married men's use of wives' personal
property, 107

Persson, Petter, compromise of, 168

Physical landscape: and separation of
married women's property rights,
40, 46, 109; and written records, 63;
and property as land, 212

Pietistic religious movements, 143

Plomgren, Anders, 149, 155, 156, 162

Polanyi, Karl, 86

Political parties, emergence of, 142,
242 (n. 5)

Politicization process: and women's
use of public sphere, 139, 141; and
Diet sessions, 142; and bankruptcy
law, 150; and public opinion, 163–64;
and married women's property
rights, 164, 205, 206

Poor relief: and family law, 12, 223
(n. 10); and individual rights, 55;
state's responsibility for, 131; and
marital rights, 175

Poverty: of widows, 10, 11, 12, 129, 131,
135, 136, 193, 199; as asset to country,
187, 249 (n. 73)

Power relations: and local courts,
61–62; and patriarchal marriage
relations, 76, 77, 78, 174, 201, 202–3,
206, 209, 214, 251 (nn. 11, 16); and
spouses' responsibilities for debts,
77–78, 80; and kin groups, 78, 80,
202; and married women's property
rights, 82–83, 97; within marital
relationship, 99; and unmarried
women, 205–6

Prenuptial agreements: public registration of, 91–92, 149–50; and married
women's property rights, 102; and
social hierarchy, 118, 239 (n. 56); and
estate money, 118–19; and marital
rights, 173

Primogeniture: and women's property
rights, 11; noble women disfavored
by, 48; Tocqueville on, 167; and preventing fragmentation of farms, 186;
and reform of inheritance laws, 187

Privacy: domestic secrecy as, 15–17;
ideals of, 16–17; increasing importance of, 85–87, 96; and marital
estates, 86, 179, 191, 212, 213; transparency contrasted with, 93–94; bankruptcy law contrasted with, 148; and
publication of legal documents, 161,
163; of marriage, 181

Probate inventories: as new legal
method, 18, 212; as compulsory, 24,
91; and personal property, 91, 93;
and social hierarchy, 93; and silver in
peasant households, 106; and land
prices, 110; and debts, 110, 113–14, 226
(n. 41); and women's economic contribution to marriage, 111–12, 113, 114,
115, 118, 138, 199, 202, 238 (n. 34); and
movable property, 113–14; and equal
marital rights, 170; and transparency,
191; and credit law, 209, 226 (n. 41);
probate accounts distinguished
from, 226 (n. 41)

Proletarianization process: and estate
money, 114–15, 135, 138, 201; and
women, 129–36, 138, 184–85, 197; and
reform of inheritance laws, 184–85,
186, 188; and fragmentation of farms,
187–88

Property law: and transparency, 14;
legal descriptions versus practical
use of property, 17, 45–46; state's
impact on, 28, 54–59, 64; and local
court records, 64; and movable
property as separate, 151–52, 153;
and restricted vision of law, 211–12.

Roberts, Michael, 14–15
Roman law, 207–8
Rückerschöld, Anna Maria, 7, 24, 130, 158, 207
Rutström, Anders, 143–44

Sahlstedt, Abraham Magnus, 241 (n. 103)
Salmon, Marylynn, 14, 77, 197, 224 (n. 18), 239 (n. 56)
Schagerborg, Eric, 131–32, 134, 135, 176
Scotland, 52–53
Scott, James C., 14, 55
Self-made men, 51, 92, 93, 153
Separation of common property, 146, 150, 151, 153, 156, 170, 177–78, 245 (n. 39)
Sjöberg, Maria, 32–33, 227 (n. 17), 229 (n. 53), 230 (n. 60)
Skytte, Johan, 66–67, 71
Slavery, 169, 205
Social control by neighbors, and support of legal system, 18
Social hierarchy: and use of legal representatives, 23; and probate inventories, 24; and reading culture, 24; and wills, 46, 53, 64; and women's property rights, 67; and credit dependence, 73; and creditworthiness, 92; and self-made men, 92; and commercialized economy, 93, 139; and legal transformations, 97; and prenuptial agreements, 118, 239 (n. 56); and surrogates, 128; and women's ability to marry, 129–32; and inheritance law, 167–68. *See also* Nobility; Peasantry
Social question: and women's property rights, 139, 199; and marital rights, 175–76
Spousal identity, and wills, 46, 49–50, 64
Stability, and taxation, 55, 56–57, 58
State: and state building in seventeenth-century Sweden, 8, 22; interest in inheritance law, 12, 57–58; and transparency, 14, 17, 99; and legi-

bility, 14, 55, 99, 223 (n. 13); and local courts, 22–23; impact on property law, 28, 54–59, 64; transfer of landed property to nobility, 45, 230 (n. 61); and credit access, 73; and property rights, 82, 235 (n. 48); king being invested with state power, 103, 109, 110, 237 (n. 5); and division of power, 169; repossession of state lands, 230 (n. 61)
Statutory law: role of, 25–26; and credit law, 26, 73, 233 (n. 19); and *bördsrätt*, 85; and redeemed land, 103–4; and enclosure movement, 108; and form of inheritance, 133, 241 (n. 100); and debts, 145; and bankruptcy, 146–47
Stiernhöök, Johan, 71–72, 79
Stowe, Harriet Beecher, 205
Surnames, 246–47 (n. 7)
Surrogates: legal stipulations concerning, 88, 124, 127, 128, 138, 201; contexts of, 89, 128–29, 236 (n. 77); and commercialized economy, 90; kin groups' right to, 101, 128, 139, 140, 199; and bankruptcy law, 152, 154; and publication of legal documents, 152, 154
Sweden: population of, 8, 19, 21, 130, 131, 189, 190, 225 (n. 29); constitution of, 169–70. *See also* Demographics; Diet; Legal code of 1734; Medieval legal code

Taxation: and inheritance law, 12; and peasant farm as basic cadastral unit, 19, 49; and peasantry, 19, 105, 224 (n. 24), 232 (n. 100); and state's influence on property system, 28; and legibility, 55, 237 (n. 96); and property claims, 55–58, 63, 64; mitigation of, 105; and Diet, 142, 242 (n. 5)
Tenants: and cadastral units, 19; and capital accumulation, 107; of Crown-owned lands, 124, 135, 203, 240 (n. 75)
Theft, and movable property in marital estates, 86

Winberg, Christer, 225 (n. 28), 227 (n. 21)

Women: access to education, 7; control of income, 8; appearances in local courts, 23; literacy skills of, 24; as "bearers of wealth," 54; debt responsibility of, 80, 85, 94, 208; restricted legal capacity of, 80–81, 121, 129, 162, 207–8, 228–29 (n. 41), 234 (n. 42), 240 (n. 66); capability for rational thinking, 83; as legally responsible actors, 83, 94, 95, 96, 97, 205, 235 (n. 52); and Roman concept of *imbecillitas sexus*, 94, 207, 208, 237 (n. 97); misogynist attitudes toward, 94–95; discursive use of images of, 95; complaints filed by, 101, 120–21, 123, 127, 133, 139, 141, 158, 159, 196; heirs filing complaints on behalf of, 121; and proletarianization, 129–36, 138, 184–85, 197; and waged work, 130; use of public sphere, 139, 141, 157–61, 163, 164, 196, 207; freedom of unmarried adult, 205–6; invisibility of, 210, 211

Women as landholders: in seventeenth-century rural Sweden, 6, 21; and demographics, 90; and acquired land, 195–96; and inherited land, 195

Women's economic contribution to marriage: law's acknowledgement of, 4, 31; inherited assets as, 5, 6, 9, 111–12, 121–22, 124–25; and skills and labor, 6–7, 84, 98–99, 174, 182–85, 207, 235 (n. 58); renegotiation of, 7; reconceptualization of, 7, 8; and privacy, 16; and inherited land, 28–29, 31, 118, 120, 121, 138, 202, 207; and social hierarchy, 97–98; and compensating practices, 101, 111–15, 117, 120, 122, 123, 129, 137–38, 173, 202, 203; and wills, 107–8, 119; and probate inventories, 111–12, 113, 114, 115, 118, 123, 138, 199, 202, 238 (n. 34);

and movable property, 171; and mortgages, 239 (n. 46)

Women's landownership: and local court records, 34–36; and frequency of sales, 57–58; in seventeenth century, 202; and women as co-owners, 203

Women's property rights: information on in unprinted legal documents, 6, 30–31; protection of, 8–12, 102, 211; and trusts, 9, 11, 12, 139, 151, 202; and compensating practices, 11, 44, 102, 111–12, 138; granting of equal rights in, 26, 28; and inherited land, 28, 134–35, 138, 241–42 (n. 104), 242 (n. 105); and kin veto, 28–40, 59, 71, 74, 76; and shares of land, 30–31, 38, 44, 57, 58, 60, 102, 110, 129, 130, 131–33; and local knowledge, 61; and personal property, 65; and social hierarchy, 67; eighteenth-century deterioration of, 99, 104–10, 130, 196, 197, 202–3; and economic dependence on men, 115; population increase linked to, 131; and social question, 139, 199; complexity of, 142; reconstruction of, 170

Women's rights: interconnectedness of, 18–19; and responsibilities, 83; and egalitarianism, 166–67, 181, 195, 197, 199; to trade, 168, 170; and contributions to society, 182–85; and France, 185, 207. *See also* Married women's property rights; Women's property rights

Women's suffrage, 206, 251 (n. 12)

Women's work: economic importance of, 6–7, 8, 98, 182–85, 198, 199, 206, 207, 250 (n. 96); and control of income, 8; and legal simplification, 15; and wills, 49–50, 51, 52; invisibility of, 98, 212; and freedom for unmarried women, 205–6

Writing skills, 24, 26, 157–58

Written land records, 25, 30, 63

www.ingramcontent.com/pod-product-compliance
Lightning Source LLC
Chambersburg PA
CBHW021810270326
41932CB00007B/128